MINIMUS

**Starting out in Latin
Teacher's Resource Book**

Barbara Bell

Joint Association of Classical Teachers

Illustrated by **Helen Forte**

CAMBRIDGE
UNIVERSITY PRESS

PUBLISHED BY THE PRESS SYNDICATE OF THE UNIVERSITY OF CAMBRIDGE
The Pitt Building, Trumpington Street, Cambridge, United Kingdom

CAMBRIDGE UNIVERSITY PRESS
The Edinburgh Building, Cambridge CB2 2RU, UK   http://www.cup.cam.ac.uk
40 West 20th Street, New York, NY 10011–4211, USA   http://www.cup.org
10 Stamford Road, Oakleigh, Melbourne 3166, Australia
Ruiz de Alarcón 13, 28014 Madrid, Spain

© Cambridge University Press 1999

NOTICE TO TEACHERS
The photocopy masters in this publication may be photocopied free of charge for classroom use within the school or institution which purchases the publication. Worksheets and photocopies of them remain in the copyright of Cambridge University Press and such photocopies may not be distributed or used in any way outside the purchasing institution. Written permission is necessary if you wish to store the material electronically.

First published 1999
Reprinted 2000

Printed in the United Kingdom at the University Press, Cambridge

Typeface Macra Palatino, Scala Sans and Tempus *System* QuarkXPress®

A catalogue record for this book is available from the British Library

ISBN: 0 521 65961 2 paperback

Illustrations by Helen Forte
Design by Angela Ashton

AUTHOR ACKNOWLEDGEMENTS
The author would like to thank the many individuals who have helped to bring this project to fruition, in particular Robin and Pat Birley at Vindolanda, Susanna Morton Braund, Lindsay Allason-Jones, Peter Jones and Rachel Wood. The author is also indebted to the advisory panel: Jean Cross, Martin Forrest, Helen Forte, Wendy Hunt and Tim Wheeler. The feedback provided by teachers who participated in the testing programme is greatly appreciated. Warmest thanks are owed to Nick, Joanna and Kate, who allowed this little mouse to take over their lives.

Contents

	Introduction	4
1	Meet the family	7
2	Food, glorious food!	10
3	Work, work, work	13
4	The best days of your life	15
5	Romans and Britons	17
6	Off to town	19
7	The military machine	22
8	Clean and healthy	24
9	A soldier's life	26
10	How beautiful!	28
11	A sad day	30
12	Gods! Hear our prayers!	32
	Photocopiable activity sheets	I–XXXV
	Glossary	
	Certificate of achievement	

Introduction

These teacher's notes are intended to outline the content of each chapter and to give ideas and suggestions for classroom work. Don't feel that you have to do every activity in every chapter; you must select what you think is appropriate to the age and ability of your pupils. Time will also be a big factor. The range of suggested activities is intended to stimulate pupils who have more time and/or who work more quickly.

Each chapter contains a core of material, which every pupil should complete. This is as follows:

- picture story;
- grasp the grammar;
- any short Latin story later in the chapter;
- the grammar and vocabulary summary pointed out by Minimus at the end of each chapter.

It is hoped that *Minimus* will be of help and interest to pupils aged approximately 7–10, in both preparatory and state primary schools.

General aims of the course

1. To introduce pupils to a real family that lived at Vindolanda (which is near Hadrian's Wall) at the beginning of the second century AD. Through the family's various adventures, pupils should learn something of what it meant to be invaded by the Romans, to serve in the Roman army, and to be the wife or child of someone serving in the army. This course is intended to complement the work the pupils are doing on the Romans in history at Key Stage 2.

    Vindolanda is a very special site, preserving the remains of eight forts, one on top of the other. Flavius's house is currently being excavated. Wherever possible, the material has been based on what is real. Hence the picture stories have been developed from the content of the Vindolanda writing tablets. Many artefacts referred to in the stories are real objects found on the site, and which can be seen in the splendid Chesterholme Museum on the site of Vindolanda. If possible, it would be excellent for pupils to visit the site. If distance precludes this, pupils will enjoy looking at similar artefacts at a nearby Roman museum.

2. To give pupils a taste of the language that the Romans spoke and brought to Britain, and which was so influential on the development of many other languages, especially English. In the limited time available, pupils do not move beyond first and second declension nouns, or meet any verb tenses other than the present. Nonetheless, it is hoped that pupils will enjoy their experience of Latin, including reading it aloud, and that they will want to do more.

    Not all those who teach this course will be Classicists. Indeed many will not have studied Latin themselves. For this reason, all the Latin passages are translated in the Teacher's Resource Book. The Latin passages are, of necessity, short and simple.

3. To help pupils understand English grammar, and to extend their English vocabulary, through the study of Latin. Most of the parts of speech which have to be known at Key Stage 2 of the National Curriculum feature in the course. Derivatives are an important feature of every chapter. Those who have studied Latin, even for a short time, usually speak with gratitude about the lasting improvement it has made to their understanding of English.

The aim of *Minimus* is not to turn seven-year-olds into Classical scholars (though that would be a pleasing spin-off!) but simply to give them a taste of a most rewarding and satisfying language. Above all, it should be fun! All pupils respond to encouragement, but this is perhaps especially true of young children. On completion of each third of the course (at the end of chapters 4, 8 and 12), pupils may be rewarded with a certificate. This is photocopiable and can be found at the back of the Teacher's Resource Book.

Course structure

Each chapter contains the following elements:

PICTURE STORY
This introduces the subject matter and language for the chapter.

WORDS TO HELP
This section lists new vocabulary from the picture story. The words are listed in the order in which they occur in the picture story.

GRASP THE GRAMMAR
This section introduces and explains grammatical concepts. It is usually followed by reinforcement activities.

ROMAN REPORT
This section contains information about Roman life. It is sometimes followed by points for discussion.

LATIN ROOTS
This section introduces English derivatives from Latin words.

MYTHOLOGY
A myth or story, told in English.

GRAMMAR SUMMARY
Minimus recaps on the key grammatical points.

WORDS TO REMEMBER
This section reinforces key vocabulary from the chapter.

Latin roots

An important aim of the course is to build pupils' English vocabulary. The Latin roots sections, which focus on derivatives, play a key role in this. Hopefully, all pupils will manage at least some of the answers. They should begin by identifying the Latin word in the chapter from which each of the underlined English derivatives comes. Once they have established the meaning of the Latin word, they should be able to guess at the meaning of the English derivative. Pupils who struggle with this could be encouraged to work on their dictionary skills. Alternatively, you could provide cards featuring the definitions to help pupils see the links between Latin and English.

The Latin roots sections are particularly suitable for individual research, possibly for homework.

Reading aloud

It is highly desirable for pupils to read their Latin aloud, if time permits. Here are some hints on Latin pronunciation:

- There are no silent letters in Latin. Pronounce every letter.
- There was no letter 'J' in the Roman alphabet: hence Iulius (pronounced Youlius).
- Evidence suggests that the Romans in Italy, and in Britain at this period, pronounced the letter 'v' as a 'w'. So the name of our cat is 'Wibrissa'!
- Romans stressed both letters in double consonants. So the double 's' in Vibrissa suggests the hissing sound of the cat.
- The letter 'c' is always hard, as in 'cat'.

Learning vocabulary

There are many different ways of learning new words. Pupils need help to develop a method which works for them. A brief discussion in class will often reveal some interesting and unorthodox methods. Here are some suggestions:

- Very few pupils have photographic memories: most benefit from writing new words down and testing themselves.
- A challenging but efficient method is to write a list of English words and ask pupils to fill in the Latin.

- Encourage pupils to think of linguistic links between new Latin words and English (or any other language with which they may be familiar). Use the Latin roots sections to reinforce this idea.
- Divide long lists of vocabulary into short sections – it's easier to learn little 'chunks'!
- Pupils can make lists of tricky items which 'won't stick'.
- It is very helpful if pupils can get friends and family to test them.
- Pupils can make cards with the Latin word on one side and the English translation on the other. They can then use the cards to test themselves and each other.
- Some pupils find it helpful to learn new words to a 'jingle' or rhythmic song.
- Others like to record new words on cassette and play them back.
- Classroom displays of vocabulary items are encouraging and effective.

Introduction: Roman Britain

The following list of place-names in Roman Britain may be useful for pupils who wish to know their nearest Roman town.

Bath **Aquae Sulis**
Caerleon **Isca Silurum**
Carlisle **Luguvalium**
Chester **Deva**
Colchester **Camulodunum**
Corbridge **Corstopitum**
Dover **Dubris**
Exeter **Isca**
Gloucester **Glevum**
Lincoln **Lindum**
London **Londinium**
St Albans **Verulamium**
York **Eboracum**

NB See photocopiable blank map of Roman Britain (activity sheet XXI).

1 Meet the family

- **subject matter:** introductions, greetings
- **materials:** activity sheets I–V
- **grammar content:** nouns

Picture story
Who are you? (pp. 2–3)

1. Minimus: I am Minimus. I am a mouse.
2. Minimus: Who are you?
   Lepidina: I am Lepidina. I am the mother.
3. Minimus: Who are you?
   Flavius: I am Flavius. I am the father.
4. Minimus: Who are you?
   Flavia: I am Flavia. I am the daughter.
5. Minimus: Who are you?
   Iulius: I am Iulius. I am the son.
6. Minimus: Who are you?
   Rufus: I am Rufus. I am a young child.
7. Minimus: Who are you?
   Candidus: I am Candidus.
   Corinthus: I am Corinthus.
   Candidus & Corinthus: We are slaves.
8. All: We are at Vindolanda!
9. Minimus: Who are you?
   Vibrissa: I am Vibrissa. I am a cat.
10. The mouse goes out.

- This story is quite demanding. Explain to pupils that Minimus (the mouse) is meeting all the members of the family and asking them who they are. Do encourage the pupils to guess the meaning – the pictures will help. Point out the vocabulary support (Words to help). It is deliberate policy not to give every new word; unfamiliar words can often be guessed from the context.
- The cat's name (**Vibrissa**) means 'Whiskers'.
- Observant pupils will notice that the use of capital letters in Latin does not follow what they have been taught to do in English. In Latin, capitals are only used for the names of people and places – not at the beginning of a sentence. You may wish to take this opportunity to revise the English rules for the use of capital letters and/or to introduce the concept of proper nouns.

Background information

- Flavius Cerialis did not come from Rome but from Batavia (now the Netherlands). He commanded the ninth cohort of Batavians. We know that Flavius and Lepidina, the prefect and his wife, had three children. The children's actual names and ages are not known, but in this course we have called them Flavia (aged 16), Iulius (aged 13) and Rufus (aged 3). Flavius is envisaged to be about 40, and Lepidina 32.
- Throughout the book, Flavius Cerialis will be referred to as Flavius, for ease of pronunciation. His house is currently being excavated at Vindolanda. Those who visit the site, and who wish to see his house, and read correspondence to and from him, should of course bear in mind his full name. Many of the letters are addressed to 'Dear Cerialis...'.
- From the correspondence between slaves which has been discovered, we know that the slaves at Vindolanda were mostly educated. Corinthus is a Greek slave, whereas Candidus is Celtic. Their different clothes are meant to reflect this. Corinthus is wearing a tunic decorated with the Greek key pattern.

He is frequently seen writing or reading; he teaches the children to read and write in chapter 4, as well as acting as a secretary. His age is 42. Candidus is skilled in a different way; he is an excellent cook and is therefore a valuable slave. He is also good at making things and, in chapter 7, he makes a wooden sword for Rufus. He is 36. Pandora, the new slave girl who arrives in chapter 3, is 25, and a skilled hairdresser.

- Each of the children wears a **bulla**. This was a lucky charm, worn around the neck. On his coming of age, a boy would dedicate his **bulla** to the household gods, and a girl would do the same on the eve of her marriage.

Grasp the grammar (p. 4)

This chapter focuses on nouns. A noun is defined here as 'a naming word for a person, a place or a thing'. The exercise on Latin boys' and girls' names (ending in **-us** and **-a** respectively) is a gentle introduction to the concept of gender, which will be developed in later chapters.

Here are some possible Roman names for pupils to use:

Boys: Augustus, Cassius, Catullus, Claudius, Fabius, Germanicus, Marcus, Neptunus, Paulus, Remus, Romulus, Tacitus, Tiberius, Vergilius.

Girls: Agrippina, Anna, Camilla, Cassandra, Diana, Drusilla, Flora, Helena, Horatia, Iulia, Lavinia, Lucia, Marcia.

Picture story
The birthday party (pp. 5–6)

Dearest Lepidina,

On 11th of September, come to my birthday. Goodbye, sister*, my soul.

Claudia

* There is some evidence to suggest that Lepidina and Claudia were in fact sisters.

① Lepidina: Hello, Claudia!
    Claudia: Hello, everyone!

② Claudia: Hello, Rufus!

③ Claudia: You are very welcome. Come! I have a present for you.

④ Lepidina: And I have a present for you.
    Flavia: Happy birthday! (*Literally*, 'May there be a happy day for you!')

⑤ Claudia: I thank you. How beautiful it is!
    Rufus: But what is it?

⑥ Claudia: It is Medusa.
    Rufus: But who is Medusa?
    Claudia: It is the famous Medusa. (*or* 'Medusa is famous.') Sit down, everyone! Once upon a time...

Background information

- The photograph on page 5 shows what the full birthday invitation looked like when it was found at Vindolanda. Writing tablets like these were found on a Roman bonfire. The soldiers decided to destroy all their records before they left the site. Fortunately, a heavy fall of rain and strong winds put out the fire and the burnt remains of these tablets are very helpful when trying to build up a picture of what life was like for those people who lived near Hadrian's Wall.

- It is difficult to read the writing on the tablet because it is written on wood and cannot be seen except with infra-red photography. It has no punctuation or word-divisions and some of the script is hard to decipher. In addition, the Latin is written in the cursive script. (There is more information on this as well as an activity sheet (XV) in chapter 4.) In this letter, the earliest Latin written by a woman in the whole Roman Empire, most of the writing was done by a scribe, but Claudia added her own farewell and her name, in a rather shaky hand.

Latin roots: answers (See activity sheet V)

1 **maternal** (from **māter**) means 'motherly'. Some pupils might like this, some not!

2 **service** (from **servī**, 'slaves'). Service stations provide essential help and serve us.

3 **pater noster** means 'Our Father' – the Lord's Prayer.

4 **infantile** (from **īnfāns**) means 'childish'. Teacher would be angry.

5 **feline** (from **fēlēs**) means 'cat-like'. Yes, you would be surprised.

6 Three times **per diem** means three times *a day*.

Suggested activities

HISTORY
- Ask pupils to consider which materials would be likely to survive being buried in the soil for nearly 2,000 years. Organic materials, such as leather and wood, which normally decay in Britain's damp climate, have survived at Vindolanda because of a lucky combination of circumstances.

ART (See activity sheets III and IV)
- Roman women wore a lot of jewellery. Some jewellery that may have been worn by Lepidina is in the museum at Vindolanda.
- At this time, Roman women wore their hair long, tied up off the face.
- Lepidina wore a long **tunica** (tunic) and a **palla** (cloak) when it was cold.
- Lepidina's beautiful, small leather sandals have also been found at Vindolanda.

MUSIC
- The pupils will enjoy singing 'Happy Birthday' in Latin. The words are as follows:
  fēlīx diēs tibi sit
  fēlīx diēs tibi sit
  fēlīx diēs cāre (for a boy)/cāra (for a girl)
  _____ (name)
  fēlīx diēs tibi sit

ENGLISH
- Ask the pupils to write an imaginary conversation between Lepidina and her friend Claudia, who is celebrating her birthday. Give them the following information to work with:
  - The two women are great friends but can't see each other very often, because of the difficulties and dangers of travel in the Roman world.
  - Both of their husbands (**Flāvius** and **Aelius**) are important men in charge of a fort. They are wealthy, educated men who can enjoy the best that money can buy. They like rich food, served in elegant surroundings. It seems likely that Flavius even entertained the Governor of Britain at the camp.
  - Rich Roman women did not do paid work. Their job was to run the home and to be in charge of the food, meals and slaves. Often they would spin and weave. Spindle whorls (the heavy weights which hold down the wool), weaving combs and needle-cases have all been found at Vindolanda. Lepidina would also be busy looking after her three children.

- After studying the myth of Perseus and Medusa, pupils could write acrostic poems (i.e. where the initial letter of each line forms the word 'Perseus' or 'Medusa'), giving the main elements of the story, for example:

  Medusa was a monster,
  Everyone was afraid of her.
  Death was the fate of…

  Pupils can then illustrate their poems or add a border of snakes.

DESIGN
- Ask the children to design a head of Medusa, remembering to include the hissing snakes. It is meant to be so frightening that it turns men into stone!

  N.B. The word 'petrify' means literally 'to make into stone'. In the New Testament, Jesus said he would make Peter the rock (**petrus**) of his church.

  The story of Perseus and Medusa was very popular among the Romans. Medusa's head can be found in many mosaics, paintings, and even on rooftiles on Roman sites.

DRAMA
- The pupils will enjoy acting out the story of Perseus and Medusa. Working in groups of three, one pupil can narrate the story while the other two mime the parts of Perseus and Medusa. Perseus will need a shield and winged sandals if possible.

GEOGRAPHY
- Use the map of the Roman Empire (see activity sheet XXII) and a modern atlas. Write a list of the countries which once belonged to the Roman Empire.

2 Food, glorious food!

- **subject matter:** food, entertaining
- **grammar content:** adjectives
- **materials:** activity sheets VI–IX

Picture story
The Governor is coming! (p. 8)

① Lepidina: Oh dear! The house is dirty.

② Flavius: Oh dear! The garden is messy.

③ Flavia: Oh dear! The (*or* My) dress is not beautiful.

④ —

⑤ Corinthus & Candidus: Oh dear! We are tired slaves.

⑥ Iulius: Hooray! Marcellus is an excellent soldier!

⑦ Minimus: Hooray! The food will be excellent!

⑧ Vibrissa: Hooray! Minimus will be fat!

- The two Latin words **ēheu** (oh dear, alas) and **euge** (hooray) are tricky to pronounce. As a general rule, try to make each of them a three-syllable word. They are onomatopoeic – **eheu** should sound like a sigh, whereas **euge** should express excitement, and the voice should lift. Try something like *ehayoo* and *ayoogay*.

- On page 9 there are some questions which aim to stimulate discussion. The adults are concerned to impress the Governor, whereas Iulius is excited to meet a military hero. The slaves are unhappy about the extra work, and Minimus and Vibrissa have their own agenda!

Grasp the grammar (p. 9)

The main point of this chapter is to introduce **adjectives** ('words used to describe nouns') and the concept of gender and adjectival agreement. The rules are deliberately kept simple (first and second declension nouns only, no mention of neuter nouns, etc.) to help children with these unfamiliar grammatical ideas.

Other new grammatical features (such as the future tense of the verb 'to be', **erit**) are glossed in the vocabulary and should not need further emphasis.

Grasp the grammar: answers

1 **tunica**; **pulchra**; feminine

2 **a** The wasp is small. **b** The whale is very big. **c** The rabbit is naughty. **d** The dolphin is friendly. **e** The horse is big. **f** The pig is dirty. **est** = is.

Here is an additional list of animals. Ask pupils to choose two or three of their favourites and to match them with a relevant adjective from page 10 of the pupil's book. Remind them that they must choose the right ending for each adjective depending on whether the noun is masculine or feminine.

masculine nouns

elephantus elephant
cycnus swan
mūs mouse
pāvō peacock
psittacus parrot
piscis fish
taurus bull
canis dog

feminine nouns

vacca cow
gallīna hen
vulpēs fox
fēlēs cat
rāna frog
mēles badger
avis bird

N.B. Some more able pupils may pick up on the fact that not all these nouns end in **-us** (masculine) or **-a** (feminine). Simply explain to them that these nouns (e.g. **fēlēs, pāvō, canis**) are *irregular*, that is that they do not follow the normal pattern. More able pupils may well be aware of irregular patterns in English (e.g. 'I went' instead of 'I goed', 'I saw' instead of 'I seed').

Here are some further suggestions for reinforcing the concept of adjectival agreement.

- A memory game, for two or more players. Lay out the animal cards (activity sheet VII) and the adjective cards (activity sheet VIII) face down. Each player picks up one card from each set. If the adjective matches the noun (if the ending is correct and if it is an appropriate adjective) the pupils will enjoy shouting **euge!** The pair is theirs. If not, they have to put them back in the same place – **ēheu!** The winner is the one with most pairs.

  You'll need to remind pupils that it's **-us** for masculine nouns and **-a** for feminine nouns.

- On activity sheet IX, write the Latin version of pupils' names in the first column. Write **est** (he/she is) in the third column. Give each child copies of the partially completed sheet and activity sheet VIII and ask them to complete the sentences with a suitable adjective. Remind them to check the adjective endings.

- Cut up the sentences children made on activity sheet IX. Use these cards together with the animal and adjective cards to make further simple sentences, for example:

  vacca benigna est. The cow is kind.
  Michaelus parvus est. Michael is small.

- The animal cards can also be used for role play (**quis es? elephantus sum!**).

Latin roots: answers (p. 11)

1 <u>pork</u> from **porcus**, pig.
2 <u>equestrian</u> from **equus**, horse. A statue of a horse.
3 <u>maximum</u> from **maximus**, very large. Yes, you would be pleased.
4 <u>minimal</u> from **minimus**, very small. No, your teacher would not be pleased.

Background information

- Pupils will enjoy discussing in what ways a Roman **cēna** was similar to a modern dinner party and in what ways it was different.

  Some similarities: Poultry, fish, fruit and cheese would have been served on the best crockery and the meal would have been accompanied by fine wine. Rubbish tips at Vindolanda have yielded fish bones, chicken bones and oyster shells. Samian pottery was the best-quality glazed tableware, featuring raised decoration (see photo on page 13 of the pupil's book). Broken pieces of dishes, bowls and cups have also been found on rubbish tips at the site. Many collections of Roman artefacts in local museums contain Samian pottery.

  Some differences: Guests reclined on a couch, leaning on their left elbows. Different use was made of cutlery: knives and spoons have been found, but the Romans did not use forks. Food was served by slaves. The normal seating plan was like this:

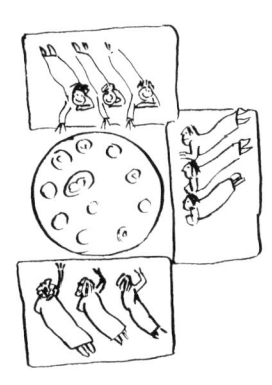

  In one Vindolanda letter, we learn that a special silver dinner service was ordered from London, for the prefects' table. Details of foodstuffs shipped into Vindolanda are given in many of the writing tablets.

- For more details of the extravagant food served at Roman banquets, the best source is the cookery book of **Apicius**.

- The Romans didn't have sugar for cooking but we know that they liked sweet food. Ask the children what they might have used instead. The Romans used honey in place of sugar. There are a number of other familiar foods which would not have been available to a Roman cook. This would make an interesting topic for discussion. Potatoes, tomatoes, sweetcorn and chocolate are all native to the Americas, and did not reach

Europe until the 16th century. Oranges, lemons and coffee come from Africa and hadn't yet arrived in Italy in Roman times. Pasta wasn't invented until the Middle Ages!

- Some vegetables and fruit might have been grown at Vindolanda but meat, fish and bread would have come from outside the fort. Sometimes it had to be brought from large towns like Eboracum (York). Ask the children how they think the food was transported in the absence of lorries, trains and planes. Supplies came in carts. There were no tin cans, plastic bottles, cardboard boxes or refrigerated containers. Liquids were transported in **amphorae**, tall pottery jars. Meat or fish might travel in barrels and was usually salted or pickled to preserve it.

- The Romans didn't have gas or electricity. How do the children think they cooked their food? A typical Roman kitchen had a cooking range rather like a brick-built barbecue, with a grid on top for pans. The fuel was either wood or charcoal.

Picture story
Dinner for the Governor (p. 12)

1. Flavius: Sit down, sir. You are very welcome.
2. Minimus: Hooray! The cheese is excellent!
3. Lepidina: Oh dear! It's the mouse! Vibrissa, get up!
4. Vibrissa: Hooray! Now Minimus is fat!
5. Rufus: Hooray! The peacock is beautiful.
6. Flavius: Rufus! Don't touch!!
7. All: Rufus! You are naughty!

Everyone is silent.

8. All: Go back to your bedroom!
9. Marcellus: Don't cry! Rufus is not naughty. Of course Rufus is curious.

Everyone smiles, especially Rufus.

10. Marcellus: Once upon a time…

Suggested activities

ENGLISH
- Ask pupils to imagine what Candidus and Corinthus might have said to each other while they were getting the dinner ready. They could then write a conversation between the two slaves. What do Candidus and Corinthus think about the Governor, Marcellus?

- 'Dinner for the Governor' is a story which lends itself well to drama.

- Ask pupils to retell the story of Daedalus and Icarus in a modern setting. It could be retitled *Dad always knows best*. Asking 'What is the moral of this story?' should also stimulate some good discussion work.

ART
- See activity sheet VI. The surprising food in the dot-to-dot puzzle is a peacock – this would certainly have been part of the special dinner for Marcellus.

- The pupils could model Roman food from salt dough, and then paint and label it in Latin (e.g. **cāseus, pāvō**) to reinforce vocabulary.

- Ask pupils to draw a colourful picture of Daedalus flying high as Icarus plummets into the sea.

COOKERY
- If time and circumstances permit, pupils will enjoy following a genuine Roman recipe. It is both simple and cheap.

Roman biscuits
You will need:
half a cup of plain wholemeal flour
2 cups of rolled oats
2 tablespoons of sesame oil
2 tablespoons of malt extract or molasses
a quarter of a cup of raisins

1. Put the raisins in a saucepan with enough water to cover them and simmer them for five minutes.
2. Mix the oats and the flour together and mix in the oil.
3. Add the raisins along with the liquid in which they were cooked and the malt/molasses. Mix together.
4. Add enough water to make a thick batter.
5. Form into shapes and place on a well-oiled baking tray. Bake for 25 minutes at 190° C (gas mark 5).

3 Work, work, work

■ **subject matter:** slaves ■ **grammar content:** verbs ■ **materials:** activity sheets X–XIV

Picture story
What are you doing? (p. 15)

1 Rufus: What are you doing?
Corinthus: I am writing.

Corinthus is writing. Rufus is watching.

2 Rufus: What are you doing?
Candidus: I am cleaning.

Candidus is cleaning. Rufus is watching.

3 Rufus: What are you doing?
Corinthus: I am reading.

Corinthus is reading.

4 Rufus: What are you doing?
Candidus: I am sweeping.

Candidus is sweeping.

5 Rufus is sitting and watching. Suddenly a slave girl enters.
Rufus: Who are you?
Pandora: I am Pandora. I am a new slave girl.

6 Corinthus and Candidus are not working now. Corinthus and Candidus are smiling.

Corinthus &
Candidus: How beautiful she is!

Grasp the grammar (p. 16)

The crucial point here is to get pupils to look at the ending of the verb to identify the subject (i.e. the person doing the action).

N.B. **scrībit** = he writes *or* he is writing. Both are acceptable translations of the present tense.

■ For some further practice, use the animal cards on activity sheet VII. Write verbs in the he/she form on the blank template (activity sheet IX) and ask pupils to construct short sentences, for example **cunīculus verrit** (the rabbit is sweeping).

Grasp the grammar: answers

1 **scrībit** he is writing; **spectat** he is watching; **pūrgat** he is cleaning; **legit** he is reading; **verrit** he is sweeping; **sedet** he is sitting down; **intrat** she enters

2 **scrībō** I am writing; **pūrgō** I am cleaning; **legō** I am reading; **verrō** I am sweeping

labōrant they are working; **rīdent** they are smiling

3 **a** he/she is writing; **b** he/she is watching; **c** I am watching; **d** I am writing; **e** they are watching; **f** you are doing; **g** they are writing; **h** you are writing

Background information

■ Slavery was an accepted part of life in the ancient world. You might become a slave by being captured in war, by being sold to pay debts, or you might be born into slavery. As there was no form of welfare state, slavery was often a better alternative to starvation. A house-slave in a good family might live comfortably; a slave working in a mine or rowing a galley would not.

■ Corinthus was probably born a slave. He has been owned by the same family all his life.

■ Candidus was born a free man, but became a slave in childhood when another Celtic tribe raided his village and killed his family. He

- has nothing to go back to. Flavius is a much better master than the Celtic chieftain who previously owned him.
- The pictures of Corinthus and Candidus on page 17 of the pupil's book indicate their different backgrounds. Corinthus has a Greek pattern on his tunic and carries a writing tablet. Candidus wears trousers in a typical Celtic tartan pattern. He is not as smartly dressed as Corinthus.

Picture story
Pandora settles in (p. 18)

1. Corinthus: Hello! I am Corinthus. I am the best, because I read.
2. Candidus: Hello! I am Candidus. I am the best, because I cook.
3. Corinthus: No, you are not the best because you don't read.
4. Candidus: No, you are not the best because you don't cook.
5. Corinthus: No, I am the best because I am handsome.
   Candidus: No, I am the best because I am strong.
6. Suddenly Rufus enters.
   Pandora: No, Rufus is the best, because he is always smiling.

Latin roots: answers (p. 20)

scrībit (he writes): scribe, script, scribble, prescription, description, inscription…

spectat (he watches): spectate, spectator, spectacle, prospect, inspect…

labōrant (they work): labour, labourer, laboratory, collaborate, laborious…

1 optimum from **optimus**, the best.
2 invalid from **validus**, strong. Invalids are sick people (not strong).
3 minimize from **minimus**, very small.
4 sedentary from **sedeō**, I sit. A job which is done sitting down – a desk-bound job.
5 introduction from **intrat**, he enters. A book which 'takes you in' to Latin.

Suggested activities

P.S.E.
- After reading the story of Pandora's box, discuss the evils in the world today (war, hunger, pollution, etc.) and find examples from the news. Then choose one to talk about in detail.

ART
- Ask pupils to draw a picture of Pandora's box with illustrations of each of the evils flying out and with Hope remaining inside. Alternatively, pupils could illustrate the whole story in comic-strip format.

R.E.
- Ask pupils to write a prayer which asks for help with the problems of hunger, war, disease, etc. for use in assembly.

ENGLISH
- The two picture stories form a useful basis for discussion work. Emphasise the different skills of the two slaves in your discussions. Following on from this, ask pupils to imagine that they are Candidus and to write his diary for a week.
- The picture stories also work well together as the basis of a drama activity.

4 The best days of your life

- **subject matter:** education, writing
- **materials:** activity sheets XV–XIX
- **grammar content:** revision (nouns, adjectives and verbs)

Picture story
A writing lesson (p. 21)

1. Flavia enters. Iulius enters.
2. Flavia and Iulius sit down.
3. Corinthus teaches.
4. Iulius writes. Flavia does not write.
5. Corinthus is not happy. Corinthus is angry.
6. Corinthus: Flavia, why aren't you writing?
   Flavia: I am bored.

Grasp the grammar: answers (p. 22)

1 **intrat** he/she enters; **sedent** they sit down; **docet** he is teaching; **scrībit** he/she is writing; **scrībis** you are writing (**est** he is; **sum** I am)

2 **a** īrātus **b** laetus **c** fessus **d** optimus **e** optima

Background information

- The picture story will lead naturally into a discussion of Roman writing and writing materials. The story is based on actual wooden writing tablets and artefacts found at Vindolanda. It is important to stress to pupils that these are real objects which can be seen in the museum at Vindolanda. At least 1,800 tablets have been discovered at the site, seven metres below ground in waterlogged conditions. When the tablets have been dried out, they are cleaned and soaked in methylated spirits for up to eight weeks to preserve them. They are then photographed using infra-red technology. The ink is then legible but the writing is still difficult to read because there is no punctuation or even word division. The standard of Latin in the tablets is high. Over 200 people are named in the tablets, which makes them a very valuable historical resource.

- Why are all the Vindolanda letters written on wood? The alternative writing material, papyrus, had to be imported from Egypt and was expensive. Wood was readily available. Roman ink was made of soot, gum and water.

- The lines copied onto Iulius's tablet are from Virgil's *Aeneid* (Book ix, lines 473 and 474). They are:

   **intereā pavidam volitāns pennāta per urbem
   nūntia Fāma ruit mātrīsque adlābitur aurīs**

   Meanwhile winged Rumour, flying through the terrified city with her news, rushes and slips into the ears of (Euryalus's) mother.

   While this piece of Latin is obviously very difficult for beginners, pupils may be intrigued to look at it and to realise that children in Britain in the second century AD were already using Virgil as a school textbook. You might also like to point out the use of a capital letter to personify a concept (**Fāma**, Rumour). This will be a hard idea for all but the oldest and most able children but, if it seems appropriate to your group, you could link this with some examples of personification in English poetry.

Picture story
Rufus! Don't touch! (p. 24)

- The only piece of Latin in this story is when Flavia says 'Rufus! Don't touch!'. This is a sentence which has already occurred – when Flavius told Rufus not to touch the peacock at the Governor's dinner in chapter 2 (page 12 of the pupil's book). Hopefully some pupils will remember this. If not, a little prompting of the original context should help.

- This story is deliberately told in English, for variety. Pupils can work in small groups to act out the story, with Flavia speaking the Latin at the appropriate moment. Groups of four work best: Flavia, Corinthus, Vibrissa and Rufus. (Groups of five have successfully used two cats!) Few props are needed. Pupils will enjoy practising the scene and performing in front of the rest of the class, possibly as a competition.

- As an extension activity, pupils could compose Latin captions or speech bubbles for this picture story, using words they have already learnt as well as the following Latin words:

  venit comes **ambulat** walks
  ātrāmentum ink **volat** goes flying
  lavat is washing **sordida** dirty
  spectat is watching
  in tablīnum into the study

- The name Rufus occurs here in the **vocative case**. No formal mention is made of case endings as yet and there is no particular need to raise the issue here. However, if pupils want to know why it doesn't say 'Rufus', it may be time to mention that nouns change their endings in Latin, just as verbs do. From their work on verbs, pupils should now be familiar with the idea of looking at word endings to see what is happening in a sentence. The idea of a different ending being used when a person is being spoken to should be sufficient at this stage. Introduce the term 'vocative' if you think your pupils can take it.

Latin roots (p. 26)

dormiō (I sleep): dormitory, dormant, dormouse...

irate from **īrātus**, angry. No, you would not be pleased.

Suggested activities

ENGLISH
- The myth of Echo and Narcissus will be a good basis for discussion about jealousy and vanity. Ask pupils to draw out the moral of the story. Pupils may need to be shown or told about the narcissus flower.

MATHS
- See activity sheet XVI. Extension activities using Roman numerals might include Latin Bingo, and comparison with numbers in French.

ART/C.D.T.
- See activity sheets XV and XVIII. Pupils will notice that the letters *j*, *w*, *x*, *y* and *z* are absent from the Vindolanda cursive script. This is because the Romans didn't use the letters *j* or *w*, and only used *x*, *y* and *z* in Greek names. If pupils want to use these letters, they should make use of these alternatives:

  for *j* – use *i*   for *w* – use *v*
  for *x* – use *cs*   for *y* – use *u*
  for *z* – use *s*

- Let pupils experiment with a dip pen on wood veneer or with a cocktail stick on Plasticine. Dip pens are available from most school supplies catalogues. They will soon discover why the cursive script is made up of open curves!

N.B. When pupils have completed chapter 4, they can be awarded a certificate to mark the end of the first third of the course. The certificate can be found on the last page of this book.

You may wish to revise and then test pupils on some or all of the vocabulary listed on page 17 before awarding the certificate. This list includes all the vocabulary items from the **Words to remember** sections in chapters 1–4.

KEY VOCABULARY FROM CHAPTERS 1–4

verbs

sum	I am
es	you are (sing.)
sumus	we are
estis	you are (pl.)
sedē!/sedēte!	sit down! (sing./pl.)
salvē!/salvēte!	hello! (sing./pl.)
nolī lacrimāre!	don't cry!
coquō	I cook
dormiō	I sleep
faciō	I do
intrō	I enter
labōrō	I work
lacrimō	I cry
legō	I read
rīdeō	I smile
scrībō	I write
sedeō	I sit
spectō	I watch

nouns

ancilla	slave girl
cibus	food
mīles	soldier
servī	slaves
vīlla	house

adjectives

bonus/bona	good
improbus/improba	naughty
novus/nova	new
optimus/optima	very good
parvus/parva	small

adverbs

nunc	now
semper	always
subitō	suddenly

pronouns

omnēs	everyone

interrogatives

cūr?	why?
quid?	what?
quis?	who?

exclamations

ēheu!	oh dear!
euge!	hooray!

5 Romans and Britons

- **subject matter:** Britons, Candidus's experiences
- **grammar content:** adverbs
- **materials:** activity sheets XX–XXI

Picture story
Britons are best! (p. 27)

1. Rufus and Flavia and Candidus are playing.
2. Rufus and Flavia and Candidus sit down.
3. —
4. Candidus: We ride quickly…
5. Candidus: We fight fiercely…
6. Candidus: We farm carefully…

- An inflated pig's bladder was often used as a football!

- The questions at the bottom of page 31 in the pupil's book should stimulate discussion. For Candidus, the Roman mosaics, roads and houses are all very well but they don't really impinge upon his life. He is no longer free, but has to obey someone else's orders. On the other hand, he is safe and well-fed, living in a warm, spacious house. His duties are not as physically demanding as farming. He is well treated by Flavius and Lepidina and is fond of the children. Perhaps he feels slightly inferior to Corinthus, the educated Greek slave.

Use Candidus's experiences to lead pupils into an imaginative discussion of what it might mean to be invaded, conquered and enslaved.

Grasp the grammar (p. 28)

This chapter focuses on adverbs (words which tell us **how an action is done** – quickly, carefully, etc.). Irregularities and complications have been deliberately avoided at this stage. Only adverbs which end in **-ter** (in Latin) and in **-ly** (in English) have been included.

Grasp the grammar: answers

1. **a** fiercely **ferōciter**; **b** carefully **dīligenter**
   Minimus's reference back to chapter 4 – the word used was **segniter** 'sloppily'.
2. -ly
3. -ter

As a reinforcement exercise, ask pupils to compose short sentences using the verbs ending in **-mus** and adverbs, and to illustrate them with pictures of Minimus and Vibrissa, for example:

dīligenter pingimus we paint carefully.

Here is some extra vocabulary:
Verbs: **cantāmus** we sing; **pingimus** we paint; **currimus** we run
Adverbs: **fortiter** loudly *or* strongly; **hilariter** cheerfully; **fēlīciter** happily; **ārdenter** eagerly; **audācter** boldly

Background information

- The quotation from Julius Caesar is from *Gallic War* 4.33. The quotation from Cicero is from *ad Atticus* 4.16.7 and the quotation from Strabo is from *Geography* 4.5.1–3.

Latin roots: answers (p. 30)

1. <u>diligent</u> from **dīligenter**, carefully. Yes, your teacher would be pleased.
2. <u>ferocious</u>
3. <u>pugnacious</u> from **pugnō**, I fight. An aggressive dog.
4. <u>accelerator</u> from **celeriter**, quickly. The car speeds up.

Picture story
Romans are best! (p. 31)

1 Flavia: The mosaics are beautiful.
Candidus: Yes.

2 Flavia: And Roman roads are straight.
Candidus: Yes.

3 Flavia: And Roman houses are comfortable.
Candidus: Yes.

4 Rufus: And now you live with us!
Candidus: Yes!

- **tesserae** are actually the individual pieces of stone which make up mosaics. The correct term for mosaics is **opus mūsivum**.

Suggested activities

ART
- Ask pupils to draw a picture of a British warrior in his chariot. They can use the following description by Julius Caesar to help:

  'All the Britons paint themselves with a blue dye called woad; this gives them a more frightening appearance in battle. They wear their hair long and the men have moustaches.'

- Pupils could make their own mosaics using black or white card as a background (A4 is suitable for individual mosaics; a class project might be bigger). Pupils should sketch out a rough design on the card. Try to persuade them not to be too ambitious – simple designs and patterns work best! Next, pupils cut different coloured paper into small pieces (about thumbnail size). They then glue their design with a glue stick and use tweezers to apply the tesserae, leaving no spaces. A more challenging project would be to use glass tesserae to make a permanent mosaic.

GEOGRAPHY
- Use the map of Roman Britain (activity sheet XXI).

  Ask pupils to mark on their map the names of Roman towns and to write their English names underneath in a different colour.

  Find out if anyone in the class has visited a Roman site and, if so, which one(s). Get pupils to mark these sites on their maps.

  Ask pupils to mark clearly the things that the Romans brought back from Britain (see quotations on page 30 of the pupil's book).

  Ask pupils to consider how long it would take to get from your school to various Roman sites:

  a) today (in a car, by train, or even by plane)

  b) in Roman times (in a cart or on foot).

  Using appropriate reference sources, ask pupils to mark in the Fosse Way, Watling Street and Ermine Street – Roman roads, parts of which we still travel on today.

6 Off to town

- **subject matter:** a trip to Eboracum (York)
- **grammar content:** consolidation
- **materials:** activity sheets XXII–XXIII

Picture story
Let's go shopping! (p. 33)

1 Flavius: I am going to York. There the weapons are splendid.

2 Lepidina: I am going to York. There the dresses are beautiful.

3 Iulius: I am going to York. There the board-games are excellent.

4 Flavia: I am going to York. There the beads are colourful.

- The normal rule in Latin is that the names of towns do not need a preposition in front of them. Therefore here **Eborācum** means 'to York'.

- The style of dress worn by women in Roman Britain at this time is tunic-shaped and is not the stola, which was worn by women in Rome. Hence **tunica** is here translated as 'dress'.

- **lūdī** is used here for board-games. In fact, it can mean any kind of game such as gladiatorial games. **lūdus** is also the word used for 'school'.

- There are some excellent examples of colourful glass beads in the York Gardens Museum. In fact, all the items that the family buy in York are based on original artefacts in the museum. York went on to become a major centre for the production of jewellery made of jet, but this had not yet begun at the time of Flavius and his family. Hence the purchase of glass beads.

Background information

- This visit to Eboracum (York) is a major undertaking. The family would have had an armed guard in case of bandits. There would be possible danger on the road out of Vindolanda. This road was known as the Stanegate, and it pre-dates Hadrian's Wall. The idea of travel being so difficult and dangerous is a tricky concept to get across to pupils. Stress that the round trip is likely to have taken about a week.

- This would be a good point at which to research travel in the ancient world. Ask pupils how they think Flavius and his family travelled from the Netherlands to Vindolanda.

The likely scenario is that Flavius would have received notice of his new command while the family was in the Netherlands. He would then have set off on the next troop ship heading for South Shields, leaving his wife and children to pack up the house and their belongings. They would then have followed on a merchant ship, trading with the north coast of Britain. Flavius would have made arrangements with his fellow commanding officer at the port (on the Humber) to accommodate his family and to send a message for someone to come and pick them up with a wagon. Flavius would only have brought with him to Britain the minimum of belongings and his horse; Lepidina was expected to bring everything else.

Picture story
Let's all go! (pp. 34–5)

1 Corinthus: I am going to York. There the pens and wax tablets are excellent

2 Candidus: Barates lives in York. He is a friend (*or* He is my friend).

③ Rufus cries.

④ Lepidina: Don't cry! Come to York!
Rufus smiles.

⑤ Lepidina: Pandora, come to York!
Pandora: Yes!

⑥ Corinthus and Candidus are smiling.

Grasp the grammar: answers (p. 36)

Mini-quiz: **1** verb **2** noun **3** adjective **4** ending

1 a The pen is excellent. **b** The pens are excellent. **c** The dress is beautiful. **d** The swords are sharp. **e** The wax tablet is broken. **f** The beads are beautiful. **g** Vibrissa is fat. **h** Pandora is beautiful. **i** Corinthus is clever. **j** Candidus is tough.

N.B. Some of the nouns in this exercise and in the picture stories are plural. Note that the adjectives still agree with nouns, and that the verb **est** (is) changes to the plural form **sunt** (are).

A day in Eboracum: answers (p. 37)

Flavius buys a sword (**gladius**).

Lepidina buys a perfume flask (**ampūlla**). This is in the York museum. It was found at Catterick, where the family spent at least one night. It is enamelled, beautiful and very rare.

Flavia buys glass beads (**pilulae**). The fashion was to wear several necklaces of different colours.

Iulius buys a board and counters (**lūdus**). The counters are in the Gardens Museum and there are game boards in various Roman museums such as Corbridge and Caerleon, and at Vindolanda itself.

Rufus chooses some little bronze animals (**animālia aēnea**). These are in the Gardens Museum in the form of brooches. They are adapted here as animal figures because of the danger of pins for a three-year-old. Bronze animals were sold as statuettes and toys. Pupils may raise the issue of small objects being dangerous for young children – a good point. Reassure them that Pandora is vigilant!

Candidus chooses a cooking pot (**mortārium**). Many of these have been found in Britain, some in York. They were used for grinding up food, herbs and so on (as in *mortar* and pestle).

Corinthus selects pens and wax tablets (**stilī et cērae**). As a slave, Corinthus cannot purchase these items himself. However, as an educated slave in charge of the children's schooling, he can advise on what to buy.

Pandora buys a wig (**capillāmentum**) not for herself, but she is employed for her hairdressing skills. Experimenting with wigs and hair dyes was popular and fashionable. The big town would be the right place to find such fashion items. In the Gardens Museum is a roll of auburn hair – not a wig, but possibly a separate hair-piece. It is rolled into a bun and still has the hairpins to keep it in place. Roman women of this period wore their hair long and pinned up, off the face.

Latin roots: answers (p. 37)

1 <u>habitat</u> from **habitat**, he lives. An animal's habitat is the place where it lives.

2 <u>acute</u> from **acūtus**, sharp. Yes, a severe pain.

3 <u>obese</u> from **obēsus**, fat.

4 <u>fractured</u> from **frāctus**, broken.

Background information

■ The wonderful, true story of Barates and his beloved Regina can be pieced together from their tombstones. His is in the museum at Corbridge; hers in the museum at South Shields and there is a copy of it in the Museum of Antiquities in Newcastle. Barates came from Palmyra in Syria. Regina was from the Verulamium (St Albans) area and was a member of the Catuvellauni tribe; we don't know where they met. Barates had to purchase Regina's freedom in order to marry her. They lived at South Shields where Barates was a **vexillārius**. One translation of this is 'flagseller'. It is likely that he traded in other good cloth and jewellery. He seems to have moved to Corbridge after Regina's death. He died aged 68. Regina died aged 30. On her tombstone, Barates laments her death, both in Latin and in his native Palmyrene script. The tombstone is elaborate; he was determined to commemorate her in a grand style. There is no record of any children; it is quite likely that she died in childbirth. We can't be certain when they lived but the second century AD seems probable. For the purposes of this story, they are imagined to be living in Eboracum (York).

- Their story illustrates perfectly the meaning of the Roman Empire – cultural mixing, travel, trade, etc. You could use the story of Barates and Regina to lead into a discussion about mixed marriages. What might be their language difficulties? How did Regina feel about moving so far north? How did Barates cope with the change in climate between Syria and Northumberland?

- The story of Barates and Regina forms the basis of a recent Channel 4 video, *Romans and Celts*.

Suggested activities

ENGLISH

- Ask pupils to work in pairs. One partner role-plays a television reporter who can travel back in time; the other plays Barates. The pupils should act out and then write an account of an interview with Barates. Help the reporters to question Barates in such a way that he has to talk about his feelings. Remind pupils that Barates is now living a very long way from home.

- Barates travelled from one end of the Empire to the other, probably following the legions. Ask pupils to write a story about some of the adventures he might have had on the way.

GEOGRAPHY

- Using an atlas and the map of the Roman Empire on page 38 of the pupil's book, work out the route that Barates took to travel from Syria to Britain.

7 The military machine

- **subject matter:** the Roman army
- **grammar content:** imperatives (commands)
- **materials:** activity sheets XXIV–XXV

Picture story
Be careful, Rufus! (p. 40)

1. Iulius: What is it?
   Flavius: It is a helmet. Rufus, don't touch!

2. Iulius: What is it?
   Flavius: It is a sword. Rufus, don't touch!

3. Iulius: What is it?
   Flavius: It is a javelin. Rufus, don't touch!

4. Iulius: What is it?
   Flavius: It is a shield. Rufus, be careful! The shield is very big.

5. Iulius: What is it?
   Flavius: It is a breastplate. Rufus, stop! The breastplate is very big.

6. Iulius: What is it?
   Flavius: It is a dagger. Rufus, leave it! It is dangerous!

7. Candidus: Look!

8. Candidus: Now Rufus is happy!

Grasp the grammar (p. 41)

This chapter sees the formal introduction of imperatives, which have already occurred simply as vocabulary items. There is no need to use the term 'imperative' unless your pupils like formal terminology – 'command' (or 'order') is descriptive and accurate.

The examples given are: **venī!** come! **surge!** get up! **redī!** go back!

N.B. Two of the nouns in the picture story are neuter (i.e. neither masculine nor feminine). This is why the endings of **scūtum** and **pīlum** are different (not **-us** or **-a**). **maximum** agrees with **scūtum**. Pupils do not need to tackle the concept of a third gender at this stage.

Simō dīcit (Simon says) (p. 41)

Remember to use the plural form (ending **-te**) as you are speaking to the whole class. Begin the game with familiar verbs in the command form. Then teach pupils some new verbs to extend the range of actions.

Familiar verbs:

scrībite!	write!	**rīdēte!**	laugh *or* smile!
sedēte!	sit!	**pūrgāte!**	clean!
surgite!	get up!	**verrite!**	sweep!
labōrāte!	work!	**legite!**	read!
lacrimāte!	cry!		

New verbs:

cōnsūmite!	eat!	**natāte!**	swim!
cantāte!	sing!	**salīte!**	jump!
dormite!	sleep!	**pingite!**	paint!
saltāte!	dance!		

For further practice, pupils can play **Simō dīcit** in pairs or in small groups. If they are working in pairs, they will need to remember to use the singular form of the imperative.

- Alternatively, one pupil could play the part of a centurion, giving orders to a group of soldiers. Any soldiers who fail to grasp the command and are therefore slow to obey, are out. The last pupil left is the best legionary soldier and gets a reward (extra pay? light duties?!). Here is a list of possible commands from the centurion:

ad signa	fall in
laxāte	stand at ease
dextrōrsum vertite	right turn
sinistrōrsum vertite	left turn
retrōrsum vertite	about turn
cōnsistite	halt
ūnum ōrdinem facite	make a single line
ūnum passum prōcēdite	one step forward
ūnum passum recēdite	one step backwards
cuneum facite	make a wedge (a wedge-shaped formation of soldiers)
gladiōs stringite	draw swords
gladiōs recondite	sheath swords
scūta tollite	lift shields to battle position
scūta dēmittite	lower shields
gradum servāte	keep in step
iter accelerāte	quicken the pace
iter tardāte	slow the pace
quiēscite (*pl.*) **quiēsce** (*sing.*)	be quiet
ab signīs discēdite	dismiss

Picture story
Do as you're told! (p. 42)

❶ Centurion: Soldiers, listen!

  The soldiers listen.

❷ Centurion: Pick up your javelins (*or* the javelins)!

  The soldiers pick up their javelins.

❸ Centurion: Carry the javelins!

  The soldiers carry the javelins.

❹ Centurion: Soldiers, go forward (*or* advance)!

  The soldiers go forward.

❺ Centurion: Put down the javelins! Make the tortoise!

  The soldiers make the tortoise.

Latin roots: answers (p. 44)

1 military from **mīlitēs**, soldiers.
2 auditorium from **audīte!**, listen.
3 porter from **portāte!**, carry.
4 proceed from **prōcēdite!**, go forward.
5 factory from **facite!**, make. A factory is where things are made.

Suggested activities

ART
- See activity sheets XXIV and XXV, which should be handed out together. When pupils have completed their Roman soldier, ask them the following questions:

  Which of his weapons did the Roman soldier throw at his enemy from a distance?
  (**pīlum** javelin)

  Which sharp weapon did he use to cut an enemy?
  (**gladius** sword)

  Which pointed weapon did he use to stab his enemy when he got really close?
  (**pugiō** dagger)

  Why are there two pieces of metal hanging down from his helmet over the sides of his face?
  (to protect his cheeks)

  Why does he wear a woollen scarf around his neck?
  (to prevent chafing from the metal rim of the helmet – and to keep warm)

  You can see soldiers' leather shoes in many Roman museums, including the one at Vindolanda. Why do you think they had nails on the soles?
  (to make the soles last longer; improved grip)

ENGLISH
- Ask pupils to imagine they are Greeks inside the Wooden Horse. They should write a poem describing their feelings on the last night of Troy.

8 Clean and healthy

- **subject matter:** Roman baths, doctors
- **materials:** activity sheets XXVI–XXVII
- **grammar content:** revision of adverbs and imperatives

Picture story
Time for a bath! (p. 46)

1. Lepidina and Flavia play cheerfully.
2. Lepidina and Flavia are in the changing room. They undress quickly.
3. Lepidina and Flavia are in the warm room. They are lying down lazily.
4. Lepidina and Flavia are in the hot room. Slave girls are scraping them skilfully.
5. Lepidina and Flavia are in the cold room. They plunge under the water for a short time.
6. Lepidina and Flavia are chatting with friends. They are happy and clean.

Grasp the grammar: answers (pp. 47–8)

1 **a** celeriter (Vibrissa and Minimus run / are running quickly.) **b** segniter (Lepidina and Flavia walk / are walking lazily.) **c** dīligenter (Pandora and Corinthus work / are working carefully.) **d** ferōciter (The Romans and the Britons fight / are fighting ferociously.) **e** breviter (Lepidina and Flavia plunge / are plunging underwater for a short time.)

Minimus visits the baths: **1** d, **2** a, **3** b, **4** c.

frīgidārium sounds like 'fridge'. <u>Tepid</u> water is warm.

- Roman toilets were usually communal. Romans used a sponge on a stick instead of toilet paper. A good example of a Roman toilet is the one at the fort at Housesteads, on Hadrian's Wall. If you can get hold of photographs of the splendid reconstruction (postcards are available), pupils will be fascinated to see what the toilets probably looked like!

Picture story
A visit to the doctor (p. 50)

1. Doctor: Hello!
   Flavius & Lepidina: Hello!
2. Doctor: Come! Sit down!
3. Doctor: Lie down! Open your eyes!
4. —
5. Doctor: Put it on three times a day!
6. Doctor: Take these twice a day!
   Flavius & Lepidina: Thank you.

- Here are the answers to the questions on page 51 of the pupil's book. Commands in the picture story: **venīte!** come! **sedēte!** sit down! **discumbe!** lie down! **oculōs aperī!** open your eyes! **impōne!** put it on! **cōnsūme!** eat!

Some of the commands end in **-te** (the plural form) because the doctor is addressing both Flavius and Lepidina.

Background information

- One of the Vindolanda writing tablets concerns soldiers who are absent from duty because they are suffering from what seems to be conjunctivitis. Pupils could be taught this term – perhaps one of their relatives has suffered from it. Stress to pupils that the Romans suffered from many of the illnesses that we do today. This might lead to a discussion about progress in medicine and how antiseptics, antibiotics and inoculations have eliminated or reduced the risk of many diseases today. There is no evidence of a hospital at Vindolanda, but tweezers, probes and spatulas have all been found. The nearest military hospital is at Housesteads, a couple of miles away.

Suggested activities

DRAMA
- Pupils could write and act out a simple play, in Latin, about a visit to the doctor (see activity sheets XXVI and XXVII).
- The wonderful story of Odysseus and the Cyclops is from Homer's *Odyssey*, Book 9. Pupils will enjoy acting it out.

ENGLISH
- We know that women used the soldiers' bath-house at Vindolanda because archaeologists have found combs, hair-pins and jewellery at the baths. Ask pupils to write a story called 'Lepidina loses her necklace'. Encourage them to include the different rooms at the bath-house and to use the correct Latin names.
- Ask pairs of pupils to take on the roles of Odysseus and a chat-show host. Odysseus has been invited onto the show to talk about his adventures with the Cyclops. Pupils should enact the scene and then write a dialogue, trying to get across the fact that Odysseus is confident and cunning.
- Pupils could make up acrostic poems using words like 'Cyclops' and 'monster'.

ART
- Pupils could illustrate the story of Odysseus and the Cyclops as a cartoon strip.
- Ask pupils to draw a picture to give their impression of what the Cyclops looked like. They should remember that he was a giant, with one eye in the centre of his forehead.

N.B. When pupils have completed chapter 8, they can be awarded a certificate to mark the end of the second part of the course. The certificate can be found on the last page of this book.

You may wish to revise and then test pupils on some or all of the vocabulary listed on page 27 before awarding the certificate. This list includes all the vocabulary items from the **Words to remember** sections in chapters 5–8.

KEY VOCABULARY FROM CHAPTERS 5–8

verbs

equitō	I ride
habitat	he lives
lūdō	I play
pugnō	I fight
audīte!	listen!
prōcēdite!	go forward!
redīte!	go back!
siste!	stop!

nouns

apodytērium	changing room
arma	weapons
caldārium	hot room
cēra	wax tablet
frīgidārium	cold room
galea	helmet
gladius	sword
lōrīca	breastplate
lūdus	game
pīlum	javelin
pugiō	dagger
scūtum	shield
stilus	pen
tepidārium	warm room
viae	streets
vīllae	houses

adjectives

callidus/callida	clever

adverbs

breviter	briefly
celeriter	quickly
dīligenter	carefully
ferōciter	fiercely
hilariter	cheerfully
prūdenter	skilfully
segniter	lazily

phrases

ita vērō	yes
nōbīscum	with us

9 A soldier's life

- **subject matter:** life in the Roman army
- **materials:** activity sheets XXVIII–XXX
- **grammar content:** prepositions

Picture story
Who's who? (p. 53)

1. Iulius: Who is he?
   Flavius: He is a standard-bearer.
2. Iulius: Who is he?
   Flavius: He is a flag-bearer.
3. Iulius: Who is he?
   Flavius: He is a horn-player.
4. Iulius: Who is he?
   Flavius: He is a centurion.

- The soldiers at Vindolanda belonged to the ninth cohort of Batavians, from the Netherlands. They were mostly auxiliary soldiers. About 25% of the troops at Vindolanda were cavalry. One of the most striking artefacts in the museum is the collection of remains of a **chamfron**, or horse's headdress. Something as fine as this must have been worn only on ceremonial occasions.

- The writing tablet concerning extra socks and pants (page 55 of the pupil's book) was the first to be discovered at Vindolanda.

- Here are some further questions which pupils might consider on the subject of life in the Roman army:

Were soldiers allowed to have families?
Officers were, but soldiers beneath the rank of centurion were not. Many soldiers had 'unofficial' families living in the civilian settlements near their fort or camp.

Where did the soldiers sleep?
In bunks in a barrack block. The commander and senior officers had houses. When they were on the march, soldiers slept eight to a tent.

Were soldiers allowed out on leave?
Yes: several of the writing tablets from Vindolanda detail soldiers' requests for leave.

Did soldiers play sports?
They trained in wrestling, and they might swim or play ball games at the baths. Soldiers kept fit with weapons drill and regular route marches.

What happened to disobedient soldiers?
They would be whipped, or made to do the worst jobs such as cleaning the latrines.

Picture story: Where are Minimus and Vibrissa? (p. 56)

1. Minimus and Vibrissa are near the ballista.
2. Minimus and Vibrissa are running round the ballista.
3. Minimus is under the ballista.
4. Vibrissa is on top of the ballista.
5. Minimus is in the ballista.
6. Vibrissa is in front of the ballista.
7. Vibrissa runs to the ballista.
8. Minimus runs away from the ballista.
9. Vibrissa is tired. Minimus is very happy!

Latin roots: answers (p. 57)

1 submarine from **sub**, under. Under the sea.
2 Under the ground.
3 circumnavigate from **circum**, round. He has sailed around the world.
4 propeller from **pro**, in front. (Usually) forwards.

Extend work on English words that use Latin prepositions by using a dictionary to check the meanings of the following words: *circumference, circumstance, submerge, sublunar, subsoil, substratum, subside, subtract*. Can pupils think of further examples? (There are plenty more.)

Quiz

This quiz tests pupils' knowledge of Roman military life. The class could be divided into two teams – legionaries and auxiliaries. You could give two points for a correct answer, awarding a bonus point if a team can answer a question their opponents fail to answer.

1. How old must Iulius be before he can join the army? (18.)
2. Which pointed weapon did soldiers throw from a distance? (The **pīlum**/javelin.)
3. What is a **gladius**? (A sword.)
4. What did the soldiers' sandals have on the soles? (Metal studs.)
5. What did these studs help to do? (Make the sandals last longer / help the soldiers to grip.)
6. What were the soldiers' practice weapons made from? (Wood.)
7. Give three ways of recognising a **centurion**. (One point for each correct answer. He carries a stick for beating the soldiers; he wears shiny shin pads called **greaves**; he wears a special helmet – the crest on a centurion's helmet went from side to side (transverse), whereas that on a soldier's helmet went from front to back.)
8. What do we call the formation when soldiers covered their heads with their shields to protect themselves? (A tortoise.)
9. Name one thing that the soldiers drank at Vindolanda. (Beer, water or milk.)
10. How did a soldier stop his helmet from scratching his neck? (He wore a woollen scarf.)
11. What other job did the standard-bearer do, apart from carrying the legion's flag into battle? (He looked after the soldiers' savings.)
12. How long would a soldier sign up for? (At least twenty years.)
13. Name three things a soldier would carry each day, apart from his heavy armour. (One point for each correct answer. Food, cooking pots, an axe for chopping wood.)
14. One soldier at Vindolanda wrote home to Mum because he was feeling cold and wanted more clothes. What three things did she send him? (One point for each correct answer. Socks, sandals and underpants.)

Use the following question as a tiebreaker if necessary.

15. What is the name of the large Roman catapult that was used to fire stone balls? (A **ballista**.)

Activity sheet XXX: answers

B	P	S	T	O	P	I	L	U	M
A	L	A	B	T	P	C	S	M	U
C	S	E	T	E	U	T	U	G	T
I	I	L	U	S	G	C	I	E	U
R	G	A	G	T	I	B	D	O	C
O	N	G	M	U	O	L	A	S	S
L	I	B	L	D	A	D	L	P	O
C	F	A	G	O	P	N	G	A	P
S	E	T	I	L	I	M	S	T	B
P	R	O	I	V	U	T	N	B	C

When pupils have identified all the words, they can write a list of them, together with their English meanings.

ballista	catapult
mīlitēs	soldiers
lōrīca	breastplate
scūtum	shield
pīlum	javelin
pugiō	dagger
gladius	sword
signifer	standard-bearer
galea	helmet
testūdō	tortoise

Suggested activities

ART
- Pupils could design a poster encouraging young men to join the Roman army.

ENGLISH
- Read W.H. Auden's poem 'Roman Wall Blues', which is about the feelings of a soldier stationed on Hadrian's Wall. Ask pupils to write down four things that made the soldier unhappy or uncomfortable. They should imagine they are the soldier and, using the information from the poem, write a letter home, describing what it is like to serve at Vindolanda.

10 How beautiful!

> ■ **subject matter:** jewellery, clothes and cosmetics ■ **materials:** activity sheets XXXI–XXXII
> ■ **grammar content:** conjunctions

Picture story
You look lovely (p. 59)

1 Lepidina: Hello, Rufus!
Rufus: Hello, mother! How beautiful you are.

2 Lepidina: Thank you, Rufus. Sit down and watch!

Lepidina is happy because Pandora works skilfully.

3 Rufus: What is this, Pandora?
Pandora: It is a wig.

4 Lepidina: Now my hair is beautiful but my ears are dirty.

5 Rufus: What is this?
Pandora: It is lip gloss.

6 Lepidina: Pandora, where are my jewels?
Pandora: Look! (*or* Here they are!)

Although Pandora works for a long time, Lepidina is not satisfied.

7 Rufus: Hooray!

8 Lepidina & Pandora: Rufus! You are naughty!

Grasp the grammar: answers (p. 60)

This chapter introduces conjunctions ('joining words'). As they are invariable (do not change their ending according to their function in the sentence), they should not present too much difficulty.

1 **quod** (because); **sed** (but); **quamquam** (although)

2 There is more than one possible set of correct answers. The likeliest are:

a and **b** but/although **c** because **d** but/although

Picture story
The romantic ring (p. 61)

1 Flavia is in the bedroom and is looking at the jewellery.

2 Flavia: What is it?
Lepidina: It is a ring. It is valuable.

3 Flavia: Why is it valuable?
Lepidina: Because it is made of gold (*or* it is golden).

4 Flavia: It is a splendid ring. (*or* The ring is splendid.)
Lepidina: Yes. The ring is a present from your father.

5 Flavia: What are these words?
Lepidina: My life. (*or* My soul.)

6 Flavia: How romantic it is!

■ Pupils may remember that Claudia called Lepidina her **anima** in the birthday party invitation in chapter 1.

■ The activity on jewellery at the bottom of page 62 is intended to combine English and science through a discussion of materials. It is hoped that the discussion will cover the size of each piece and the complexity of its design, as well as the value and rarity of the material of which it is made. You could ask pupils to bring in some especially interesting pieces to illustrate these points.

- Answer to Minimus's question at the top of page 62: The conjunction is **et**, meaning 'and'.

Latin roots: answers (p. 62)

1. precious
2. donation
3. <u>animated</u> from **anima**, life. They would be speaking in a lively manner.
4. <u>verbose</u> from **verba**, words. The story is too wordy.

Suggested activities

C.D.T.
- Ask pupils to design a piece of Roman jewellery. It might be beads (Roman women liked to wear several strings of different coloured beads), a brooch, a bracelet or earrings. (See activity sheet XXXI for ideas.)
- Weave your own piece of Roman cloth, like the textiles found at Vindolanda. (See activity sheet XXXII.) The cloth found at Vindolanda is now rather dull in colour because the original colours have faded, but it would have been brightly coloured with vegetable dyes.

SCIENCE
- Draw pupils' attention to the Latin names of certain metals. It may help them to remember the chemical symbols:

  Au **aurum** gold
  Ag **argentum** silver
  Pb **plumbum** lead
  Sn **stannum** tin
  Cu **cuprum** copper
  Fe **ferrum** iron

ENGLISH/DRAMA/R.E.
- The Midas story teaches that greed for gold brought about unhappiness. Compare this with other stories which have a moral, such as the story of the Prodigal Son (Luke 15.11–32). Discuss the links between the two stories. This could lead to a general discussion about parables, fables and allegories.
- Small groups could act out fables such as Aesop's. Give each group a fable to act out in not more than three minutes. Ask the rest of the class to guess the moral of the tale.

ART
- Ask pupils to draw King Midas in his palace, beginning to turn things to gold. They should draw some objects which he hasn't yet touched, so that the picture is not totally yellow.

11 A sad day

- **subject matter:** death and burial
- **grammar content:** concept of subject and object
- **materials:** activity sheet XXXIII

Picture story
Bad news (p. 64)

1. Candidus receives a letter.
2. Barates is very sad because Regina is dead.
3. —
4. Lepidina looks after Candidus.
5. Corinthus gets the horse and cart ready.
6. Pandora looks after the family.

Grasp the grammar: answers (p. 65)

Linguistically, this is the most demanding chapter as it introduces the concepts of subject and object, and of case endings. Give pupils plenty of practice in identifying the subject and the object in English sentences (as in the exercise on page 66 of the pupil's book). There is no mention of the terms 'nominative' and 'accusative'. It is up to you to decide whether it is appropriate to introduce these terms to your particular pupils. All they really need to know is that nouns (like verbs and adjectives) change their endings depending upon the job they are doing in the sentence.

1. a Vibrissa (s) <u>chases</u> Minimus (o).
   b Minimus (s) <u>chases</u> Vibrissa (o).
   c Minimus (s) <u>eats</u> cheese (o).
   d Vibrissa (s) <u>eats</u> mice (o).
   e Flavius and Lepidina (s) <u>praise</u> Candidus (o).
   f Candidus (s) <u>roasts</u> a peacock and a dormouse (o).
   g Candidus and Corinthus (s) <u>like</u> Pandora (o).
   h Pandora (s) <u>loves</u> Rufus (o).

Latin roots: answers (p. 66)

1. accepts
2. letters
3. a keeping the bodies of dead people before burial
   b someone who will die eventually
   c they never die; the gods

Picture story
Goodbye to Regina (p. 67)

1. Barates carries a wreath.
2. Flavius carries a lamp. Lepidina carries a ring.
3. A sculptor carves a splendid inscription.
4. —
5. Flavius and Lepidina put (down) the lamp and the ring into the pot.
6. Barates places the wreath onto the tomb.

Background information

- The story here is based on what we know of Barates and Regina. Barates was introduced as a friend of Candidus in chapter 6, when the family visited York (Eboracum). What we know of Barates and Regina has been deduced from their tombstones. This chapter provides an opportunity for pupils to learn some of the principles of decoding Roman inscriptions – see Suggested activities below (and activity sheet XXXIII).

Suggested activities

HISTORY

- Visit a local museum which contains some Roman tombstones. Using the inscription on Regina's tomb as a pattern, ask pupils to try to decipher one of the tombstones.

  N.B. The abbreviation STIP is common on military tombstones. It is short for STIPENDIA and is usually followed by Roman numerals. This refers to the number of years that a soldier spent in the Roman army. (See activity sheet XXXIII.)

- With pupils, work through the Latin inscription on Regina's tomb (pictured on page 70 of the pupil's book). It reads:

  DM.REGINA.LIBERTA.ET.CONIVGE.
  BARATES.PALMYRENVS.NATIONE
  CATVALLAVNA.AN.XXX

Key

DM (Dis manibus)	to the gods of the Underworld
Regina	her name
Liberta	freedwoman
Coniuge	wife (N.B. The letter 'u' is normally shown as a 'v' in inscriptions.)
Barates Palmyrenus	Barates' name and home. He came from Palmyra, in Syria.
Natione Catvallauna	Regina belonged to the Catuvellauni tribe.
AN (annos)	how many years she lived
XXX	30*

Underneath the Latin inscription is a sentence in Barates' native Palmyrene, reading from right to left, which means 'Regina, the freedwoman of Barates, alas!'

*This is a good point at which to revise Roman numerals.

- Ask pupils to go and look at some tombstones in a local cemetery. What are the similarities between 'modern' inscriptions and Roman ones?

  Similarities: name of deceased, expressions of grief of surviving relatives.

  Differences: no dates given on Roman tombstones; many Roman tombs had elaborate carved pictures, recording the life and achievements of the deceased.

- Point out that it is in his native tongue rather than in Latin that Barates feels free to express his grief (**alas!**).

- The carving shows Regina with her jewel box (she holds the key) and her spindles and balls of wool. She is sitting in a high basket chair. She is wearing earrings. This is a traditional view of a Roman married woman (**mātrōna**). The significance of the large hat is not known. Ask pupils to speculate!

ART

- Pupils can colour the picture of a Roman tombstone on activity sheet XXXIII. They should make the Latin inscription stand out clearly.

12 Gods! Hear our prayers!

- **subject matter:** religion
- **grammar content:** revision
- **materials:** activity sheets XXXIV–XXXV

Picture story
Rufus is ill (p. 71)

1. Rufus is eating nothing because he is hot.
2. Lepidina is anxious and summons the doctor.
3. Corinthus and Candidus are not working because they are worried.
4. Although Flavia and Iulius are frightened, they are playing in the garden.
5. Minimus and Vibrissa are sad and are not running.
6. Flavius is anxious but writes a letter.

Grammar revision: answers (p. 72)

callidus means 'clever'.

1. a **calidus** hot; **anxia** anxious; **sollicitī** worried; **pavidī** frightened; **trīstēs** sad; **anxius** anxious

   b Singular: **calidus**, **anxia** and **anxius**. Plural: **sollicitī**, **pavidī** and **trīstēs**.

2. a **quod** because; **et** and; **quod** because; **quamquam** although; **et** and; **sed** but

3. The verbs which end in **-t** are singular (he/she). The verbs which end in **-nt** are plural (they).

4. Because it is in the plural form (the command is being given to more than one goddess).

   Flavius: Jupiter! Hear our prayers! Accept the wine!

   Candidus: Mother goddesses! Hear my prayer!

   N.B. Jupiter is spelt with two 'p's in Latin.

5. There is more than one correct solution to this matching game. This should lead to some revision of and reflection on the characters as they have appeared earlier in the book. This is the most appropriate pairing:

a	**Lepīdina Rūfum tenet.**	Lepidina cuddles (*or* holds) Rufus.
b	**Flāvius sacrificium facit.**	Flavius (as the **pater familias** – father of the household) makes a sacrifice.
c	**Iūlius versum recitat.**	Iulius recites some poetry (*or* a verse).
d	**Flāvia suāviter cantat.**	Flavia sings sweetly.
e	**Candidus plaustrum facit.**	Candidus makes a toy cart (because he is good at making things).
f	**Corinthus fābulam nārrat.**	Corinthus tells a story.
g	**Pandōra capillōs pectit.**	Pandora combs his hair (because she is a hairdresser).
h	**medicus medicāmentum portat.**	The doctor brings medicine.
i	**Minimus cāseum dat.**	Minimus gives cheese.
j	**Vibrissa Rūfum lambit.**	Vibrissa licks Rufus.

Roman report (p. 74)

Play a simple game of Pelmanism to follow work on the Greek and Roman gods and goddesses. Make a set of twelve small green cards with the Greek names of the Olympian gods. Make another set of twelve pink cards with the gods' equivalent Roman names. A simple symbol drawn on the cards might be helpful (e.g. a trident for Poseidon/Neptune; a musical instrument for Apollo; a bow and arrow for Artemis/Diana). Pupils play this game in small groups of 2–4. Put the cards face down on the table. Pupils turn over a pink and a green card, the aim being to find a pair with the Greek and Roman words for the same god/goddess. If they do not match, the cards must be replaced on the table, face down. The winner is the pupil to collect the most pairs in a given time.

Picture story
All's well that ends well... (p. 75)

1. Now Rufus is not hot.
2. Suddenly Rufus gets up.
3. Now Rufus smiles.
4. Everyone smiles.

- Rufus has probably picked up some minor but nasty bug. Cold water brings his temperature down and all the attention from the rest of the family brings about a speedy recovery.

valēte! Farewell!

Suggested activities

SCIENCE
- Discuss how medical treatments have developed since Roman times. How would a modern-day doctor treat a child with a high temperature and an infection? Children could do some research on this topic – for example, into the discovery of penicillin and the development of antibiotics.

N.B. When pupils have completed chapter 12, they can be awarded a certificate to mark the end of the course. The certificate can be found on the last page of this book.

You may wish to revise and then test pupils on some or all of the vocabulary listed on page 36 before awarding the certificate. This list includes all the vocabulary items from the **Words to remember** sections in chapters 9–12.

KEY VOCABULARY FROM CHAPTERS 9–12

verbs

accipit	receives
cantat	sings
dat	gives
facit	makes
nārrat	tells
parat	prepares
pōnit	places/puts
portat	carries

nouns

epistula	letter
fābula	story
vīnum	wine

adjectives

fessus/fessa	tired
laetus/laeta	happy
mortuus/mortua	dead

phrase

grātiās tibi agō	I thank you

adverbs

diū	for a long time
nunc	now
suāviter	sweetly

interrogatives

cur?	why?
quid?	what?
quis?	who?
ubi?	where?

prepositions

ad	to
circum	around
ē	from / out of
in	in/on
prō	in front of
prope	near
sub	under
super	on top of

Meet the family

Name: _____ Date: _____

Colour the picture of the family and write in their names. Who is the strange girl on the left? You'll find out in chapter 3.

Chapter 1

© Cambridge University Press 1999

Family tree

II

Name: _____ Date: _____

Flavius
pater

Write in everyone's name...

...and write in the Latin word too.

© Cambridge University Press 1999

Chapter 1

Cut-out Lepidina

III

Name: _____ Date: _____

Photocopy the picture onto thin card. Colour in Lepidina and her clothes, and dress her up. Stick her jewellery on. Cut out carefully – don't cut the tabs off! Cut along the two heavy lines on her **palla** so that it will slip on over her head. Fold along the dotted lines on the base to make her stand up.

Don't use really bright colours for Lepidina's **tunica** and **palla** because they were dyed with natural dyes. Only the Emperor was allowed to wear purple.

© Cambridge University Press 1999

Chapter 1

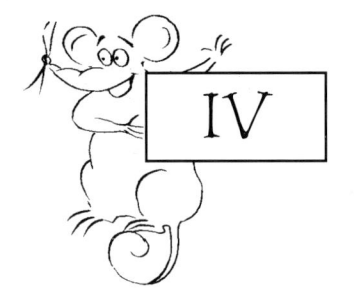

Design a birthday card

IV

Name: ——————————— Date: ———————

Use the Latin you know from chapter 1 to make your own birthday card or party invitation.

Here are some reminders:

fēlīx diēs tibi sit	Happy birthday to you.
euge!	Hooray!
dōnum tibi habeō	I have a present for you.
exspectātissimus es	You are very welcome.
venī ad diem nātālem meum	Come to my birthday party.

Cut out or copy these pictures to decorate your card.

© Cambridge University Press 1999

Chapter 1

Latin roots

Name: _____ Date: _____

More than two-thirds of all the words we use in English have come to us from Latin or Classical Greek. You have already learnt a number of Latin words which lead into English.

The answer to each of the following questions involves a Latin word that you have already met, so look back at the picture stories in chapter 1 or at the birthday invitation on page 5 if you are stuck. If you are still having problems, use a dictionary. The word underlined in each sentence gives you a clue.

1. You are feeling unhappy and your teacher treats you in a <u>maternal</u> fashion. Are you pleased?

2. Why are <u>service</u> stations on motorways so called?

3. Which well-known Christian prayer begins **"<u>pater noster</u>"**?

4. How would your teacher react if your class behaved in an <u>infantile</u> way?

5. Would you be surprised if your pet dog behaved in a <u>feline</u> manner?

6. If a doctor prescribes you medicine three times **<u>per diem</u>**, how often will you take it?

© Cambridge University Press 1999

Chapter 1

A tasty surprise!

Name: _____ Date: _____

Join the dots to find a creature that the Romans loved to eat.

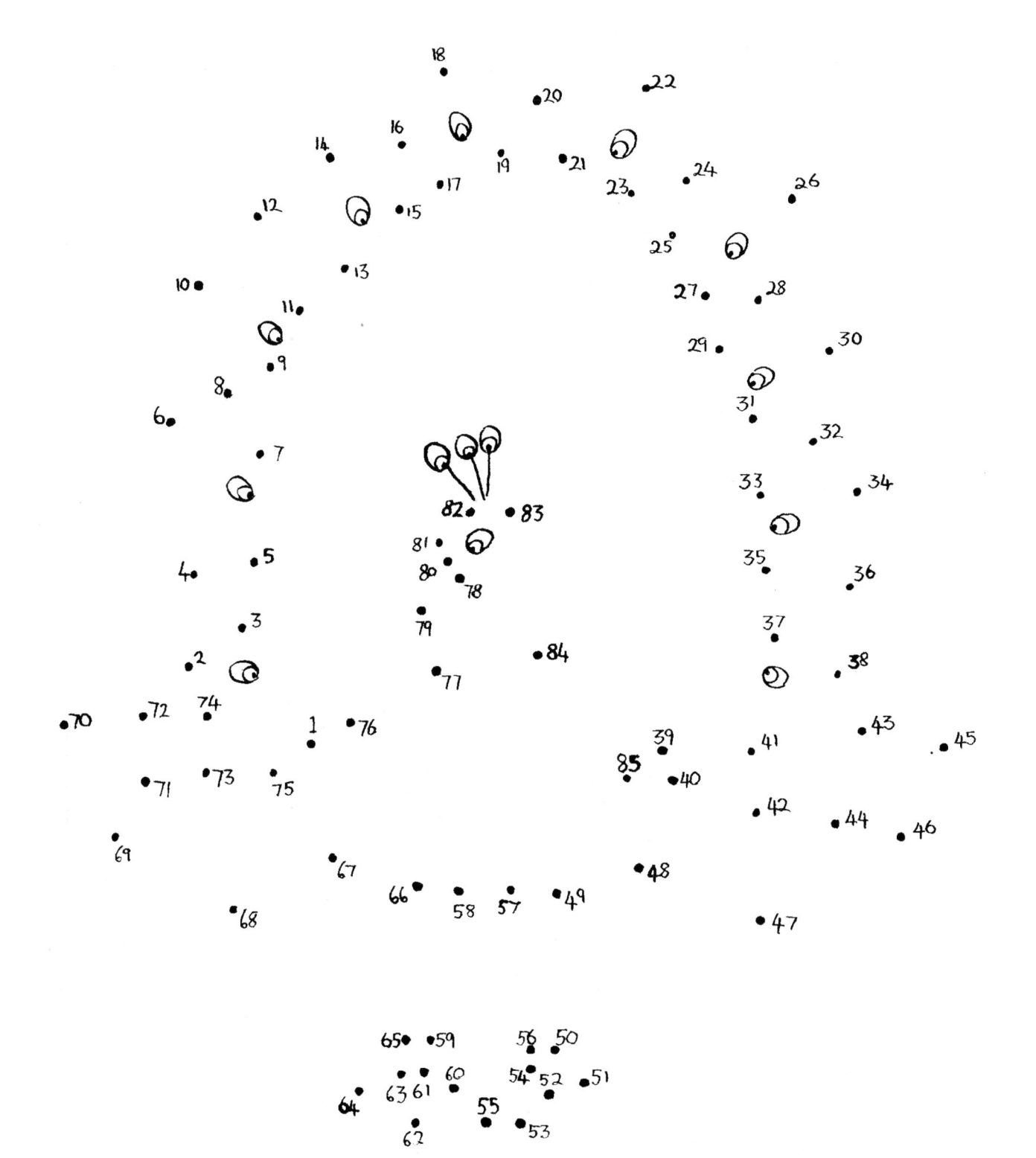

Animal nouns

VII

Name: _____ Date: _____

bālaena	cunīculus
rāna	porcus
delphīnus	vespa
mūs	vacca
taurus	gallīna

© Cambridge University Press 1999

Chapter 2

VIII Adjectives

Name: _____ Date: _____

sordidus	sordida
callidus	callida
magnus	magna
parvus	parva
optimus	optima
bonus	bona
maximus	maxima
improbus	improba
fōrmōsus	fōrmōsa
strēnuus	strēnua
ignāvus	ignāva
benignus	benigna

Describe your friends!

Name: _____ Date: _____

Chapter 2

© Cambridge University Press 1999

What am I doing?

Name: _____ Date: _____

verrō

pūrgō

rīdeō

legō

scrībō

lacrimō

spectō

sedeō

dormiō

Match the Latin with the English.

I am reading. _legō_____

I am crying. _____

I am looking. _____

I am sitting. _____

I am writing. _____

I am cleaning. _____

I am sleeping. _____

I am sweeping. _____

I am smiling. _____

© Cambridge University Press 1999

Chapter 3

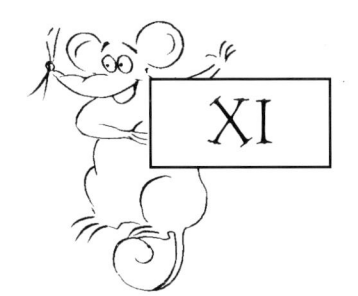

XI What are the people doing?

Name: _____ Date: _____

1 quis dormit? _____

2 quis rīdet? _____

3 quis sedet? _____

4 quis coquit? _____

5 quis legit? _____

6 quis spectat? _____

7 quis lacrimat? _____

8 quis scrībit? _____

© Cambridge University Press 1999   Chapter 3

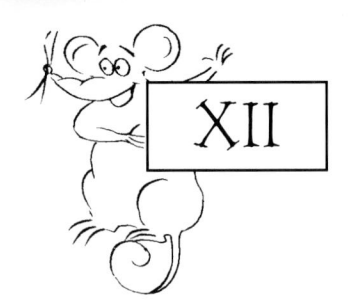

XII What are the animals doing?

Name: _____   Date: _____

Write the correct sentence under each picture.

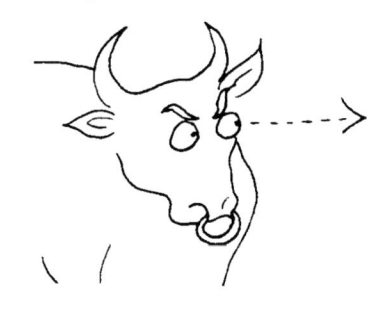

_____   _____   _____

_____   _____   _____

_____   _____   _____

mūs coquit	vespa scrībit	gallīna pūrgat
vacca sedet	elephantus verrit	rāna legit
delphīnus rīdet	taurus spectat	fēlēs dormit

© Cambridge University Press 1999

Chapter 3

XIII The six verb endings

Name: _____ Date: _____

> These tables show the verb endings for four Latin verbs. Can you fill in the English? I've done the first one for you!

labōrō	I am working	scrībō	
labōrās	you are working	scrībis	
labōrat	he or she is working	scrībit	
labōrāmus	we are working	scrībimus	
labōrātis	you are working	scrībitis	
labōrant	they are working	scrībunt	

dormiō		pingō	
dormīs		pingis	
dormit		pingit	
dormīmus		pingimus	
dormītis		pingitis	
dormiunt		pingunt	

© Cambridge University Press 1999

Chapter 3

I'm the best because…

XIV

Name: _____ Date: _____

Draw a picture of yourself in the first box, and fill in the speech bubble with a Latin sentence like the ones in the picture story.

You need to say:

> **optimus/optima sum quod…**
> I'm the best because…

Here are some verbs and phrases you could use:

scrībō I write   **rīdeō** I smile   **legō** I read
currō I run   **pingō** I paint   **equitō** I ride

fōrmōsus/fōrmōsa sum I'm handsome/pretty
callidus/callida sum I'm clever

> Now draw another picture in the second box. You could draw your friend, your teacher – or me! How will you need to change the Latin in the speech bubble?

© Cambridge University Press 1999

Chapter 3

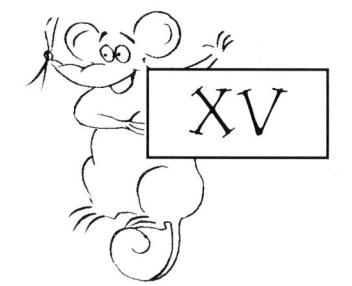

Roman writing

Name: _____ Date: _____

The writing tablets which have been found at Vindolanda are difficult to read. This is partly because they are dirty, and partly because there is no punctuation and no spaces between the words. What's more, the tablets are written in a Roman style of handwriting called the **cursive script**.

Here's what it looked like:

This box shows the actual size of a writing tablet. Try writing a short message to a friend, in English, using the cursive script.

© Cambridge University Press 1999

Chapter 4

Roman numerals

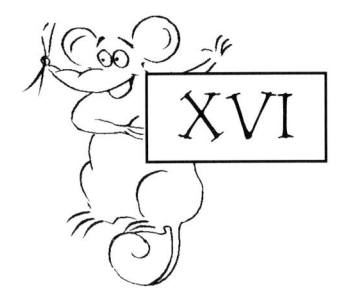

XVI

Name: _____ Date: _____

The Romans wrote their numbers differently from the way we write them today. Here's how the Romans used to write some of their numbers:

1	I	11	XI	50	L
2	II	12	XII	100	C
3	III	13	XIII	1000	M
4	IV	14	XIV		
5	V	15	XV		
6	VI	16	XVI		
7	VII	17	XVII		
8	VIII	18	XVIII		
9	IX	19	XIX		
10	X	20	XX		

We call these numbers "Roman numerals" and they're still used sometimes today. Can you think of any examples?

Practice with numbers

Write your answers in Roman numerals.

1. How old are you? _____
2. Write down the number of your house or flat. _____
3. How many people are there in your class? _____
4. Write down your date of birth. _____
5. If this is someone's date of birth, when was he born? MCMLI _____

Numbers in words

Here are the Latin numbers from 1 to 10 in words:

1. ūnus/ūna
2. duo
3. trēs
4. quattuor
5. quīnque
6. sex
7. septem
8. octō
9. novem
10. decem

How many derivatives (English words which come from Latin) can you find from these Latin numbers?

For example: five babies born on the same day to the same mother are called… Which sea creature has eight legs?

Have a competition to see who can find the most. A dictionary will be a great help!

© Cambridge University Press 1999

Chapter 4

Match the English to the Latin

Name: _____ Date: _____

Write the correct English word or phrase in each box.

sum
es
sumus
estis

sedēte!
salvē!
omnēs

quis?
quid?

I am
what?
everyone
you are ✶
you are ✶✶
sit down ✶✶
who?
hello
we are

Make your own seal-stone

XVIII

Name: _____ Date: _____

You will need:

- Plasticine
- a cocktail stick
- a smooth, flat surface (e.g. an old mirror, or a piece of formica)
- plaster of Paris mixed to a pouring consistency
- red Plasticine or modelling clay.

1	Roll out a thin, flattish strip of Plasticine, about 4 cm x 2 cm. Form it into a ring, and stick it down firmly on your flat surface.	
2	Make a tiny figure out of Plasticine to fit inside the ring. You could make an eagle, a wreath, a hand, an eye, a sun or a design of your own. It must be flat on the back. Use a cocktail stick to decorate and adjust the figure.	
3	Stick the figure down firmly inside the wall of the ring, flat side down.	
4	Pour liquid plaster of Paris into the ring and fill it up to the top of the wall. Pour the plaster slowly, popping any bubbles with the cocktail stick. Leave it to set hard.	
5	Peel off the Plasticine wall. Carefully dig out the Plasticine figure using the cocktail stick. Trim off any overhanging edges. The seal-stone is finished.	
6	Press a ball of modelling clay or red Plasticine into the hollow in your stone. Flatten the ball out. Peel it up carefully to produce a seal.	

© Cambridge University Press 1999

Chapter 4

Writing a Roman letter

XIX

Name: _____ Date: _____

You will need:
- a dip pen
- black ink
- a hole-punch
- string
- red Plasticine or modelling clay
- a thin, flat piece of wood (about 6 cm x 4 cm). The grain should run horizontally

1. The letters found at Vindolanda are in Latin but they are written in a strange-looking alphabet.

   a b c d
   e f g h
   i k l m
   n o p q
   r s t u/v

   Try writing your name with it!

2. Imagine that you are living at Vindolanda in AD 100. You could be one of the family or a soldier at the fort. Write a short letter to a friend or relation in another part of the Roman Empire. For example:

   > Dear Mother
   > It's really cold here at the fort. The commander is not bad but the food is terrible and the soldier in the bunk next to mine snores. Love to Dad and to all my sixteen brothers and sisters,
   >   your son
   >   Lucius

3. Copy your letter onto a piece of thin wood, using a dip pen and ink. You will probably notice that writing rounded letters makes your pen splatter like this:

   Open strokes work better:

   Now do you see why the Vindolanda writers developed those strangely shaped letters?

4. Seal your letter. Punch a hole at the right-hand side, and tie a piece of string through it. Seal the string with a flattened ball of Plasticine or modelling clay. If you have made your own seal-stone, use it! If not, press a coin into the clay to make a decorative seal.

© Cambridge University Press 1999

Chapter 4

Cut-out Celtic warrior

XX

Name: _____ Date: _____

Photocopy the picture onto thin card and colour it in. Draw dots and spirals of blue war paint on the warrior's face and chest. Give his clothes a checked pattern. Cut the pieces out carefully, and stick the weapons onto the warrior's hands. Fold along the dotted lines on the base to make him stand up.

Give your warrior a Celtic name, like Audurdic, Bruccius, Suobnus or Caratius.

© Cambridge University Press 1999

Chapter 5

Roman Britain

Name: _____ Date: _____

© Cambridge University Press 1999

Chapter 5

The Roman Empire in AD 97–102

Name: _____ Date: _____

XXII

- Britain
- Italy
- Rome
- BLACK SEA
- MEDITERRANEAN SEA

Chapter 6

© Cambridge University Press 1999

What does Rufus think?

XXIII

Name: _____ Date: _____

1 Write an adjective in each of the thought bubbles below. Remember that the ending must match the noun! The first one has been done for you.

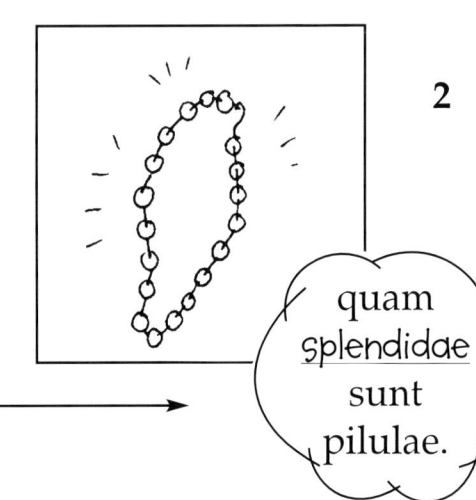

2 Now cut out the bubbles and stick them onto the matching pictures.

quam splendidae sunt pilulae.

splendidae
malus
callidus
acūtus
obēsa
pulchra

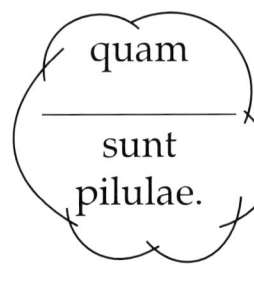

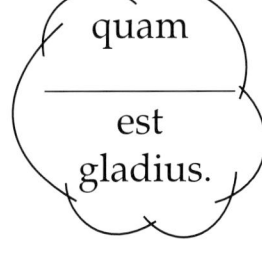

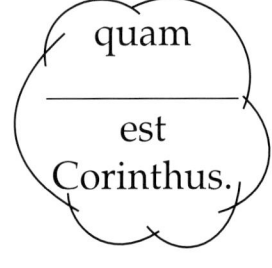

quam _____ sunt pilulae.

quam _____ est gladius.

quam _____ est Corinthus.

quam _____ est tunica.

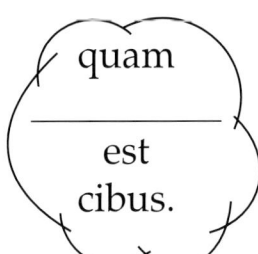

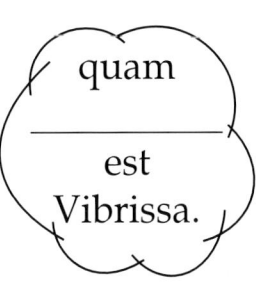

quam _____ est cibus.

quam _____ est Vibrissa.

© Cambridge University Press 1999

Chapter 6

Work out the weapons (1)

XXIV

Name: _____ Date: _____

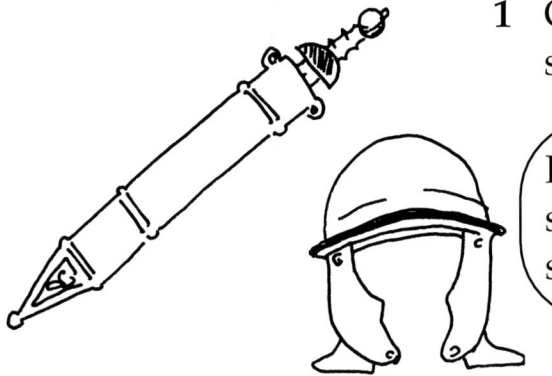

1. Colour in the Roman soldier on activity sheet XXV.

   His tunic should be red, and his shield too. The pattern on the shield should be yellow.

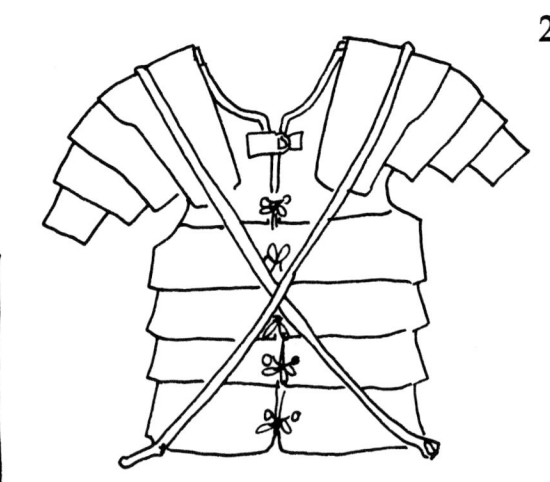

2. Colour in and cut out the weapons and equipment on this page and stick them onto the soldier.

   Put the shield under his left hand, and the javelin in his right. The sword should hang by his right side, and the dagger by his left. His shoes (**caligae**) go on his feet – of course! His breastplate goes on his chest, and his helmet on his head.

3. Fill in the Latin names for the weapons in the spaces provided on activity sheet XXV. (Look back at the picture story if you need some help.)

4. Now give your soldier a Roman name and write it in the box at the bottom of the page.

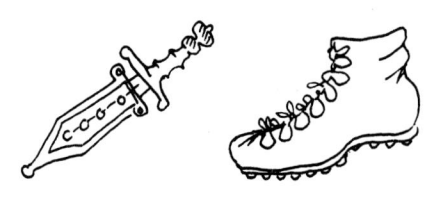

© Cambridge University Press 1999

Chapter 7

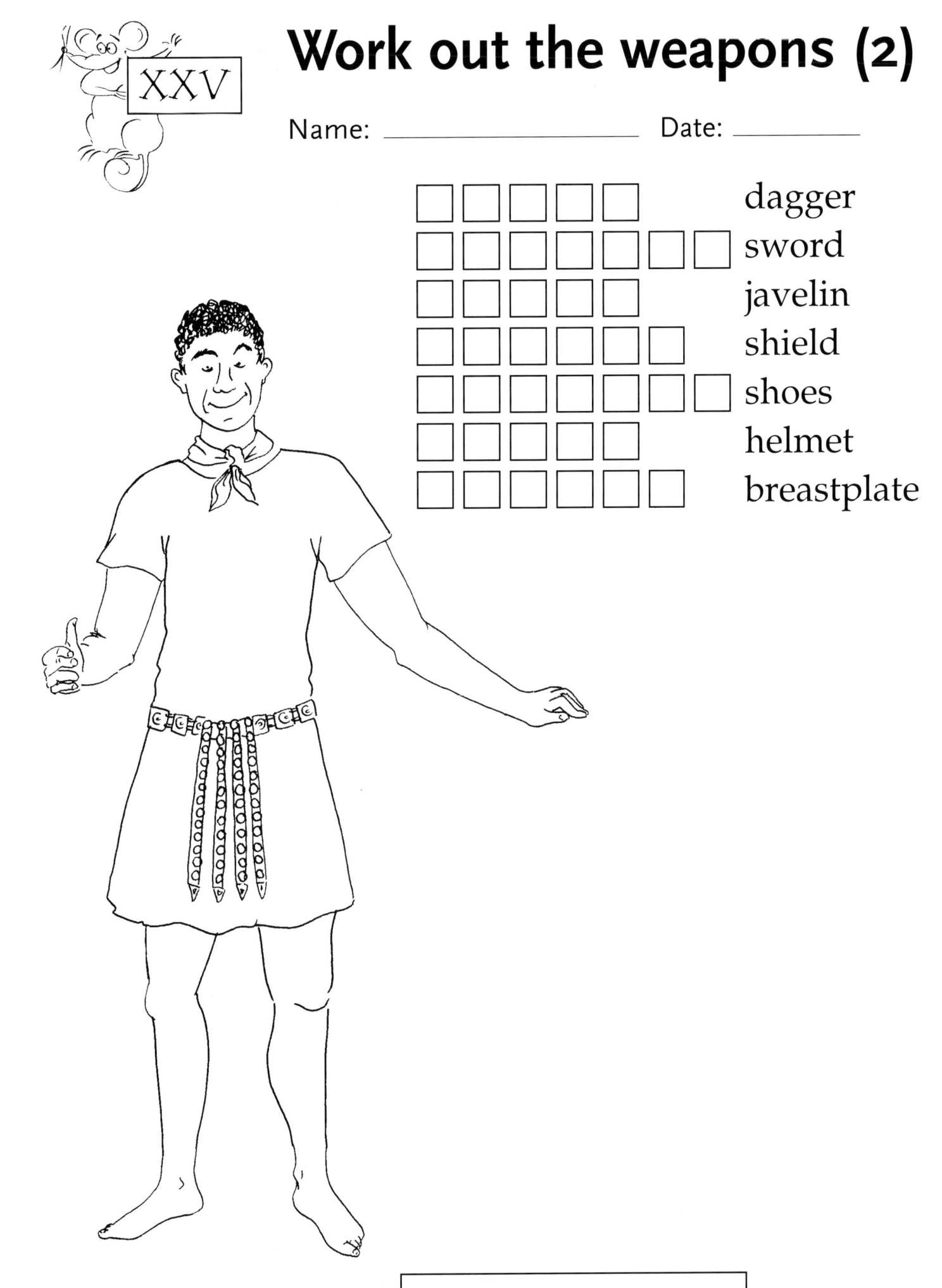

Work out the weapons (2)

Name: _____ Date: _____

☐	☐	☐	☐	☐			dagger
☐	☐	☐	☐	☐	☐	☐	sword
☐	☐	☐	☐	☐			javelin
☐	☐	☐	☐	☐	☐		shield
☐	☐	☐	☐	☐	☐	☐	shoes
☐	☐	☐	☐	☐			helmet
☐	☐	☐	☐	☐	☐		breastplate

Chapter 7

Doctor! Doctor! (1)

XXVI

Name: _____ Date: _____

Can you find the English for these Latin words? They are all parts of the body. (Look at the numbers and the clues in the sentences below.)

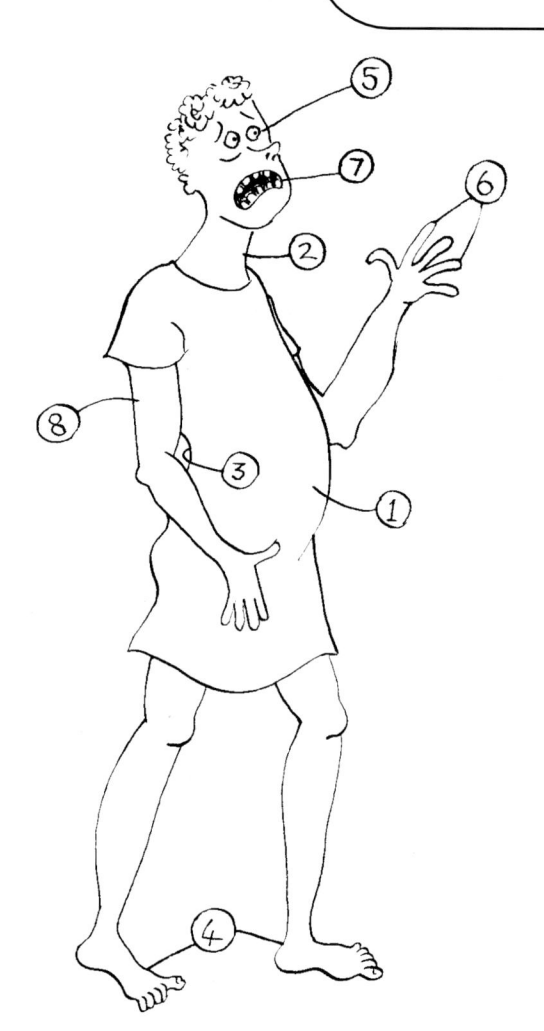

bracchium	
dentēs	
collum	
venter	
pedēs	
digitī	
dorsum	
oculī	

1. A **ventriloquist** is supposed to speak from the stomach.
2. You wear your **collar** on this part of your body.
3. A shark's **dorsal** fin is on its back.
4. You press **pedals** with these.
5. You look through **binoculars** with these.
6. You have five **digits** on each hand.
7. A **dentist** looks after these.
8. A **bracelet** goes on this part of your body.

© Cambridge University Press 1999

Chapter 8

XXVII Doctor! Doctor! (2)

Name: _____   Date: _____

Practise using the Latin words for different parts of the body. Act out a scene between a doctor and a patient. You could use the conversation from the picture story on page 50 or you could make up your own. Here are some sentences to help you:

Patient		Doctor	
salvē!	Hello!	**intrā!**	Come in!
venter mihi dolet.	My stomach hurts.	**discumbe!**	Lie down.
collum mihi dolet.	My neck hurts.	**ubī tibi dolet?**	Where does it hurt?
bracchium mihi dolet.	My arm hurts.	**quid tibi dolet?**	What hurts?
dorsum mihi dolet.	My back hurts.	**hoc cōnsūme...**	Eat this...
oculī mihi dolent.	My eyes hurt.	**hoc bibe...**	Drink this...
pedēs mihi dolent.	My feet hurt.	**impōne unguentum...**	Put the ointment on...
dentēs mihi dolent.	My teeth hurt.	**... bis per diem!**	... twice a day!
digitī mihi dolent.	My fingers hurt.	**dēbeō tē secāre.**	I'll have to operate.
		valē!	Goodbye!

"AAAAAAAH!" is the same in Latin and in English!

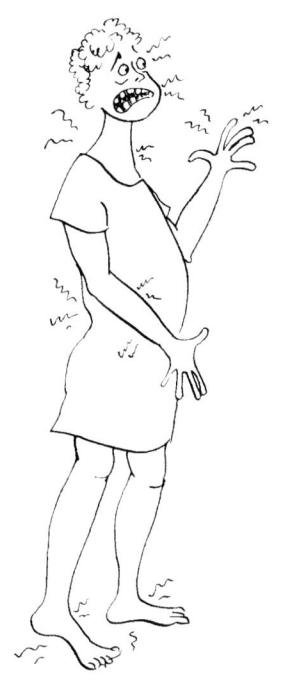

© Cambridge University Press 1999

Chapter 8

Cut-out auxiliary soldier

XXVIII

Name: _____ Date: _____

Photocopy the picture onto thin card. Colour in the soldier and his armour and weapons. His tunic and scarf are red, his shield is black with a green wreath and his mail shirt is grey. Cut out the pieces carefully and stick the soldier's kit in place. Fold along the dotted lines on the base to make him stand up.

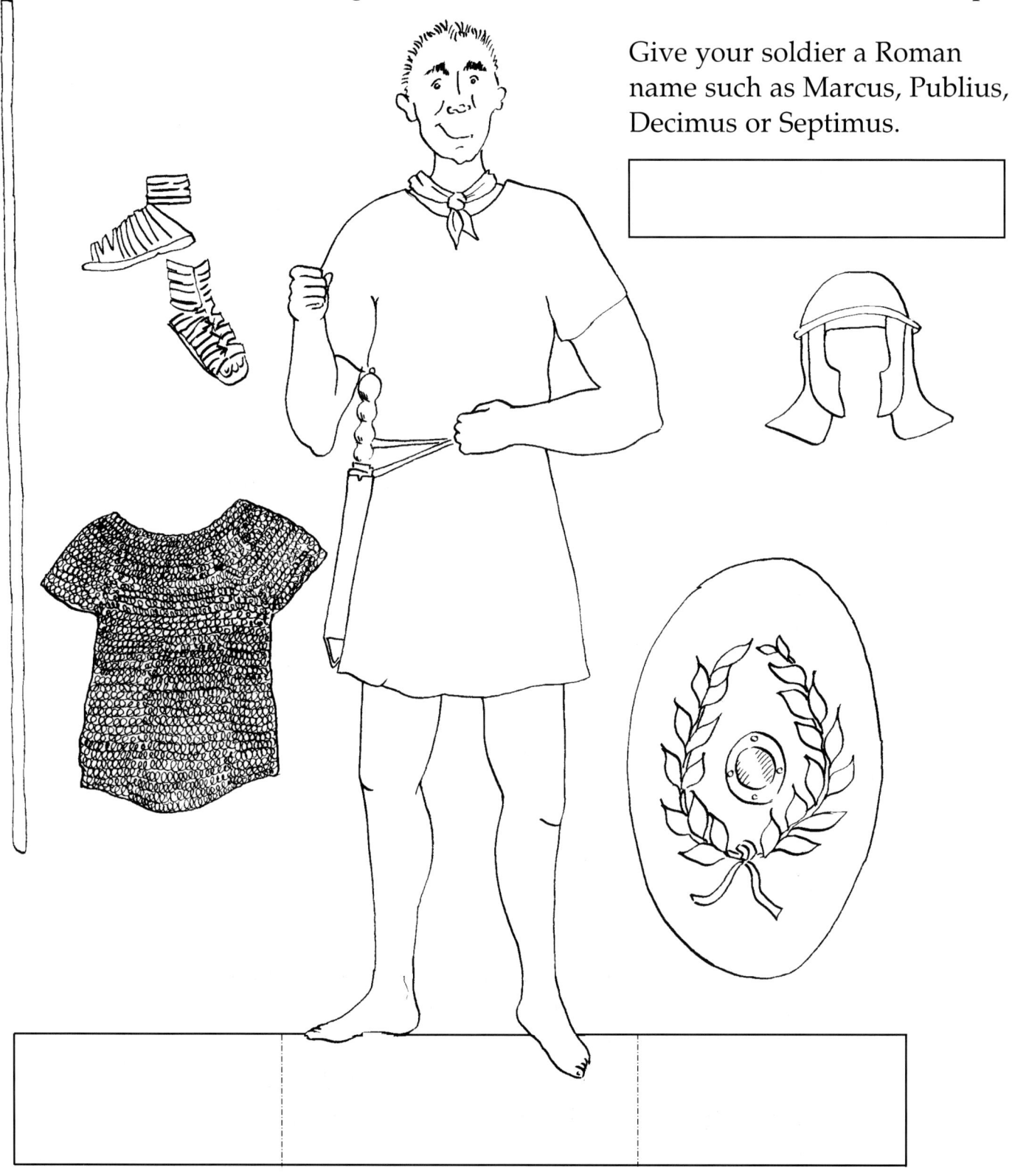

Give your soldier a Roman name such as Marcus, Publius, Decimus or Septimus.

© Cambridge University Press 1999

Chapter 9

A letter home

XXIX

Name: _____ Date: _____

> Imagine that you are a Roman soldier stationed at the fort at Vindolanda. Write a letter home to your family telling them about your life in a fort in Roman Britain. Here is some information to help you:

- **What was it like living in the north of Britain?** Cold! Roman soldiers often came from hot countries. They wore cloaks to keep the cold out – warm, hooded cloaks were a British speciality. They might also wear short leather trousers under their tunics, and woollen socks in their boots.

- **Where did the soldiers live?** In barrack blocks, with eight soldiers sharing a room with bunk-beds. The officers had better rooms, and the fort commander had a big house. The barrack rooms had shutters, not glass in the windows, so it wouldn't have been much fun on a windy February day.

- **Were soldiers allowed to have their families with them in the fort?** Ordinary soldiers weren't allowed to marry officially, though some may have had wives or girlfriends living in the village next to the fort. However, the commander's family lived with him at the fort. Archaeologists at Vindolanda have dug up women's shoes and a child's little boot.

- **Were soldiers paid a lot? What did they spend their money on?** Soldiers were fairly well paid. They often managed to save money. (The standard-bearer looked after the soldiers' savings bank.) Soldiers didn't usually have to buy their own kit or food. They might spend their money on beer, gambling, or on paying a scribe to write letters for them.

- **What did the soldiers do when they weren't fighting?** They worked on building the Wall, or roads, or forts. They practised with their weapons. They went on long marches to keep fit. They patrolled the Wall or the roads near it, or escorted supply carts safely from one fort to another.

© Cambridge University Press 1999

Chapter 9

A letter home

Name: _____ Date: _____

- **Did the soldiers have any spare time?** Yes; they had time to visit the fort's bath-house every day, or for a game, or for reading or drawing. They might visit their family, or go to the nearest city (York) if they had a longer period of leave.

- **What happened if a soldier was injured in battle?** The fort had a doctor to take care of him. Roman doctors could treat many injuries and do operations. Bigger forts would have had a hospital.

- **How might a soldier get into trouble?** By being lazy, not keeping his kit polished, losing things, or being rude to the centurion.

- **What happened to disobedient soldiers?** They might be consigned to barracks or whipped, or made to do the worst jobs like cleaning the latrines (toilets). Roman forts had toilets, often with a stream running through to flush them.

- **What did the soldiers eat?** Bread, porridge and bacon were the most important things. We know that chickens and pigs were kept at Vindolanda.

- **What were the army trumpets for?** The trumpets, which were in the shape of a big circle, were sounded to tell soldiers when to get up or go to bed, and when to change the guard. They were also used to signal an emergency.

- **What was the armour like?** Itchy! (It was probably very easy to catch lice in your tunic.) Soldiers wore a scarf to stop the armour rubbing on their necks.

- **What did soldiers ask for from home?** Olives, perhaps, or warm socks! They might ask for money, although many soldiers actually sent money home to their parents.

© Cambridge University Press 1999

Chapter 9

Wordsearch

Name: _____ Date: _____

Search the word square below to find these words, which are connected with soldiers and the army:

ballista   pugiō
mīlitēs   gladius
lōrīca   signifer
scūtum   galea
pīlum   testūdō

Remember the words can go from right to left, bottom to top and diagonally!

B	P	S	T	O	P	I	L	U	M
A	L	A	B	T	P	C	S	M	U
C	S	E	T	E	U	T	U	G	T
I	I	L	U	S	G	C	I	E	U
R	G	A	G	T	I	B	D	O	C
O	N	G	M	U	O	L	A	S	S
L	I	B	L	D	A	D	L	P	O
C	F	A	G	O	P	N	G	A	P
S	E	T	I	L	I	M	S	T	B
P	R	O	I	V	U	T	N	B	C

Can you remember what each word means?

© Cambridge University Press 1999

Chapter 9

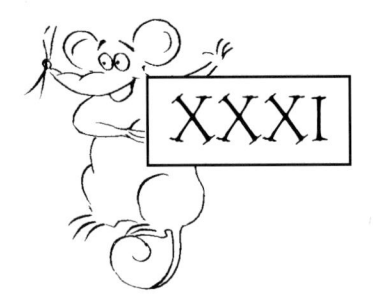

Roman jewellery

Name: _____ Date: _____

If you would like to dress up as Lepidina or Flavia, here are some ideas on choosing or even making jewellery.

Rings: simple gold or silver, with inset seal-stones.

Bracelets: wire or plain metal bangles, gold links or snake bracelets.

Pins: straight pins made of bone, ivory, glass or metal, were used to hold clothes or hair in place.

Earrings: gold hoop shapes, or wire hooks with glass beads or pearls.

Brooches: used to fasten cloaks, closed like a safety-pin.

Necklaces: strings of amber, pearls, glass beads, gold beads.

Brooch

You need: a large safety-pin, thin card, masking tape, glue, tiny beads or fine wire, silver or bronze paint.

1 Cut 2 shapes like this.

2 Tape the long edges together.

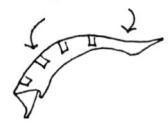

3 Decorate with beads or coils of fine wire.

4 Glue to pin.

5 Paint.

Bracelet

You need: a cardboard tube that fits your wrist (e.g. a crisp tube), tiny beads, fine string, thick thread, gold paint.

1 Cut a 5 cm ring from the tube, and cut it in half.

2 Make 2 holes at each end of both pieces.

3 Make plaits with the thick thread. Thread the tiny beads onto the fine string.

4 Stick plaits, rows of beads and lines of thread onto the bracelet. Paint it all gold.

5 Tie the halves together to form a hinge. Tie the strings at the open ends. These will fasten your bracelet.

© Cambridge University Press 1999

Weaving

XXXII

Name: _____ Date: _____

The Romans made their clothes from cloth which they wove from wool. You can try weaving too!

You will need:

a piece of stiff card around 15 cm × 15 cm with zigzags cut into two opposite edges, like this:

a bobbin made from a smaller piece of stiff card cut to this shape:

scissors

different coloured wool.

1. Wind the wool around the card, anchoring it in the notches as shown in the picture.

   Tie the ends securely. You should have an even number of strings.

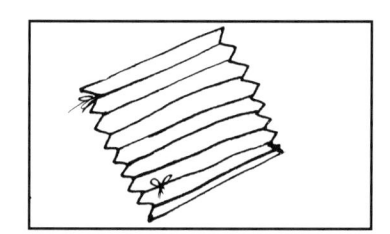

2. Wind some wool around the bobbin.

3. Tie the end of the wool onto one of the outer strings. Now feed the bobbin in and out of the strings. When you reach the end of the row, go back in the opposite direction. Push the rows up so they fit snugly together.

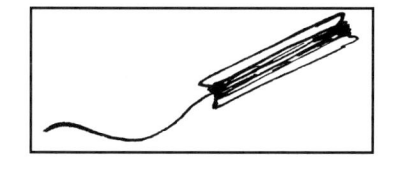

4. You can change the colour of the wool in your bobbin to make stripes in your cloth. Remember to tie off the first colour before you change.

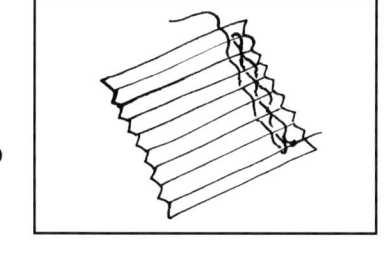

5. When you have filled the card, tie the end securely. Cut the strings on the back of the card. Divide the cut strings into pairs and knot them together as close to the weaving as possible.

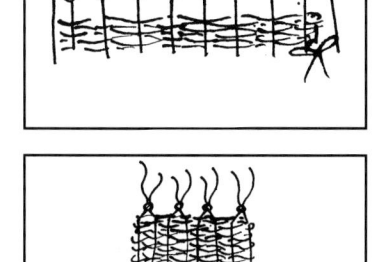

   Now you have a piece of cloth, just like the Romans made!

© Cambridge University Press 1999

Chapter 10

Reading Roman tombstones

XXXIII

Name: _____ Date: _____

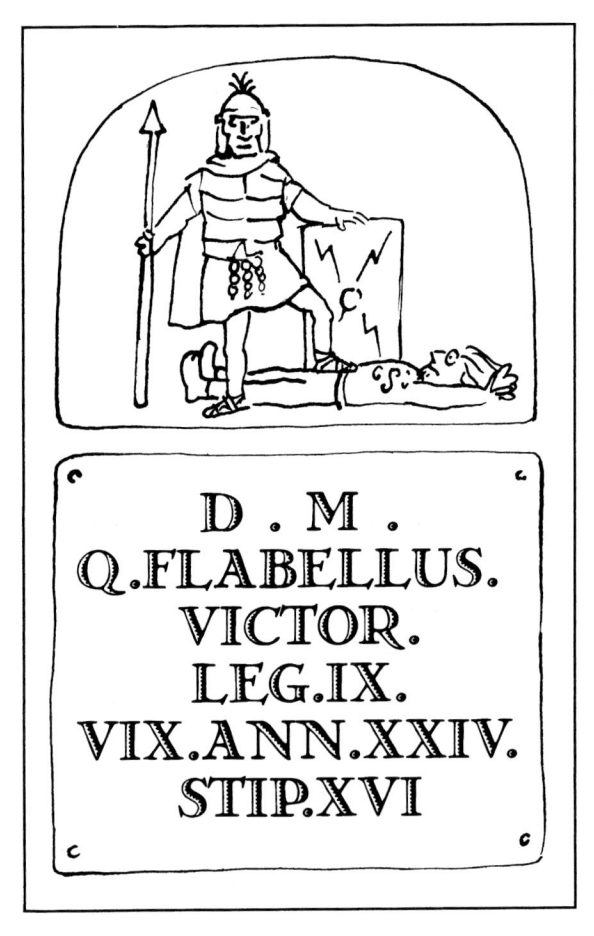

You can learn a lot about Roman people from the inscriptions on their tombstones, but you need to understand their 'code'.
Often, the sculptor made words shorter to save space. Look at this soldier's tombstone, and use the list here to help you translate the inscription.

D.M. = **dis manibusque** = to the spirits of the dead.
LEG. is short for **legiō**, and tells you which regiment the soldier served in.

```
D . M .
Q.FLABELLUS.
VICTOR.
LEG.IX.
VIX.ANN.XXIV.
STIP.XVI
```

VIX. = lived
ANN. = years
STIP. tells you how long the soldier served in the army.

What does the inscription say?

Now design a tombstone yourself. Draw a portrait of the dead person in the top panel. Write your inscription in the lower panel. Use capital letters only, and put dots between words.

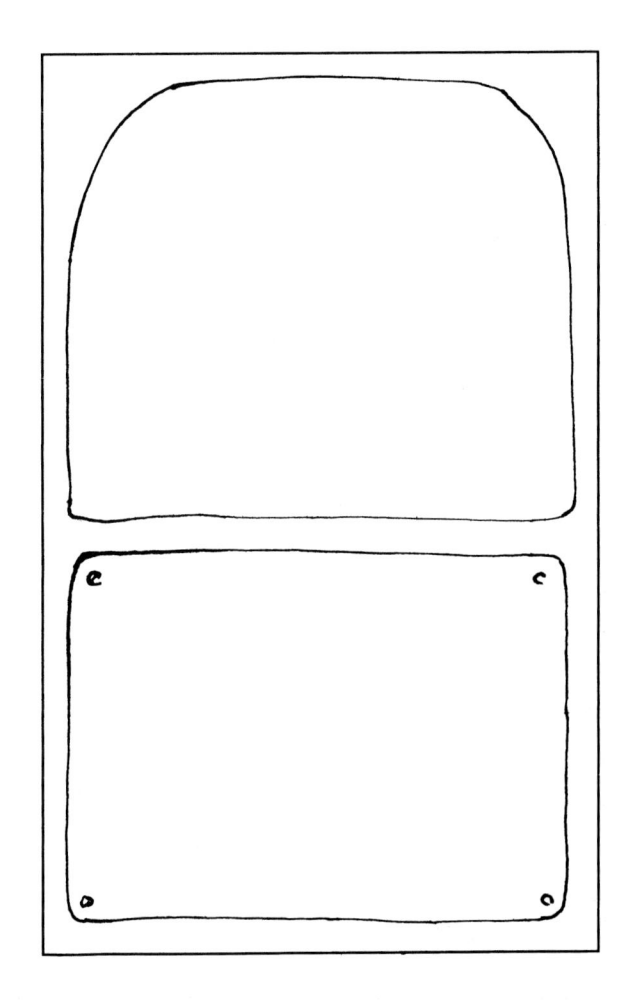

© Cambridge University Press 1999

Chapter 11

The twelve Olympians

XXXIV

Name: _____ Date: _____

The twelve most important Greek gods and goddesses lived on Mount Olympus, so they are known as 'the Olympians'. The Romans worshipped the same gods but gave most of them new names. Can you remember their Greek and Roman names? (There's a list in chapter 12 if you need help!)

Fill in the gaps in the table below. Then, using a library, try to find out what area of life each god was in charge of. For example, Zeus was King of the gods and ruler of Mount Olympus; he was also god of the weather. Add any information you can find to the table.

Greek name	Roman name	In charge of
Zeus		the gods; Olympus; weather
	Juno	
Apollo	Apollo	
	Diana	
Ares		
Demeter		
	Mercury	
Poseidon		
	Venus	
Hephaestus		
	Bacchus	
Athena		

© Cambridge University Press 1999

Chapter 12

Make a Latin door sign

XXXV

Name: _____ Date: _____

- Photocopy onto thin card.
- Decorate the sign with pictures of Minimus and his friends.
- Carefully cut out the circle below and the large rectangle.
- Cut out the round hole at the top of the rectangle and the window at the bottom.
- Position the large circle behind the rectangle so that one of the words shows through the window.
- Pierce both pieces of card with a brass paper fastener through the tiny hole at the centre.
- Hang it from your doorknob.
- The four messages are:
  dormiō I'm sleeping
  scrībō I'm writing
  absum I'm away
  intrāte! come in!

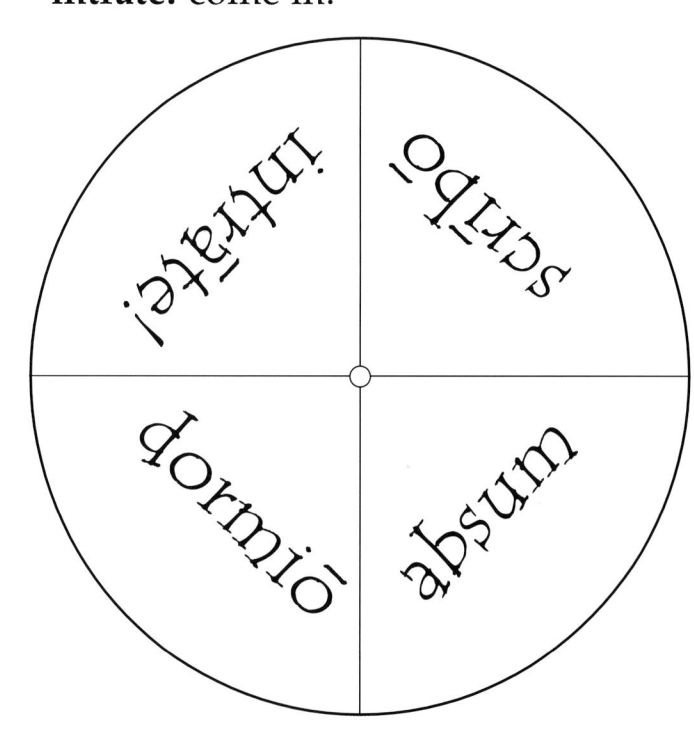

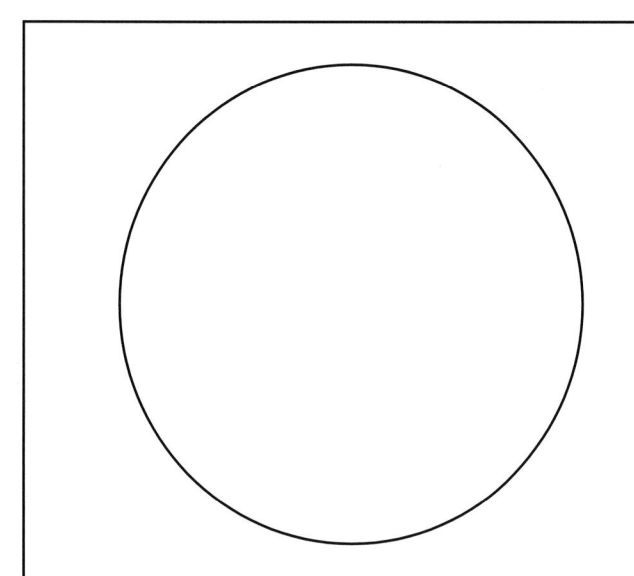

salvēte!

© Cambridge University Press 1999

Chapter 12

GLOSSARY

A

accipit	receives
acūtus, acūta	sharp
ad	to
ambula!	walk!
amīcus	friend
ampūlla	flask
anima	soul
animālia aēnea	bronze animals
ānulus	ring
aperī!	open!
in apodytēriō	in the changing room
arma	weapons
audīte!	hear!
aurēs	ears
avis	bird

B

bālaena	whale
ballista	catapult
benignus, benigna	kind
bis per diem	twice a day
bonus, bona	good
breviter	briefly

C

in caldāriō	in the hot room
callidissimus, callidissima	very clever
callidus, callida	clever
canis	dog
cantō	I sing
capillāmentum	wig
capillī	hair
cāseus	cheese
cavē!	be careful!
celeriter	quickly
cērae	wax tablets
cibus	food
circum	around
colimus	we farm

commodus, commoda	convenient
cōnsūme!	eat!
contentus, contenta	content
coquō	I cook
cubiculum	bedroom
cunīculus	rabbit
cūr?	why?
cūriōsus, cūriōsa	curious
currunt	they run

D

delphīnus	dolphin
dēmittite!	put down!
diēs nātālis	birthday
dīligenter	carefully
dīrēctus, dīrēcta	straight
discumbe!	lie down!
diū	for a long time
docet	teaches
dōnum	present
dormiō	I sleep
dūrus, dūra	tough

E

Eborācum	to York
ecce!	look!
ēheu!	oh dear!
elephantus	elephant
epistula	letter
equus	horse
erit	will be
et	and
euge!	hooray!
exit	he/she goes out
exspectātissimus	very welcome
exuunt	they take off

F

facis	you make
facit	makes
facite!	make!

fāmōsus, fāmōsa	famous
fatīgātus, fatīgāta	bored
fēlēs	cat
fēlīx diēs tibi sit	happy birthday
ferōciter	ferociously
fessus, fessa	tired
fīlia	daughter
fīlius	son
fōrmōsus, fōrmōsa	beautiful
in frīgidāriō	in the cold room

G
galea	helmet
gallīna	hen
garriunt	they chat
gemmae	jewels
gladius	sword
grātiās tibi agō	I thank you
gravis	heavy

H
habeō	I have
habitās	you live
hortus	garden

I
ibi	there
ignāvus, ignāva	lazy
impōne!	put on!
improbus, improba	naughty
in	in/on
īnfāns	young child
intrat	he enters
īrātus, īrāta	angry
ita vērō	yes

L
labōrō	I work
lacrimat	he cries
laetissimus, laetissima	very happy
laetus, laeta	happy

legit	he reads
legō	I read
lōrīca	breastplate
lūdī	games
lūdunt	they play

M

magnus, magna	big
malus, mala	bad
māter	mother
maximus, maxima	very big
meum	mine
mīles	soldier
minimē	no
minimus, minima	very small
mortārium	mortar
mūs	mouse

N

nōbīscum	with us
nōlī lacrimāre!	don't cry!
nōlī tangere!	don't touch!
nōmen	name
nōn	not
novus, nova	new
nunc	now

O

obēsus, obēsa	fat
ōlim	once
omnēs	all
optimē	very well
optimus, optima	very good

P

parvus, parva	small
pater	father
pāvō	peacock
perīculōsus, perīculōsa	dangerous
pilulae	beads
pīlum	javelin

piscis	fish
porcus	pig
portāte!	carry!
pretiōsus, pretiōsa	precious
prō	in front of
prōcēdite!	go forward!
prope	near
prūdenter	carefully
psittacus	parrot
pugiō	dagger
pugnō	I fight
pulcher, pulchra	beautiful
pūrgō	I clean

Q

quam	how
quam celerrimē	as quickly as possible
quī estis?	who are you?
quid est?	what is it?
quis es?	who are you?
quod	because
quoque	also

R

rādunt	they scrape
rāna	frog
recumbunt	they recline
redī!	go back!
relinque!	leave!
rīdent	they are smiling
Rōmānae	Roman

S

salvē	hello
scīlicet	of course
scrībō	I write
scūtum	shield
sed	but
sedēte!	sit!
segniter	carelessly
semper	always

servī	slaves
servus	slave
siste!	stop!
sordidus, sordida	dirty
soror	sister
spectat	he is watching
splendidus, splendida	splendid
squālidus, squālida	dirty
stilī	pens
strēnuus, strēnua	energetic
sub	beneath
subitō	suddenly
sum	I am
sūmite!	pick up!
sumus	we are
super	above
surge!	get up!

T

taurus	bull
in tepidāriō	in the warm room
tesserae	mosaics
tibi	for you
trīs per diem	three times a day
tristissimus, tristissima	very sad
tunica	tunic; dress

V

vacca	cow
vādō	I go
valē	goodbye
validus, valida	strong
variae	various
venī!	come!
verrō	I sweep
vespa	wasp
viae	streets
vīlla	house
vir optime	sir

OPTIMĒ!

This is to certify that

_____

a pupil at

_____

has completed and understood

chapters _____

of the MINIMUS course

EUGE!

signed _____

© Cambridge University Press 1999

Stimmt! 1

Teacher's Guide

TO DOWNLOAD YOUR EDITABLE SCHEME OF WORK, GO TO :

www.pearsonschools.co.uk/stimmtschemesofwork

PASSWORD:ZICKZACK

ALWAYS LEARNING   PEARSON

Published by Pearson Education Limited, Edinburgh Gate, Harlow, Essex, CM20 2JE.

www.pearsonschoolsandfecolleges.co.uk

Edited by Sarah Langman Scott
Cover photo © Pearson Education: Jörg Carstensen

Text © Pearson Education Limited 2013

First published 2013
16 15 14 13
10 9 8 7 6 5 4 3 2 1

British Library Cataloguing in Publication Data
A catalogue record for this book is available from the British Library

ISBN 978 1 447 96022 5

Copyright notice
All rights reserved. No part of this publication may be reproduced in any form or by any means (including photocopying or storing it in any medium by electronic means and whether or not transiently or incidentally to some other use of this publication) without the written permission of the copyright owner, except in accordance with the provisions of the Copyright, Designs and Patents Act 1988 or under the terms of a licence issued by the Copyright Licensing Agency, Saffron House, 6–10 Kirby Street, London EC1N 8TS (www.cla.co.uk). Applications for the copyright owner's written permission should be addressed to the publisher.

This product is accompanied by downloadable editable Word files. Pearson Education Limited is not responsible for the quality, accuracy or fitness for purpose of the materials contained in the Word files once edited. To revert to the original Word files, redownload them from the given URL.

Printed in the UK by Henry Ling Ltd.

Acknowledgements
Every effort has been made to contact copyright holders of material reproduced in this book. Any omissions will be rectified in subsequent printings if notice is given to the publishers.

Contents

Introduction   4

Kapitel 1	**Meine Welt und ich**	15
Kapitel 2	**Familie und Tiere**	53
Kapitel 3	**Freizeit – juhu!**	93
Kapitel 4	**Schule ist klasse!**	132
Kapitel 5	**Gute Reise!**	169

Introduction

Course description

Stimmt! is a differentiated 11–14 German course in three stages – *Stimmt! 1* for Year 7, *Stimmt! 2* for Year 8 and *Stimmt! 3* for Year 9. In Year 7 pupils can be assessed at National Curriculum Levels 1 to 5.

Stimmt! 1 and *Stimmt! 2* are suitable for use on their own as a two-year Key Stage 3 course.

The course has been written to reflect the world pupils live in, using contexts familiar to them in their everyday lives and teaching them the vocabulary that they need to communicate with young German people of their own age on topics that interest and stimulate them. They are introduced to young German people and given insight into the everyday life and culture of Germany and other German-speaking countries, encouraging intercultural understanding.

At the same time, *Stimmt!* ensures that pupils are taught the language learning skills and strategies that they need to become independent language learners. The elements of the 2014 Programme of Study for Key Stage 3 Modern Languages (grammar and vocabulary, and linguistic competence) are fully integrated into the course. In addition, pupils have the chance to experience cross-curricular studies and are given regular opportunities to develop and practise the personal learning and thinking skills required to operate as independent enquirers, creative thinkers, reflective learners, team workers, self-managers and effective participators.

Stimmt! ActiveTeach (see details on pp. 5–6) provides easy-to-use and exciting technology designed to add dynamism and fun to whole-class teaching. For individual pupil use, *Stimmt! ActiveLearn* (see details on pp. 6–7) provides a wealth of exciting differentiated material for pupils to access individually via computers or mobile devices, in class or for homework.

Differentiation

Stimmt! 1 and *2* provide one book each for the whole ability range. Pupil requirements are catered for in the following ways:

- There are differentiated activities at a range of NC Levels in listening, speaking, reading and writing throughout the Pupil Book.
- Ideas are given in the Teacher's Guide for reinforcing and extending the Pupil Book activities.
- *Skills* spreads towards the end of every chapter contain in-depth work and some higher level activities which give pupils the opportunity to work on language learning skills at a deeper level and pull their learning together, producing longer pieces of speaking and writing.
- The *Extra* section at the back of the Pupil Book provides extra reading and writing activities at reinforcement and extension levels.
- The workbooks are differentiated at two levels: reinforcement (*Übungsheft A*) and extension (*Übungsheft B*).

Stimmt! 3 is differentiated by means of parallel books:

Stimmt! 3 Rot   NC Levels 3–7
Stimmt! 3 Grün   NC Levels 3–6

Stimmt! 1

Pupil Book

- One book for the whole ability range in Year 7
- Full coverage of the 2014 Programmes of Study for Key Stage 3 MFL
- Assessment right from the start at National Curriculum Level 4
- Exciting video introducing pupils to the lives of young people in Germany
- Fully integrated grammar explanations and practice ensuring logical and rigorous progression
- In-depth work on listening, speaking, reading and writing skills to promote greater levels of achievement and linguistic competences
- Integrated cross-curricular work linking to topics covered
- Fully integrated opportunities for PLTS

The Pupil Book consists of five core chapters which are subdivided as follows:

- A fun, double-page opener quiz to wet pupils' appetites for a new topic and make them aware of things that they may already know about it.
- Four double-page core units (five in Chapters 1 and 2) – these contain the core material that must be taught to ensure that all the key language and grammar is covered in Year 7.
- Two double-page skills units (one in Chapters 1 and 2) which allow pupils to work on one receptive skills and one productive skill in greater depth.
- *Lernzieltest* – this is a checklist of 'I can' statements, allowing pupils to check their progress as part of Assessment for Learning.
- *Wiederholung* – optional revision activities that can be used as a 'mock' test preceding the

end of chapter *Kontrollen* in the Assessment Pack.

- *Grammatik* – two pages where the key grammar points introduced in the chapter are explained fully and accompanied by practice activities.
- *Wörter* – two pages of word lists for vocabulary learning and revision, with an *Strategie* tip box to help pupils acquire the skills they need to learn vocabulary more effectively.
- *Projektzone* – one or two optional units in which no new grammar is introduced, but which extend the chapter topic into an exciting cultural and practical context which allows for cross curricular and project work.

At the back of the Pupil Book there are three further sections:

- *Extra* – self-access differentiated reading and writing activities. *Extra A* contains reinforcement activities for lower-ability pupils, and *Extra B* contains extension activities for higher-ability pupils. These are ideal for use as homework.
- Verb tables – two pages showing the present tense conjugation of regular verbs, the three most common irregular verbs: *fahren, sein,* and *haben*, the *lesen/sehen* pattern of irregular verbs and modal verbs as well as the future tense.
- *Wortschatz* – a comprehensive German-English glossary, organised alphabetically and containing all the vocabulary encountered in *Stimmt! 1*. There is also a list of classroom language and of the German rubrics used in the Pupil Book.

Teacher's Guide

The Teacher's Guide contains all the support required to help you use *Stimmt! 1* effectively in the classroom:

- Clear and concise teaching notes, including lesson starters, plenaries and PLTS references for every unit
- Full cross-referencing to the 2014 National Curriculum Programmes of Study
- Overview grids for each chapter highlighting grammar content and skills coverage
- Answers to all the activities
- The complete audioscript for all the listening activities in the *Stimmt! 1* Pupil Book
- Guidance on using the course with the full ability range

With the Teacher's Guide there is an accompanying customisable Scheme of Work offering complete help with planning, and showing how the course covers the National Curriculum Programme of Study.

The Teacher's Guide and Scheme of Work are available in the following ways:

- As a printed, spiral-bound book (Scheme of Work supplied as downloadable word files with instructions on how to access them inside the front cover).
- Alternatively both the complete Teacher's Guide content and Scheme of Work can be purchased and accessed as word files online (via the ActiveTeach Library). From there they can be downloaded and printed off as necessary.

ActiveTeach

ActiveTeach is a powerful and motivating resource combining the 'book on screen' and a wealth of supporting materials – providing you with the perfect tool for whole-class teaching.

- Use the on-screen Pupil Book with all the listening activities included.
- Zoom in on areas of text and activities to facilitate whole-class teaching.
- Build your own lessons and add in your own resources to help personalise learning.
- Use fun and motivating electronic flashcards to teach new vocabulary.
- Consolidate language using the whole-class interactive games.
- Use the video clips to introduce your pupils to the lives of young German people.
- Teach and revise grammar using PowerPoint® presentations, followed by interactive grammar activities on key grammar points.
- Download and print off a variety of extra worksheets for starters, plenaries, consolidation of grammar, thinking skills, language-learning skills, extended reading comprehensions, self assessment and vocab lists. These are ideal for follow-up work, cover lessons and homework.
- You can also download and print off worksheets with a current topical and cultural focus. These are updated half-termly, and, once up online, will remain there to be accessed or downloaded at any time.

The wide variety of worksheets in *ActiveTeach* (mentioned above) can be used to consolidate and extend pupils' learning as follows:

Kapitel 1

Grammar: Regular verbs in the present tense

Thinking skills: Cracking the code

Extension: Question time!

Kapitel 2

Learning skills: Plural nouns

Extension: Monster families

Grammar: Verbs

Kapitel 3

Extension: Out of this world!

Thinking skills: It's only logical

Grammar: Using the present tense to express future plans

Kapitel 4

Grammar: Word order

Extension: In Lisa's room

Learning skills: Dealing with new words

Kapitel 5

Extension: Modal verbs

Grammar: The future tense

Learning skills: How do I remember everything?

These worksheets can be found in the page resources section of the relevant page or by searching by keyword or resource type in the ActiveTeach search.

Audio Files

The audio files for the course contain all the recorded material for the listening activities in the Pupil Book. These audio files are also contained on ActiveTeach so only teachers who do not purchase ActiveTeach will need to buy the audio files. The different types of activities can be used for presentation of new language, comprehension and pronunciation practice. The material includes dialogues, interviews and songs recorded by native speakers.

After purchasing the audio files for Stimmt!, you can access and download them online from the ActiveTeach Library. From there they can be saved onto your computer or network for future use.

Please note: the audio files and ActiveTeach do not contain the listening material for the end-of-chapter tests and end-of-year test. This material can be found in the Assessment Pack (see right).

Workbooks

There are two parallel workbooks to accompany Stimmt! 1: one for reinforcement (Übungsheft A) and one for extension (Übungsheft B). There is one page of activities for each double-page unit in the Pupil Book. The workbooks fulfil a number of functions:

- They provide self-access reading and writing activities designed to offer the pupils enjoyable ways of consolidating and practising the language they have learned in each unit.
- They give extra practice in grammar, as well as reading and writing skills, with integrated activities throughout the workbooks.
- Revision pages at the end of each chapter (Wiederholung) help pupils revise what they have learned during the chapter.
- Chapter word lists (Wörter) with English translations are invaluable for language learning homework.
- The Mein Fortschritt pages at the end of each chapter allow pupils to record their National Curriculum level for each skill and set themselves improvement targets for the next chapter.
- Level descriptors in pupil-friendly language at the back of the workbooks allow pupils to see what they must do to progress through the levels in all four skills.

The Workbooks are available as print books sold in packs of 8 or can be downloaded as PDFs from the ActiveTeach Library.

Assessment Pack

The Assessment Pack contains all the assessment material required to assess pupils in Year 7 against the National Curriculum Attainment Targets, as well as self-assessment sheets.

- End of chapter tests in all four skills – listening, speaking, reading and writing
- End-of-year test in all four skills
- Covers Levels 1 to 5
- Optional Extra Level 5 test
- Target setting sheets

The audio material supports the listening tests. The assessment pages and the audio can be downloaded online from the ActiveTeach Library. There you will find Word files and PDF versions of the test sheets, alongside the audio files for the listening tests.

ActiveLearn

ActiveLearn is a motivating new digital resource for individual pupil use in school or at home. It is accessed online and follows the same topics as the Pupil Book. The ActiveCourse part of the product comprises sequences of exercises that will help pupils to work on their language skills, in particular listening, reading, grammar and vocab.

Activities in the ActiveLearn ActiveCourse are structured in the following way:

- Interactive listening skills activities at two levels (reinforcement (A) and extension (B))

matched to each core teaching unit (Units 1–4 of each chapter, or 1–5 of Chapters 1 and 2).
- Interactive reading skills activities at two levels (lower and higher) matched to each core teaching unit (Units 1–4 of each chapter, or 1–5 of Chapters 1 and 2).
- Interactive grammar activities, one per core unit, covering key grammar points.
- Key vocabulary from each core unit, drilled and tested through a unique system of activities.

Pupils' performance in the activities is tracked and recorded, making it easy for themselves and teachers to review their progress throughout the year.

In addition, through *ActiveLearn*, it is possible to purchase a digital version of their Pupil Book (the *ActiveBook*, accessed online) which includes all the audio files for the listening activities in the Pupil Book.

Grammar coverage

Grammar is fully integrated into the teaching sequence in *Stimmt!* to ensure that pupils have the opportunity to learn thoroughly the underlying structures of the German language. All units have a grammar objective so that pupils can see clearly which grammar structures they are learning. The key grammar points are presented in the *Stimmt! Grammatik* boxes on the Pupil Book pages and fuller explanations and practice are provided in the *Grammatik* pages at the end of each chapter. In addition, there are grammar PowerPoint® presentations in *ActiveTeach* for presenting new grammar concepts to classes, followed by interactive practice activities that can be used with whole classes or for individual practice.
Worksheets focusing on the key grammar topics taught in *Stimmt! 1* are also provided in *ActiveTeach* and can be printed off for individual pupil use.

Grammar points explained and practised in *Stimmt! 1*:
- Article 'the' (*der, die, das*)
- Article 'a' (*ein, eine*) and negative (*kein, keine*)
- Present tense of *sein, haben, fahren, lesen, sehen*
- Present tense of regular verbs
- Possessive adjectives *mein(e), dein(e), sein(e), ihr(e)*
- Accusative after *haben* and *es gibt*
- Pronouns
- Plural of nouns
- Modal verbs: *können, dürfen*
- *Formal/informal modes of address*
- *Adjectival agreement*
- Ordinal numbers
- Forming questions
- Using *gern/nicht gern*

- Word order (with expressions of time)
- Talking about the future using the present tense
- Using *weil*
- *How to say 'his' and 'her'*
- Prepositions: *in, an, auf, neben*
- Using *man*
- Using *ich möchte*
- The future tense with *werden*

Coverage of the National Curriculum Programme of Study in *Stimmt! 1*

In *Stimmt!* the 2014 National Curriculum Programme of Study is covered comprehensively. The Programme of Study is as follows

1 Grammar and vocabulary

Pupils should be taught to:
- identify and use tenses or other structures which convey the present, past, and future as appropriate to the language being studied
- use and manipulate a variety of key grammatical structures and patterns, including voices and moods, as appropriate
- develop and use a wide-ranging and deepening vocabulary that goes beyond their immediate needs and interests, allowing them to give and justify opinions and take part in discussion about wider issues
- use accurate grammar, spelling and punctuation.

2 Linguistic competence

Pupils should be taught to:
- listen to a variety of forms of spoken language to obtain information and respond appropriately
- transcribe words and short sentences that they hear with increasing accuracy
- initiate and develop conversations, coping with unfamiliar language and unexpected responses, making use of important social conventions such as formal modes of address
- express and develop ideas clearly and with increasing accuracy, both orally and in writing
- speak coherently and confidently, with increasingly accurate pronunciation and intonation
- read and show comprehension of original and adapted materials from a range of different sources, understanding the purpose, important ideas and details, and provide an accurate English translation of short, suitable material

- read literary texts in the language, such as stories, songs, poems and letters, to stimulate ideas, develop creative expression and expand understanding of the language and culture
- write prose using an increasingly wide range of grammar and vocabulary, write creatively to express their own ideas and opinions, and translate short written text accurately into the foreign language.

Activities throughout *Stimmt!* are specifically designed to give pupils opportunities to cover the Programme of Study. As the Programme of Study is intended to represent learning through Years 7, 8 and 9, not all aspects of it are covered in Book 1. However *Stimmt!* 1 and 2 cover the Programme of Study in full. After Book 2, Pupils could either move on to GSCE if time is short, or continue with *Stimmt!* 3 (which also covers the Programme of Study) in Year 9.

The table below outlines the points from the Programme of Study in short form, and shows examples of where they are covered in *Stimmt! 1*. The content of the course is also matched to the Programme of Study unit by unit throughout this Teacher's Guide.

1 Grammar and vocabulary (GV)	
GV1 Tenses	K2 U3, K3 U4, K5 U4
GV2 Grammatical structures	K2 U2, K4 U1, K4 U4, K5 U2.
GV3 Developing vocabulary	K2 PZ, K3 PZ, K5 U4
Opinions and discussions	K2 U3, K3 U2, K4 U1
GV4 Accuracy	K1 U6
2 Linguistic competence (LC)	
LC1 Listening and responding	K2 U4, K3 U5, K4 U2, K5 U5
LC2 Transcription	K2 U1, K2 U5, K5 U5, K5 U6
LC3 Conversation	K1 U1, K2 U6, K4 U3, K5 U2
Conversation (dealing with the unexpected)	K2 U6, K3 U2, K5 U4
Conversation (using modes of address)	K2 U2, K5 U2

LC4 Expressing ideas (speaking)	K2 U5, K4 U6, K5 U1, K5 U4
Expressing ideas (writing)	K1 U6, K3 U6, K5 U6
LC5 Speaking coherently and confidently	K2 U1, K2 U6, K4 U6, K5 U4
Accurate pronunciation and intonation	K1 U1, K2 U1, K3 U1, K4 U6,
LC6 Reading comprehension	K2 PZ2 (authentic text), K4 U5, K5 U6 (authentic text), K5 PZ (authentic text)
Translation into English	K2 U4, K3 U6, K4 Gr, K5 Gram
LC7 Literary texts	K1 U2, K2 PZ1, K4 U6
LC8 Writing creatively	K1 U6, K2 U2, K3 U2, K5 U6
Translation into German	K2 U3, K3 U4, K4 Gr, K5 Gram

National Curriculum Levels in *Stimmt!*

The 2014 National Curriculum no longer includes Level Descriptors for Levels 1-8 and exceptional performance. In order to ensure sound progression, as well as to aiding progress tracking and reporting, *Stimmt!* keeps the levels in place, using the level descriptors as they were in the previous Curriculum. In the course they feature in the following ways:

- All activities in the course are levelled (in the Teacher's Guide) from Levels 1-7
- End-of-chapter tests for *Stimmt!* have been written using the old National Curriculum Levels to indicate the level of challenge
- Workbooks contain self-assessment and target setting pages based around the old National Curriculum Levels.

As the new National Programmes of Study become established in schools from 2014, their use in *Stimmt!*, as well as the use of the older NC Level descriptors, will be reviewed to make sure that the course provides the most valid and up-to-date account of how achievement is measured and progress is tracked.

© Pearson Education Ltd 2013. Copying permitted for purchasing institution only. This material is not copyright free.

Coverage of Personal Learning and Thinking Skills in *Stimmt! 1*

Activities supporting PLTS development are included throughout the course. One PLTS is identified in each unit, with Chapters 1–5 all featuring the full range of PLTS. Each PLTS is given in the table below, with a selection of examples and details of how they meet the curriculum requirements.

Personal Learning and Thinking Skills	
I Independent enquirers	Pupil Book activities throughout the course (e.g. K1 U3 Ex 5, K2 U2 Ex 2, K4 U3 Ex 3)
C Creative thinkers	Regular activities developing skills strategies (how to improve listening/speaking, etc.) (e.g. K2 U6 Ex 1); Starters requiring pupils to apply logic and make connections (e.g. K1 U1); regular activities encouraging pupils to identify patterns and work out rules (e.g. K2 U1 Ex 6); activities requiring creative production of language (e.g. K4 U2 Ex 10)
R Reflective learners	Ongoing opportunities to assess work and identify areas for improvement (e.g. K1 U6 Ex 8), including all *Lernzieltest* and Plenaries (e.g. K4 U5 Plenary)
T Team workers	Regular pairwork activities (e.g. K3 U3), including many Starters; regular peer assessment (e.g. K1 U6 Ex 9)
S Self-managers	Ongoing advice on managing learning (e.g. K2 U6), including strategies to improve learning (e.g. K5 U6)
E Effective participators	Opportunities throughout the course for pupils to contribute (e.g. K2 U6), including presentations (e.g. K5 U4) and all Plenaries (e.g. K1 U1)

Pupils may find the following short forms useful as a reference in class:

I am a/an ...		Today I ...
Independent enquirer	I	worked on my own to find out something new
Creative thinker	C	used what I know to work out or create something new
Reflective learner	R	thought about what I've learned and how I can improve
Team worker	T	worked well with other people
Self-manager	S	took responsibility for improving my learning
Effective participator	E	took part in the lesson in a positive way

Coverage of the Foundation Certificate of Secondary Education in German (Revised Specification) in *Stimmt! 1*

Stimmt! can be used to teach the Key Stage 3 FCSE qualification from AQA. The following table shows where each of the FCSE units and sub-topics for the Revised Specification (2014) can be taught using *Stimmt! 1*. Many of the FCSE units and sub-topics that do not appear in *Stimmt! 1* are covered in *Stimmt! 2* or *Stimmt! 3 Rot/Grün*.

Unit 1 – Relationships, family and friends

Sub-topics	Where in *Stimmt! 1*
Reading and listening	
Family and step family	Chapter 2, Unit 3
Personal details about family	Chapter 2, Unit 4
Mini biography of family *(Set A only)*	
Rank in family *(Set B only)*	
Personal details about friends *(Set B only)*	
Girlfriend, boyfriend	
Relationships and reasons for good and bad relations within family and friends	
Issues *(Set B only)*	
Taking sides in an argument *(Set B only)*	
Pets	Chapter 2, Unit 1, Chapter 2, Unit 2
Clothes *(Set A only)*	
Family celebrations	Chapter 2, Unit 5
Prepositions	
Numbers	Chapter 1, Unit 2
Speaking and writing	
Personal information	Chapter 1, Unit 1, Chapter 1, Unit 5, Chapter 1, Unit 6, Chapter 1, Projektzone
Family/friends	Chapter 2, Unit 3, Chapter 3, Unit 5
Meeting up with friends/activities	
Descriptions	Chapter 2, Unit 4, Chapter 2, Unit 6
Hobbies/free-time activities	Chapter 3, Unit 1

Unit 2 – Education and future plans

Sub-topics	Where in *Stimmt! 1*
Reading and listening	
Education	
School – teachers problems transport	Chapter 4, Unit 3
timetable uniform	Chapter 4, Unit 2
facilities	Chapter 4, Unit 4, Chapter 4, Unit 6
type of school *(Set A only)* location *(Set A only)* subjects	Chapter 4, Unit 1
rules *(Set A only)* school clubs *(Set A only)* sport progress report *(Set A only)* items in school bag *(Set B only)*	
Future plans	
Plans for after school	
Plans for jobs and careers	
Plans for future study	
Advantages and disadvantages of jobs	
Advantages and disadvantages of staying on at school *(Set B only)*	
Time	
Prepositions of place	
Alphabet *(Set A only)*	
Numbers *(Set A only)*	
Sequence *(Set B only)*	
Speaking and writing	
Physical description of school	
School activities	
Opinions	Chapter 4, Unit 1
Uniform	
Future plans	

Unit 3 – Holidays and travel

Sub-topics	Where in *Stimmt! 1*
Reading and listening	
Holidays	Chapter 5, Unit 4
Types of holiday	
Camping *(Set A only)*	
Activities *(Set A only)*	
Travel	
Accommodation	
Weather on holiday	
Problems on holiday *(Set B only)*	
Holiday experiences *(Set B only)*	
Speaking and writing	
Destination	Chapter 5, Projektzone
Travel	
Accommodation	
Activities	Chapter 5, Unit 4, Chapter 5, Projektzone

Unit 4 – Leisure

Sub-topics	Where in *Stimmt! 1*
Reading and listening	
Hobbies	Chapter 3, Unit 1
Free time/hobbies	Chapter 3, Unit 1, Chapter 3, Unit 2, Chapter 3, Unit 3, Chapter 3, Unit 4, Chapter 3 Projektzone
Television	
Films *(Set A only)*	
Cinema *(Set B only)*	
Music	
Gardening *(Set A only)*	
Going out *(Set A only)*	
Theatre visit *(Set A only)*	
Clubs	
Around town *(Set B only)*	Chapter 5, Unit 2
Leisure centre *(Set B only)*	

Speaking and writing	
Hobbies/activities	Chapter 3, Unit 1, Chapter 3, Unit 2
Preferences	Chapter 1, Unit 4
Going out	
Pocket money	

Unit 5 – Healthy lifestyle

Sub-topics	Where in *Stimmt! 1*
Reading and listening	
Healthy living	
Food/drink *(Set B only)*	
Healthy/unhealthy eating *(Set A only)*	
Fast food *(Set A only)*	
Exercise *(Set A only)*	
Life as a footballer *(Set B only)*	
Sports	
Leisure centres *(Set A only)*	
Alcohol	
Smoking	
Illness	
Chemist's *(Set B only)*	
Stress *(Set A only)*	
Exam pressure	
Health farms *(Set A only)*	
Speaking and writing	
State of health	
Activities	Chapter 3, Unit 1
Eating and drinking	
Opinions	

Unit 6 – Food and drink

Sub-topics	Where in *Stimmt! 1*
Reading and listening	
Food/drink vocabulary items	Chapter 5, Unit 3
Eating out	Chapter 5, Unit 3
Opinions about food and drink	
Shopping for food	
Unhealthy/healthy food choices	

Speaking and writing	
Food and drink habits	
Eating out	
Opinions about food and drink	

Unit 7 – Local area and environment

Sub-topics	Where in *Stimmt! 1*
Reading and listening	
Facilities	Chapter 5, Unit 1, Chapter 5, Unit 5, Chapter 5, Unit 6
Locations	
Preferences	
Environment	
Recycling	
Weather	
Speaking and writing	
Local area	Chapter 1, Unit 3
Activities	Chapter 5, Unit 6
Environment	

Unit 8 – Celebrations

Sub-topics	Where in *Stimmt! 1*
Reading and listening	
Birthdays	Chapter 2, Unit 5
Various festivals	Chapter 2, Projektzone
Parties	
Celebrating *(Set A only)*	
Engagements and weddings	
Celebrating success *(Set A only)*	
Carnival	
End of exams	
Speaking and writing	
Parties	
Opinions	
Special celebrations	Chapter 2, Projektzone

Games and other teaching suggestions

Reading aloud

There are many reading activities in the Pupil Book which give scope for further activities.

1. You can use the texts to practise reading aloud. As an incentive, award five points to a pupil who can read a text without any errors. Points could also be given to teams, depending on seating arrangements – tables, rows, sides of the room.
2. Set a challenge – 'I bet no one can read this without a single mistake' or ask a volunteer pupil to predict how many mistakes he/she will make before having a go, then seeing if he/she can do better than predicted.
3. Texts could be read round the class with pupils simply reading up to a full stop and then passing it on to someone else in the room. They enjoy this activity if it is fast. Alternatively, pupils can read as much or as little as they want before passing it on.
4. You can also read a text, pause and have the pupils say the next word.

Reading follow-up

Motivation and participation can be enhanced by dividing the class into two teams and awarding points. Once they know a text very well, pupils should be able to complete a sentence from memory, hearing just the beginning. Move from a word to a phrase to a sentence: i.e. you say a word, the pupils give the word in a short context and then in a longer context.

1. You read aloud and stop (or insert the word 'beep') for pupils to complete the word or sentence.
2. You read aloud and make a deliberate mistake (either pronunciation or saying the wrong word). Pupils put up their hand as soon as they spot a mistake.
3. *Hot potato*: Pupils read a bit and pass it on quickly to someone who may not be expecting it.
4. *Marathon*: A pupil reads aloud until he/she makes a mistake. Pupils have to put up their hand as soon as they hear a mistake. A second pupil then takes over, starting at the beginning again and trying to get further than the previous pupil.
5. *Random reading*: You read a phrase at random and the pupils have to say the next bit.
6. You can play music and get the pupils to pass an object round the class. When the music stops, the person with the object has a turn. Let a pupil control the music, facing away from the class.

Mime activities

Mimes are a motivating way to help pupils to learn words.

1. You say a word, for example a job, sport or hobby, or an adjective, and the pupils mime it. This can be done silently with the whole class responding. Alternatively, it can be done as a knock-out game starting with six volunteers at the front who mime to the class as you say each word. Any pupil who does the wrong mime or who is slow to react is knocked out. Impose a two-minute time limit.
2. Pupils say a word or phrase and you mime it – but only if the pupils say it correctly. This really puts you on the spot and gets the pupils trying very hard. You could also insist that the pupils say it from memory.
3. You mime and pupils say the word or phrase.
4. Send five or six pupils out of the room. They each have to decide on an adjective which sums up their character. They return to the room individually or together, each one miming their character adjective. The remaining pupils then guess the adjective. Get them to use a sentence, e.g. *Daniel ist lustig.*
5. *Ein Freiwilliger / Eine Freiwillige*: One person goes out of the room. The rest of the class decides on a character adjective to mime. The volunteer comes back into the room and has to guess the adjective that the class is miming. Again, encourage the use of whole sentences.
6. *Class knock-down*: As above, but this time everyone in the class can choose different qualities to mime. The volunteer returns to the room with everyone doing his/her own mime. The volunteer points to each pupil and names the character adjective. If the volunteer is correct, the pupil sits down. This works well as a timed or team activity. The aim is to sit your team down as quickly as possible.
7. A version of charades is a good activity at the end of the lesson. Organise two teams, A and B. Have all the adjectives written down on separate cards, masculine forms only. Put the cards in a pile at the front. A volunteer from Team A comes to the front, picks up the first card and mimes it. The rest of the team must not see the word on the card. Anyone from Team A can put up his/her hand and is then invited by the volunteer to say the word. If correct, the volunteer picks up the next card and mimes it. The aim is to get through the whole list as quickly as possible. Note down the time for Team A. Team B then tries to beat that time.

Exploiting the songs

1. Pupils sing along. Fade out certain bits while they continue. When most of them know the song quite well you can pause the audio to let them give you the next line by heart. Then try

the whole chorus, followed by a few verses completely from memory.
2 You could try the 'pick up a song' game: you fade the song after a few lines, the pupils continue singing, and then you fade the song up again towards the end and they see whether they have kept pace with the recording.

Translation follow-up

Motivation and participation can be enhanced by dividing the class into two teams and awarding points. Once they know the text very well, you should be able to say any word, phrase or sentence from the text at random for the pupils to translate into English without viewing the text.

1 You translate the text and stop (or insert the word 'beep') for pupils to complete the word or sentence.
2 You translate, making a deliberate mistake. Pupils put up their hand as soon as they spot a mistake.
3 *Hot potato*: A pupil translates a bit and passes it on quickly to someone who may not be expecting it.
4 *Marathon*: A pupil translates until he/she makes a mistake. Pupils have to put up their hand as soon as they hear a mistake. A second pupil then takes over, starting from the beginning again and trying to get further than the previous pupil.
5 *Random translation*: You read a phrase in German at random and the pupils have to translate it.
6 One half of the class has their books open, the other half has them closed. The half with their books open reads a sentence in German at random. The other side has to translate. Do about five then swap round.
7 You can play music and get the pupils to pass an object round. When the music stops, the person with the object has a turn. Let a pupil control the music, facing away from the class.

Writing follow-up (text dissection)

Whiteboards are a useful tool. They do not need to be issued to every pupil. Pupils can work in pairs or groups or they can pass the whiteboards on. You could also divide the class into teams, with one whiteboard per team.

After reading a text in some detail:

1 Display some anagrams of key words from the text and ask pupils to write them correctly. You will need to prepare these in advance and check carefully. Award points for correct answers on each board.
2 Display some jumbled phrases from the text, e.g. *spiele Ich Basketball gern.*. Pupils rewrite the phrase correctly in their exercise books or on the board. They could work in teams, producing one answer per team on paper.

3 Display an incorrect word or phrase in German and ask pupils to spot the mistake and correct it. This can also be done as 'spot the missing word' or 'spot the word that is in the wrong place'.
4 Ask pupils to spell certain words from memory. Differentiate by first reading out a few words in German and then giving a few in English for them also to write out in German.
5 *Mini-Diktat*: Read four or five short sentences in German for pupils to write out. Again, this could be a group exercise.
6 Give pupils phrases in English to write out in German.

Comprehension follow-up

1 Ask questions in English about the text.
2 Ask questions in German about the text.
3 True or false?
4 Who … ?

Vocabulary treasure hunt

1 Find the word for …
2 Find (three) opinions.

Grammar treasure hunt

1 Find (three) adjectives.
2 Find (two) feminine adjectives.
3 Find a verb in the nous form.
4 Find a plural noun.
5 Find a negative.

A variation on pairwork

Musical pass the mobile phone: One pupil controls the music, facing away from the class. While the music is playing, a toy or old mobile phone is passed from pupil to pupil. As soon as the music stops, the music operator (who is ideally also equipped with a phone) says the first statement of a dialogue. The other pupil who has ended up with the phone replies. They can, if they like, disguise their voice. The music operator tries to guess who is speaking. The game then continues.

KAPITEL 1

Meine Welt und ich

Unit & Learning objectives	Programme of Study references	Key Language	Grammar and other language features
1 Hallo! (pp. 8–9) • Introducing yourself • Learning how to pronounce German words	**GV2** Grammatical structures (definite and indefinite article) **LC1** Listening and responding **LC5** Accurate pronunciation and intonation	Hallo! Ich heiße … Wie heißt du? Guten Tag! Wie geht's? Und dir? Gut./Nicht schlecht. Tschüs! Auf Wiedersehen!	• The definite (*der, die, das*) and indefinite (*ein, eine, ein*) article (nominative singular) • Active learning • Pronunciation of *s* and *ß*
2 Eins, zwei, drei … (pp. 10–11) • Counting to 19 • Using the verb *sein* (to be)	**GV1** Tenses (*sein* simple present) **LC1** Listening and responding	Numbers 1–19 Wie alt bist du? Ich bin … Jahre alt.	• The verb *sein* (simple present, singular) • Using key words to help pronunciation • Asking someone's age
3 Ich wohne in Deutschland (pp. 12–13) • Using the German alphabet • Using the verb *wohnen* to say where you live	**GV1** Tenses (present) **LC3** Conversation **LC5** Accurate pronunciation and intonation	Wo wohnst du? Ich wohne in … Er/Sie wohnt in … Das ist in … England Schottland Wales Nordirland Irland Wie schreibt man das (Haus)? Das schreibt man (H–A–U–S).	• The verb *wohnen* (simple present, singular) • Pronunciation of *ä, ö, ü* and *ß*

Meine Welt und ich – **KAPITEL**

Unit & Learning objectives	Programme of Study references	Key Language	Grammar and other language features
4 Meine Welt is wunderbar! (pp. 14–15) • Describing your character • Using *mein(e)* and *dein(e)*	**GV3** Developing vocabulary **LC1** Listening and responding **LC3** Conversation	freundlich launisch kreativ intelligent sportlich laut faul musikalisch lustig Ich bin sehr/ziemlich/nicht … Was ist deine(e) …? Mein(e) … ist … der Lieblingssport der Lieblingsmonat die Lieblingsmusik die Lieblingszahl die Lieblingssendung die Lieblingsfußballmannschaft das Lieblingsspiel das Lieblingsland das Lieblingsauto	• The indefinite article (*ein*, *mein*, *dein*) • Using connectives • Cognates
5 Meine Sachen (pp. 16–17) • Asking and answering questions about your belongings • Using the verb *haben* + the indefinite article	**GV2** Grammatical structures (accusative) **LC3** Conversation **LC6** Reading comprehension	Wie? Was? Wo? Woher? Wer?	• Singular paradigm of *haben* • Introduction to the accusative • Asking questions
6 Writing Skills: Ich über mich (pp. 18–19) • Preparing a poster presentation • Checking your work	**GV4** Accuracy (grammar, spelling) **LC2** Transcription **LC8** Writing creatively		
Lernzieltest und Wiederholung (pp. 20–21) Pupils' checklist and practice exercises			

© Pearson Education Ltd 2013. Copying permitted for purchasing institution only. This material is not copyright free.

Meine Welt und ich – KAPITEL 1

Unit & Learning objectives	Programme of Study references	Key Language	Grammar and other language features
Grammatik (pp. 22–23) Detailed grammar summary and practice exercises			• Nouns, gender and articles • Verbs • The present tense – regular verbs • The present tense – irregular verbs
Projektzone: Supertrumpf (pp. 26–27) • Learning about famous people • Creating 'super trumps' cards	**LC2** Transcription **LC4** Expressing ideas (speaking) **LC8** Writing creatively		• Using *ich denke …* to say what you think about something

1 Hallo! (Pupil Book pp. 6–9)

Meine Welt und ich – KAPITEL

Learning objectives
- Introducing yourself
- Learning how to pronounce German words

Programme of Study
GV2 Grammatical structures (definite and indefinite article)
LC1 Listening and responding
LC5 Accurate pronunciation and intonation

FCSE links
Unit 1 – Relationships, Family and Friends (Personal information)

Grammar
The definite (*der*, *die*, *das*) and indefinite (*ein*, *eine*, *ein*) article (nominative singular)

Key Language
Hallo!
Ich heiße …
Wie heißt du?
Guten Tag!
Wie geht's?
Und dir?
Gut./Nicht schlecht.
Tschüs!
Auf Wiedersehen!

PLTS
S Self-managers

Cross-curricular
Design and technology: inventions

Resources
Audio files:
01_Kapitel1_Einheit1_Aufgabe1
02_Kapitel1_Einheit1_Aufgabe2
03_Kapitel1_Einheit1_Aufgabe3
04_Kapitel1_Einheit1_Aufgabe5
05_Kapitel1_Einheit1_Aufgabe8

Workbooks:
Übungsheft 1 A&B, page 2

ActiveTeach:
Starter 1 resource
p.008 Class game
p.008 Exercise 1 video
p.009 Grammar practice
p.009 Grammar presentation

ActiveLearn:
Listening A, Listening B
Reading A, Reading B
Grammar, Vocabulary

Kapitel 1 Quiz pp. 6–7

Answers

1 Das ist …
1 c 2 b 3 a

2 Das ist …
1 b 2 c 3 a

3 Was ist das?
1 d 2 b 3 a 4 c

4 Woher kommen diese Dinge?
Auto – Deutschland
Mozart – Österreich
Paella – Spanien
Kaffee – Brasilien
Pizza – Italien

5 Welches Auto kommt nicht aus Deutschland?
Ford

6 Finde ein deutsches Beispiel.
a *Auto* – *Volkswagen* **b** Supermarkt – Aldi
c Sportmode – Adidas **d** Energiesysteme – Siemens **e** Bonbons – Haribo

(Other answers are possible.)

Starter 1

Aim
To introduce *Stadt-Land-Fluss* as a vocabulary builder and encourage pupils to recycle vocabulary already seen.

Pupils copy down the grid (Starter 1 resource) and are given the letter 'S'. They then find a German word for each of the categories (*Stadt, Land, Fluss, Objekt, Ort, Tier*) from either this spread or the chapter opener spread. (Rivers have been included as they are in the name of the game, but categories can be adapted as required and locations are not restricted to Germany.) A dictionary could be used for extension or for beginning to use a bilingual dictionary. Points are awarded for the number of correct answers, with pupils being awarded 1 point per word and 2 points if they have a different word to everyone else. The first pupil to finish shouts *Halt!* and everyone has to stop.

Stadt-Land-Fluss grids can be bought in German in different designs and are always popular with pupils. Eventually pupils could come up with their own categories and once they know the alphabet, they can be asked to choose a letter. As pupils learn more vocabulary, extra categories can be added to test different topics.

Hallo! | Meine Welt und ich – **KAPITEL 1**

1 Sieh dir das Video auf ActiveTeach an. Hör zu und mach mit. (1–16)
(Listening L1)

Listening. Pupils watch the video. They imitate the gestures shown to represent words which contain key sounds.

These particular words were chosen with the following rationale: They are all:

- nouns, so they are consistent in format, i.e. all capitals
- easy to depict in visual form
- concrete rather than abstract
- easy to do with unambiguous actions (the gestures are based on British Sign Language where applicable and other obvious signs where not)
- engaging words, either because they are enjoyable to say, the pictures will be interesting, or both
- memorable.

If you don't have access to ActiveTeach, listen to the audio and ask pupils to make up their own actions for each word.

Audioscript

1 – *Jo-Jo*
2 – *Vogel*
3 – *Wildwassersport*
4 – *Zickzack*
5 – *Haus*
6 – *Freund*
7 – *Eis*
8 – *Biene*
9 – *Bär*
10 – *Löwe*
11 – *Tür*
12 – *Mäuse*
13 – *Buch*
14 – *Schlange*
15 – *Spitzbart*
16 – *Sterne*

2 Hör zu. Welches Wort ist das? Mach die richtige Geste. (1–8) (Listening L1)

Listening. Pupils listen to a word and make the appropriate gesture. They repeat the gesture they have seen in the video or have made up.

Audioscript

1 – *Spitzbart*
2 – *Vogel*
3 – *Bär*
4 – *Schlange*
5 – *Biene*
6 – *Mäuse*
7 – *Eis*
8 – *Sterne*

3 Hör zu. Was passt nicht? (1–6)
(Listening L1)

Listening. Pupils listen to four words and in each case identify the odd one out, i.e. the word that does not contain the same key sound.

Audioscript

1 – *Schlange, Schokolade, Zickzack, Schuh*
2 – *Jo-Jo, Jacke, Biene, Japan*
3 – *Zickzack, Konzert, Pizza, Sterne*
4 – *Spitzbart, Bär, Käse, Träne*
5 – *Freund, Eis, Deutsch, Feuer*
6 – *Buch, Schlange, Frankreich, acht*

Answers

1 Zickzack **2** Biene **3** Sterne **4** Spitzbart **5** Eis **6** Schlange

4 Partnerarbeit. Partner(in) A sagt das Wort, Partner(in) B macht die richtige Geste. (Speaking L1)

Speaking. Pupils work in pairs. One pupil reads out the words, the other has to make the appropriate gesture. After four words the roles are reversed. Encourage pupils to use all 16 words from exercise 1.

Starter 2

Aim

To introduce some German names and reflect on similarities and differences between German and English spelling patterns.

Pupils create a table with two columns:

Jungennamen   ***Mädchennamen***

Pupils write the names under the headings, deciding whether they think the names are boys' or girls' names (suggested names: Lukas, Leoni, Finn, Lena, Jonas, Lara, Jan, Maximilian, Elias).

This is also an opportunity for discussion about names in different languages and for reflection on similarities and differences.

© Pearson Education Ltd 2013. Copying permitted for purchasing institution only. This material is not copyright free.

Hallo! | Meine Welt und ich – KAPITEL

5 Hör zu und lies. (1–3) (Listening L2)

Listening. Pupils listen to the audio and read alongside the three short dialogues.

Audioscript

1 – *Hallo, ich heiße Julian. Wie heißt du?*
– *Guten Tag! Ich heiße Maja.*
2 – *Wie geht's, Maja?*
– *Gut, danke. Und dir?*
– *Nicht schlecht.*
3 – *Tschüs, Maja.*
– *Auf Wiedersehen, Julian.*

6 Partnerarbeit. Mach einen Dialog. (Speaking L3)

Speaking. In pairs pupils create a dialogue following the example in the pupil book.

This dialogue lends itself to repetition and roles should be swapped each time the dialogue is repeated. Learners could keep their own names throughout or be invited to introduce themselves with a different name each time.

The idea is that pupils memorise the dialogue. At speed this demands a high level of concentration and is a lot of fun. Asking learners to repeat the dialogue with different moods/intonation, then replacing one of the lines with a gesture also works memory, sustains concentration and promotes enjoyment of speaking.

Point pupils to the Pronunciation box to help with the pronunciation of *heiße*.

Extension

Pupils could be encouraged to add lines to their dialogue, borrowing from the captioned dialogue in exercise 5. If they keep the number of lines odd and keep recycling the dialogue they will quickly memorise all parts of it.

Grammatik

Use the *Grammatik* box to introduce the concept of gender and the three definite and indefinite articles. There is more information and practice in the grammar unit on pupil book p. 22.

7 Was passt zusammen? Verbinde die Person mit der Erfindung. Sprich die Wörter aus. (Reading L1)

Reading. Pupils match inventor to invention and say the words out loud to practise the German pronunciation of these brands.

Answers

1 c 2 d 3 e 4 b 5 a

8 Hör zu und überprüfe. (1–5) (Listening L1)

Listening. Pupils listen to the audio and check their answers to exercise 7.

Audioscript

1 – *Rudolf Diesel – c der Dieselmotor*
2 – *Adi Dassler – d die Marke Adidas*
3 – *Wilhelm Conrad Röntgen – e das Röntgenbild*
4 – *Ferdinand Porsche – b das Auto Porsche*
5 – *Karlheinz Brandenburg – a das MP3-Format*

Reinforcement

For further practice:

Wie heißt du? Was ist deine Erfindung?

Felix Hoffmann – aspirin
Karl Benz / Gottlieb Daimler – car
Konrad Zuse – computer
Heinrich Focke – helicopter
Oskar Barnack – pocket camera
Manfred von Ardenne – television
Ottomar Heinsius von Mayenburg – toothpaste

Plenary

Give pupils a character card (any character will do, e.g. celebrities, sportspeople, cartoon characters). They introduce themselves as their character to their partner, who gives them verbal feedback using the 'two stars and a wish' approach using the checklist below:

- Saying hello / goodbye
- Giving your name
- Saying how you are feeling
- Good pronunciation

Partners should then swap roles.

Alternative plenary

Use ActiveTeach p.008 Class Game to review German pronunciation.

Hallo! | Meine Welt und ich – **KAPITEL 1**

Workbook A, page 2

Answers

1 1 f 2 c 3 g 4 d 5 b 6 a 7 e

2 4 Hallo! Ich heiße Tobi. Wie heißt du?
5 Guten Tag! Ich heiße Christina.
3 Wie geht's, Christina?
2 Gut, danke. Und dir?
7 Nicht schlecht.
6 Auf Wiedersehen, Tobi.
1 Tschüs, Christina.

3 1 Hallo! Wie **heißt** du?
Ich **heiße** Roselyn.
Wie **geht's**, Roselyn?
Gut, danke.
2 Guten Tag! **Wie** heißt du?
Ich heiße Heather. Wie geht's?
Nicht **schlecht**. Und **dir**?
Gut, **danke**.

Workbook B, page 2

Answers

1 1 Buch 2 Bär 3 Tür 4 Biene

2 1 f 2 a 3 b 4 d 5 c 6 e

3 1 Hallo! Wie heißt du? *Hello! What's your name?*
2 Ich heiße Ben. Wie heißt du? *My name's Ben. What's your name?*
3 Ich heiße Nadia. Wie geht's, Ben? *My name's Nadia. How are you, Ben?*
4 Gut, danke. Und du? *Well, thanks. And you?*
5 Nicht schlecht. *Not bad.*
6 Auf Wiedersehen. *Goodbye.*

4 das Röntgenbild, ein Röntgenbild
der Dieselmotor, ein Dieselmotor
das MP3-Format, ein MP3-Format
das Auto Porsche, ein Auto Porsche
die Marke Adidas, eine Marke Adidas

© Pearson Education Ltd 2013. Copying permitted for purchasing institution only. This material is not copyright free.

Meine Welt und ich – KAPITEL

2 Eins, zwei, drei ... (Pupil Book pp. 10–11)

Learning objectives
- Counting to 19
- Using the verb *sein* (to be)

Programme of Study
GV1 Tenses (*sein* simple present)
LC1 Listening and responding

FCSE links
Unit 1 – Relationships, Family and Friends (Numbers)

Grammar
The verb *sein* (simple present, singular)

Key Language
Numbers 1–19
Wie alt bist du?
Ich bin ... Jahre alt.

PLTS
T Team workers

Cross-curricular
Mathematics: numbers 1–19

Resources
Audio files:
06_Kapitel1_Einheit2_Aufgabe1
07_Kapitel1_Einheit2_Aufgabe2
08_Kapitel1_Einheit2_Aufgabe3
09_Kapitel1_Einheit2_Aufgabe6
10_Kapitel1_Einheit2_Aufgabe7
Workbooks:
Übungsheft 1 A&B, page 3
ActiveTeach:
Starter 1 resource
p.010 Flashcards
p.011 Grammar presentation
Plenary resource
ActiveLearn:
Listening A, Listening B
Reading A, Reading B
Grammar, Vocabulary

Starter 1

Aim

To review the idea of gender and the different words for 'the' in German.

Explain that words need to be sorted into the different categories according to the German word for 'the' which is in front of each word. Pupils write the words onto the *der/die/das* balloons (Starter 1 resource) according to the article. Pupils are asked to explain what the difference is, why they have put the words on the particular balloons and then to colour-code the balloons to help them to remember the difference. Words from unit 1 should be used to recycle the vocabulary. Extension work would be to put the same words onto the *ein/ein/eine* balloons. Pupils should be asked to reflect why they have grouped the words in the way they have.

Suggested words:
- das Auto
- der Supermarkt
- die Sportmode
- der Vogel
- der Freund
- die Freundin
- das Haus
- das Buch

1 Hör zu und sing mit. (Listening L1)

Listening. Pupils listen to the song and sing along.

Audioscript

– Ich heiße Max, ich bin die Nummer eins
  Nummer eins, eins, eins ist der Beste.
– Ich heiße Jens, ich bin die Nummer zwei
  Nummer zwei, zwei, zwei ist der Beste.
– Ich heiße Emma, bin die Nummer drei
  Nummer drei, drei, drei ist die Beste.
– Ich heiße Klaus, ich bin die Nummer vier
  Nummer vier, vier, vier ist der Beste.
– Eins, zwei, drei, vier
– Ich heiße Anna, bin die Nummer fünf
  Nummer fünf, fünf, fünf ist die Beste.
– Ich heiße Paul, ich bin die Nummer sechs
  Nummer sechs, sechs, sechs ist der Beste.
– Ich heiße Mia, ich bin die Nummer sieben
  Nummer sieben, sieben ist die Beste.
– Ich heiße Jan, ich bin die Nummer acht
  Nummer acht, acht, acht ist der Beste.
– Eins, zwei, drei, vier, fünf, sechs, sieben, acht
– Ich heiße Finn, ich bin die Nummer neun
  Nummer neun, neun, neun ist der Beste.
– Ich heiße Leah, bin die Nummer zehn
  Nummer zehn, zehn, zehn ist die Beste.
– Ich heiße Sara, bin die Nummer elf
  Nummer elf, elf, elf ist die Beste.

© Pearson Education Ltd 2013. Copying permitted for purchasing institution only. This material is not copyright free.

Eins, zwei, drei ... | Meine Welt und ich – **KAPITEL 1**

- *Ich heiße Noah, bin die Nummer zwölf*
  Nummer zwölf, zwölf, zwölf ist der Beste.
- *Eins, zwei, drei*
  Vier, fünf, sechs
  Sieben, acht, neun
  Zehn, elf, zwölf

2 Hör noch mal zu. Wer ist das? Schreib die Zahl und den Namen auf. (1–12) (Listening L2)

Listening. Pupils listen again to the audio and write down the names and numbers mentioned in the song. The names are given in the book in random order.

Audioscript

For transcript see exercise 1.

Answers

1 Max 2 Jens 3 Emma 4 Klaus 5 Anna 6 Paul
7 Mia 8 Jan 9 Finn 10 Leah 11 Sara 12 Noah

Extension

Some pupils could try to write down both number and name with the book closed.

3 Lies den Reim vor. Dann hör zu und überprüfe. (Listening/Speaking L1)

Listening/Speaking. Pupils read the rhyme out loud, then listen to the audio and read it out to check pronunciation.

Refer pupils to the *Tip* box, which encourages them to compare their key words (in this case *Eis*) with words in the poem to help with pronunciation. Words with sounds that match the unit 1 key words are:

- *Zickzack – zwei, Polizei, Offizier, zehn*
- *Vogel – vier*
- *Biene – vier, Offizier, sieben, auf Wiedersehen*
- *Tür – fünf*
- *Buch – acht, Nacht*
- *Freund – neun*

The rhyme is a traditional German children's rhyme.

Audioscript

Eins, zwei, Polizei
drei, vier, Offizier
fünf, sechs, alte Hex'
sieben, acht, gute Nacht!
Neun, zehn, auf Wiedersehen!

Starter 2

Aim

Pupils play a game of bingo to practise numbers 1–12. This is a variant on the usual game and in this version, pupils write six numbers on a piece of paper in a vertical list. If a number from the top or the bottom is called out, pupils may rip the number off. If the number called out is on their paper but in the middle, they may not rip the number off. The winner is the pupil who has ripped off all their numbers first. This game offers more opportunities to hear the numbers than in the usual game, as the caller may call each number more than once.

Alternative starter 2

Use ActiveTeach p.010 Flashcards to review and practise numbers 1–12.

4 Was passt zusammen? Finde die Paare. (Reading L1)

Reading. Pupils match the numbers (written as words) to the relevant figures.

Answers

dreizehn – 13
vierzehn – 14
fünfzehn – 15
sechzehn – 16
siebzehn – 17
achtzehn – 18
neunzehn – 19

5 Löse die Rechenaufgaben. (Writing L1–2)

Writing. Pupils solve maths questions and write the answers as words.

Answers

1 drei + zwölf = fünfzehn
2 neun + zwei = elf
3 sechs + sieben = dreizehn
4 neunzehn – elf = acht
5 acht + vier = zwölf
6 siebzehn – drei = vierzehn

© Pearson Education Ltd 2013. Copying permitted for purchasing institution only. This material is not copyright free.

Eins, zwei, drei ... | Meine Welt und ich – **KAPITEL**

6 Hör zu. Wie alt sind sie? (1–6) (Listening L2)

Listening. Pupils listen to six dialogues in which children are asked about their age. Pupils write down the age given as a response in each case.

Audioscript

1 – *Wie alt bist du, Julia?*
  – *Ich bin zwölf Jahre alt.*
2 – *Wie alt bist du, Lukas?*
  – *Ich bin sechzehn Jahre alt.*
3 – *Wie alt bist du, Mia?*
  – *Ich bin vierzehn Jahre alt.*
4 – *Wie alt bist du, Jonas?*
  – *Ich bin dreizehn Jahre alt.*
5 – *Wie alt bist du, Laura?*
  – *Ich bin elf Jahre alt.*
6 – *Wie alt bist du, Moritz?*
  – *Ich bin fünfzehn Jahre alt.*

Answers
1 12 *2* 16 *3* 14 *4* 13 *5* 11 *6* 15

Grammatik

Use the *Grammatik* box to introduce the singular of the verb *sein*, stressing that since it is irregular and it is a verb that pupils will use frequently, they do need to learn it. There is more information and practice in the grammar unit on pupil book p. 23.

7 Hör noch mal zu. Wie heißen sie? (1–6) (Listening L2)

Listening. Pupils listen to the dialogues (from exercise 6) again and write down the name of each speaker.

Audioscript

For transcript see exercise 6.

Answers
1 Julia *2* Lukas *3* Mia *4* Jonas *5* Laura
6 Moritz

8 Partnerarbeit. Sieh dir Aufgabe 7 an. Du bist Julia, Lukas, Mia ... Mach Dialoge. (Speaking L3)

Speaking. Using the dialogues from exercise 6, pupils assume the roles of the speakers. In pairs they ask and respond to questions about their age.

Refer pupils to the *Tip* box. It points out that both German and English put the words in the same order.

9 Schreib deinen Dialog aus Aufgabe 8 auf. (Writing L2–3)

Writing. Pupils write out their dialogue from exercise 8.

Plenary

For pupils to establish whether they have met the lesson objectives of counting to 19 and using the verb 'to be'.

Pupils play a game of dominoes practising the numbers 1–19 and the verb *sein*. The Plenary resource can be used or pupils can make their own set of dominoes to play with and take home. This is intended as a reading exercise and a visual/kinaesthetic approach to remembering the vocabulary.

Workbook A, page 3

© Pearson Education Ltd 2013. Copying permitted for purchasing institution only. This material is not copyright free.

Eins, zwei, drei … | **Meine Welt und ich** – KAPITEL 1

Answers

1 **1** eins **2** zwei **3** drei **4** vier **5** fünf **6** sechs
7 sieben **8** acht **9** neun **10** zehn

2 **a** Ich bin elf Jahre alt.
b Ich bin sechzehn Jahre alt.
c Ich bin dreizehn Jahre alt.
d Ich bin fünfzehn Jahre alt.
e Ich bin neunzehn Jahre alt.
f Ich bin zwölf Jahre alt.

Workbook B, page 3

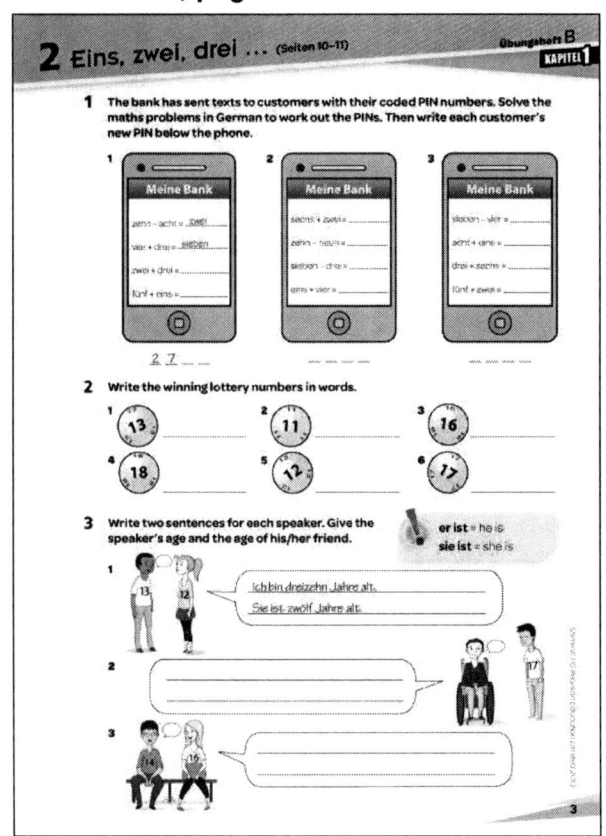

Answers

1 **1** zwei, sieben, fünf, sechs – 2756
2 acht, eins, vier, fünf – 8145
3 drei, neun, neun, sieben – 3997

2 **1** dreizehn **2** elf **3** sechzehn **4** achtzehn
5 zwölf **6** siebzehn

3 **1** Ich bin dreizehn Jahre alt. Sie ist zwölf Jahre alt.

2 Ich bin fünfzehn Jahre alt. Er ist siebzehn Jahre alt.

3 Ich bin vierzehn Jahre alt. Sie ist sechzehn Jahre alt.

Meine Welt und ich – KAPITEL

3 Ich wohne in Deutschland (Pupil Book pp. 12–13)

Learning objectives
- Using the German alphabet
- Using the verb *wohnen* to say where you live

Programme of Study
GV1 Tenses (present)
LC3 Conversation
LC5 Accurate pronunciation and intonation

FCSE links
Unit 7 – Local Area and Environment (Local area)

Grammar
The verb *wohnen* (simple present, singular)

Key Language
Wo wohnst du?
Ich wohne in …
Er/Sie wohnt in …
Das ist in …
England
Schottland
Wales
Nordirland
Irland
Wie schreibt man das (Haus)?
Das schreibt man (H–A–U–S).

PLTS
T Team workers

Cross-curricular
Geography: map of Germany

Resources
Audio files:
11_Kapitel1_Einheit3_Aufgabe1
12_Kapitel1_Einheit3_Aufgabe2
13_Kapitel1_Einheit3_Aufgabe4
14_Kapitel1_Einheit3_Aufgabe8
Workbooks:
Übungsheft 1 A&B, page 4
ActiveTeach:
Starter 1 resource
Starter 2 resource
p.013 Grammar presentation
p.013 Video: Episode 1
p.013 Exercise 5 grid
p.013 Grammar worksheet
p.013 Thinking skills worksheet
ActiveLearn:
Listening A, Listening B
Reading A, Reading B
Grammar, Vocabulary

Starter 1

Aim

To review numbers from 1–19.

Pupils play a game of bingo in groups of four, with one pupil as the caller and the other three pupils as the players (Starter 1 resource). This could be played a number of times to give each pupil an opportunity to be the caller.
Alternatively, the caller could be given the role as an extension task.

Caller and player cards could be laminated for future use; pupils could mark off numbers with whiteboard pens.

---

1 Hör zu, lies und mach mit.
(Listening L1)

Listening. Pupils listen to the alphabet chant, read the sounds and join in.

Refer pupils to the *Tip* box and talk about the *Umlaut* and the 'ess tsett' (*Eszett*).

Audioscript

- A, B, C, D, E, F, G
- A, B, C, D, E, F, G
- H, I, J, K, L, M, N
- H, I, J, K, L, M, N
- O, P, Q, R, S, T, U
- O, P, Q, R, S, T, U
- V, W, X, Y, Z
- V, W, X, Y, Z
- A, B, C, D, E, F, G
- A, B, C, D, E, F, G
- H, I, J, K, L, M, N
- H, I, J, K, L, M, N
- O, P, Q, R, S, T, U
- O, P, Q, R, S, T, U
- V, W, X, Y, Z
- V, W, X, Y, Z

2 Hör zu. Wo wohnen sie? Schreib den Namen der Stadt auf. (1–6) (Listening L2, Writing L1)

Listening/Writing. Pupils listen to find out where the people live. They listen as the names of the towns are spelled out. Pupils copy and complete the table with the name of each town.

Audioscript

1 – *Wo wohnst du, Indra?*
 – *Ich wohne in Erfurt. Erfurt schreibt man E-R-F-U-R-T. E-R-F-U-R-T. Erfurt. Das ist in Thüringen.*
2 – *Who wohnst du, Felix?*
 – *Ich wohne in Leipzig. Leipzig schreibt man L-E-I-P-Z-I-G. L-E-I-P-Z-I-G. Leipzig. Ich wohne in Leipzig und das ist in Sachsen.*

© Pearson Education Ltd 2013. Copying permitted for purchasing institution only. This material is not copyright free.

Ich wohne in Deutschland | Meine Welt und ich – **KAPITEL 1**

3 – Und du, Lena? Wo wohnst du?
– Ich wohne in Straubing. Straubing schreibt man S-T-R-A-U-B-I-N-G. S-T-R-A-U-B-I-N-G. Straubing. Ich wohne in Straubing und das ist in Bayern.
4 – Wo wohnst du, Kai?
– Ich wohne in Kassel. Das schreibt man K-A-S-S-E-L. K-A-S-S-E-L. Kassel. Das ist in Hessen.
5 – Leoni, wo wohnst du?
– Ich wohne in Duisburg. Duisburg schreibt man D-U-I-S-B-U-R-G. D-U-I-S-B-U-R-G. Duisburg. Das ist in Nordrhein-Westfalen.
6 – Und du, Markus? Wo wohnst du?
– Ich wohne in Braunschweig. Das schreibt man B-R-A-U-N-S-C-H-W-E-I-G. B-R-A-U-N-S-C-H-W-E-I-G. Ich wohne in Braunschweig und das ist in Niedersachsen.

Answers
1 E-R-F-U-R-T. Erfurt.
2 L-E-I-P-Z-I-G. Leipzig.
3 S-T-R-A-U-B-I-N-G. Straubing.
4 K-A-S-S-E-L. Kassel.
5 D-U-I-S-B-U-R-G. Duisburg.
6 B-R-A-U-N-S-C-H-W-E-I-G. Braunschweig.

3 Sieh dir die Karte an. Rate mal: Was sind die Lieblingsfußballmannschaften der Personen in Aufgabe 2? (1–6) (Reading L1)

Reading. Pupils look at the map of Germany. The map shows the six *Bundesländer* (federal states) from exercise 2 as well as the towns of six famous German football teams. Pupils guess which are the favourite football teams of the people interviewed in exercise 2. Note that the answers are given in exercise 4, where pupils listen for them.

4 Hör zu und überprüfe. (1–6) (Listening L2)

Listening. Pupils listen and check their answers to exercise 3.

Audioscript

1 – Indra, was ist deine Lieblingsfußballmannschaft?
– Meine Lieblingsfußballmannschaft ist der VfB Stuttgart.
2 – Und Felix, was ist deine Lieblingsfußballmannschaft?
– Meine Lieblingsfußballmannschaft ist Hertha BSC.
3 – Lena, hast du eine Lieblingsfußballmannschaft?
– Ja, meine Lieblingsfußballmannschaft ist der FC Bayern München!
4 – Und Kai, was ist deine Lieblingsfußballmannschaft?
– Meine Lieblingsfußballmannschaft ist Borussia Dortmund.
5 – Leoni, was ist deine Lieblingsfußballmannschaft?
– Meine Lieblingsfußballmannschaft ist Schalke 04.
6 – Und du, Markus? Was ist deine Lieblingsfußballmannschaft?
– Meine Lieblingsfußballmannschaft ist der VfL Wolfsburg.

Answers
1 Indra – d VfB Stuttgart
2 Felix – b Hertha BSC
3 Lena – c Bayern München
4 Kai – e Borussia Dortmund
5 Leoni – f Schalke 04
6 Markus – a VfL Wolfsburg

Starter 2

Aim

To review the alphabet and recycle vocabulary from previous units.

Pupils each have a copy of the grid (Starter 2 resource), which has columns for *Stadt* (town), *Land* (country), *Objekt* (object), *Ort* (place), *Name* (name) and *Nummer* (number). One pupil chooses a letter, giving the letter in German. All pupils then find a German word beginning with that letter for each of the columns on the grid. The words can be taken either from this unit or the previous one. Points are awarded for the number of correct answers, with pupils being awarded 1 point per word and 2 points if they have a different word to everyone else. The first pupil to finish shouts 'Halt!' and everyone has to stop. (This can be done more than once with different letters.)

Use a bilingual dictionary to help pupils at the beginning. As an extension activity, some pupils could use a monolingual dictionary.

© Pearson Education Ltd 2013. Copying permitted for purchasing institution only. This material is not copyright free.

Ich wohne in Deutschland | Meine Welt und ich – KAPITEL

> **Grammatik**
>
> Use the *Grammatik* box to draw pupils' attention to the singular paradigm of *wohnen*. There is more opportunity to practise this in the grammar unit on pupil book p. 23.

5 Lies die Texte. Schreib die Tabelle ab und füll sie aus. (Reading L3)

Reading. Pupils read the texts. They then copy and complete the table with details of each person's name, age and home town.

> **Answers**
> 1 Maja, 13, München
> 2 Helgo, 12, Bad Hersfeld
> 3 Paula, 13, Bonn

6 Partnerarbeit. Partner(in) A ist eine der Personen von Aufgabe 5. Partner(in) B stellt Fragen. (Speaking L3)

Speaking. Pupils work in pairs. Partner A assumes the role of one of the people from exercise 5. Partner B asks Partner A questions to find out their name, age and where they live.

7 Schreib über dich. (Writing L2)

Writing. Pupils write about themselves using the language skills they have acquired through the recent exercises. They must include the following details: their name, their age, where they live and where that is. They should also put two questions to the reader.

8 Hör zu. Wie schreibt man das? Schreib die sechs Wörter auf. (Listening L2)

Listening. Pupils listen as Indra spells words in a spelling bee. They write down the six words Indra has to spell.

Use the *Tip* box to draw pupils' attention to how to spell words containing letters with umlauts, as well as the letter ß.

> **Audioscript**
>
> – Hallo und willkommen bei uns im Studio. Hier ist Indra. Indra kommt aus Erfurt, in Deutschland. Hallo, Indra!
> – Hallo!
> – Also, Indra, deine Minute beginnnnnnnnnnnnt … jetzt. Wie schreibt man ‚Hello'?
> – Hallo. Das schreibt man H–A–L–L–O.
> – Thirteen.
> – Dreizehn. D–R–E–I–Z–E–H–N.
> – England.
> – England. E–N–G–L–A–N–D.
> – Goatee beard.
> – Spitzbart. S–P–I–T–Z–B–A–R–T.
> – Seventeen.
> – Siebzehn. S–I–E–B–Z–E–H–N.
> – Book.
> – Buch. B–U–C–H.
> – Super, Indra, alles richtig!

> **Answers**
> H–A–L–L–O. Hallo.
> D–R–E–I–Z–E–H–N. Dreizehn.
> E–N–G–L–A–N–D. England.
> S–P–I–T–Z–B–A–R–T. Spitzbart.
> S–I–E–B–Z–E–H–N. Siebzehn.
> B–U–C–H. Buch.

9 Partnerarbeit: Ein Rechtschreibwettbewerb. Wähl acht Wörter aus. (Speaking L2)

Speaking. Pupils work in pairs. Partner A chooses eight words, and gives Partner B one of the words in English. Partner B must say the word in German and then spell the word out. When Partner B has spelled all of Partner A's words, pupils swap roles.

You may wish to display the following words for pupils to use during this exercise: *Ich passe* (pass), *Leerzeichen/Abstand* (space), *Bindestrich* (hyphen).

> **Plenary**
>
> **Aim**
>
> For pupils to establish whether they have met the lesson objective of saying where they live.
>
> Pupils should work in pairs. Each pupil receives a character card. Any character will work for this exercise; for example, celebrities, sportspeople, cartoon characters. Partner A should introduce themselves in character to Partner B. Partner B must give Partner A verbal feedback using the 'two stars and a wish' approach and referring to the checklist (Plenary resource):
>
> - Saying hello / goodbye
> - Giving your name
> - Spelling your name
> - Saying how you are feeling
> - Saying how old you are

© Pearson Education Ltd 2013. Copying permitted for purchasing institution only. This material is not copyright free.

Ich wohne in Deutschland | Meine Welt und ich – **KAPITEL 1**

- Saying where you live
- Good pronunciation

Partners should then swap roles.

Workbook A, page 4

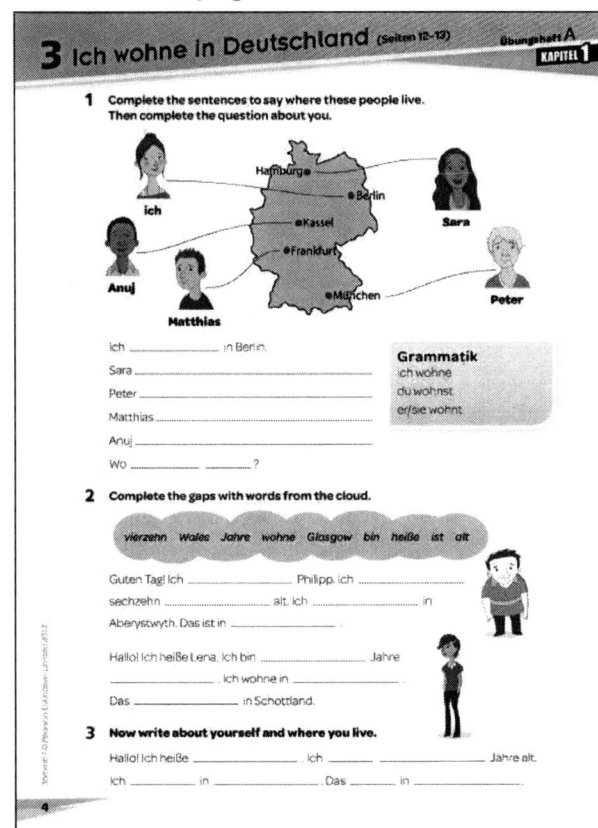

Answers

1 Ich wohne in Berlin.

Sara wohnt in Hamburg.

Peter wohnt in München.

Matthias wohnt in Frankfurt.

Anuj wohnt in Kassel.

Wo wohnst du?

2 Guten Tag! Ich **heiße** Philipp. Ich **bin** sechzehn **Jahre** alt. Ich **wohne** in Aberystwyth. Das ist in **Wales**.

Hallo! Ich heiße Lena. Ich bin **vierzehn** Jahre **alt**. Ich wohne in **Glasgow**. Das **ist** in Schottland.

3 Pupils' own answers.

Workbook B, page 4

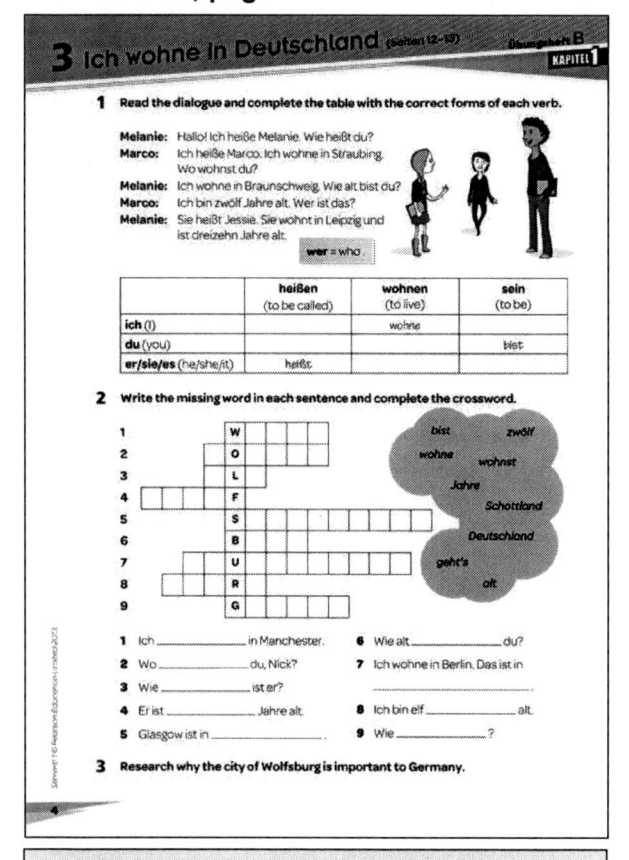

Answers

1 ich heiße, du heißt, er/sie/es heißt

ich wohne, du wohnst, er/sie/es wohnt

ich bin, du bist, er/sie/es ist

2 1 wohne 2 wohnst 3 alt 4 zwölf
5 Schottland 6 bist 7 Deutschland 8 Jahre
9 geht's

3 Wolfsburg is home to Volkswagen AG, and was originally built to house workers producing the original VW Käfer/Beetle. All VW print advertisements feature cars with number plates prefixed with 'WOB', alluding to their heritage.

Worksheet 1

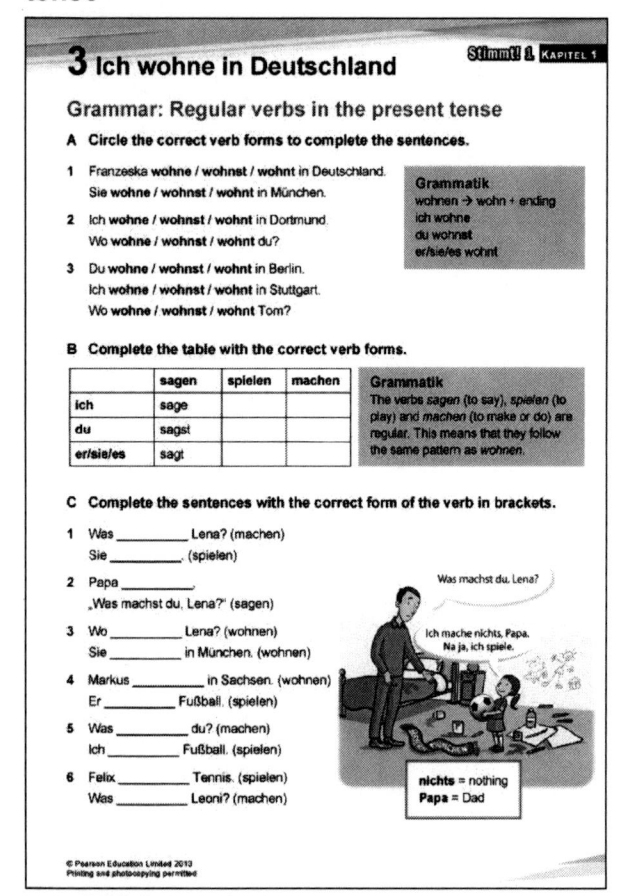

Grammar: Regular verbs in the present tense

3 Ich wohne in Deutschland

Grammar: Regular verbs in the present tense

A Circle the correct verb forms to complete the sentences.

1. Franzeska wohne / wohnst / wohnt in Deutschland.
   Sie wohne / wohnst / wohnt in München.
2. Ich wohne / wohnst / wohnt in Dortmund.
   Wo wohne / wohnst / wohnt du?
3. Du wohne / wohnst / wohnt in Berlin.
   Ich wohne / wohnst / wohnt in Stuttgart.
   Wo wohne / wohnst / wohnt Tom?

Grammatik
wohnen → wohn + ending
ich wohne
du wohnst
er/sie/es wohnt

B Complete the table with the correct verb forms.

	sagen	spielen	machen
ich	sage		
du	sagst		
er/sie/es	sagt		

Grammatik
The verbs sagen (to say), spielen (to play) and machen (to make or do) are regular. This means that they follow the same pattern as wohnen.

C Complete the sentences with the correct form of the verb in brackets.

1. Was _____ Lena? (machen)
   Sie _____. (spielen)
2. Papa _____,
   „Was machst du, Lena?" (sagen)
3. Wo _____ Lena? (wohnen)
   Sie _____ in München. (wohnen)
4. Markus _____ in Sachsen. (wohnen)
   Er _____ Fußball. (spielen)
5. Was _____ du? (machen)
   Ich _____ Fußball. (spielen)
6. Felix _____ Tennis. (spielen)
   Was _____ Leoni? (machen)

Was machst du, Lena?
Ich mache nichts, Papa. Na ja, ich spiele.

nichts = nothing
Papa = Dad

Answers

A 1 Franzeska wohnt in Deutschland. Sie wohnt in München.
2 Ich wohne in Dortmund. Wo wohnst du?
3 Du wohnst in Berlin. Ich wohne in Stuttgart. Wo wohnt Tom?

B ich: spiele, mache
du: spielst, machst
er / sie / es: spielt, macht

C 1 Was macht Lena? Sie spielt.
2 Papa sagt, „Was machst du, Lena?"
3 Wo wohnt Lena? Sie wohnt in München.
4 Markus wohnt in Sachsen. Er spielt Fußball.
5 Was machst du? Ich spiele Fußball.
6 Felix spielt Tennis. Was macht Leoni?

Worksheet 2

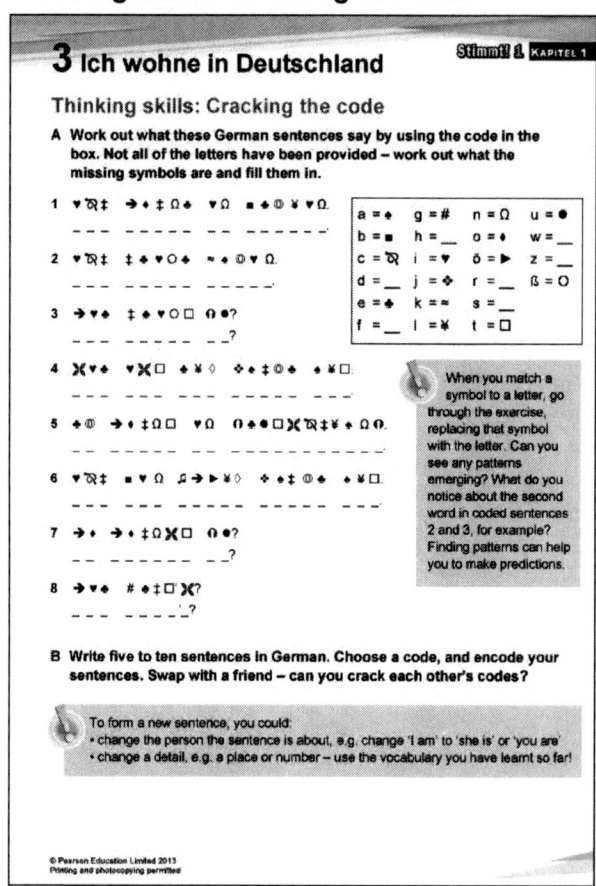

Thinking Skills: Cracking the code

3 Ich wohne in Deutschland

Thinking skills: Cracking the code

A Work out what these German sentences say by using the code in the box. Not all of the letters have been provided – work out what the missing symbols are and fill them in.

When you match a symbol to a letter, go through the exercise, replacing that symbol with the letter. Can you see any patterns emerging? What do you notice about the second word in coded sentences 2 and 3, for example? Finding patterns can help you to make predictions.

B Write five to ten sentences in German. Choose a code, and encode your sentences. Swap with a friend – can you crack each other's codes?

To form a new sentence, you could:
• change the person the sentence is about, e.g. change 'I am' to 'she is' or 'you are'
• change a detail, e.g. a place or number – use the vocabulary you have learnt so far!

Answers

A d = ☊ f = ◇ h = ‡ r = ⓞ s = �ö
w = → z = ♪

1 Ich wohne in Berlin.
2 Ich heiße Karin.
3 Wie heißt du?
4 Sie ist elf Jahre alt.
5 Er wohnt in Deutschland.
6 Ich bin zwölf Jahre alt.
7 Wo wohnst du?
8 Wie geht's?

B Pupils' own answers.

Ich wohne in Deutschland | Meine Welt und ich – **KAPITEL 1**

Video

The video component provides opportunities for speaking activities in a plausible and stimulating context. The *Studio Stimmt!* team – Audrey and Mesut – operate from their headquarters in Hamburg. With the help of their reporters on location – Alwin, Katharina, Ciara, Felix, Leoni and Benno – they are making video reports about their life in Hamburg in response to questions they have received from teenagers in the UK.

Each video is between three and four minutes long.

Episode 1

We meet Mesut and Audrey from *Studio Stimmt!* They are responding to an email from an English pupil, Sam, who has written asking questions about them and their friends.

Answers

A Before watching

  1 Mesut is a boy and Audrey is a girl.

  2 Wie heißt du? Wie alt bist du? Wo wohnst du?

B Watch

  1 Germany

  2 Wo wohnst du?

  3 Alwin / Katharina / Ciara / Felix / Leoni / Benno

  4 This is where they live.

C Watch again

  1 Manchester

  2 Which member of the *Studio Stimmt!* team:

   a) Alwin

   b) Mesut

   c) Katharina

  3 Italy

  4 11

D Discuss with your partner

  1 Welcome to *Studio Stimmt!*

  2 Benno says he is 19 and lives in Namibia in Africa.

Remaining answers will vary.

© Pearson Education Ltd 2013. Copying permitted for purchasing institution only. This material is not copyright free.

4 Meine Welt is wunderbar! (Pupil Book pp. 14–15)

Meine Welt und ich – **KAPITEL**

Learning objectives
- Describing your character
- Using *mein(e)* and *dein(e)*

Programme of Study
GV3 Developing vocabulary
LC1 Listening and responding
LC3 Conversation

FCSE links
Unit 4 – Leisure (Preferences)

Grammar
Possessive adjectives (*mein, dein*)

Key Language
freundlich
launisch
kreativ
intelligent
sportlich
laut
faul
musikalisch
lustig
Ich bin sehr/ziemlich/nicht ...
Was ist deine(e) ...?
Mein(e) ... ist ...
der Lieblingssport
der Lieblingsmonat
die Lieblingsmusik
die Lieblingszahl
die Lieblingssendung
die Lieblingsfußballmannschaft
das Lieblingsspiel
das Lieblingsland
das Lieblingsauto

PLTS
T Team workers

Resources
Audio files:
15_Kapitel1_Einheit4_Aufgabe2
16_Kapitel1_Einheit4_Aufgabe5
17_Kapitel1_Einheit4_Aufgabe6
Workbooks:
Übungsheft 1 A&B, page 5
ActiveTeach:
p.014 Flashcards
p.014 Class game
p.015 Grammar practice
p.015 Grammar presentation
Plenary resource
ActiveLearn:
Listening A, Listening B
Reading A, Reading B
Grammar, Vocabulary

Starter 1

Aim
To review spellings.

Pupils work in pairs and see how many words from the list below they can spell correctly in one minute. They keep score to decide on a winner. Pupils give each other feedback on their pronunciation and their spelling, focusing on which letters they have had difficulty remembering. As an extension, pupils guess what they think the characteristics mean in English.

- *freundlich*
- *launisch*
- *kreativ*
- *intelligent*
- *sportlich*
- *laut*
- *faul*
- *musikalisch*
- *lustig*

1 Was passt zusammen? Finde die Paare. (Reading L1)

Reading. Pupils match the pictures to the vocabulary.

Refer pupils to the *Tip* box to reminds them that cognates – words in English and German which share the same or similar meanings – are a useful way to grow vocabulary.

Answers
1 c 2 f 3 d 4 e 5 g 6 h 7 i 8 a 9 b

2 Hör zu und überprüfe. (1–9) (Listening L2)

Listening. Pupils check the answers to exercise 1.

Audioscript

1 – c – *kreativ. Ich bin kreativ.*
2 – f – *laut. Ich bin laut.*
3 – d – *intelligent. Ich bin intelligent.*
4 – e – *sportlich. Ich bin sportlich.*
5 – g – *faul. Ich bin faul.*
6 – h – *musikalisch. Ich bin musikalisch.*
7 – i – *lustig. Ich bin lustig.*
8 – a – *freundlich. Ich bin freundlich.*
9 – b – *launisch. Ich bin launisch.*

3 Schreib fünf Sätze über dich. Benutze die Adjektive aus Aufgabe 1. (Writing L2)

Writing. Pupils write five sentences about themselves, using the adjectives in exercise 1.

© Pearson Education Ltd 2013. Copying permitted for purchasing institution only. This material is not copyright free.

Meine Welt is wunderbar! | **Meine Welt und ich** – **KAPITEL 1**

Refer pupils to the skills box, which encourages them to use connectives and intensifiers to make their writing more interesting.

The skills feature looks at ways of making sentences longer and more interesting by using connectives.

4 Lies die Texte vor. Wer bin ich? (Reading L3, Speaking L1)

Reading/Speaking. Pupils read aloud the four short texts and match the person described to the person in the photo.

Answers
1 Wolfgang Amadeus Mozart 2 Lena Schöneborn 3 Albert Einstein 4 Franka Potente

Starter 2
Aim To review characteristics. Pupils play a miming game in pairs/groups of four or as a whole class. Each person takes it in turns to mime a characteristic and pupils must guess in German. This could also be played as a beat-the-teacher game, where the teacher thinks of one of the characteristics and the class have to guess which characteristic (s)he is thinking of. There are various beat-the-teacher templates available free to download on the internet such as a splat-the-teacher PowerPoint, which pupils really enjoy. **Alternative starter 2** Use ActiveTeach p.014 Flashcards to review and practise adjectives of personality.

5 Hör zu und überprüfe. (1–4) (Listening L2)

Listening. Pupils listen to check the answers to exercise 4.

Audioscript

1 – *Ich bin sehr kreativ und auch musikalisch. Ich bin ziemlich lustig, aber ich bin auch launisch. Wer bin ich?*
   – *Ich bin Wolfgang Amadeus Mozart!*
2 – *Ich bin sehr sportlich und intelligent. Ich bin nicht faul. Wer bin ich?*
   – *Ich bin Lena Schöneborn!*

3 – *Ich bin sehr intelligent und kreativ. Ich bin ziemlich freundlich, aber ich bin nicht sportlich. Wer bin ich?*
   – *Ich bin Albert Einstein!*
4 – *Ich bin sehr freundlich und auch lustig. Ich bin ziemlich sportlich. Wer bin ich?*
   – *Ich bin Franka Potente!*

6 Hör zu und lies. Was ist die richtige Reihenfolge? (Listening L2)

Listening. Pupils read the numbered sentences. They then listen to the audio and note which order they hear the sentences in.

Audioscript
– *Mein Lieblingsmonat ist Dezember.* – *Meine Lieblingszahl ist vier.* – *Meine Lieblingssendung ist „Batman" und meine Lieblingsmusik ist sehr laut.* – *Meine Lieblingsfußballmannschaft ist Bayern München, aber mein Lieblingssport ist Tennis.*

Answers
3, 2, 5, 1, 4, 6

Grammatik
Pupils use the table in the *Grammatik* box to help them use the correct form of the possessive adjective (*mein/meine, dein/deine*). There is more information and practice in the grammar unit on pupil book p. 22.

7 Partnerarbeit. Wie bist du? Was ist dein(e) Lieblings ...? (Speaking L3)

Speaking. Pupils work in pairs, and describe themselves and their favourite things to each other.

8 Schreib fünf Sätze über deine Lieblingssachen. (Writing L3)

Writing. Pupils write five sentences about their favourite things.

© Pearson Education Ltd 2013. Copying permitted for purchasing institution only. This material is not copyright free.

Meine Welt is wunderbar! | **Meine Welt und ich** – KAPITEL

Plenary

Aim

For pupils to establish whether they have met the lesson objectives (describing their character and using *mein* and *dein* to discuss their favourite things).

Pupils play the jigsaw game in pairs or small groups (Plenary resource). The pieces need to be copied onto card and then cut out before playing. Pupils match the two halves of a German word using their knowledge of gender and the indefinite article. They then match the English meaning to the German word.

Alternative plenary

Use ActiveTeach p.014 Class Game to review adjectives of personality.

Workbook A, page 5

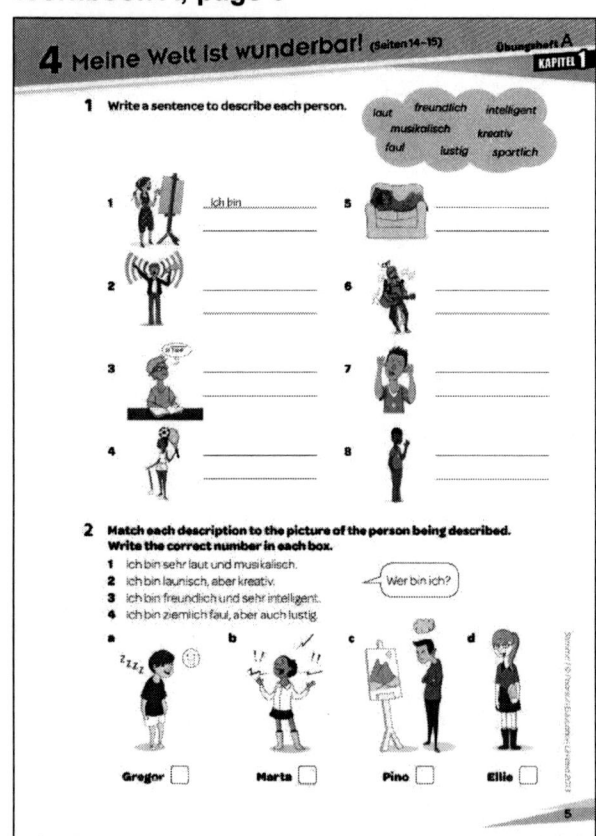

Answers

1   1 Ich bin kreativ.
    2 Ich bin laut.
    3 Ich bin intelligent.
    4 Ich bin sportlich.
    5 Ich bin faul.
    6 Ich bin musikalisch.
    7 Ich bin lustig.
    8 Ich bin freundlich.
2   Gregor – 4   Marta – 1   Pino – 2   Ellie – 3

Workbook B, page 5

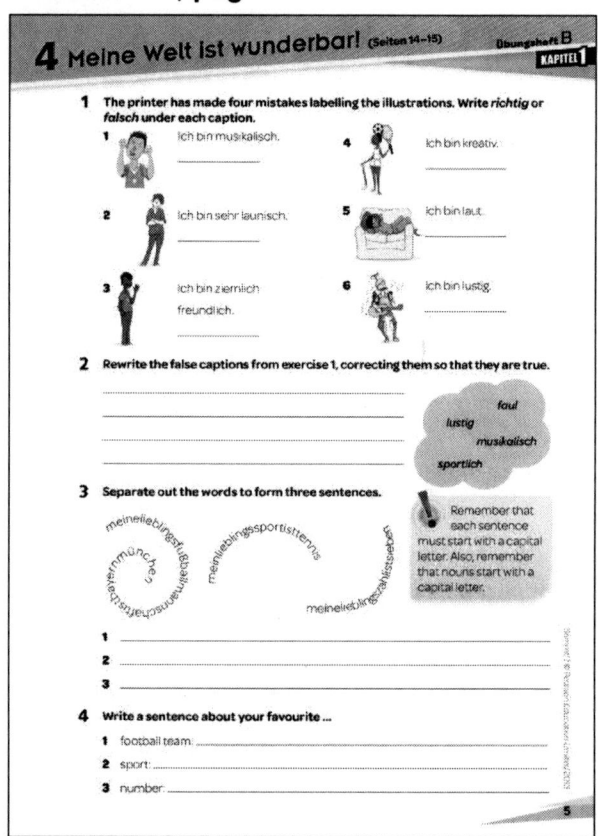

Answers

1   1 falsch 2 richtig 3 richtig 4 falsch 5 falsch
    6 falsch
2   1 ich bin lustig.
    4 Ich bin sportlich.
    5 Ich bin faul.
    6 Ich bin musikalisch.
3   1 Meine Lieblingsfußballmannschaft ist Bayern München.
    2 Mein Lieblingssport ist Tennis.
    3 Meine Lieblingszahl ist sieben.
4   1 Meine Lieblingsfußballmannschaft ist …
    2 Mein Lieblingssport ist …
    3 Meine Lieblingszahl ist …

© Pearson Education Ltd 2013. Copying permitted for purchasing institution only. This material is not copyright free.

Meine Welt und ich – KAPITEL 1

5 Meine Sachen (Pupil Book pp. 16–17)

Learning objectives	Grammar	Resources
• Asking and answering questions about your belongings • Using the verb *haben* + the indefinite article **Programme of Study** **GV2** Grammatical structures (accusative) **LC3** Conversation **LC6** Reading comprehension **FCSE links** Unit 1 – Relationships, Family and Friends (Personal information)	Introduction to the accusative Singular paradigm of *haben* **Key Language** Wie? Was? Wo? Woher? Wer? **PLTS** **C** Creative thinkers	**Audio files:** 18_Kapitel1_Einheit5_Aufgabe1 19_Kapitel1_Einheit5_Aufgabe5 **Workbooks:** Übungsheft 1 A&B, page 6 **ActiveTeach:** p.016 Grammar practice p.016 Grammar presentation (1) p.016 Grammar presentation (2) p.017 Class game p.017 Video: Episode 2 p.017 Extension reading activity p.017 Extension worksheet Plenary resource **ActiveLearn:** Listening A, Listening B Reading A, Reading B Grammar, Vocabulary

Starter 1

Aim

To review the key vocabulary and structures from the previous unit.

Pupils are asked to work in pairs to make as long a sentence as possible using the characteristics from last unit, the verb *sein* and the connectives. The words could either be displayed on the board, pupils could use the vocabulary list or the unit in the pupil book. For a greater challenge pupils could be given no guidance as to which words to use and left to determine for themselves what their sentences should be.

Pupils could repeat the miming game for the characteristics from unit 4 (Starter 2).

Pupils could also re-do the jigsaw puzzles from the last unit.

1 Hör zu. Wer ist das? (1–3)
(Listening L3)

Listening. Pupils listen to the interviews and decide which of the boys pictured is talking.

Audioscript

1 – Hast du einen Computer?
– Nein, aber ich habe eine Wii, eine Gitarre und einen iPod.

2 – Hast du einen Computer?
– Ja, ich habe einen Computer. Ich habe auch einen Fußball und ein Keyboard.

3 – Hast du einen Computer?
– Ja, und ich habe auch ein Handy und eine Schlange und ein Skateboard.

Answers

1 Max 2 Andreas 3 Jonas

Grammatik

The *Grammatik* box presents the singular paradigm of the irregular verb *haben*. There is more information and practice in the grammar unit on pupil book p. 23.

The *Grammatik* box also introduces the idea that the masculine word for 'a' changes its spelling after *haben* and most other verbs.

2 Partnerarbeit. Mach Dialoge.
(Speaking L3)

Speaking. Pupils work in pairs and ask each other about the things that they have.

The *Tip* box reminds pupils that in order to ask 'Do you have …?' all they need to do is to swap the verb and the subject.

Meine Sachen | **Meine Welt und ich** – KAPITEL

3 Sieh dir Aufgabe 1 an. Was haben Andreas, Jonas und Max? Schreib Sätze. (Writing L3)

Writing. Pupils write sentences about the things that Andreas, Jonas and Max have.

Answers

1 Andreas hat einen Computer, einen Fußball und ein Keyboard.
2 Jonas hat einen Computer, ein Handy, eine Schlange und ein Skateboard.
3 Max hat eine Wii, eine Gitarre und einen iPod.

Starter 2

Aim

To review the use of the accusative after the verb *haben*.

Put a giant *EN* on the board and asks pupils to complete a think-pair-share activity where they have to write a reason why these letters are on the board.

- Think = the pupils have three minutes to individually think in silence about the letters.
- Pair = the pupils compare their ideas in pairs to decide on a reason.
- Share = the pupils work in groups of four to write out a reason, which is then shared with the class.

Pupils could re-use the masculine, feminine, neuter balloons as a visual representation of the rule.

4 Füll die Lücken mit dem richtigen Fragewort aus. (Reading L3)

Reading. Pupils read sentences and insert the correct question word from a selection provided.

The *Tip* box reminds pupils that in German the question word comes first, followed by the verb.

Answers

1 Wie 2 Wie 3 Wo 4 Was 5 Wie
6 Wo 7 Woher 8 Wer

5 Hör zu und lies das Interview. (Listening/Reading L3–4)

Listening/Reading. Pupils listen to and read a short interview.

Some vocabulary is glossed for support.

Audioscript

– Guten Tag und willkommen bei Radio Eins. Und heute hören wir ein Interview mit Thomas. Hallo, Thomas! Hast du eine Wii?
– Ja! Ich habe eine Wii und mein Lieblingsspiel ist FIFA.
– Super, Thomas. Danke. Und hast du noch etwas?
– Ich habe auch einen Vogel. Er kommt aus Australien.
– Ein Vogel aus Australien? Toll. Und …?
– Ich habe eine Schlange. Sie ist siebzehn Jahre alt.
– Und bist du musikalisch? Hast du einen iPod?
– Ja! Ich habe einen iPod. Mein iPod kommt aus China.
– Interessant! Mm. Und hast du ein Handy? Woher kommt es?
– Ja, ich habe ein Handy. Es kommt aus Finnland.
Mein Lieblingsklingelton ist „Gummibär" – er ist sehr laut!

6 Lies das Interview noch mal. Schreib fünf Informationen über Thomas und seine Sachen auf Englisch auf. (Reading L4)

Reading. Pupils write down five sentences about Thomas and his belongings, using material from the written interview. A variety of answers are possible.

Answers [Five from the following]

Thomas has a Wii.
His favourite Wii game is FIFA.
Thomas has a bird.
His bird is from Australia.
He has a snake.
His snake is 17 years old.
He has an iPod.
His iPod comes from China.
He has a mobile phone.
His phone comes from Finland.
His favourite ringtone is "Gummy Bear".
"Gummy Bear" is very loud.

Meine Sachen | Meine Welt und ich – **KAPITEL 1**

Extension

An alternative version of this reading activity is provided on ActiveTeach (p.017 Extension reading activity. Reading Level 4, Writing Level 3–4). Pupils read the interview again and work out which of the statements 1–8 are true and which are false. They correct the false statements.

Answers

1 Richtig.
2 Falsch. Thomas' Lieblingsspiel ist FIFA.
3 Falsch. Der Vogel kommt aus Australien.
4 Falsch. Thomas hat einen Vogel und eine Schlange.
5 Falsch. Die Schlange ist 17 Jahre alt.
6 Richtig.
7 Falsch. Das Handy kommt aus Finnland.
8 Richtig.

7 Partnerarbeit. Mach ein Interview. (Speaking L3–4)

Speaking. In pairs pupils interview each other to find out about their character and belongings. The pupil book provides some suggestions to start them off.

8 Sieh dir die Antworten an. Schreib die passenden Fragen auf. (Writing L2)

Writing. Pupils write their own questions appropriate to the answers provided in the pupil book.

Answers

1 Was ist dein Lieblingsspiel?
2 Wie alt ist dein Vogel?
3 Wie bist du?
4 Was hat Max?
5 Hast du ein Handy?
6 Hast du einen Fußball?

Plenary

Aim

For pupils to establish whether they have met the lesson objective of asking and answering questions about their belongings.

Pupils play a speaking chain game, where the class is split into two halves. Each half of the class is competing against the other half of the class to ask and answer as many questions as possible in the shortest time possible. The half of the class not competing must keep score and keep a check on the time. Start off by asking pupil 1 a question (from the unit), which the pupil must answer in German. This pupil then asks their neighbour a question and their neighbour must answer in German before asking a question of the next person.

For an extra challenge, suggest that a different question must be asked each time. Pupils may consult their notes or not, depending on the level of challenge desired.

Pupils could also complete a jigsaw, practising the question words and matching questions and answers (Plenary resource).

Alternative plenary

Use ActiveTeach p.017 Class Game to review questions.

Workbook A, page 6

Answers

1
  1 Ich habe einen Computer.
  2 Ich habe eine Schlange.
  3 Ich habe eine Gitarre.
  4 Ich habe ein Keyboard.
  5 Ich habe einen Fußball.
  6 Ich habe ein Skateboard.
  7 Ich habe eine Wii.

© Pearson Education Ltd 2013. Copying permitted for purchasing institution only. This material is not copyright free.

Meine Sachen | Meine Welt und ich – **KAPITEL**

8 Ich habe ein Handy.
9 Ich habe einen iPod.
2 1 Wie – What's your name?
   2 Wo – Where do you live?
   3 Wie – How old are you?
   4 Wie – What sort of person are you?
   5 Wo – Where is Hanover?
   6 Was – What's your favourite sort of music?
3 Pupils' own answers.

3 1 Ich heiße Gabi.
   2 Ich wohne in Kiel, in Deutschland.
   3 Ich komme aus Swansea. Das ist in Wales.
   4 Ich bin sportlich, lustig und sehr laut.
   5 Meine Lieblingssendung ist „Die Simpsons".
   6 Ich habe ein iPad und einen Computer.

Worksheet

Extension: Question time!

Workbook B, page 6

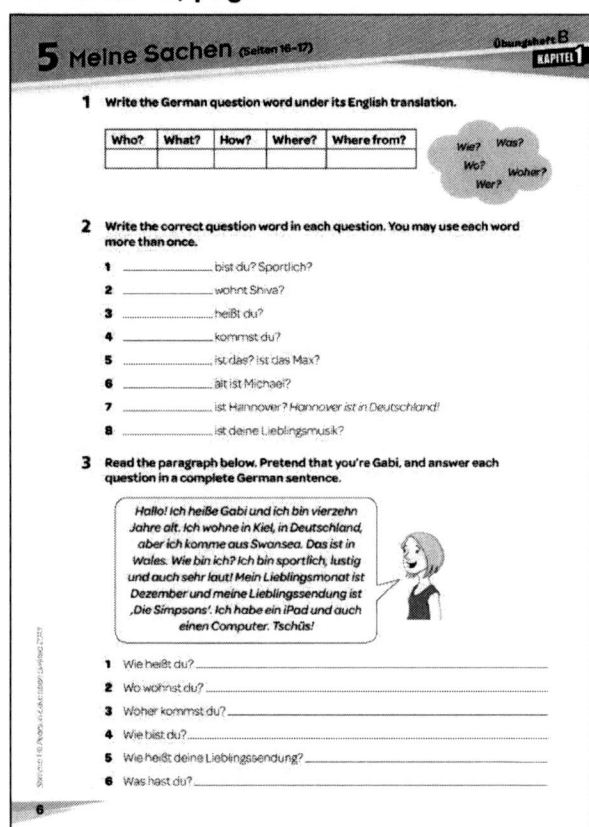

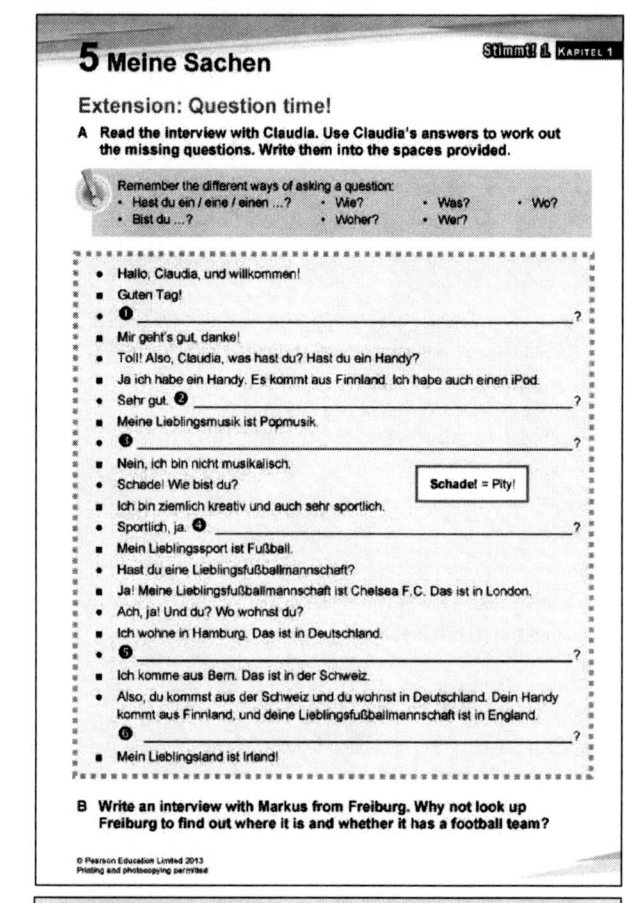

Answers

1 Who? – Wer?
   What? – Was?
   How? – Wie?
   Where? – Wo?
   Where from? – Woher?
2 1 Wie 2 Wo 3 Wie 4 Woher 5 Wer 6 Wie
   7 Wo 8 Was

Answers

A 1 Wie geht's?
   2 Was ist deine Lieblingsmusik?
   3 Bist du musikalisch?
   4 Was ist dein Lieblingssport?
   5 Woher kommst du?
   6 Was ist dein Lieblingsland?
B Pupils' own answers.

© Pearson Education Ltd 2013. Copying permitted for purchasing institution only. This material is not copyright free.

Meine Sachen | **Meine Welt und ich –** KAPITEL 1

Video

Episode 2

Mesut and Audrey and their friends are discussing what they are like and what their favourite things are.

> **Answers**
>
> **A Before watching**
>   1 Ich bin / Meine Lieblingssache ist
>   2 Wie bist du? / Was ist deine Lieblingssache?
>   3 freundlich, launisch, kreativ, intelligent, sportlich, laut, faul, musikalisch, lustig
>
> **B Watch**
>   1 Leonie
>   2 Katharina and Mesut
>   3 launisch (moody)
>   4 freundlich und lustig (friendly and funny)
>
> **C Watch again**
>   1 Which one of the following adjectives does Mesut not use to describe himself? loud
>   2 intelligent and kreativ (intelligent and creative)
>   3 True or false?
>   a) Felix is loud – true
>   b) Katharina describes herself as moody – false – it's Audrey she describes as moody
>   c) Audrey agrees that Alwin is friendly – true
>   d) Benno's favourite thing is sport – false (he says his favourite sport is sleeping!)
>   4 Match each person to their favourite number.
>   Audrey – 13 Katharina – 8 Ciara – 18
>   Benno – 16 Alwin – 1 Mesut – 3
>
> **D Discuss with your partner**
>   1 Because he is boasting about how great he is.
>   2 It's the rival team to Mesut's team.
>   3 Guess.
>   4 They both say the other one is moody. They don't like each other.
>   5 Sorry.
> Remaining answers will vary.

© Pearson Education Ltd 2013. Copying permitted for purchasing institution only. This material is not copyright free.

Meine Welt und ich – KAPITEL

6 Writing Skills: Ich über mich (Pupil Book pp. 18–19)

Learning objectives
- Preparing a poster presentation
- Checking your work

Programme of Study
GV4 Accuracy (grammar, spelling)
LC2 Transcription
LC8 Writing creatively

FCSE links
Unit 1 – Relationships, Family and Friends (Personal information)

Key Language
No new key language. Pupils develop writing skills using key language from the chapter.

PLTS
R Reflective learners

Resources
Audio files:
20_Kapitel1_Einheit6_Aufgabe3
Workbooks:
Übungsheft 1 A&B, page 7
ActiveTeach:
Starter 1 resource
Starter 2 resource
Plenary resource

Starter 1

Aim

To review masculine, feminine and neuter articles.

Pupils are given a blank grid to complete (Starter 1 resource). They then compare their grid with that of their partner and make any changes necessary based on their review.

For extension, pupils make a sentence using a word from each column.

For support include the missing words beneath the grid.

1 *Mein* oder *meine*? Füll die Lücken aus. (Writing L1–2)

Writing. Pupils fill in the gaps using the correct word for 'my'.

The skills feature reminds pupils to use the right word for 'the', 'a', 'my', 'your' and gives a reference table.

Answers
1 mein Lieblingswort
2 mein Lieblingssport
3 meine Lieblingsmusik
4 mein Lieblings-T-Shirt
5 mein Lieblingsspiel
6 meine Lieblingssache

Extension
Pupils should copy out the six nouns in exercise 1 and then change to 'your favourite …' without referring to the pupil book. (AT4.2)

2 Schreib Sätze über deine Lieblingssachen. Benutze die Bilder. (Writing L3)

Writing. Pupils write out six sentences about their favourite things, using the pictures provided as a guide. They check their answers in exercise 3.

Answers
1 *Meine Lieblingszahl ist sieben.*
2 Mein Lieblingsauto ist ein Mercedes.
3 Mein Lieblingsland ist Japan.
4 Meine Lieblingsfußballmannschaft ist Bayern München.
5 Mein Lieblingsklingelton ist „Gummibär".
6 Meine Lieblingssendung ist „Batman".

3 Hör zu und überprüfe. (1–6) (Listening L2)

Listening. Pupils listen to the audio and check their answers to exercise 2.

Audioscript
1 – Meine Lieblingszahl ist sieben.
2 – Mein Lieblingsauto ist ein Mercedes.
3 – Mein Lieblingsland ist Japan.
4 – Meine Lieblingsfußballmannschaft ist Bayern München.
5 – Mein Lieblingsklingelton ist „Gummibär".
6 – Meine Lieblingssendung ist „Batman".

4 Schreib den Text ab und füll die Lücken aus. (Reading L3/Writing L2)

Reading. Pupils copy out the text and fill in the gaps using the words provided. The skills box reminds pupils that they need to use a capital letter for *all* nouns in German.

Extension
More able pupils could be encouraged to translate the text, once completed, into English.

Answers
1 heiße 2 Jahre 3 wohne 4 ist 5 Deutschland 6 sehr 7 Lieblingssport

Ich über mich | Meine Welt und ich – **KAPITEL 1**

5 Mach das Buch zu. Schreib Sätze über dich. (Writing L3–4)

Writing. Pupils write a short piece about themselves, including their name, age, where they live and what they are like.

The skills feature provides some useful tips on what to check in their work to minimise mistakes; for example gender of nouns.

Starter 2

Aim

To practise the key verbs from the unit with other useful vocabulary.

Pupils play a battleships game in pairs. On the grid provided (Starter 2 resource) they draw four boats. They then guess where each other's boats are using the grid headings (which construct a sentence in German). They will need to know key phrases such as: *getroffen/gesunken*.

For a greater challenge, use pictures of objects on the grids instead of the words. Pupils could also choose their own items and make up their own games.

6 Was sagen sie? Schreib Texte für Boris und Anita. (Writing L3–4)

Writing. Pupils write about a male and female character using the stimulus pictures provided.

Refer pupils to the skills feature further down the page, which reminds pupils to use connectives and qualifiers to add interest to their writing.

Suggested answers

1 Ich heiße Boris. Ich bin sechzehn Jahre alt. Ich wohne in Australien. Ich bin sportlich und intelligent.

2 Ich heiße Anita. Ich bin neunzehn Jahre alt. Ich wohne in Amerika. Ich bin musikalisch und faul.

7 Sieh dir das Poster an. Du bist Matthias. Beantworte die Fragen. (Reading/Writing L3–4)

Reading/Writing. From the poster stimulus provided, pupils answer the questions in the first person, using full sentences.

Answers

1 Ich bin vierzehn Jahre alt.
2 Ich wohne in Köln (in Deutschland).
3 Ich bin sportlich (, aber nicht musikalisch).
4 Meine Lieblingssport ist Basketball.
5 Mein Lieblingsauto kommt aus Italien.
6 Mein Lieblingsspiel ist FIFA.
7 Mein iPod kommt aus China.

8 Sieh dir Aufgabe 7 an. Mach dein eigenes Poster. Schreib über dich. Dann überprüfe dein Poster mit Hilfe der Checkliste. (Writing L3–4)

Writing. Pupils create a poster about themselves using the example in exercise 7. They then check their own work against the checklist provided.

The skills feature reminds pupils to use connectives and qualifiers to make their work more interesting.

9 Lies den Text von deinem Partner/deiner Partnerin und überprüfe ihn mit Hilfe der Checkliste. (Reading L4)

Reading. Working in pairs, pupils read their partner's poster texts and check them using the checklist provided in the pupil book.

Plenary

Aim

To focus on written work, including spellings, grammar and punctuation.

Pupils use the grids (Plenary resource) to self- and peer-assess each other's written work.

They then set themselves a target for improvement and give their partner a target for improvement.

© Pearson Education Ltd 2013. Copying permitted for purchasing institution only. This material is not copyright free.

Workbook A, page 7

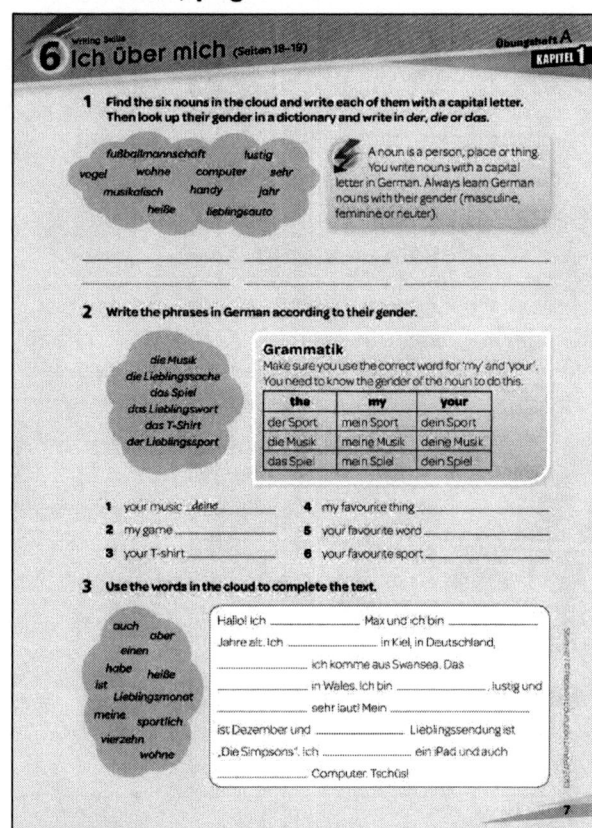

Answers

1. die Fußballmannschaft
   der Vogel
   der Computer
   das Handy
   das Lieblingsauto
   das Jahr

2. 1 deine Musik
   2 mein Spiel
   3 dein T-Shirt
   4 meine Lieblingssache
   5 dein Lieblingswort
   6 dein Lieblingssport

3. Hallo! Ich **heiße** Max und ich bin **vierzehn** Jahre alt. Ich **wohne** in Kiel, in Deutschland, **aber** ich komme aus Swansea. Das **ist** in Wales. Ich bin **sportlich**, lustig und **auch** sehr laut! Mein **Lieblingsmonat** ist Dezember und **meine** Lieblingssendung ist „Die Simpsons". Ich **habe** ein iPad und auch **einen** Computer. Tschüs!

Workbook B, page 7

Answers

1. masculine: der ein mein dein
   feminine: die eine meine deine
   neuter: das ein mein dein

2. 1 Ich heiße Osman.
   2 Ich wohne in Deutschland.
   3 Ich bin ganz freundlich und auch kreativ.
   4 Ich habe ein Handy.
   5 Wo wohnst du?

3. Ich heiße … Ich wohne … Ich bin … Ich habe …, etc.

© Pearson Education Ltd 2013. Copying permitted for purchasing institution only. This material is not copyright free.

Meine Welt und ich – KAPITEL 1

Lernzieltest und Wiederholung (Pupil Book pp. 20–21)

Lernzieltest

Pupils use this checklist to review language covered in the chapter, working on it in pairs in class or on their own at home. There is a Word version on ActiveTeach which can be printed out and given to pupils. Encourage them to follow up any weakness they identify. There are Target Setting Sheets included in the Assessment Pack, and an opportunity for pupils to record their own levels and targets on the *Mein Fortschritt* page in the Workbooks. You can also use the *Lernzieltest* checklist as an end-of-chapter plenary option.

Wiederholung

These revision exercises can be used for assessment purposes or for pupils to practise before tackling the assessment tasks in the Assessment Pack.

Resources

Audio files:
21_Kapitel1_Wiederholung_Aufgabe1
22_Kapitel1_Wiederholung_Aufgabe2

Workbooks:
Übungsheft 1 A&B, pages 8–9

Active Teach:
p.020 Lernzieltest checklist

1 Hör zu. Wie schreibt man das? Ist Davids Antwort richtig (✓) oder falsch (✗)? (Listening L1)

Listening. Pupils listen to the audio and decide if David is spelling the given word correctly or not.

Audioscript

1 – *Hallo und willkommen bei uns im Studio. Hier ist David. Er kommt aus England. Guten Tag, David!*
 – *Hallo!*
 – *Also, David, deine Minute beginnnnnnnnnnnnt … jetzt! Snake.*
 – *Die Schlange. S–C–H–L–A–N–G–E.*
2 – *Germany.*
 – *Deutschland. D–E–U–T–C–H–L–A–N–D.*
3 – *To live.*
 – *Wohnen. W–O–H–N–E–N.*
4 – *Musical.*
 – *Musikalisch. M–U–S–I–K–A–L–I–S–C–H.*
5 – *Favourite sport.*
 – *Der Lieblingssport. L–E–I–B–L–I–N–G–S–P–O–R–T.*
6 – *Mobile phone.*
 – *Das Handy. H–E–N–D–Y.*
 – *Danke schön, David. Ziemlich gut!*

Answers
1 ✓ 2 ✗ 3 ✓ 4 ✓ 5 ✗ 6 ✗

2 Hör zu. Schreib den Text ab und füll die Lücken auf Englisch aus. (Listening L3)

Listening. Pupils copy out the text. They then listen to the audio and fill in the gaps in English.

Audioscript

– *Hallo! Ich heiße Miriam und ich bin vierzehn Jahre alt. Ich komme aus Amerika, aber ich wohne jetzt in Berlin. Ich bin sehr sportlich und mein Lieblingssport ist Tennis. Ich habe ein Handy, eine Wii und einen iPod und meine Lieblingsband ist Tokio Hotel.*

Answers
1 Miriam 2 14 3 America 4 Berlin 5 sporty 6 favourite sport 7 mobile phone 8 favourite band

3 Partnerarbeit. Mach Interviews. (Speaking L3)

Speaking. Working in pairs, pupils interview each other to find out about who they are and what their favourite things are. Prompt questions and answers are provided in the pupil book.

4 Lies das Porträt. Beantworte die Fragen auf Englisch. (Reading L3)

Reading. Pupils read the text and answer questions in English.

Some vocabulary is glossed for support.

© Pearson Education Ltd 2013. Copying permitted for purchasing institution only. This material is not copyright free.

Lernzieltest und Wiederholung | Meine Welt und ich – **KAPITEL**

Answers

1 Stern is seven years old.
2 Stern is funny and fairly intelligent, but also very loud.
3 Stern's family has a snake, a bird and a fish.
4 His favourite thing is very loud pop music.

5 Wie bist du? Sieh dir Aufgabe 4 an. Schreib ein Porträt in der Ich-Form.
(Writing L3–4)

Writing. Using the example in exercise 4, pupils write a profile in the first person about whoever or whatever they like.

Workbook A, page 8

Answers

1 1 Vogel 2 FIFA 3 ein Porsche
   4 Australien 5 Rugby

2 Pupils' own answers:
   1 Meine Lieblingssendung ist …
   2 Meine Lieblingsfußballmannschaft ist …
   3 Mein Lieblingsspiel ist …
   4 Mein Lieblingssport ist …

3 Hallo! Ich **heiße** Lina und ich **wohne** in Walsrode. Das ist in **Deutschland**. Ich bin fünfzehn **Jahre** alt. Ich bin **sportlich** und **ziemlich** intelligent, **aber** ich bin **nicht** faul. Mein **Lieblingssport** ist Hockey und **meine** Lieblingsmusik ist Pop. Ich **habe** einen Vogel aus Amerika. Er ist **freundlich** und sehr laut!

Workbook A, page 9

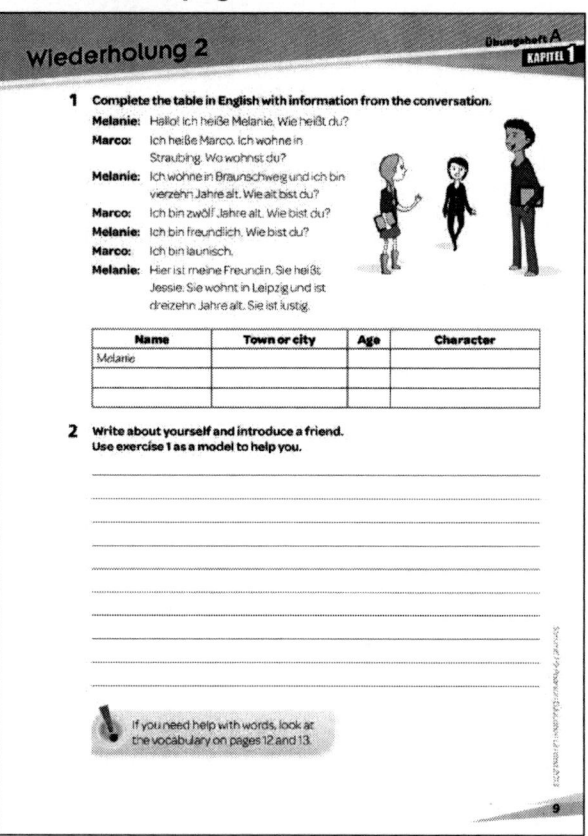

Answers

1 Melanie, Braunschweig, 14, friendly
  Marco, Straubing, 12, moody
  Jessie, Leipzig, 13, funny

2 Pupils' own answers:
  Ich heiße … und ich bin … Jahre alt. Ich wohne in … Ich bin …
  Mein/e Freund/in heißt … und er/sie ist … Jahre alt. Er/Sie wohnt in … Er/Sie ist …

© Pearson Education Ltd 2013. Copying permitted for purchasing institution only. This material is not copyright free.

Lernzieltest und Wiederholung | Meine Welt und ich – **KAPITEL 1**

Workbook B, page 8

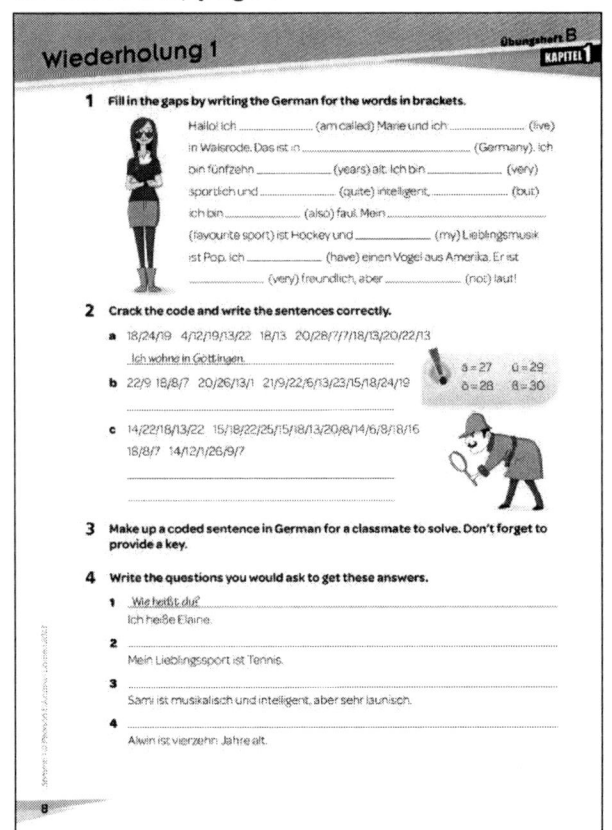

Wiederholung 1

1 Fill in the gaps by writing the German for the words in brackets.

Hallo! Ich _____ (am called) Marie und ich _____ (live) in Walsrode. Das ist in _____ (Germany). Ich bin fünfzehn _____ (years) alt. Ich bin _____ (very) sportlich und _____ (quite) intelligent, _____ (but) ich bin _____ (also) faul. Mein _____ (favourite sport) ist Hockey und _____ (my) Lieblingsmusik ist Pop. Ich _____ (have) einen Vogel aus Amerika. Er ist _____ (very) freundlich, aber _____ (not) laut!

2 Crack the code and write the sentences correctly.

a 18/24/19 4/12/19/13/22 18/13 20/28/7/7/18/13/20/22/13
  Ich wohne in Göttingen.

b 22/9 18/8/7 20/26/13/1 21/9/22/6/13/23/15/18/24/19

c 14/22/18/13/22 15/18/22/25/15/18/13/20/8/14/6/8/18/16
  18/8/7 14/12/1/26/9/7

ä = 27 ü = 29
ö = 28 ß = 30

3 Make up a coded sentence in German for a classmate to solve. Don't forget to provide a key.

4 Write the questions you would ask to get these answers.

1 Wie heißt du?
   Ich heiße Elaine.
2 _____
   Mein Lieblingssport ist Tennis.
3 _____
   Sami ist musikalisch und intelligent, aber sehr launisch.
4 _____
   Alwin ist vierzehn Jahre alt.

Workbook B, page 9

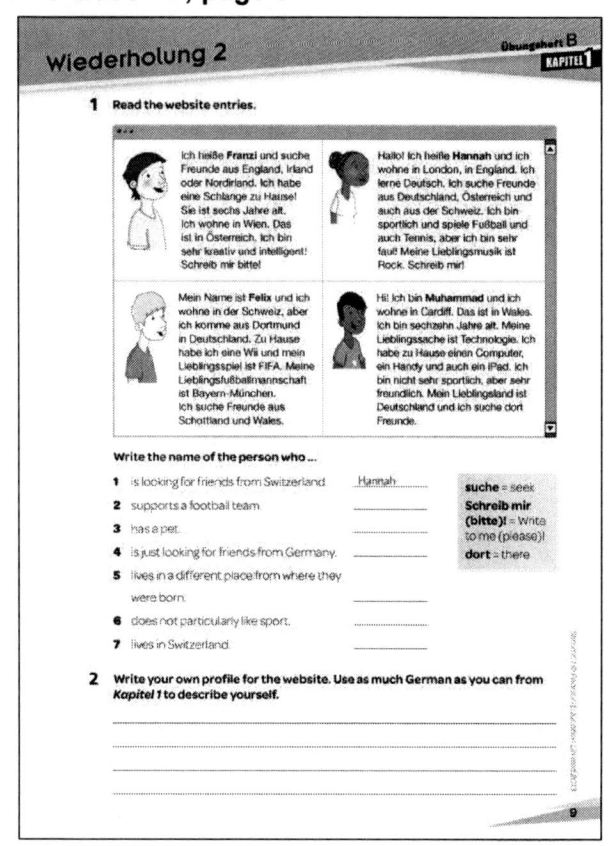

Wiederholung 2

1 Read the website entries.

Ich heiße **Franzi** und suche Freunde aus England, Irland oder Nordirland. Ich habe eine Schlange zu Hause! Sie ist sechs Jahre alt. Ich wohne in Wien. Das ist in Österreich. Ich bin sehr kreativ und intelligent! Schreib mir bitte!

Hallo! Ich heiße **Hannah** und ich wohne in London, in England. Ich lerne Deutsch. Ich suche Freunde aus Deutschland, Österreich und auch aus der Schweiz. Ich bin sportlich und spiele Fußball und auch Tennis, aber ich bin sehr faul! Meine Lieblingsmusik ist Rock. Schreib mir!

Mein Name ist **Felix** und ich wohne in der Schweiz, aber ich komme aus Dortmund in Deutschland. Zu Hause habe ich eine Wii und mein Lieblingsspiel ist FIFA. Meine Lieblingsfußballmannschaft ist Bayern-München. Ich suche Freunde aus Schottland und Wales.

Hi! Ich bin **Muhammad** und ich wohne in Cardiff. Das ist in Wales. Ich bin sechzehn Jahre alt. Meine Lieblingssache ist Technologie. Ich habe zu Hause einen Computer, ein Handy und auch ein iPad. Ich bin nicht sehr sportlich, aber sehr freundlich. Mein Lieblingsland ist Deutschland und ich suche dort Freunde.

Write the name of the person who ...

1 is looking for friends from Switzerland. Hannah
2 supports a football team. _____
3 has a pet. _____
4 is just looking for friends from Germany. _____
5 lives in a different place from where they were born. _____
6 does not particularly like sport. _____
7 lives in Switzerland. _____

suche = seek
Schreib mir (bitte)! = Write to me (please)!
dort = there

2 Write your own profile for the website. Use as much German as you can from *Kapitel 1* to describe yourself.

Answers

1 Hallo! Ich **heiße** Marie und ich **wohne** in Walsrode. Das ist in **Deutschland**. Ich bin fünfzehn **Jahre** alt. Ich bin **sehr** sportlich und **ganz** intelligent, **aber** ich bin **auch** faul. Mein **Lieblingssport** ist Hockey und **meine** Lieblingsmusik ist Pop. Ich **habe** einen Vogel aus Amerika. Er ist **sehr** freundlich, aber **nicht** laut!

2 1 Ich wohne in Göttingen.

2 Er ist ganz freundlich.

3 Meine Lieblingsmusik ist Mozart.

3 Pupils' own answers.

4 1 Wie heißt du?

2 Was ist dein Lieblingssport?

3 Wie ist Sami?

4 Wie alt ist Alwin?

Answers

1 1 Hannah 2 Felix 3 Franzi 4 Muhammad
5 Felix 6 Muhammad 7 Felix

2 Pupils' own answers.

Meine Welt und ich – KAPITEL

Grammatik (Pupil Book pp. 22–23)

The *Stimmt!* Grammatik section provides a more detailed summary of key grammar covered in the chapter, along with further exercises to practise these points.

Grammar topics
Nouns, gender and articles
Verbs
The present tense – regular verbs
The present tense – irregular verbs

Resources
Workbooks:
Übungsheft 1 A&B, page 10
Active Teach:
p.022 Grammar practice
p.022 Grammar presentation
p.023 Grammar practice
p.023 Grammar presentation (1)
p.023 Grammar presentation (2)
p.023 Grammar presentation (3)

Nouns, gender and articles

1 Change 'the' to 'a' and find the English meaning for each noun in the *Wortschatz*. (Reading L2)

Answers
1 *eine Lampe* – a lamp
2 *ein Apfel* – an apple
3 *ein Computer* – a computer
4 *eine Tabelle* – a table (chart)
5 *ein Kuli* – a pen/biro
6 *ein Lineal* – a ruler
7 *ein Haus* – a house
8 *ein Fenster* – a window
9 *ein Lehrer* – a teacher (male)
10 *eine Lehrerin* – a teacher (female)

2 Look up the genders of these nouns in the *Wortschatz*. Write the correct word for 'the' and the English meaning. (Reading L2)

Answers
1 *Buch – (das)*, book
2 *Freund – (der)*, friend
3 *Eis – (das)*, ice/ice cream
4 *Schlange – (die)*, snake
5 *Schokolade – (die)*, chocolate
6 *Vogel – (der)*, bird
7 *Handy – (das)*, mobile phone
8 *Schule – (die)*, school
9 *Nacht – (die)*, night
10 *Band – (die)*, band

3 Copy these compound nouns. Write each part in the correct colour for gender. Write the correct article and English meaning for each compound noun. (Reading L2)

Answers
1 *der Wassersport* – water sport (*der* and *sport* in blue, *Wasser* in green)
2 *das Spielauto* – toy car (all in green)
3 *der Wasserpark* – water park (*der* and *park* in blue, *Wasser* in green)
4 *das Musikspiel* – music game (*das* and *spiel* in green, *Musik* in red)
5 *die Sportschule* – sports school (*die* and *schule* in red, *Sport* in blue)

Verbs

4 Find the six infinitives from the verbs below. Write the English meaning. Check in the *Wortschatz* any you are unsure of. (Reading L2)

Answers
trinken – to drink
schwimmen – to swim
hören – to hear
gehen – to go
lernen – to learn
spielen – to play

© Pearson Education Ltd 2013. Copying permitted for purchasing institution only. This material is not copyright free.

Grammatik | Meine Welt und ich – **KAPITEL 1**

The present tense – regular verbs

5 Write out these parts of the verb *singen* (to sing) in the present tense and translate into English. (Writing L2)

> **Answers**
>
> *ich singe* – I sing
>
> *du singst* – you sing
>
> *er/sie/es singt* – he/she/it sings

6 Write out these sentences using the correct form of the verb (given in square brackets) in the present tense. Underline the subject each time. (Writing L2)

> **Answers**
>
> 1 <u>Ich</u> trinke Tee.
>
> 2 Wo wohnst <u>du</u>?
>
> 3 <u>Wayne Rooney</u> spielt Fußball.
>
> 4 <u>Arnold Schwarzenegger</u> wohnt in Kalifornien.
>
> 5 <u>Ich</u> komme aus England.
>
> 6 <u>Mein iPod</u> kommt aus China.

The present tense – irregular verbs

7 Fill in the gaps in these sentences with the correct part of either *haben* or *sein*, then translate the sentences into English. (Reading L2)

> **Answers**
>
> 1 Wie alt **bist** du? – How old are you?
>
> 2 Er **ist** freundlich, lustig und sehr intelligent. – He is friendly, funny and very intelligent.
>
> 3 **Hast** du einen iPod? – Do you have an iPod?
>
> 4 Was **ist** dein Lieblingsname? – What is your favourite name?
>
> 5 Ich **habe** ein Handy und eine Wii. – I have a mobile phone and a Wii.
>
> 6 Sie **ist** sehr musikalisch und sie hat eine Gitarre. – She is very musical and she has a guitar.

Workbook A, page 10

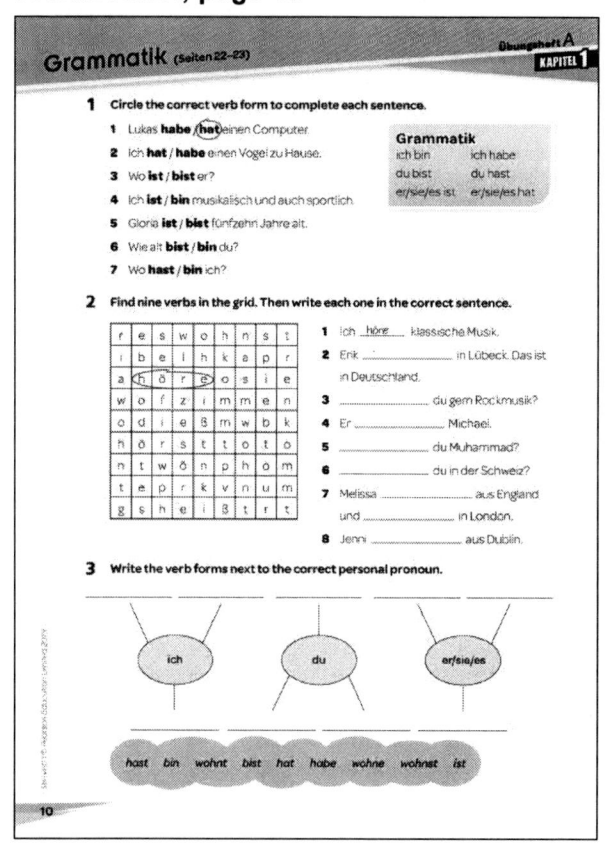

> **Answers**
>
> 1 1 hat 2 habe 3 ist 4 bin 5 ist 6 bist 7 bin
>
> 2 1 höre 2 wohnt 3 Hörst 4 heißt 5 Heißt 6 Wohnst 7 kommt; wohnt 8 kommt
>
> 3 ich bin, habe, wohne
>
> du hast, bist, wohnst
>
> er/sie/es wohnt, hat, ist

© Pearson Education Ltd 2013. Copying permitted for purchasing institution only. This material is not copyright free.

Grammatik | Meine Welt und ich – KAPITEL

Workbook B, page 10

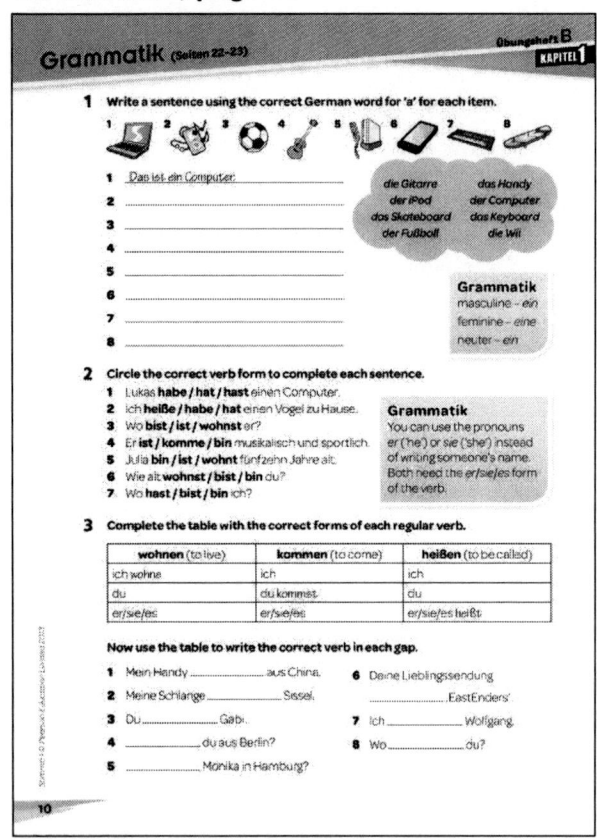

Answers

1
1 Das ist ein Computer.
2 Das ist ein iPod.
3 Das ist ein Fußball.
4 Das ist eine Gitarre.
5 Das ist eine Wii.
6 Das ist ein Handy.
7 Das ist ein Keyboard.
8 Das ist ein Skateboard.

2 1 hat 2 habe 3 ist 4 ist 5 ist 6 bist 7 bin

3 ich **wohne**, du **wohnst**, er/sie/es **wohnt**
ich **komme**, du **kommst**, er/sie/es **kommt**
ich **heiße**, du **heißt**, er/sie/es **heißt**

4 1 kommt 2 heißt 3 heißt 4 Kommst 5 Wohnt 6 heißt 7 heiße 8 wohnst

Meine Welt und Ich – KAPITEL 1

Projektzone: Supertrumpf (Pupil Book pp. 26–27)

The *Projektzone* is one or two optional units in which no new grammar is introduced, but in which the chapter topic is extended into an exciting cultural and practical context which allows for cross-curricular and project work.

Learning objectives
- Learning about famous people
- Creating 'super trumps' cards

Programme of Study
LC2 Transcription
LC4 Expressing ideas (speaking)
LC8 Writing creatively

FCSE links
Unit 1 – Relationships, Family and Friends (Personal information)

PLTS
C Creative thinkers

Cross-curricular
History: famous people

Resources
Audio files:
23_Kapitel1_Projektzone_Aufgabe1
24_Kapitel1_Projektzone_Aufgabe3
ActiveTeach:
Starter 1 resource
Starter 2 resource
Plenary resource

Starter 1

Aim

To introduce the idea of inventors and inventions.

Pupils have a list of inventors and their inventions (Starter 1 resource). They match them individually and then compare with their partner, making logical guesses as to the meanings of the new vocabulary. Pupils could be encouraged to use a dictionary if necessary. Alternatively, pupils could be given the dates, inventions and inventors as cut-out cards to match up in pairs or groups of four.

Go online to research more ideas.

1 Was hörst du? Wähl die richtige Antwort aus: a oder b? (Listening L2)

Listening. Pupils listen to the audio and choose the correct answer (a or b).

They then go on to discuss their answers in exercise 2.

Use the *Tip* box to tell pupils the vocabulary for saying what you think about something.

Audioscript

1 – [SOUND OF VERY FEW NOTES OF BACH PRELUDE]
2 – [SOUND OF A HANDBALL MATCH]
3 – [SOUND OF THE HIGH-POWERED ENGINE OF A CAR]
4 – [SOUND OF SOMEONE BRUSHING THEIR TEETH – MANUAL TOOTHBRUSH]

Answers
1 a 2 b 3 b 4 a

2 Gruppenarbeit. Diskutier deine Meinungen mit deiner Gruppe.
(Speaking L3–4)

Speaking. In groups, pupils discuss what they think about the answers to exercise 1.

Some vocabulary is glossed for support.

3 Hör zu und lies. Schreib den Text ab und füll die Lücken aus. (Listening L3)

Listening. Pupils listen to the audio and look at the text. They copy out the text and fill in the gaps with the correct piece of missing text.

Some vocabulary is glossed for support.

Audioscript

– Er heißt Albert Einstein. Er kommt aus Deutschland. Er ist Physiker. Er ist sehr intelligent und ziemlich kreativ. Er ist aber nicht besonders musikalisch und gar nicht sportlich. Seine Lieblingssache ist die Relativität.

Answers
1 Einstein 2 kommt 3 Er 4 ist 5 intelligent 6 nicht 7 sportlich 8 Lieblingssache

Extension

More able pupils could be encouraged to translate the text, once completed, into English.

4 Sieh dir Aufgabe 3 an. Schreib den Text in der Ich-Form. (Writing L4)

Writing. Pupils re-write the text from exercise 3 in the first person.

© Pearson Education Ltd 2013. Copying permitted for purchasing institution only. This material is not copyright free.

Supertrumpf | **Meine Welt und ich –** KAPITEL

Answers

Ich heiße Albert Einstein. **Ich komme** aus Deutschland. **Ich bin** Physiker. **Ich bin** sehr intelligent und ziemlich kreativ. **Ich bin** aber nicht besonders musikalisch und gar nicht sportlich. **Meine** Lieblingssache ist die Relativität.

Starter 2

Aim

To introduce the concept of a 'super trump'.

Pupils are given a template for a 'super trumps' card (Starter 2 resource). They also have words to fit in each category. In pairs they build up the card to reveal information about an inventor.

5 Lies den Text. Schreib die Supertrumpfkarte ab und füll sie auf Deutsch aus. (Reading L4)

Reading. Pupils read the text and complete the 'super trumps' card in German.

Some vocabulary is glossed for support.

Answers

Name: Sebastian Vettel
Kommt aus: Heppenheim, Deutschland
Wohnt in: *der* Schweiz
kreativ: 2
intelligent: 7
sportlich: *10*
lustig: 5
musikalisch: 7
Lieblingssache: Autos

6 Lies die Supertrumpfkarten. Wähl eine Karte aus. Schreib einen Text in der Ich-Form dazu. Suche die Infos im Internet oder frag deinen Lehrer/deine Lehrerin. (Writing L3–4)

Writing. Pupils choose one of the 'super trumps' cards displayed in the pupil book and write a text based on it in the first person.

Pupils can look for information on the computer or ask the teacher.

7 Wähl drei Personen aus und finde Informationen über sie. Schreib drei Supertrumpfkarten. (Writing L3–4)

Writing. Pupils choose three famous people (see below for some ideas), collect some information about them and create three 'super trumps' cards.

8 Schreib einen Text zu einer Karte. Benutze die er/sie-Form. (Writing L3–4)

Writing. Pupils create a piece of writing based on one of the 'super trumps' cards displayed in the pupil book.

Name suggestions, choose ten names

Usain Bolt
Rebecca Adlington
Cheryl Cole
Prince William
Lady Gaga
Cristiano Ronaldo
Lionel Messi
Johnny Depp
Barack Obama
Jessica Ennis
Victoria Pendleton
Bradley Wiggins
Tom Daley
Mo Farah

German-speaking 'celebrities'

Bastian Schweinsteiger
Heidi Klum
Angela Merkel
Adi Dassler
Ferdinand Porsche
Hans Riegel
Levi Strauss
Ludwig van Beethoven
Albert Einstein
Michael Schumacher
Franka Potente
Arnold Schwarzenegger
Roger Federer
Wolfgang Amadeus Mozart
Anne Frank
Johann Wolfgang von Goethe

© Pearson Education Ltd 2013. Copying permitted for purchasing institution only. This material is not copyright free.

Supertrumpf | **Meine Welt und ich** – **KAPITEL 1**

Plenary

Aim

For pupils to establish whether they have met the unit objectives of learning about famous people and creating 'super trumps' cards.

Pupils use their newly created cards to play a game of 'super trumps' in pairs or groups of four.

All the cards are dealt out. The first player chooses one category from their top card and reads out the value in German. The other players then use their top card and read out the value of the same category as the first player. The highest value wins the round and takes the cards from the other players. The winner is the player who has the most (or all) cards at the end of the game.

Character points:

sehr [✓✓] = 10

ziemlich [✓] = 7

nicht besonders [–] = 5

gar nicht [✗] = 2

Alternatively, pupils could complete an information gap speaking exercise (Plenary resource) on asking and answering questions in German.

Meine Welt und ich – KAPITEL

Extra (Pupil Book pp. 120–121)

Self-access reading and writing

A Reinforcement

1 Schreib die Zahlen als Wörter auf. Dann sag die Zahlen. (Writing L2)

Writing. Pupils write out in words the numbers on the illustrations and then say the numbers out loud to themselves.

The *Tip* box reminds pupils that they can use the page numbers on the pupil book to check their spelling.

Answers
1 neun 2 sieben 3 acht 4 sechzehn 5 zwölf

2 Verbinde die Worthälften und schreib die Charaktereigenschaften richtig auf. Schreib auch das englische Wort auf. (Reading L1)

Reading. Pupils match the halves of words together to make a complete word. They then write out the word correctly and translate it into English.

Answers
1 *freundlich* – friendly 2 *faul* – lazy
3 *launisch* – moody 4 *intelligent* – intelligent
5 *laut* – loud 6 *kreativ* – creative
7 *musikalisch* – musical 8 *lustig* – fun

3 Wie heißt das auf Deutsch? Verbinde die Wörter. Schreib sie auf. (Writing L2)

Writing. Pupils translate the English into German by combining words from the selection provided. They then write the word out.

The *Tip* box reminds pupils that they will need to use some words more than once.

Answers
1 *Fußballmannschaft*
2 Lieblingsname
3 Oktoberfest
4 Lieblingsland
5 Hockeymannschaft
6 Lieblingsmädchenname

4 Ein Interview mit einem Außerirdischen. Wähl die richtige Antwort aus. (Reading L2)

Reading. Pupils answer multiple-choice questions.

Answers
1 a 2 b 3 a 4 a 5 b 6 a 7 b

B Extension

1 Lies die Sätze vor und sieh dir das Bild an. Richtig oder falsch? (Reading L2)

Reading. Pupils read the questions and look at the illustration, then decide if the questions are true or false.

The *Tip* box reminds pupils that reading a text out loud can help with understanding it.

Answers
1 *Falsch* 2 Falsch 3 Richtig 4 Falsch 5 Falsch
6 Richtig

2 Korrigiere die falschen Sätze aus Aufgabe 1 und schreib sie richtig auf. (Writing L2)

Writing. Pupils write out the incorrect statements in exercise 1 correctly. Words are provided to help.

Answers
1 *Meine Schlange heißt Noah.*
2 Mein Lieblingseis ist Vanille.
4 Mein Lieblingsauto ist ein Porsche.
5 Ich komme aus Deutschland.

3 Lies die Texte und schreib den richtigen Namen auf. (Reading L3)

Reading. Pupils read the texts then match the person to the sentences given.

Answers
1 *Elias* 2 Elias 3 Max 4 Sofie 5 Max 6 Katrin

4 Schreib einen Text über dich und deine Lieblingssachen. Benutze die Texte aus Aufgabe 3. (Writing L3)

Writing. Pupils write a text about themselves and their favourite things. They can adapt the texts from exercise 3. Pupils must include:

- their name and age
- where they live
- their character
- two or three favourite things.

© Pearson Education Ltd 2013. Copying permitted for purchasing institution only. This material is not copyright free.

KAPITEL 2

(Pupil Book pp. 28–51)

Familie und Tiere

Unit & Learning objectives	Programme of Study references	Key Language	Grammar and other language features
1 Extreme Haustiere (pp. 30–31) • Talking about pets • Using pronouns	**GV2** Grammatical structures (plurals, pronouns) **GV3** Developing vocabulary **LC3** Conversation	Hast du ein Haustier? Ich habe … einen Hund einen Goldfisch einen Hamster eine Katze eine Maus eine Schlange ein Kaninchen ein Pferd ein Meerschweinchen dick faul frech freundlich groß intelligent klein kreativ lang launisch laut lustig musikalisch niedlich schlank sportlich Goldfische Hamster Hunde Kaninchen Katzen Mäuse Meerschweinchen Pferde Schlangen	• Pronouns • Pronunciation of -d and Pf- • Using kein to say you have no pet • Plural of nouns

© Pearson Education Ltd 2013. Copying permitted for purchasing institution only. This material is not copyright free.

Familie und Tiere – **KAPITEL**

Unit & Learning objectives	Programme of Study references	Key Language	Grammar and other language features
2 Supertiere (pp. 32–33) • Talking about 'superpets' • Using *kann* + infinitive	**GV2** Grammatical structures (using *können*) **LC1** Listening and responding **LC2** Transcription	Wie ist er/sie/es? Er/Sie/Es ist … cool gemein kräftig schlau schnell superintelligent superlustig süß Er/Sie kann … fliegen Flöte/Fußball/Wii spielen Italienisch sprechen (schnell) laufen lesen Rad fahren schwimmen singen springen tanzen	• Using *können* with the infinitive • Adding '*super*' to adjectives • Improving fluency by using connectives and the correct pronouns
3 Meine Familie (pp. 34–35) • Talking about family members and age • More practice of present tense verbs	**GV1** Tenses (present) **GV3** Opinions and discussions **LC8** Translation into German	Numbers 20–100 Hast du Geschwister? Das ist die Familie … meine Mutter mein Vater meine Eltern meine Großeltern Die … Personen wohnen in … Er wohnt in … Meine Großeltern wohnen mit uns zusammen. Es gibt … Personen in meiner Familie. Ich habe eine Schwester/zwei Brüder/einen Bruder/zwei Schwestern. keine Geschwister ein Einzelkind	• Full paradigm of regular present tense (*wohnen*) • Ways of saying 'you' • Vocabulary for group talk • Vocabulary for step-families and half-siblings (*Stief…* and *Halb…*)

© Pearson Education Ltd 2013. Copying permitted for purchasing institution only. This material is not copyright free.

Familie und Tiere – **KAPITEL 2**

Unit & Learning objectives	Programme of Study references	Key Language	Grammar and other language features
4 Die Farben der Welt (pp. 36–37) • Describing family members • Using adjectives with nouns	**GV4** Accuracy (grammar) **LC4** Expressing ideas (writing) **LC6** Translation into English	schwarz weiß grau braun rot orange gelb grün blau indigoblau violett lila rosa schwarze/braune/blonde/rote Haare lange/kurze/mittellange Haare blaue/braune/grüne/graue Augen	• Adjectival agreement • Full paradigm of irregular verb *haben* • Using *hell-* and *dunkel-* to qualify colours • Working out meanings from context
5 Alles Gute! (pp. 38–39) • Talking about birthdays • Using ordinal numbers (first, twentieth, and so on)	**GV2** Grammatical structures (ordinal numbers) **LC4** Expressing ideas (writing) **LC5** Accurate pronunciation and intonation	Januar Februar März April Mai Juni Juli August September Oktober November Dezember Ich habe am …(s)ten … Geburtstag. Ich habe (heute) Geburtstag.	• Ordinal numbers (saying when someone's birthday is) • Pronouncing the months of the year (cognates) • Recognising numbers when listening
6 Speaking Skills: Eine Superfamilie (pp. 40–41) • Developing speaking skills • Practising asking and answering questions	**GV2** Grammatical structures (question words) **LC1** Listening and responding **LC4** Expressing ideas (speaking)		• Question words • Adding details to answers • Importance of understanding question words • Talking about a topic • Plural of some foreign nouns (add *–s*)

© Pearson Education Ltd 2013. Copying permitted for purchasing institution only. This material is not copyright free.

Familie und Tiere – KAPITEL

Unit & Learning objectives	Programme of Study references	Key Language	Grammar and other language features
Lernzieltest und Wiederholung (pp. 42–43) Pupils' checklist and practice exercises			• Improving spoken fluency by adding detail, using connectives and using correct pronunciation • Adapt texts to create an original
Grammatik (pp. 44–45) Detailed grammar summary and practice exercises			• Plural of nouns • The present tense – regular verbs • The present tense – *haben* • Modal verbs • Pronouns
Projektzone 1: Frohe Weihnachten! (pp. 48–49) • Learning about Christmas • Finding out about German traditions	**GV3** Developing vocabulary **LC1** Listening and responding **LC6** Reading comprehension		
Projektzone 2: Prost Neujahr! (pp. 50–51) • Learning about New Year celebrations • Giving a presentation	**GV3** Developing vocabulary **LC5** Speaking coherently and confidently **LC6** Reading comprehension		

Familie und Tiere – KAPITEL 2

1 Extreme Haustiere (Pupil Book pp. 28–31)

Learning objectives	Key Language	Resources
• Talking about pets • Using pronouns **Programme of Study** **GV2** Grammatical structures (plurals, pronouns) **GV3** Developing vocabulary **LC3** Conversation **FCSE links** Unit 1 – Relationships, Family and Friends (Pets) **Grammar** Plural of nouns Pronouns **PLTS** C Creative thinkers	Hast du ein Haustier? Ich habe … einen Hund (plural -e) einen Goldfisch (-e) einen Hamster (-) eine Katze (-n) eine Maus (Mäuse) eine Schlange (-n) ein Kaninchen (-) ein Pferd (-e) ein Meerschweinchen (-) dick faul frech freundlich intelligent klein / groß kreativ lang launisch laut lustig musikalisch niedlich schlank sportlich	**Audio files:** 25_Kapitel2_Einheit1_Aufgabe1 26_Kapitel2_Einheit1_Aufgabe3 **Workbooks:** Übungsheft 1 A&B, page 14 **ActiveTeach:** Starter 1 resource Starter 2 resource p.030 Grammar presentation p.030 Flashcards p.031 Learning skills worksheet Plenary resource **ActiveLearn:** Listening A, Listening B Reading A, Reading B Grammar, Vocabulary

Kapitel 2 Quiz pp. 28–29

Answers

1 a 2 c 3 c 4 a 5 b 6 b

The *Tip* box suggests that pupils say the names out loud to help.

Starter 1

Aim

To introduce the new vocabulary from the unit and to encourage pupils to make logical guesses about the meaning of new vocabulary.

Pupils are asked to match two lists of vocabulary, one with the words in German and one with the words in English (Starter 1 resource). After they have matched the words, they compare first with their partner and then within their group of four (think-pair-share). Ask for feedback on how they made their decisions and to reflect on the strategies they have used to work out the meaning of new words.

Pupils could also be asked to write the new vocabulary on their *der/die/das* balloons. Another possibility could be to ask the pupils what they think the learning objective of the day's lesson should be.

Answers

1 D 2 G 3 F 4 H 5 C 6 I 7 A 8 B 9 E

1 Hör zu. Wie heißen die Tiere? (1–9) (Listening L2)

Listening. Pupils listen to the audio and work out the names of the pets. The pupil book gives pictures of the animals as well as their names to help.

Audioscript

1 – *Hast du ein Haustier?*
 – *Ja, ich habe einen Hund. Mein Hund heißt Romeo.*

2 – *Hast du ein Haustier?*

© Pearson Education Ltd 2013. Copying permitted for purchasing institution only. This material is not copyright free.

Extreme Haustiere | **Familie und Tiere –** KAPITEL

– Ja, ich habe einen Goldfisch. Mein Goldfisch heißt Gollum.
3 – Und du, hast du ein Haustier?
– Ja, ich habe einen Hamster. Er heißt Blitz.
– Ach so, dein Hamster heißt Blitz.
4 – Ich habe eine Katze.
– Eine Katze? Wie heißt sie?
– Meine Katze heißt China.
5 – Hast du ein Haustier?
– Ich habe eine Maus.
– Wie heißt deine Maus?
– Sie heißt Mitzi.
6 – Hast du ein Haustier?
– Ich habe eine Schlange.
– Eine Schlange?
– Ja, sie heißt Pippi.
7 – Ich habe ein Haustier: ein Kaninchen.
– Ja? Und wie heißt dein Kaninchen?
– Es heißt Nudel.
8 – Ich habe ein Pferd.
– Ein Pferd. Toll. Wie heißt es?
– Mein Pferd heißt Elvis.
9 – Hast du ein Haustier?
– Oh ja, ich habe ein Meerschweinchen.
– Und wie heißt dein Meerschweinchen?
– Schnuffel. Es heißt Schnuffel.

Answers
1 Romeo 2 Gollum 3 Blitz 4 China 5 Mitzi
6 Pippi 7 Nudel 8 Elvis 9 Schnuffel

2 Sieh dir die Bilder an und schreib Sätze. (Writing L2)

Writing. Using the pictures in the pupil book, pupils write pairs of sentences about the animals. Remind pupils that masculine nouns change *ein* to *einen* after the verb *haben*.

Answers
1 Ich habe einen Hund. Er heißt Romeo.
2 Ich habe einen Goldfisch. Er heißt Gollum.
3 Ich habe einen Hamster. Er heißt Blitz.
4 Ich habe eine Katze. Sie heißt China.
5 Ich habe eine Maus. Sie heißt Mitzi.

6 Ich habe eine Schlange. Sie heißt Pippi.
7 Ich habe ein Kaninchen. Es heißt Nudel.
8 Ich habe ein Pferd. Es heißt Elvis.
9 Ich habe ein Meerschweinchen. Es heißt Schnuffel.

Grammatik

Use the *Grammatik* box to talk about pronouns. Remind pupils that German nouns can be masculine, feminine or neuter, and that the pronoun (*er/sie/es*) must also be masculine, feminine or neuter.

There is more information and practice in the grammar unit on pupil book p. 45.

3 Hör zu. Welches Haustier ist das und wie ist es? (1–5) (Listening L3)

Listening. Pupils listen to the audio and identify the pet and its main characteristics. Pupils take notes or, to make the activity more challenging, write full sentences.

Audioscript

1 – Wie ist deine Schlange?
– Meine Schlange ist freundlich.
– Freundlich?!
– Ja, Pippi ist sehr freundlich und sie ist auch lang … sehr sehr lang!
2 – Wie ist dein Kaninchen?
– Nudel ist frech und auch kreativ. Ja, mein Kaninchen ist frech und kreativ!
3 – Du hast ein Meerschweinchen. Wie ist es?
– Ach, es ist niedlich. Schnuffel ist sooo niedlich.
– Aber es ist auch dick, ja?
– Okay, ja, es ist dick … aber niedlich!
4 – Mein Hamster heißt Blitz.
– Wie ist er? Ist er faul?
– Oh nein, er ist nicht faul. Er ist sportlich und schlank.
– Sportlich und schlank … das ist gut.
5 – Du hast einen Goldfisch, ja?
– Ja, er heißt Gollum.
– Wie ist er? Ist er intelligent?
– Nein, er ist nicht intelligent, aber er ist lustig.

Extreme Haustiere | **Familie und Tiere** – KAPITEL 2

> **Answers**
> 1 *Schlange, freundlich, lang*
> 2 *Kaninchen, frech, kreativ*
> 3 *Meerschweinchen, niedlich, dick*
> 4 *Hamster, (nicht faul), sportlich, schlank*
> 5 *Goldfisch, nicht intelligent, lustig*

4 Partnerarbeit. Sieh dir die Aufgaben 1–3 an. Stell und beantworte Fragen. (Speaking L3)

Speaking. Working in pairs, pupils take turns to ask each other questions and to answer them, basing their questions on material and vocabulary explored in exercises 1–3.

Refer pupils to the *Tip* box which introduces *kein*.

Use the *Aussprache* box to help pupils with remembering how to pronounce *–d* and *Pf–*.

> **Starter 2**
> **Aim**
> To review the formation of plural nouns.
>
> Pupils have two sets of cards, one containing singular nouns using vocabulary from the unit and from Chapter 1 and one showing plural noun endings (Starter 2 resource).
>
> First pupils match the plural endings to the nouns, asking a partner to check their work once they have finished (Double check the work if necessary).
>
> In pairs, pupils then play a memory game using both sets of cards placed face down on a flat surface. They turn over two cards at a time and when they find a match, they keep the cards. The winner is the person who has the most matched cards at the end of the game.
>
> **Alternative starter 2**
> Use ActiveTeach p.030 Flashcards to review and practise names of pets.

5 Partnerarbeit. Finde die Tiere. (Speaking L3)

Speaking. Working in pairs, pupils examine the illustration and point out aloud the animals they find within it.

> **Grammatik**
> The *Grammatik* box presents some of the different ways of forming the plural in German (add no ending, add *–n*, add *–e* or add an umlaut on the first vowel and an *–e* at the end).
>
> There is more information and practice in the grammar unit on pupil book p. 44.

6 Schreib die Tabelle (Grammatik) ab. Schreib die Mehrzahl der Tiere (Aufgabe 5) in die richtige Spalte. (Writing L1)

Writing. Pupils copy the table from the *Grammatik* box and then order the plural forms of the animals listed in exercise 5 in the correct column. Encourage pupils to work out patterns for plural forms of nouns. For plurals with 's' – with cognates like *Hotels, Fotos, Lamas* – see pupil book p. 40 and pp. 44–45.

> **Answers**
> **add no ending:** *Hamster*, Kaninchen, Meerschweinchen
> **add *–n*:** *Katzen*, Schlangen
> **add *–e*:** *Pferde*, Hunde, Goldfische
> **add an *Umlaut* (¨) on the first vowel and *–e* at the end:** *Mäuse*

7 Schreib eine E-Mail über ein Haustier und stell Fragen. (Writing L3–4)

Writing. Pupils describe in an email a pet, perhaps their own or perhaps an 'extreme' pet. Pupils can add a picture if they like.

8 Partnerarbeit. Deck deine E-Mail (Aufgabe 7) zu und sprich über dein Haustier. Dein Partner/Deine Partnerin schreibt alles auf. (Speaking L4, Listening L3–4)

Speaking/Listening. Without looking at their writing from exercise 7, pupils talk about the pet that they wrote about. The partner transcribes the information given about the pet.

Extreme Haustiere | **Familie und Tiere** – KAPITEL

Plenary

Aim

For pupils to establish whether they have met the lesson objective of talking about pets.

The class is split into two groups to play a speed-dating activity. One group is seated or standing facing the other. Each pupil in group A has a set of questions to ask and each pupil in group B has a card for an animal (Plenary resource). Pupils have one minute to ask and answer questions about the animal before a signal (bell/alarm) prompts them to stop. Pupils in group B then move to the left to start speaking to their new partner. Once every pupil in group B has been interviewed by every pupil in group A the groups swap roles.

Mia: mice; Max and Moritz; Max is really cute, Moritz is quite cheeky

Erik: snakes; Tibor and Magnus; Tibor is very long, Magnus is slim

Philippa: guinea-pig; Maik; fat and lazy

3 Pupils' own answers.

Workbook B, page 14

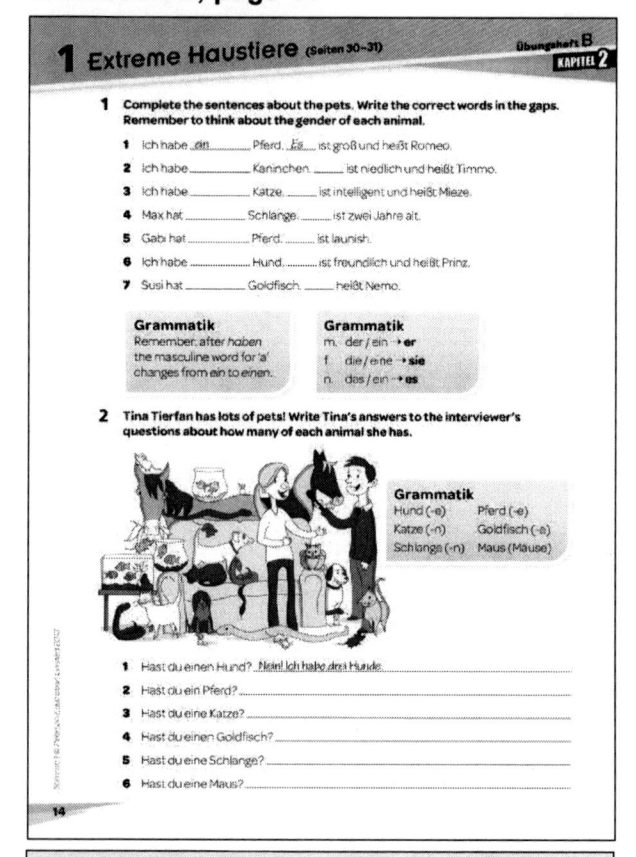

Workbook A, page 14

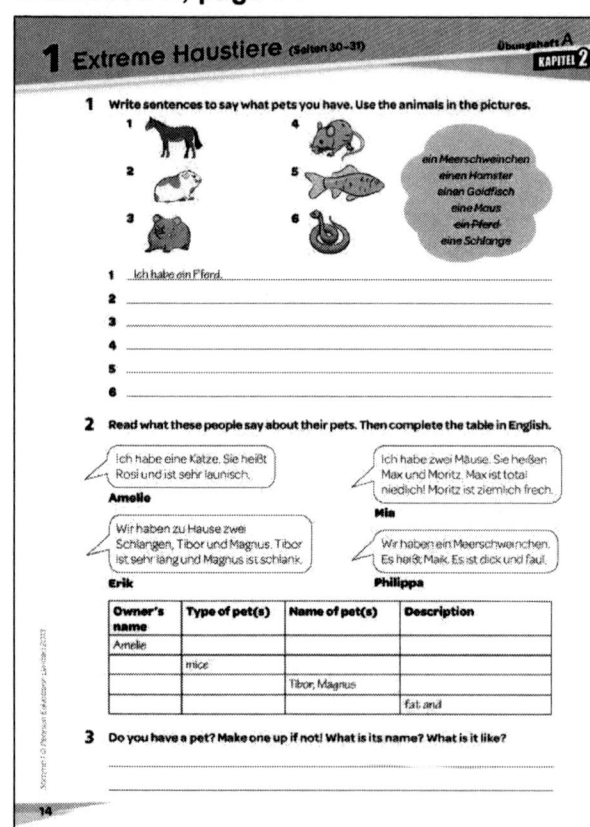

Answers

1 1 Ich habe ein Pferd.
   2 Ich habe ein Meerschweinchen.
   3 Ich habe einen Hamster.
   4 Ich habe eine Maus.
   5 Ich habe einen Goldfisch.
   6 Ich habe eine Schlange.

2 **Amelie**: cat; Rosi; moody

Answers

1 1 ein, Es
   2 ein, Es
   3 eine, Sie
   4 eine, Sie
   5 ein, Es
   6 einen, Er
   7 einen, Er

2 1 Nein! Ich habe drei Hunde.
   2 Nein! Ich habe zwei Pferde.
   3 Nein! Ich habe vier Katzen.
   4 Nein! Ich habe sieben Goldfische.
   5 Nein! Ich habe fünf Schlangen.
   6 Nein! Ich habe acht Mäuse.

© Pearson Education Ltd 2013. Copying permitted for purchasing institution only. This material is not copyright free.

Extreme Haustiere | Familie und Tiere – **KAPITEL 2**

Worksheet

Learning skills: Plural nouns

1 Extreme Haustiere

Learning skills: Plural nouns

German plurals form in patterns. Although most English plurals form in the same pattern (you add –s), there are actually many other English plural patterns. Thinking about these patterns will help you to make sense of German plural patterns.

A What are the plurals of these English words? What patterns can you see?

1 fish _____   2 sheep _____   3 goose _____
4 tooth _____   5 knife _____   6 wife _____
7 mouse _____   8 louse _____

B Which other English plurals can you think of that don't just end in –s? Write as many as you can in a minute. Can you find any more patterns?

C Draw lines to match these new words to their plurals.

1 der Frosch (frog)   a die Biber
2 die Kuh (cow)   b die Bälle
3 die Eule (owl)   c die Eulen
4 der Biber (beaver)   d die Otter
5 die Pflanze (plant) e die Frösche
6 der Otter (otter)   f die Kühe
7 der Stern (star)   g die Sterne
8 der Ball (ball)   h die Pflanzen

Some plural forms you already know are:
Kaninchen (-) → zwei Kaninchen
Katze (-n) → zwei Katzen
Fisch (-e) → zwei Fische
Maus ("-e) → zwei Mäuse

D Complete the table of plural patterns with the nouns and their plurals from activity C.

(-)	(-n)	(-e)	("-e)
			Frosch → Frösche

© Pearson Education Limited 2013
Printing and photocopying permitted

Answers

A (no change in the plural) **1** fish **2** sheep
(oo → ee) **3** geese **4** teeth (fe → ves)
5 knives **6** wives (ouse → ice) **7** mice **8** lice

B Teachers to discuss with pupils.

C 1 e 2 f 3 c 4 a 5 h 6 d 7 g 8 b

D column 1: Biber → Biber, Otter → Otter
column 2: Eule → Eulen, Pflanze → Pflanzen
column 3: Stern → Sterne
column 3: Frosch → Frösche, Kuh → Kühe, Ball → Bälle

2 Supertiere (Pupil Book pp. 32–33)

Familie und Tiere – KAPITEL

Learning objectives
- Talking about 'superpets'
- Using *kann* + infinitive

Programme of Study
GV2 Grammatical structures (using *können*)
LC1 Listening and responding
LC2 Transcription

FCSE links
Unit 1 – Relationships, Family and Friends (Pets)

Grammar
More about *können*

PLTS
T Team workers

Key Language
Wie ist er/sie/es?
Er/Sie/Es ist …
cool
gemein
kräftig
schlau
schnell
superintelligent
superlustig
süß
Er/Sie kann …
fliegen
Flöte/Fußball/Wii spielen
Italienisch sprechen
(schnell) laufen
lesen
Rad fahren
schwimmen
singen
springen
tanzen

Resources
Audio files:
27_Kapitel2_Einheit2_Aufgabe1
28_Kapitel2_Einheit2_Aufgabe3
29_Kapitel2_Einheit2_Aufgabe4
Workbooks:
Übungsheft 1 A&B, page 15
ActiveTeach:
Starter 1 resource
p.033 Grammar presentation
p.033 Flashcards
Plenary resource
ActiveLearn:
Listening A, Listening B
Reading A, Reading B
Grammar, Vocabulary

Starter 1

Aim

To introduce the concept of 'superpets'.

- Revise personality adjectives: *doof, faul, intelligent, laut, lustig, kreativ, sportlich* by writing them with missing vowels for pupils to complete or as anagrams for pupils to solve.
- Display words for pets from unit 1. Pupils group the pets under *der/die/das*. For more able pupils, add some plurals as an extra category.
- Pupils are given sets of cards (Starter 1 resource). They match the two halves of the names of the different superpets and then translate the names into English.
- Pupils think of names for the remaining pets (this can be done as a dictionary skills exercise).
- Pupils think of names to give the following animals to turn them into superpets.

- *Kaninchen*
- *Meerschweinchen*
- *Pferd*
- *Goldfisch*
- *Katze*

- Pupils could also re-do the speed-dating plenary game from unit 1.

1 Hör zu. Welches Supertier ist das? (1–5) (Listening L2)

Listening. Pupils look at the illustrations of five superpets, work out what kind of animal they are and then predict what qualities they might have. Pupils then listen to the audio and match the pet described to the illustration.

With weaker groups, use flashcards of the new adjectives to introduce the new vocabulary before doing the exercise.

Audioscript

1 – *Mein Supertier ist sportlich und schnell und er ist sehr süß. Wie heißt er?*
2 – *Hier ist mein Supertier. Sie ist kreativ und superlustig. Ja, sie ist cool. Wie heißt sie?*
3 – *Das ist mein Lieblingssupertier. Sie ist intelligent und schlau, aber faul. Wie heißt sie?*
4 – *Mein Supertier ist cool und er ist superintelligent. Wie heißt er?*
5 – *Das ist mein Supertier. Er ist laut, kräftig und gemein. Wie heißt er?*

© Pearson Education Ltd 2013. Copying permitted for purchasing institution only. This material is not copyright free.

Supertiere | **Familie und Tiere** – KAPITEL 2

Answers

1 d Harald Hamsterheld *2* b Marta Megamaus
3 e Sigi Superschlange *4* a Walter
Wunderwellensittich *5* c Hermann Horrorhund

2 Beantworte die Fragen. (Reading L2)

Reading. Start by asking some of the questions orally before pupils read and write their answers. Some pupils could omit questions 6–8.

Answers

1 Harald Hamsterheld
2 Sigi Superschlange
3 Marta Megamaus
4 Walter Wunderwellensittich
5 Hermann Horrorhund
6 Er ist superintelligent und cool.
7 Sie ist kreativ, superlustig und cool.
8 Er ist sportlich, schnell und süß.

Extension

Follow up exercise 2 by asking questions orally about the personality of all the superpets. This could be extended to members of the class or to famous personalities, etc.

3 Hör zu. Was kann das Supertier machen? Welches Bild ist das? (1–5) (Listening L2)

Listening. Pupils listen to the audio and work out what the animals can do and then match the animal to the picture.

The *Tip* box on p. 32 alerts pupils to different ways of forming 'super' adjectives.

Follow up with questions for pupils, for example, *Wer kann schwimmen? Kannst du schwimmen?*

Audioscript

1 – *Megamaus kann fliegen und Flöte spielen. Sie kann auch Wii spielen.*
2 – *Hamsterheld kann Rad fahren und schnell laufen.*
3 – *Wunderwellensittich kann lesen. Er kann auch singen und Italienisch sprechen.*
4 – *Horrorhund kann springen und Fußball spielen.*
5 – *Superschlange kann sehr gut schwimmen und tanzen.*

Answers

1 b *2* e *3* d *4* a *5* c

4 Hör noch einmal zu. Wer ist das? (Listening L2)

Listening. Pupils listen to the audio again and write the name of the superpet being described.

Audioscript

For transcript see exercise 3.

Answers

1 Megamaus
2 Hamsterheld
3 Wunderwellensittich
4 Horrorhund
5 Superschlange

Starter 2

Aim

To review giving information about the superpets.

Pupils work in groups of four. Each pupil secretly writes the name of one of the superpets on a sticky note, which is then stuck on another group member's forehead (without them seeing the name). Each pupil in turn then has to guess which superpet they are by asking questions to which the answer can only be *ja/nein*. Questions could include:

Bin ich cool / gemein / kräftig / schlau / schnell / superintelligent / superlustig / süß?

Bin ich ein Junge oder ein Mädchen?

Habe ich ein Buch / eine Sonnenbrille / eine Flöte / eine Wii / ein Schwimmbad?

Alternative starter 2

Use ActiveTeach p.033 Flashcards to review and practise using *kann* + the infinitive.

5 Schreib Sätze über die fünf Supertiere. (Writing L2–3)

Writing. Pupils write sentences about the five superpets. They could listen again to exercise 3 to check their answers.

Answers

As transcript for exercise 3 or similar.

© Pearson Education Ltd 2013. Copying permitted for purchasing institution only. This material is not copyright free.

Grammatik

Use the *Grammatik* box to show pupils how to use *kann* + infinitive, pointing out that the infinitive comes at the end of the sentence. There is more information and practice in the grammar unit on pupil book p. 45.

6 Partnerarbeit. Partner(in) A beschreibt ein Supertier, Partner(in) B rät. (Speaking L3)

Speaking. Working in pairs, pupils take it in turns to describe a superpet. Their partner guesses which superpet they are describing.

7 Beschreib dein Lieblingssupertier. Du kannst auch ein Bild malen.
(Writing L3–4)

Writing. Pupils describe their favourite superpet. This could be done as an individual or group activity. Point out the *Tip* box to remind pupils to use connectives to make their work interesting and to check that they have used the correct pronoun.

The *Tip* box also reminds pupils to use connectives to make their writing more fluent.

Extension

Pupils could include a description of where their superpet lives or comes from, how old it is, what it has, etc. to recycle and reinforce previous language.

Plenary

Aim

For pupils to establish whether they have met the lesson objective of using *kann* + infinitive.

Pupils play a game of noughts and crosses (Plenary resource) with a partner, practising the key structures from the unit. (This can also be displayed on the IWB and played as a whole-class game.) One pupil chooses a phrase to translate into German. If they get it right they can put 0 or X in that part of the grid. The game is played as a traditional noughts and crosses game.

Workbook A, page 15

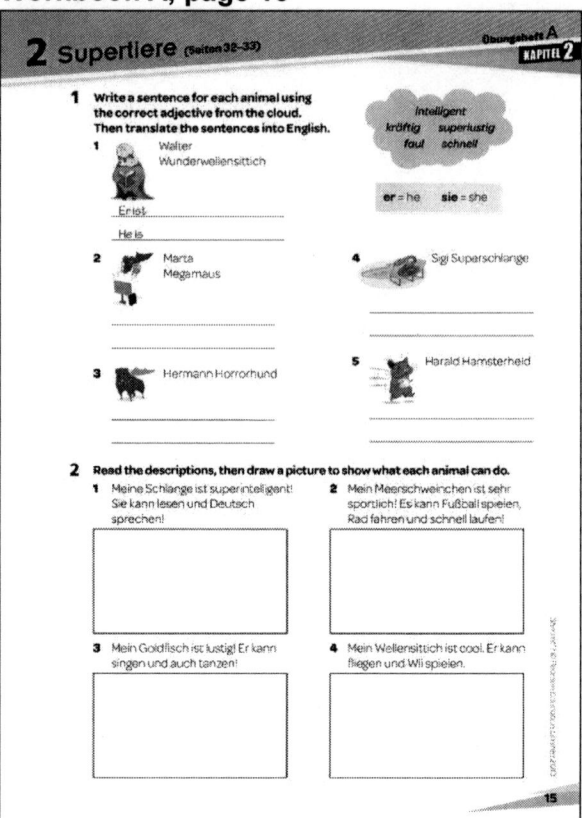

Answers

1
1 Er ist intelligent. / He is intelligent.
2 Sie ist superlustig. / She is really funny.
3 Er ist kräftig. / He is powerful.
4 Sie ist faul. / She is lazy.
5 Er ist schnell. / He is fast.

2 Pupils' own illustrations.

Workbook B, page 15

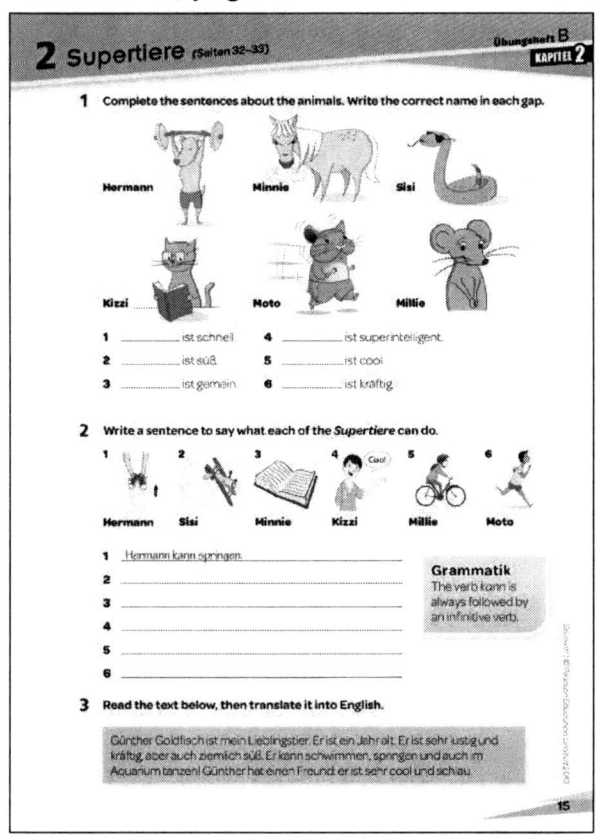

Answers

1 1 **Moto** ist schnell.
   2 **Millie** ist süß.
   3 **Minnie** ist gemein.
   4 **Kizzi** ist superintelligent.
   5 **Sisi** ist cool.
   6 **Hermann** ist kräftig.

2 1 Hermann kann springen.
   2 Sisi kann fliegen.
   3 Minnie kann lesen.
   4 Kizzi kann Italienisch sprechen.
   5 Millie kann Fahrrad fahren.
   6 Moto kann laufen.

3 Günther the goldfish is my favourite animal. He is one year old. He is very funny and strong, but also quite sweet. He can swim, jump and also dance in the aquarium! Günther also has a friend: he is very cool and smart.

3 Meine Familie (Pupil Book pp. 34–35)

Familie und Tiere – **KAPITEL**

Learning objectives
- Talking about family members and age
- More practice of present tense verbs

Programme of Study
GV1 Tenses (present)
GV3 Opinions and discussions
LC8 Translation into German

FCSE links
Unit 1 – Relationships, Family and Friends (Family/friends)

Grammar
The regular verb *wohnen*
Ways of saying 'you'

PLTS
T Team workers

Key Language
Numbers 20–100
Hast du Geschwister?
Das ist die Familie …
meine Mutter
mein Vater
meine Eltern
meine Großeltern
Die … Personen wohnen in …
Er wohnt in …
Meine Großeltern wohnen mit uns zusammen.
Es gibt … Personen in meiner Familie.
Ich habe eine Schwester/zwei Brüder/einen Bruder/zwei Schwestern.
keine Geschwister
ein Einzelkind

Resources
Audio files:
30_Kapitel2_Einheit3_Aufgabe1
31_Kapitel2_Einheit3_Aufgabe2
32_Kapitel2_Einheit3_Aufgabe3
33_Kapitel2_Einheit3_Aufgabe5
34_Kapitel2_Einheit3_Aufgabe7
Workbooks:
Übungsheft 1 A&B, page 16
ActiveTeach:
Starter 1 resource
Starter 2 resource
p.034 Flashcards
p.035 Flashcards (1)
p.035 Flashcards (2)
Plenary resource
ActiveLearn:
Listening A, Listening B
Reading A, Reading B
Grammar, Vocabulary

Starter 1

Aim

To introduce the numbers above 20.

Pupils match the written numbers to the numerals and then check they have the right answers using the pupil book (Starter 1 resource).

1 Hör zu und wiederhole. (Listening L1)

Listening. Pupils listen to the audio and repeat the numbers that they hear. For more practice, point randomly at numbers in the illustration for the pupils to identify.

Audioscript
- zwanzig, zwanzig
- dreißig, dreißig
- vierzig, vierzig
- zwanzig, dreißig, vierzig
- fünfzig, fünfzig
- sechzig, sechzig
- siebzig, siebzig
- fünfzig, sechzig, siebzig
- achtzig, achtzig
- neunzig, neunzig
- hundert, hundert
- achtzig, neunzig, hundert

2 Hör zu und wiederhole. (Listening L1)

Listening. Pupils listen to the audio and repeat the numbers that they hear.

Audioscript
- einundzwanzig
- zweiundzwanzig
- dreiundzwanzig
- fünfunddreißig
- dreiundvierzig
- achtundfünfzig
- siebenundsechzig
- neunundsiebzig
- sechsundachtzig
- vierundneunzig

3 Hör zu. Welche Zahl ist das? (a–f) (Listening L1)

Listening. Pupils should look at pairs of numbers and sound them out to themselves. Then they listen to the audio and decide which of a choice of two numbers they hear.

Audioscript
- a – siebenunddreißig
- b – vierundsechzig
- c – siebenundachtzig

© Pearson Education Ltd 2013. Copying permitted for purchasing institution only. This material is not copyright free.

Meine Familie | **Familie und Tiere –** KAPITEL 2

- d – dreiundsechzig
- e – neunzig
- f – fünfzig

Answers

a 37 b 64 c 87 d 63 e 90 f 50

4 Gruppenarbeit. Rate mal: Wie alt sind sie? Was denkst du? (Speaking L2)

Speaking. Working in small groups, pupils discuss among themselves how old they think that the people in the illustrations are. They check their ideas by listening to the audio in exercise 5.

Some vocabulary is glossed for support. The *Tip* box gives some colloquial vocabulary to make group talk livelier.

5 Hör zu und überprüfe. (1–4) (Listening L2)

Listening. Pupils check their work from exercise 4.

Audioscript

1 – *Wie alt sind Sie?*
– *Ich bin achtundzwanzig Jahre alt und ich komme aus Berlin.*
2 – *Hallo, ich heiße Richard und ich bin fünfundvierzig Jahre alt.*
3 – *Guten Tag, ich heiße Beate. Ich bin dreiundfünfzig Jahre alt und ich komme aus der Schweiz. Meine Familie wohnt in Zürich.*
4 – *Wie alt sind Sie, Herr Steppat?*
– *Wie alt ich bin? Ich bin sehr alt! Ich bin siebenundachtzig Jahre alt. Gut, nicht?*
– *Siebenundachtzig – ja, das ist toll.*

Answers

1 28 2 45 3 53 4 87

Extension

Pupils note down any other details about the speakers. They could also say what they think the people are like – leave it to their imagination.

6 Sieh dir die Bilder an und lies. (Reading L3)

Reading. Pupils look at the photos and read the texts.

Some vocabulary is glossed for support.

7 Hör zu. Welche Familie ist das? (1–5) (Listening L3)

Listening. Pupils listen to the audio again and decide which of the two families each person is from.

Audioscript

1 – *Hast du Geschwister?*
– *Ja, ich habe einen Bruder und zwei Schwestern.*
2 – *Und du, hast du Geschwister?*
– *Oh ja, ich habe eine Schwester und zwei Brüder. Das finde ich furchtbar!*
3 – *Hast du Geschwister?*
– *Nein, ich bin Einzelkind.*
4 – *Wie viele Personen gibt es in deiner Familie?*
– *Es gibt sechs Personen in meiner Familie: meine Mutter, meinen Vater, meine zwei Brüder, meine Schwester … und mich!*
5 – *Es gibt fünf Personen in meiner Familie.*
– *Du hast also Geschwister.*
– *Nein, ich habe keine Geschwister, aber meine Großeltern wohnen mit uns zusammen.*

Answers

1 A (die Familie Sennhauser) 2 A (die Familie Sennhauser) 3 B (die Familie Oberheim) 4 A (die Familie Sennhauser) 5 B (die Familie Oberheim)

Extension

Pupils identify names of speaker for each part of the recording.

8 Wie heißt das auf Deutsch? (Writing L3)

Writing. Pupils write down the German translation of the English sentences.

The *Tip* box gives the vocabulary for stepbrother and half-sister, and encourages pupils to think how they could adapt this information to make other nouns they might need.

Answers

1 Ich habe einen Bruder und eine Schwester.
2 Ich habe vier Schwestern und zwei Brüder.
3 Ich bin Einzelkind.

© Pearson Education Ltd 2013. Copying permitted for purchasing institution only. This material is not copyright free.

Meine Familie | **Familie und Tiere –** KAPITEL

4 Hast du Geschwister?
5 Es gibt drei Personen in meiner Familie.
6 Ich habe eine Stiefschwester und einen Halbbruder.

Starter 2
Aim
To revise the verb *wohnen*.

Pupils build the verb and match the German phrases to the English phrases. A grid containing the full paradigm of *wohnen* separated into pronoun and verb, and a translation is cut up and pupils match the components (Starter 2 resource). They then compare with their partner before the exercise is corrected with the class. The activity could be timed with merits awarded for the first pupil to correctly match all the components.

Alternative starter 2
Use ActiveTeach p.035 Flashcards to review and practise language for family members.

Grammatik
Use the *Grammatik* box to look at regular verbs. The full present paradigm of the regular verb *wohnen* (to live) is presented here.

There is more information and practice on regular verbs in the grammar unit on pupil book p. 44.

There is also an opportunity to look at the three different ways of saying 'you' in German: *du*, *ihr* and *Sie*.

9 Partnerarbeit. Wähl eine Person aus Aufgabe 6. Beantworte Fragen.
(Speaking L4)

Speaking. Working in pairs, pupils take it in turns to choose a person from exercise 6. Their partner asks questions until they successfully identify the person in question.

10 Schreib ein paar Sätze über deine Familie. (Writing L3–4)

Writing. Pupils write a few sentences about their family.

Plenary
Aim
For pupils to establish whether they have met the lesson objective of using all the parts of present tense verbs.

Pupils play a game of snakes and ladders using a home-made verb dice (Plenary resource). Pupils throw the dice and move according to the number of points for each pronoun (see below). If pupils make their own dice, they can re-use these in subsequent lessons and take them home for extra practice.

Ich = 1 point
Du = 2 points
Er = 3 points
Wir = 4 points
Ihr = 5 points
Sie = 6 points

Workbook A, page 16

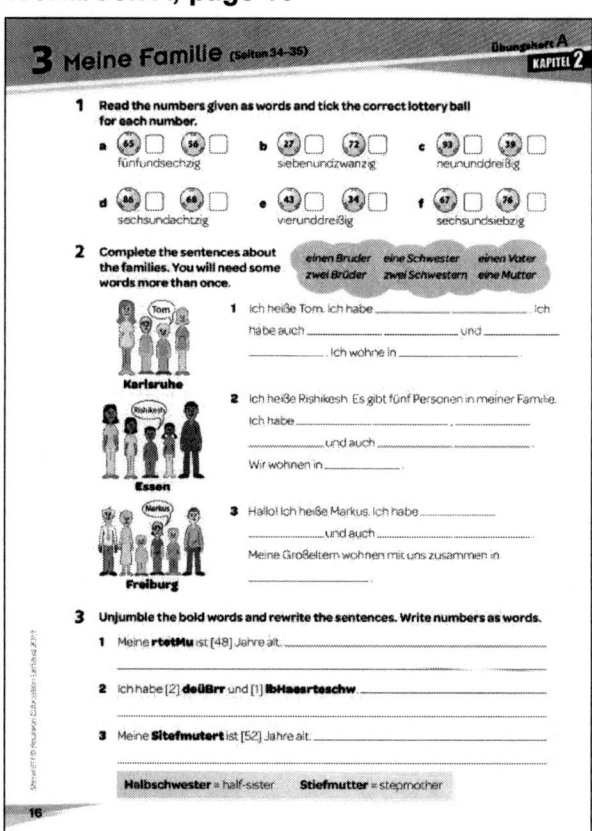

Answers
1 a 65 b 27 c 39 d 86 e 34 f 76
2 1 Ich heiße Tom. Ich habe **eine Mutter**. Ich habe auch **einen Bruder** und **eine Schwester**. Ich wohne in **Karlsruhe**.
2 Ich heiße Rishikesh. Es gibt fünf Personen

© Pearson Education Ltd 2013. Copying permitted for purchasing institution only. This material is not copyright free.

Meine Familie | **Familie und Tiere** – KAPITEL 2

in meiner Familie. Ich habe **eine Mutter**, **einen Vater** und auch **zwei Schwestern**. Wir wohnen in **Essen**.

3 Hallo! Ich heiße Markus. Ich habe **einen Vater** und auch **zwei Brüder**. Meine Großeltern wohnen mit uns zusammen in **Freiburg**.

3 1 Meine Mutter ist achtundvierzig Jahre alt.

2 Ich habe zwei Brüder und eine Halbschwester.

3 Meine Stiefmutter ist zweiundfünfzig Jahre alt.

23 – dreiundzwanzig

2 Ich heiße Tom. Ich bin vierzehn Jahre alt. Es gibt vier Personen in meiner Familie. Meine Mutter ist **zweiundvierzig** Jahre alt. Ich habe einen Bruder. **Er** ist **fünf** Jahre alt. Ich habe eine Schwester. **Sie** ist **sieben** Jahre alt. Wir wohnen in **Oban**.

Ich heiße Katja. Ich bin zwölf Jahre alt. Es gibt fünf Personen in meiner Familie. Ich habe einen Vater. Er ist siebenundvierzig Jahre alt. Meine Mutter ist einundfünfzig Jahre alt. Ich habe einen Bruder. Er ist neunzehn Jahre alt. Ich habe eine Schwester. Sie ist zehn Jahre alt. Wir wohnen in Köln.

3 Pupils' own answers.

Workbook B, page 16

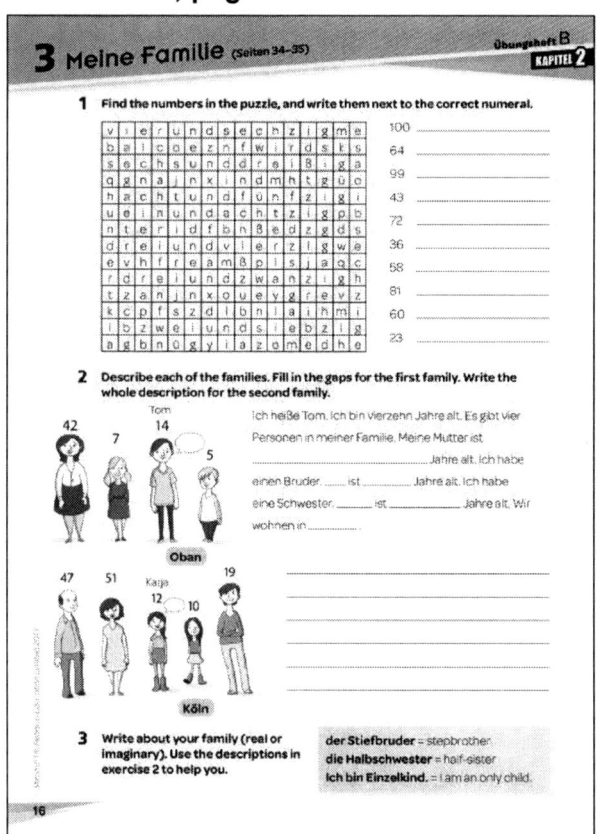

Answers

1 100 – hundert

64 – vierundsechzig

99 – neunundneunzig

43 – dreiundvierzig

72 – zweiundsiebzig

36 – sechsunddreißig

58 – achtundfünfzig

81 – einundachtzig

60 – sechzig

© Pearson Education Ltd 2013. Copying permitted for purchasing institution only. This material is not copyright free.

Familie und Tiere – KAPITEL

4 Die Farben der Welt (Pupil Book pp. 36–37)

Learning objectives	Key Language	Resources
• Describing family members • Using adjectives with nouns **Programme of Study** **GV4** Accuracy (grammar) **LC4** Expressing ideas (writing) **LC6** Translation into English **FCSE links** Unit 1 – Relationships, Family and Friends (Personal details about family, Descriptions) **Grammar** Adjectival agreement Full paradigm of irregular verb *haben* **PLTS** **R** Reflective learners	schwarz weiß grau braun rot orange gelb grün blau indigoblau violett lila rosa schwarze/braune/blonde/rote Haare lange/kurze/mittellange Haare blaue/braune/grüne/graue Augen	**Audio files:** 35_Kapitel2_Einheit4_Aufgabe1 36_Kapitel2_Einheit4_Aufgabe2 **Workbooks:** Übungsheft 1 A&B, page 17 **ActiveTeach:** Starter 1 resource p.036 Flashcards p.037 Extension reading activity p.037 Grammar presentation p.037 Video: Episode 3 p.037 Extension worksheet p.037 Grammar worksheet **ActiveLearn:** Listening A, Listening B Reading A, Reading B Grammar, Vocabulary

Starter 1

Aim

To review numbers 20–100.

Pupils play a game of bingo in groups of four, with one pupil as the caller and the other three pupils as the players. This could be played a number of times to give each pupil an opportunity to be the caller. Alternatively, the caller could be given the role as an extension task. Use different numbers to target numbers the class finds most challenging.

Caller cards and player cards (Starter 1 resource) can be laminated for future use. Pupils can cross off numbers with a whiteboard pen.

Pupils could also play the verb snakes and ladders game from unit 3.

1 Hör zu, lies und sing mit.
(Listening L1)

Listening. Pupils listen to the audio, read the text and sing along.

Also go through the colours on the umbrella illustration and check pronunciation – pupils should try pronouncing them first.

Alternatively, this could be performed as a rap, possibly as a 'chain rap' which goes round the class, each pupil saying a word in turn and as fast as possible.

Some vocabulary is glossed for support.

Another useful song can be found in various versions online:

„Grün, grün, grün sind alle meine Kleider."

Audioscript

- *Das Regenbogenlied*
- *Rot, orange, gelb, grün, blau, indigoblau, violett.*
- *Rot, orange, gelb, grün, blau, indigoblau, violett.*
- *Regenbogen hier,*
- *Regenbogen da;*
- *hier bunt, da bunt,*
- *überall bunt, bunt.*
- *Rot, orange, gelb, grün, blau, indigoblau, violett*

2 Hör zu. Wer ist das? (1–5)
(Listening L2)

Listening. Pupils listen to the audio and work out who is who by listening to the description and matching it to the illustration.

Audioscript

1 – *Diese Person hat mittellange rote Haare und grüne Augen.*
2 – *Diese Person hat kurze braune Haare und graue Augen.*
3 – *Diese Person hat braune Augen und lange schwarze Haare.*

© Pearson Education Ltd 2013. Copying permitted for purchasing institution only. This material is not copyright free.

Die Farben der Welt | Familie und Tiere – **KAPITEL 2**

4 – *Diese Person hat kurze blonde Haare und blaue Augen.*
5 – *Diese Person hat braune Augen und lange grüne, blaue und blonde Haare.*

Answers
1 *Sophia* 2 Jonas 3 Laura 4 Tobias
5 Vanessa

Grammatik

Use the *Grammatik* box to introduce the idea that adjectives change their spelling according to the nouns that they describe. For hair and eyes, adjectives need to add an *–e*.

3 Partnerarbeit. Wer ist das? Stell und beantworte Fragen. (Speaking L3)

Speaking. Working in pairs, pupils take it in turns to ask and answer questions about the people illustrated in exercise 2 (or about other pupils).

Starter 2

Aim

To review descriptions of hairstyle and colour and eye colour.

Pupils play a game of guess who. This can be played in pairs, in groups of four or as a whole class. A pupil chooses a picture and their partner/group members/the class have to guess who they have chosen by asking questions with yes/no answers. Pictures of celebrities or generic pictures with a variety of combinations of hairstyle and colour and eye colour could be used.

Alternative starter 2

Use ActiveTeach p.036 Flashcards to review and practise language for describing hair and eyes.

4 Lies den Text. Schreib die Sätze ab und korrigiere sie. (Reading L4)

Reading. Pupils read Markus' description of himself and his family. They then write out the statements and correct them.

Some vocabulary is glossed for support. A *Tip* box encourages pupils to expand their vocabulary of colours by adding *hell-* and *dunkel-* to the basic colour word.

It also encourages pupils to look at the context of an (unknown) word to help them work out for themselves the meaning.

Answers
1 Markus hat **blaue** Augen.
2 Finn hat **blonde** Haare.
3 Elena ist **klein**.
4 Sabine ist **zweiundvierzig** Jahre alt.
5 Oma und Opa haben **graue** Haare.
6 Bono ist **dunkelbraun**.

Extension

An alternative version of this exercise is provided on ActiveTeach (p.037 Extension reading activity, Reading L4). The text is different and the questions follow a different format. Some vocabulary is glossed for support.

Answers
1 Sie kommt/kommen aus Stuttgart/Südwestdeutschland.
2 Finn ist 13 Jahre alt.
3 Finn ist lustig.
4 Sie heißen Sabine und Ralf.
5 Oma und Opa/Sie wohnen in München.
6 Oma/Sie kann Flöte spielen.
7 Opa ist süß.
8 Er heißt Bono.

5 Finde die Paare und übersetze sie ins Englische. (Reading L3)

Reading. Pupils match the sentence halves and then translate the complete sentence into English.

Answers
1 d – *We have brown eyes.*
2 f – I have short hair.
3 a – Do you have light blue eyes?
4 e – He has grey eyes and hair.
5 b – My mother has red hair.
6 c – My sisters have long hair.

Grammatik

Use the *Grammatik* box to introduce the irregular verb *haben*. There is more information and practice on *haben* in the grammar unit on pupil book p. 45.

© Pearson Education Ltd 2013. Copying permitted for purchasing institution only. This material is not copyright free.

Die Farben der Welt | Familie und Tiere – KAPITEL

6 Beschreib dich und zwei Familienmitglieder. (Writing L3–4)

Writing. Pupils describe themselves and two members of their family as fully as they can.

Remind pupils to include as much information as possible, such as name, age, hair, eyes, size and personality using all that they have learned, and to use connectives and qualifiers to make their writing more fluent.

This activity is a good opportunity for peer assessment.

Plenary

Aim

For pupils to establish whether they have met the lesson objective of describing family members.

Pupils work in pairs and take it in turns to choose a family without telling their partner which they have chosen. They then describe the various family members and their partner has to guess which family they have chosen. The partner then gives feedback on their spoken work and sets them a target for improvement.

Award one, two or three stars for each of these categories:

- Names
- Ages
- Describing hairstyle and colour
- Describing eye colour
- Size
- Personalities
- Sounding German
- Speaking without hesitation

Alternative plenary

Use ActiveTeach p.036 Class Game to review language for describing hair and eyes.

Workbook A, page 17

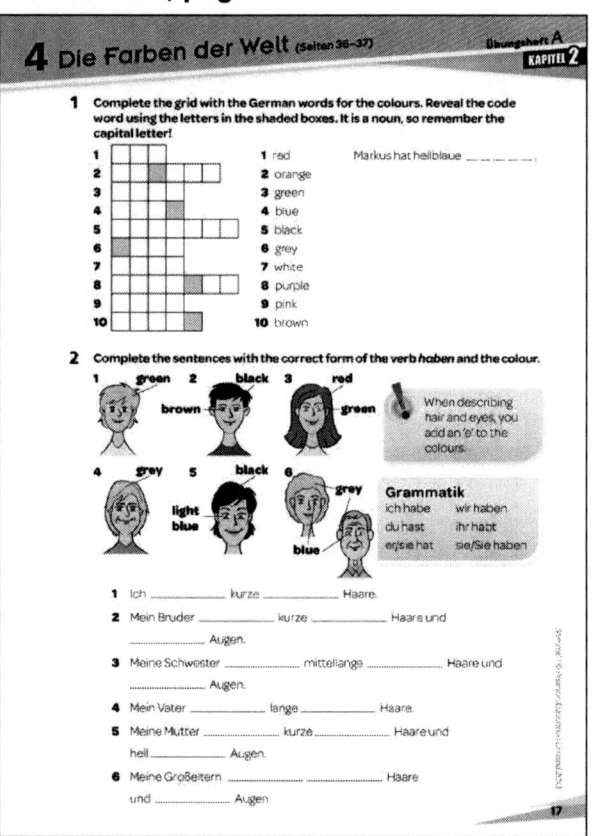

Answers

1 1 rot 2 orange 3 grün 4 blau 5 schwarz 6 grau 7 weiß 8 violett 9 rosa 10 braun

Markus hat hellblaue **Augen**.

2 1 Ich **habe** kurze **grüne** Haare.

2 Mein Bruder **hat** kurze **schwarze** Haare und **braune** Augen.

3 Meine Schwester **hat** mittellange **rote** Haare und **grüne** Augen.

4 Mein Vater **hat** lange **graue** Haare.

5 Meine Mutter **hat** kurze **schwarze** Haare und **hellblaue** Augen.

6 Meine Großeltern **haben graue** Haare und **blaue** Augen.

© Pearson Education Ltd 2013. Copying permitted for purchasing institution only. This material is not copyright free.

Die Farben der Welt | Familie und Tiere – **KAPITEL 2**

Workbook B, page 17

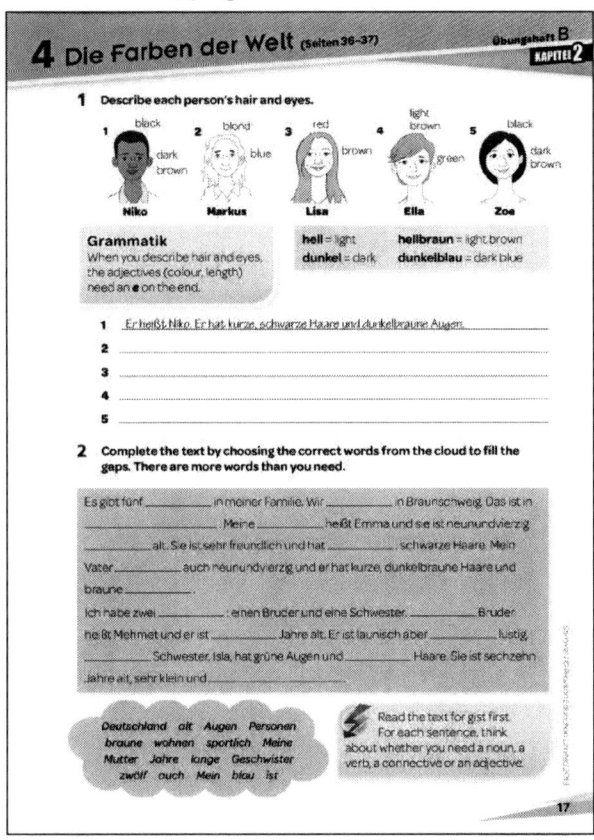

Answers

1 1 Er heißt Niko. Er hat kurze, schwarze Haare und dunkelbraune Augen.
2 Er heißt Markus. Er hat lange, blonde Haare und blaue Augen.
3 Sie heißt Lisa. Sie hat lange, rote Haare und braune Augen.
4 Sie heißt Ella. Sie hat kurze, hellbraune Haare und grüne Augen.
5 Sie heißt Zoe. Sie hat mittellange, schwarze Haare und dunkelbraune Augen.

2 Es gibt fünf Personen in meiner Familie. Wir **wohnen** in Braunschweig. Das ist in **Deutschland**. Meine **Mutter** heißt Emma und sie ist neunundvierzig **Jahre** alt. Sie ist sehr freundlich und hat **lange**, schwarze Haare. Mein Vater **ist** auch neunundvierzig und **er** hat kurze, dunkelbraune Haare und braune **Augen**. Ich habe zwei **Geschwister**: einen Bruder und eine Schwester. **Mein** Bruder heißt Mehmet und er ist **zwölf** Jahre alt. Er ist launisch aber **auch** lustig. **Meine** Schwester, Isla, hat grüne Augen und **braune** Haare. Sie ist sechzehn Jahre alt, sehr klein und **sportlich**.

Worksheet 1

Grammar: Verbs

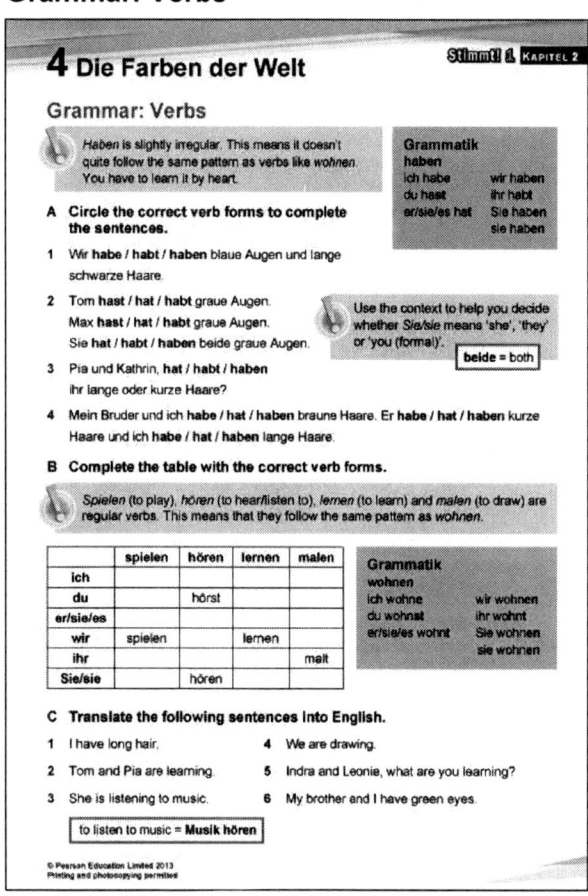

Answers

A 1 Wir haben blaue Augen und lange schwarze Haare.
2 Tom hat graue Augen. Max hat graue Augen. Sie haben beide graue Augen.
3 Pia und Kathrin, habt ihr lange oder kurze Haare?
4 Mein Bruder und ich haben braune Haare. Er hat kurze Haare und ich habe lange Haare.

B ich: spiele, höre, lerne, male
du: spielst, hörst, lernst, malst
er/sie/es: spielt, hört, lernt, malt
wir: spielen, hören, lernen, malen
ihr: spielt, hört, lernt, malt
Sie/sie: spielen, hören, lernen, malen

C 1 Ich habe lange Haare.
2 Tom und Pia lernen.
3 Sie hört Musik.
4 Wir malen.
5 Indra und Lenie, was lernt ihr?
6 Mein Bruder und ich haben grüne Augen.

© Pearson Education Ltd 2013. Copying permitted for purchasing institution only. This material is not copyright free.

Die Farben der Welt | Familie und Tiere – KAPITEL

Worksheet 2

Extension: Monster families

4 Die Farben der Welt Stimmt! 1 KAPITEL 2

Extension: Monster families

A Match each picture below to the correct text.

1. Mein Vater ist ein Monster. Er ist sehr groß, dick und blau. Er hat lange gelbe Zähne und einen grünen Spitzbart. Er ist musikalisch, intelligent und superfreundlich. Mein Vater spielt Fußball und Gitarre. Wir wohnen zusammen in einem Schloss.

2. Ich habe zwei Brüder. Sie heißen Frankenstein und Benjamin. Sie sind fünf Jahre alt und sie sind Zwillinge. Sie sind Monster. Sie sind lila und haben sehr lange Finger und rote Krallen. Sie haben blonde Haare. Wir haben einen Biber. Er heißt Justin.

3. Meine Mutter ist eine Hexe. Sie heißt Athelberta. Sie ist klein und schlank. Sie hat lange hellblaue Haare und grüne Augen. Sie kann fliegen und tanzen. Sie hat eine Schnee-Eule. Meine Mutter hat einen Zauberstab und sie spielt Flöte – sie hat eine Zauberflöte.

a = ___ b = ___ c = ___

B Use the pictures and the vocabulary you already know to work out the meanings of these new words from the texts.

Deutsch	Englisch
Zähne	
Schloss	
Zwillinge	
Finger	
Krallen	
Hexe	
Zauberstab	

German uses a lot of compound nouns. These are nouns made up of more than one word. You can break these compound nouns down to work out what they mean. E.g. you already know that *Flöte* means flute. You can work out from the picture that *Zauber* must mean magic, therefore *Zauberflöte* = magic flute. You should now be able to use this knowledge, along with the picture, to work out the meaning of *Zauberstab*.

C Draw and describe a monster family and their pets. Try to use some of the new vocabulary you have learnt in your descriptions. Can you include a compound word using *Zauber*?

© Pearson Education Limited 2013
Printing and photocopying permitted

Answers

A a 2 b 1 c 3

B Zähne, teeth

Schloss, castle

Zwillinge, twins

Finger, fingers

Krallen, claws

Hexe, witch

Zauberstab, magic wand

Video

Episode 3

Katharina and Alwin are looking at family photos, and using them to describe their own families and their friends' families.

Answers

A Before watching

Answers will vary.

B Watch

1. a) Alwin has a brother and a sister.
   b) Mesut has a brother.
   c) Leoni has two brothers and two sisters.
   d) Audrey has no brothers and sisters.
   e) Katharina has a brother.

2 Match the person to their pet.

Leoni – Minnie the cat

Katharina – Charlie the dog

Alwin – No pet

C Watch again

1 True or false?

a) false b) true c) false d) true e) false

2 Felix's grandmother has unusual hair.

D Discuss with your partner

1 Today we are talking about families.

2 She gets mixed up about which photo is Mesut's family and which is Benno's family.

3 Really?

4 She gets mixed up about which girl is an only child, Leoni or Audrey.

5 No. Their body language at the end suggests that they think it was a disaster, and Alwin says, "Oh man, we didn't do that very well!"

6 Pupils' own answers.

© Pearson Education Ltd 2013. Copying permitted for purchasing institution only. This material is not copyright free.

Familie und Tiere – KAPITEL 2

5 Alles Gute! (Pupil Book pp. 38–39)

Learning objectives	Key Language	Cross-curricular
• Talking about birthdays • Using ordinal numbers (first, twentieth, and so on) **Programme of Study** **GV2** Grammatical structures (ordinal numbers) **LC4** Expressing ideas (writing) **LC5** Accurate pronunciation and intonation **FCSE links** Unit 1 – Relationships, Family and Friends (Family celebrations) Unit 8 – Celebrations (Birthdays) **Grammar** Ordinal numbers (saying when someone's birthday is) **PLTS** C Creative thinkers	Januar Februar März April Mai Juni Juli August September Oktober November Dezember Ich habe am …(s)ten … Geburtstag. Ich habe (heute) Geburtstag.	**Mathematics:** dates and months and ordinal numbers **Resources** **Audio files:** 37_Kapitel2_Einheit5_Aufgabe2 38_Kapitel2_Einheit5_Aufgabe4 39_Kapitel2_Einheit5_Aufgabe5 40_Kapitel2_Einheit5_Aufgabe7 **Workbooks:** Übungsheft 1 A&B, page 18 **ActiveTeach:** Starter 2 resource p.039 Video: Episode 4 Plenary resource **ActiveLearn:** Listening A, Listening B Reading A, Reading B Grammar, Vocabulary

Starter 1

Aim

To introduce the months.

Use a set of A4 cards with dates written on them. Eight pupils are each given a card and asked to stand at the front of the class and put themselves into chronological order. Continue to choose different sets of eight pupils until every pupil has had an opportunity to play the game. Pupils could then be asked to reflect on the similarities and differences between the months in German and English and how dates are presented.

1 Sieh dir die Kalender an. Wie spricht man die Monate aus? Versuch es mal. (Reading L2)

Reading. Pupils look at the calendar in the pupil book and have a go at pronouncing the months in German. Draw their attention to the *Tip* box for help with this.

The *Tip* box reminds pupils that cognates (words that look the same as their English equivalent) sound different in German pronunciation. Pupils can use what they already know of German to predict how a word should be pronounced.

2 Hör zu und überprüfe. (Listening L2)

Listening. Pupils listen to the audio to check how to pronounce the months in German.

Audioscript

– *Januar, Februar, März,*
– *April, Mai, Juni,*
– *Juli, August, September,*
– *Oktober, November, Dezember.*

3 Wann haben sie Geburtstag? Finde die Paare. (Reading L2)

Reading. Pupils match the text to the illustrations.

You could create a wall display of birthdays: *Alex hat am 11. Januar Geburtstag*, etc.

Answers
1 d 2 e 3 f 4 c 5 b 6 a

4 Hör zu. Wähl das richtige Datum aus. (1–8) (Listening L3)

Listening. Pupils listen to the audio and match the dates to the audio.

Refer pupils to the *Tip* box for extra help on how to listen for the date.

Audioscript

1 – *Wann hast du Geburtstag?*
  – *Ich habe am 19. September Geburtstag.*
2 – *Hallo, Katja. Wann hast du Geburtstag?*
  – *Am 15. Juni. Ich habe am 15. Juni Geburtstag.*

© Pearson Education Ltd 2013. Copying permitted for purchasing institution only. This material is not copyright free.

Alles Gute! | Familie und Tiere – KAPITEL

3 – *Wann hat dein Bruder Geburtstag?*
   – *Mein Bruder hat am 3. März Geburtstag.*
4 – *Felix, wann hast du Geburtstag?*
   – *Ich habe am 31. Juli Geburtstag.*
5 – *Und wann hat deine Schwester Geburtstag?*
   – *Sie hat am 29. Februar Geburtstag.*
   – *Am 29. Februar – das ist nur alle vier Jahre!*
6 – *Du bist 13 Jahre alt, ja?*
   – *Ja, richtig.*
   – *Wann hast du Geburtstag?*
   – *Ich habe am 1. August Geburtstag.*
7 – *Und dein Bruder, wann hat er Geburtstag?*
   – *Er hat am Heiligabend Geburtstag, also am 24. Dezember.*
8 – *Nicole, wann hast du Geburtstag?*
   – *Im November. Ich habe am 7. November Geburtstag. Ich bin jetzt 15 Jahre alt.*

Answers
1 e 2 d 3 b 4 h 5 g 6 a 7 f 8 c

Starter 2

Aim
To review saying when your birthday is.

Pupils conduct a survey in the class to find out when most pupils were born; which is the most popular month for birthdays, for example? They use the grid to keep a tally chart (Starter 2 resource).

Grammatik
The *Grammatik* box reminds pupils that ordinal numbers (first, second, third, etc.) are used to talk about dates. It shows pupils how to create them in German.

5 Hör zu und sprich nach. (Listening L2)
Listening. Pupils listen to German ways of saying Happy Birthday.

Audioscript
– *Ich habe heute Geburtstag!!*
– *Alles Gute zum Geburtstag!*
– *Herzlichen Glückwunsch!*
– *Zum Geburtstag viel Glück!*

6 Wann haben deine Familie und Freunde Geburtstag? Schreib mindestens vier Geburtstage auf. (Writing L3)
Writing. Pupils write out in full the dates of four birthdays that they know of.

7 Sieh dir die Vampire an und hör zu. Schreib Steckbriefe für Bella, Onkel Einstein und Mondschein. (Listening L4)
Listening. Pupils listen to the audio and look at the illustrations of the vampire family. They then write profiles for three of the vampires.

Some vocabulary is glossed for support.

Audioscript
– *Hallo! Ich bin Vlad, ich bin ziemlich groß, freundlich und ich habe schwarze Haare. Ich wohne in Transsilvanien und ich habe am 13. November Geburtstag. Das ist heute! Ich bin 13 Jahre alt – ich habe viel Glück! Hier sind einige Fotos von meiner Geburtstagsparty. Da bin ich mit meinem Lieblingsessen: Blutorangen!*
– *Bella ist meine kleine Schwester. Sie ist nicht sehr groß, aber sie ist frech und sie hat kurze rote Haare. Sie hat am 11. Dezember Geburtstag. Sie ist 10 Jahre alt. Ach ja, sie hat ein Haustier, eine Fledermaus. Niedlich!*
– *Und das hier ist mein Onkel Einstein – er hat lange graue Haare, aber er ist nur 99 Jahre alt. Er hat am 14. März Geburtstag. Er ist lustig und sehr intelligent.*
– *Und zuletzt kommt meine Mutter. Sie heißt Mondschein und sie ist sehr freundlich. Sie ist 78 Jahre alt, mittelgroß, ziemlich dick und sie hat blaue Haare. Ihr Hund heißt Wolfgang. Er ist auch freundlich, aber doof!*
– *So, ... zurück zur Party!*

Answers
Name: *Bella*

Alles Gute! | Familie und Tiere – **KAPITEL 2**

Alter: *10*

Geburtstag: *11. Dezember*

Merkmale: *nicht sehr groß, frech, kurze rote Haare*

Haustier: *eine Fledermaus*

Name: *Onkel Einstein*

Alter: *99*

Geburtstag: *14. März*

Merkmale: *lustig, sehr intelligent, lange graue Haare*

Haustier: *–*

Name: *Mondschein (Mutter)*

Alter: *78*

Geburtstag: *–*

Merkmale: *mittelgroß, ziemlich dick, sehr freundlich, blaue Haare*

Haustier: *einen Hund (Wolfgang – freundlich, doof)*

8 Partnerarbeit. Sieh dir die Vampire und deine Steckbriefe an. Beschreib die Vampire. Dein Partner/Deine Partnerin schreibt alles auf. (Speaking L4)

Speaking. Working in pairs, pupils use the vampire illustrations and profiles that they have created to talk about the vampires. The partner transcribes the information given about the vampires.

This is a good opportunity for peer assessment – give some guidelines on what to listen for, etc.

Plenary

Aim

For pupils to establish whether they have met the lesson objectives of talking about birthdays and using ordinal numbers.

Pupils complete an information gap speaking activity (Plenary resource) in which they find out famous people's birthdays. Questions are asked as in the example:

Wann hat … Geburtstag? Er/Sie hat am … … Geburtstag.

Workbook A, page 18

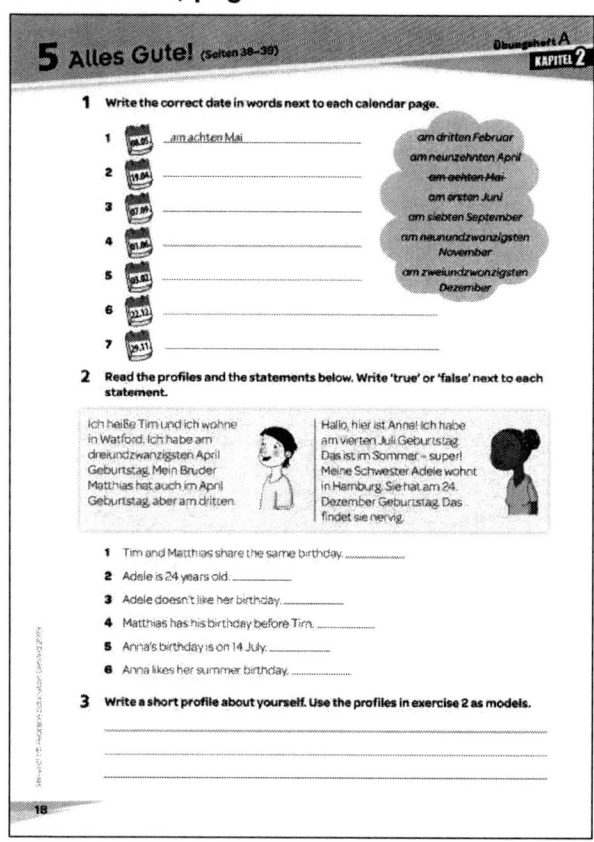

Answers

1
1 am achten Mai
2 am neunzehnten April
3 am siebten September
4 am ersten Juni
5 am dritten Februar
6 am zweiundzwanzigsten Dezember
7 am neunundzwanzigsten November

2
1 false
2 false
3 true
4 true
5 false
6 true

3 Pupils' own answers.

© Pearson Education Ltd 2013. Copying permitted for purchasing institution only. This material is not copyright free.

Alles Gute! | Familie und Tiere – KAPITEL

Workbook B, page 18

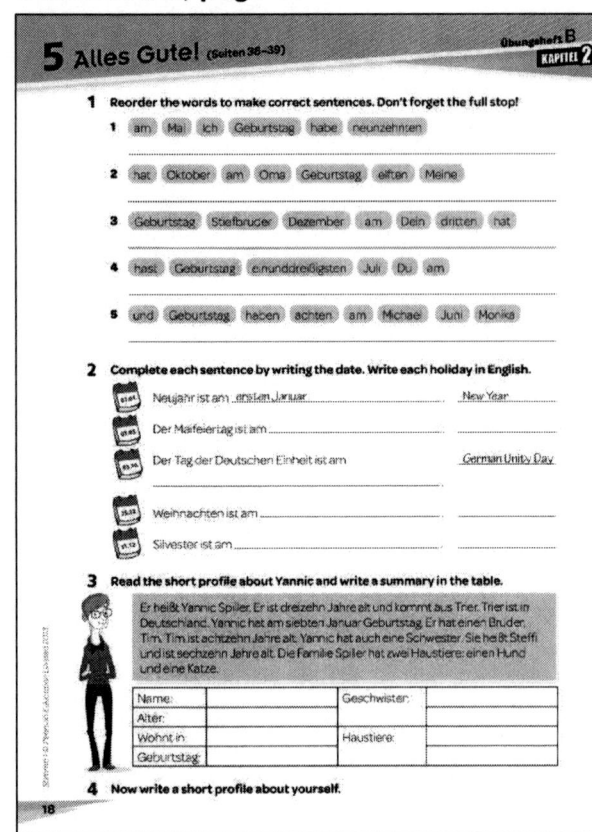

Answers

1
1 Ich habe am neunzehnten Mai Geburtstag.
2 Meine Oma hat am elften Oktober Geburtstag.
3 Dein Stiefbruder hat am dritten Dezember Geburtstag.
4 Du hast am einunddreißigsten Juli Geburtstag.
5 Monika und Michael (*or* Michael und Monika) haben am achten Juni Geburtstag.

2 Neujahr ist am **ersten Januar**. / New Year
Der Maifeiertag ist am **ersten Mai**. / May Day
Der Tag der deutschen Einheit ist am **dritten Oktober**. / German Unity Day
Weihnachten ist am **fünfundzwanzigsten Dezember**. / Christmas Day
Silvester ist am **einunddreißigsten Dezember**. / New Year's Eve

3 Name: Yannic Spiller
Alter: dreizehn
Wohnt in: Trier, Deutschland
Geburtstag: am siebten Januar
Geschwister: einen Bruder, Tim, 18; eine Schwester, Steffi, 16
Haustiere: einen Hund; eine Katze

4 Pupils' own answers.

Video

Episode 4

Leoni and Felix are at a petting zoo, where they meet some extraordinary animals!

Answers

A Before watching
Answers will vary.

B Watch
1 Animals mentioned are:
Hund, Goldfisch, Katze, Pferd, Kaninchen, Maus, Wellensittich, Schwein
2 freundlich; lustig
3 The budgie, Walter Wellensittich, and the dog, Theo Hund.

C Watch again
1 Placido (Pferd) – singing
Einstein (Kaninchen) – counting
Houdini (Maus) – knowing people's birthdays
Walter (Wellensittich) – flying
Theo (Hund) – playing football
Schnitzel (Schwein) – speaking
2 a) Leoni's dog is fat and lazy.
 b) Felix has a cat and a goldfish. He says his goldfish is sweet.
 c) Felix asks Leoni if her dog can sing.
3 May 24th

D Discuss with your partner
1 The goldfish, as he describes it as sweet but describes his cat as noisy, cheeky and mean.
2 Because Walter is a bird, so of course he can fly. It's not really a super-power.
3 She is saying, "Really?"
4 He says Felix is cheeky. Felix is surprised about this.
5 Pupils' own opinion.

Familie und Tiere – **KAPITEL 2**

6 Speaking Skills: Eine Superfamilie
(Pupil Book pp. 40–41)

Learning objectives
- Developing speaking skills
- Practising asking and answering questions

Programme of Study
GV2 Grammatical structures (question words)
LC1 Listening and responding
LC4 Expressing ideas (speaking)

FCSE links
Unit 1 – Relationships, Family and Friends (Descriptions)

Grammar
Question words

Key Language
No new key language. Pupils develop speaking skills using key language from the chapter.

PLTS
R Reflective learners

Cross-curricular
Art and design: drawing for description

Resources
Workbooks:
Übungsheft 1 A&B, page 19
ActiveTeach:
Starter 1 resource
Starter 2 resource
Plenary resource

Starter 1

Aim

To develop speaking skills.

Pupils play a board game (Starter 1 resource) using a dice, to practise giving information about their families. They use as much German as possible – anyone using English has to go back a space! For each square they land on, pupils must say a sentence about their family, using the given infinitive. Anyone who makes a mistake in their sentence must go back a space.

Key phrases include:
- *Jetzt bin ich dran.* It's my turn now.
- *Du schwindelst!* You're cheating.
- *Du bist dran.* It's your turn.
- *Das ist falsch.* That's not right.
- *Das ist richtig.* That's right.

This spread provides plenty scope for extended question and answer work by the teacher or in groups, leading up to a productive task that can vary in length and complexity depending on the ability of the pupil.

1 Partnerarbeit. Sieh dir die Superfamilie an. Stell und beantworte Fragen. (Speaking L2–3)

Speaking. Working in pairs, pupils look at the illustration of *Die Vergessbaren* and take it in turns to ask and answer the questions listed about the superfamily.

The *Tip* box notes that the plural of some German words is formed by simply adding –s.

Refer pupils to the skills feature to encourage them to expand upon their answers.

Questions can be asked in any order, but the numbers can be used to make a game out of this. Pupils shake two dice to decide which question to ask (2–8). To provide a bit of a competition element, if pupils get the answer right, they are awarded the same number of points as numbers on the dice. There is also some degree of peer assessment (you only get the points if you get the answer right).

Some vocabulary is glossed for support.

Grammatik
Use the *Grammatik* box to review German question words and to remind pupils that the verb goes after the question word.

2 Hier sind die Antworten. Was sind die Fragen? Finde die Paare und lies die Fragen und Antworten vor. (Reading L3)

Reading. Pupils match the questions to the answers, reading the pairs out loud when they have done so to practise pronunciation. This could be done as a class or pair work activity.

If necessary, point out the use of *machen* in questions with *was?* (*Was kann er/sie machen?*)

The skills feature reminds pupils to be sure that they understand the question words, and that the verb in a question and answer will often be the same.

Answers
1 d **2** e **3** h **4** j **5** b **6** i **7** g **8** a **9** f **10** c

3 Partnerarbeit. Deck diese Seite zu. Stell und beantworte Fragen. (Speaking L3–4)

© Pearson Education Ltd 2013. Copying permitted for purchasing institution only. This material is not copyright free.

Eine Superfamilie | **Familie und Tiere** – KAPITEL

Speaking. Working in pairs, pupils cover up the page in the pupil book and take it in turns to ask and answer questions about the superfamily.

As preparation for this activity, ask pupils to make brief notes to remind themselves of the questions and answers, maybe two words per item:

1 Vater – Siegfried.

Pupils then display these notes as a reminder while doing exercise 3.

Alternatively (or as well) ActiveTeach could be used to display p. 40 as a reminder for pupils.

This could be done individually or as a class activity.

they've chosen by asking questions with yes/no answers. Pupils can ask up to five questions before guessing who has been chosen. If they can't guess, then the pupil who chose the profile wins a point. At the end of the game, the pupil with the most points is the winner.

Pupils use the peer-assessment format presented in the pupil book on p. 41, awarding each other stars according to the following categories:

- Pronunciation of *w, ö, ü, ei/ie*
- Speaking without hesitation
- originality/fun

Starter 2

Aim

To practise asking and answering questions about other people.

Using sets of cards in a jigsaw format (Starter 2 resource) pupils match the two halves of the questions and then find the correct answer.

4 Erfinde eine Superfamilie. Mal ein Bild und beantworte die Fragen der Klasse. (Speaking L4)

Speaking. Pupils invent and draw their own superfamily. This could be prepared as a homework exercise. Include a reference to websites where pupils can produce their own avatars, etc. as an alternative to drawing.

Scan in examples of pupils' work and use on an IWB for the class to base their questions on.

This activity provides an opportunity for peer assessment.

Refer pupils to the skills feature on talking about a topic. It will not only help with the preparation of their presentation, but also to cope with unfamiliar language and unexpected responses during questions from the class.

Plenary

Aim

For pupils to establish whether they have met the lesson objectives of developing speaking skills and asking and answering questions.

Pupils work in groups of four. They each have a worksheet with four profile pages from a social networking site (Plenary resource). The first pupil chooses one profile, without telling the other pupils which one they've chosen. The other three pupils have to guess which profile

Workbook A, page 19

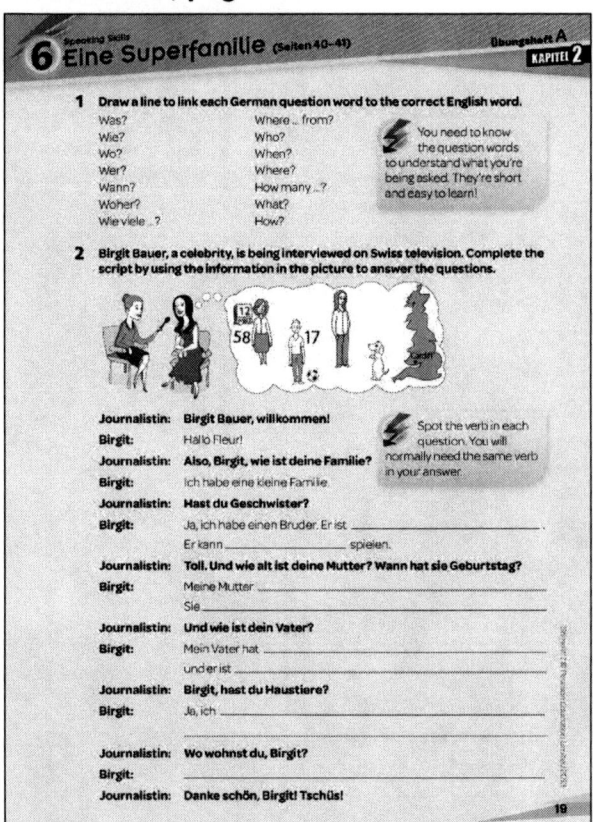

Answers

1 Was? – What?
  Wie? – How?
  Wo? – Where?
  Wer? – Who?
  Wann? – When?
  Woher? – Where … from?
  Wie viele …? – How many …?

2 Possible answers:
  – Er ist **siebzehn Jahre alt**. Er kann **Fußball** spielen.

© Pearson Education Ltd 2013. Copying permitted for purchasing institution only. This material is not copyright free.

– Meine Mutter ist **achtundfünfzig Jahre alt**.
Sie hat **am zwölften März Geburtstag**.

– Mein **Vater hat lange Haare** und er **ist total freundlich**.

– Ja, ich **habe einen Hund**.

– **Ich wohne in Cardiff. Das ist in Wales.**

2 Wie alt ist sie?
3 Wo wohnt sie?
4 Wie ist sie?
5 Wann hat sie Geburtstag?

4 Pupils' own answers.

Workbook B, page 19

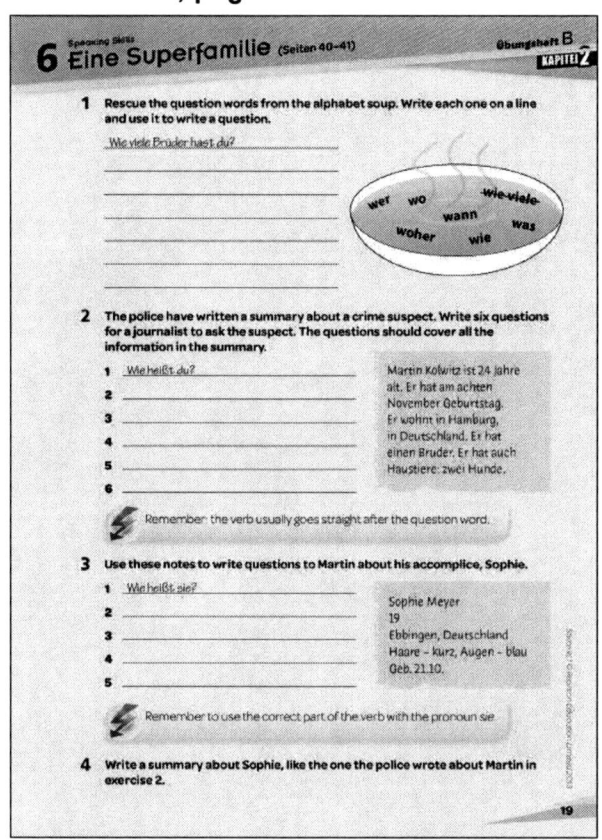

Answers

1 Possible answers:
  Wie viele Brüder hast du?
  Wann hast du Geburtstag?
  Wer ist das?
  Wo wohnst du?
  Woher kommst du?
  Wie heißt du?
  Was ist dein Lieblingssport?

2 1 Wie heißt du?
  2 Wie alt bist du?
  3 Wann hast du Geburtstag?
  4 Wo wohnst du?
  5 Hast du Geschwister?
  6 Hast du Haustiere?

3 1 Wie heißt sie?

Familie und Tiere – KAPITEL

Lernzieltest und Wiederholung (Pupil Book pp. 42–43)

Lernzieltest
Pupils use this checklist to review language covered in the chapter, working on it in pairs in class or on their own at home. There is a Word version on ActiveTeach which can be printed out and given to pupils. Encourage them to follow up any weakness they identify. There are Target Setting Sheets included in the Assessment Pack, and an opportunity for pupils to record their own levels and targets on the *Mein Fortschritt* page in the Workbooks. You can also use the *Lernzieltest* checklist as an end-of-chapter plenary option.

Wiederholung
These revision exercises can be used for assessment purposes or for pupils to practise before tackling the assessment tasks in the Assessment Pack.

Resources
Audio files:
41_Kapitel2_Wiederholung_Aufgabe1
Workbooks:
Übungsheft 1 A&B, pages 20–21
ActiveTeach:
p.042 Lernzieltest checklist
p.043 Exercise 1 grid

---

1 Hör zu. Schreib die Tabelle ab und füll sie aus. (1–6) (Listening L2)

Listening. Pupils listen to the audio and complete a copy of the table in their own books.

Audioscript

Wiederholung

1 – Hast du ein Haustier?
– Ja, ich habe eine Katze. Sie heißt Emma und sie ist schwarz.

2 – Wie heißt dein Kaninchen?
– Mein Kaninchen heißt Frodo. Es ist ziemlich klein und grau.

3 – Ich habe ein Pferd. Es ist braun und es ist sehr groß.
– Wie heißt dein Pferd?
– Es heißt Polo.

4 – Hast du ein Haustier?
– Ja, ich habe einen Hund. Er ist weiß … klein und weiß.

5 – Ich habe eine Schlange.
– Eine Schlange?!
– Ja, sie ist grün und rot.
– Grün und rot – super!

6 – Hast du ein Haustier?
– Ja, ich habe ein Meerschweinchen. Es ist süß.
– Und die Farbe?
– Es ist braun und weiß.

Answers
1 d, k
2 b, j
3 e, g
4 f, h
5 a, i&l
6 c, g&h

2 Partnerarbeit. Beschreib das Aussehen und den Charakter einer Person. Dein Partner/Deine Partnerin schreibt alles auf. (Speaking L2)

Speaking. In pairs, pupils take it in turns to describe the appearance and character of one of the three people in the illustration. The partner transcribes the information given about the appearance.

The *Tip* box reminds pupils to improve the quality of their speaking by saying as much as they can, by linking sentences using connectives, and by paying attention to the pronunciation, especially *ei/ie*, *z* and *ch*.

3 Lies die E-Mail. Finde die vier richtigen Sätze. (Reading L2)

Reading. Pupils read the text and work out which four of the eight sentences given below it are correct.

Answers
1, 5, 6, 7 are correct

© Pearson Education Ltd 2013. Copying permitted for purchasing institution only. This material is not copyright free.

Lernzieltest und Wiederholung | Familie und Tiere – **KAPITEL 2**

4 Schreib einige Sätze über deine Familie. (Writing L3–4)

Writing. Pupils write a few sentences about their family including:
- name
- age and birthday
- appearance
- character
- likes or dislikes
- pets.

The *Tip* box suggests that pupils can adapt another text – in this case the one in exercise 3 – to create their own original.

Workbook A, page 20

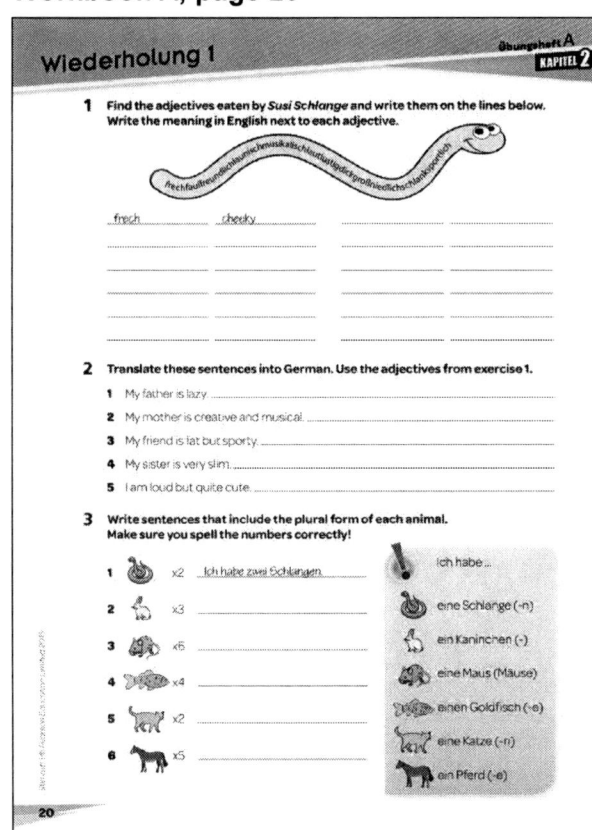

niedlich / cute
schlank / slim
sportlich / sporty

2 1 Mein Vater ist faul.
2 Meine Mutter ist kreativ und musikalisch.
3 Mein Freund ist dick aber sportlich.
4 Meine Schwester ist sehr schlank.
5 Ich bin laut aber ganz niedlich.

3 1 Ich habe zwei Schlangen.
2 Ich habe drei Kaninchen.
3 Ich habe sechs Mäuse.
4 Ich habe vier Goldfische.
5 Ich habe zwei Katzen.
6 Ich habe fünf Pferde.

Workbook B, page 20

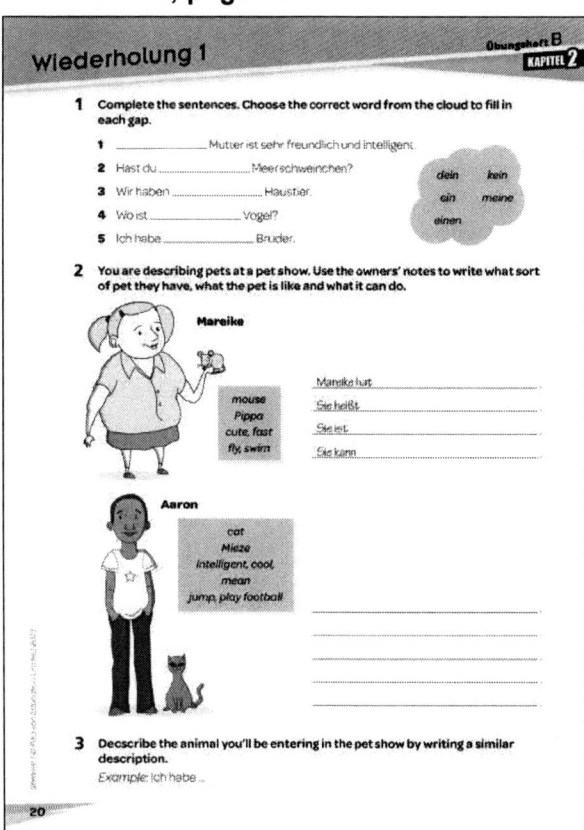

Answers

1 frech / cheeky
faul / lazy
freundlich / friendly
launisch / moody
musikalisch / musical
laut / loud
lustig / funny
dick / fat
groß / tall

Answers

1 1 Meine 2 ein 3 kein 4 dein 5 einen

2 Mareike hat eine Maus.
Sie heißt Pippa.
Sie ist niedlich und schnell.
Sie kann fliegen und schwimmen.
Aaron hat eine Katze.
Sie heißt Mieze.

© Pearson Education Ltd 2013. Copying permitted for purchasing institution only. This material is not copyright free.

Lernzieltest und Wiederholung | Familie und Tiere – KAPITEL

Sie ist intelligent, cool und gemein.
Sie kann springen und Fußball spielen.
3 Pupils' own answers.

4 Possible answers:
1 Mareike hat blaue Augen.
2 Hast du schwarze Haare?
3 Sie hat kurze Haare und braune Augen.

Workbook A, page 21

Workbook B, page 21

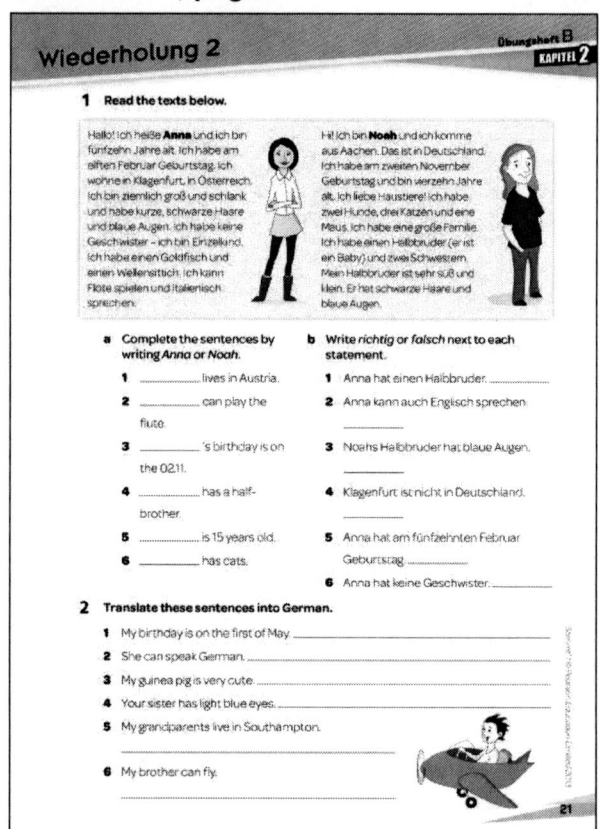

Answers
1 achtundzwanzig
   sechsundvierzig
   siebenundsechzig
   dreiundsiebzig
   neunundachtzig
2 1st – die erste Ameise
   3rd – die dritte Ameise
   5th – die fünfte Ameise
   10th – die zehnte Ameise
   18th – die achtzehnte Ameise
   21st – die einundzwanzigste Ameise
   25th – die fünfundzwanzigste Ameise
3 a blaue b schwarze c mittellange
   d braune e kurze

Answers
1 a 1 Anna 2 Anna 3 Noah 4 Noah 5 Anna
   6 Noah
  b 1 falsch 2 falsch 3 richtig 4 richtig
   5 falsch 6 richtig
2 1 Ich habe am ersten Mai Geburtstag.
  2 Sie kann Deutsch sprechen.
  3 Mein Meerschweinchen ist sehr niedlich.
  4 Deine Schwester hat hellblaue Augen.
  5 Meine Großeltern wohnen in Southampton.
  6 Mein Bruder kann fliegen.

Familie und Tiere – **KAPITEL 2**

Grammatik (Pupil Book pp. 44–45)

The *Stimmt!* Grammatik section provides a more detailed summary of key grammar covered in the chapter, along with further exercises to practise these points.

Grammar topics
Plural of nouns
The present tense – regular verbs
The present tense – *haben*
Modal verbs
Pronouns

Resources
Workbooks:
Übungsheft 1 A&B, page 22
ActiveTeach:
p.044 Grammar presentation

Plural of nouns

1 Write the plural of these nouns in full. (Writing L2)

Answers
1 Haustiere 2 Schwestern 3 Freunde 4 Handys 5 Mannschaften 6 Väter 7 Meerschweinchen 8 Wölfe

2 Say whether each noun is singular (S), plural (P) or could be either (S/P). (Reading L2)

Answers
1 P 2 P 3 S/P 4 S 5 P 6 S

The present tense – regular verbs

3 Write out each sentence using the correct form of *wohnen*. Think carefully about who or what is doing the action (the subject of the sentence). (Writing L2)

Answers
1 Wir **wohnen** in Braunschweig.
2 Wo **wohnst** du?
3 Ich **wohne** in Freiburg.
4 Mein Vater heißt Karl. Er **wohnt** nicht in Freiburg.
5 Meine Schwester **wohnt** auch in Freiburg.
6 Meine Großeltern **wohnen** in der Schweiz.

4 Which form of 'you' should you use when talking to each of these people? Write *du*, *ihr* or *Sie*. (Writing L2)

Answers
1 du 2 Sie 3 ihr 4 Sie 5 du 6 Sie

The present tense – *haben*

5 Match the pairs, then translate the sentences into English. (Reading L2)

Answers
1 c I have a dog.
2 e My friend has two cats.
3 a Do you have a pet?
4 f We don't have a rabbit.
5 b What do you have, Mr Schmidt?
6 d Does Marina have a snake?

Modal verbs

6 Translate into German. There are words in the box to help you. (Writing L3)

Answers
1 Er kann Wii spielen.
2 Du kannst schnell laufen.
3 Ich kann schwimmen.
4 Kannst du schwimmen?
5 Ich kann Fußball spielen.
6 Meine Schwester kann gut singen.

Pronouns

7 Fill in the correct pronoun. (Writing L2)

Answers
1 Er 2 Es 3 Sie 4 Sie 5 Er 6 Er

© Pearson Education Ltd 2013. Copying permitted for purchasing institution only. This material is not copyright free.

Workbook A, page 22

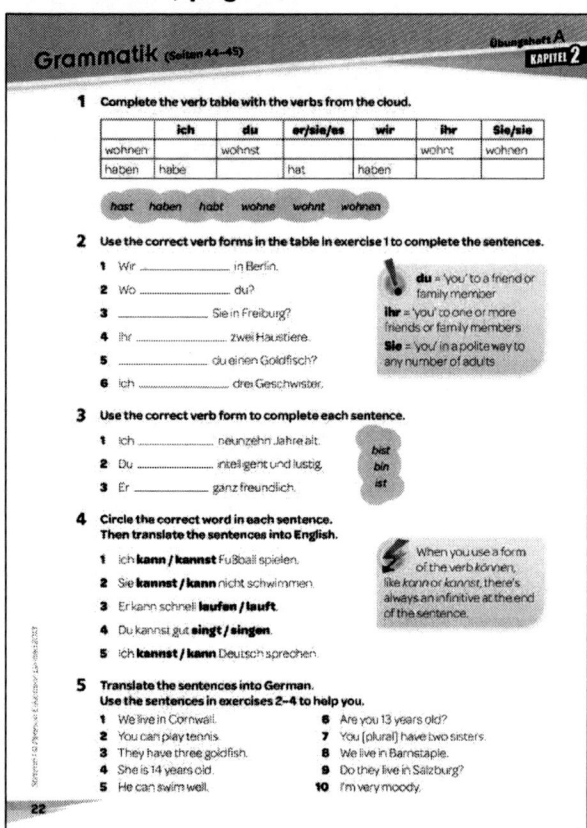

Answers

1 ich wohne; er/sie/es wohnt; wir wohnen
du hast; ihr habt; Sie/sie haben

2 1 wohnen 2 wohnst 3 Wohnen 4 habt
5 Hast 6 habe

3 1 bin 2 bist 3 ist

4 1 kann – I can play football.
2 kann – She can't swim.
3 laufen – He can run fast.
4 singen – You can sing well.
5 kann – I can speak German.

5 1 Wir wohnen in Cornwall.
2 Du kannst Tennis spielen.
3 Sie haben drei Goldfische.
4 Sie ist vierzehn Jahre alt.
5 Er kann gut schwimmen.
6 Bist du dreizehn Jahre alt?
7 Ihr habt zwei Schwestern.
8 Wir wohnen in Barnstaple.
9 Wohnen sie in Salzburg?
10 Ich bin sehr launisch.

Workbook B, page 22

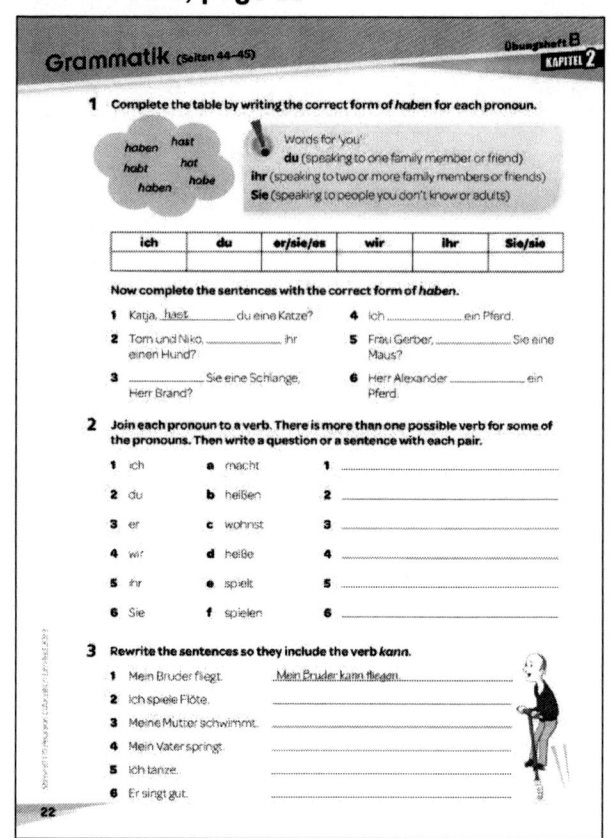

Answers

1 ich – habe   du – hast   er/sie/es – hat
Wir – haben   Ihr – habt   Sie/sie – haben
1 hast 2 habt 3 Haben 4 habe
5 haben 6 hat

2 1 d – ich heiße
2 c – du wohnst
3 a/e – er macht/spielt
4 b/f – wir heißen/spielen
5 a/e – ihr macht/spielt
6 b/f – Sie heißen/spielen
Questions/sentences: pupils' own answers.

3 1 Mein Bruder kann fliegen.
2 Ich kann Flöte spielen.
3 Meine Mutter kann schwimmen.
4 Mein Vater kann springen.
5 Ich kann tanzen.
6 Er kann gut singen.

Familie und Tiere – **KAPITEL 2**

Projektzone 1: Frohe Weihnachten!

(Pupil Book pp. 48–49)

The *Projektzone* is one or two optional units in which no new grammar is introduced, but in which the chapter topic is extended into an exciting cultural and practical context which allows for cross-curricular and project work. **Learning objectives** • Learning about Christmas • Finding out about German traditions	**Programme of Study** **GV3** Developing vocabulary **LC1** Listening and responding **LC6** Reading comprehension **FCSE links** Unit 8 – Celebrations (Various festivals, Special celebrations) **PLTS** **I** Independent enquirers	**Resources** **Audio files:** 42_Kapitel2_Projektzone1_Aufgabe1 43_Kapitel2_Projektzone1_Aufgabe2 44_Kapitel2_Projektzone1_Aufgabe4 44a_Kapitel2_Projektzone1_Kulturzone **ActiveTeach:** Starter 1 resource

Starter

Aim

To learn about Christmas and New Year celebrations.

Pupils match the vocabulary for Christmas and New Year celebrations (Starter 1 resource). They then work out what the following are in German – Christmas/holiday (2 words). Ask how they worked out the new words and about the strategies they used?

1 Hör zu. Was machst du zu Weihnachten? (1–7) (Listening L2)

Listening. Pupils listen to the audio and decide what the people in the audio do for Christmas, matching the text to the photograph.

Audioscript

1 – *Was machst du zu Weihnachten?*
– *Zu Weihnachten? Ich singe Weihnachtslieder.*
  Ja, Weihnachtslieder singen ist lustig.
2 – *Was machst du zu Weihnachten?*
– *Ich mache einen Skiurlaub. Wir fahren zu Weihnachten nach Österreich und machen einen Skiurlaub. Super!*
3 – *Und du, was machst du zu Weihnachten?*
– *Oh, das ist ganz einfach: Ich esse schöne Sachen. Mmm, lecker!*
4 – *Was machst du zu Weihnachten?*
– *Zu Weihnachten denke ich natürlich an Jesus Christus und ich gehe in die Kirche.*
5 – *Und du, was machst du zu Weihnachten?*
– *Ich habe Schulferien. Zwei Wochen, keine Schule – super!*
6 – *Was machst du zu Weihnachten?*
– *Zu Weihnachten bekomme ich Geschenke. Das ist cool. Ich bekomme Geschenke von Mama und Papa, von den Großeltern, von meiner Schwester, von Freunden – so viele Geschenke! Fantastisch!*
7 – *Und du, was machst du zu Weihnachten?*
– *Ich schmücke den Weihnachtsbaum. Der Weihnachtsbaum hat rote und goldene Dekorationen – sehr schön.*

Answers
1 c 2 f 3 a 4 e 5 g 6 b 7 d

2 Hör zu und lies. Rate mal: Was bedeuten diese Phrasen? (Listening L2)

Listening. Pupils look at the photos in exercise 1 again and match the photos to the English text.

The *Tip* box reminds pupils to use a dictionary and look up words that they are unsure of.

Audioscript

– *Lebkuchen*
– *Ich bin katholisch.*
– *Ich esse Truthahn.*
– *Stille Nacht, heilige Nacht*
– *Ich bin evangelisch.*
– *Weihnachten im Schnee*
– *Weihnachtsfernsehprogramm*

Answers
1 Gingerbread.   2 I am Roman Catholic.
3 I eat turkey.
4 'Silent night, holy night'.
5 I am Protestant.   6 Christmas in the snow.
7 Christmas television schedule

© Pearson Education Ltd 2013. Copying permitted for purchasing institution only. This material is not copyright free.

Frohe Weihnachten! | **Familie und Tiere – KAPITEL**

3 Partnerarbeit. Was machst du zu Weihnachten? (Speaking L2)

Speaking. Working in pairs, pupils talk about what they do at Christmas.

4 Hör zu und lies. (Listening L3)

Listening. Pupils listen to the audio and read the text in the pupil book.

Some vocabulary is glossed for support.

Audioscript

1 – Meine Stadt hat einen Weihnachtsmarkt. Ich kaufe Bonbons und Weihnachtsgeschenke auf dem Weihnachtsmarkt.
2 – Der Nikolaus kommt in der Nacht zum 6. Dezember und wir essen schöne Sachen am Nikolaustag – lecker!
3 – Der 24. Dezember heißt Heiligabend. Wir sagen „Frohe Weihnachten!" und wir gehen am Nachmittag in die Kirche. Wir singen Weihnachtslieder.
4 – Der Weihnachtsmann oder das Christkind kommt am Abend und wir öffnen die Geschenke vor dem Weihnachtsbaum. Das ist super!
5 – Am Abend essen wir ein traditionelles Weihnachtsessen: Gans mit Blaukraut und Kartoffeln. Mmm, lecker!
6 – Der 25. Dezember heißt „der erste Weihnachtstag" – das ist ein Feiertag. Der 26. Dezember („der zweite Weihnachtstag") ist auch ein Feiertag.

(The rhyme in the *Kulturzone* is a traditional German Christmas poem.)

Audioscript

Advent, Advent,

ein Lichtlein brennt!

Erst eins, dann zwei,

dann drei, dann vier,

dann steht das Christkind

vor der Tür!

5 Beantworte die Fragen auf Englisch. (Reading L4)

Reading. Pupils answer the questions in English using information from the text in exercise 4.

Answers

1 at the Christmas market
2 Christmas presents
3 6 December
4 Christmas Eve, 24 December
5 goose, red cabbage, potatoes
6 25 and 26 December

6 Finde Informationen über einen Weihnachtsmarkt und mach ein Poster. (Writing L3–4)

Writing. Pupils research Christmas markets and put together a poster about one of their own choosing.

Several towns in German-speaking countries have Christmas markets and lots of information can be found online. There are also German Christmas markets in various UK locations (Birmingham, Leeds, Manchester, Edinburgh, Belfast, London …).

Plenary

Split the class up into teams. Allow each team three minutes to jot down as many facts as they can remember about how *Christmas* is celebrated in Germany. Give two points for each completely correct answer, one for an answer with an error. The winning team is the one with the most points.

© Pearson Education Ltd 2013. Copying permitted for purchasing institution only. This material is not copyright free.

Familie und Tiere – KAPITEL 2

Projektzone 2: Prost Neujahr! (Pupil Book pp. 50–51)

The *Projektzone* is one or two optional units in which no new grammar is introduced, but in which the chapter topic is extended into an exciting cultural and practical context which allows for cross-curricular and project work.

Learning objectives
- Learning about New Year celebrations
- Giving a presentation

Programme of Study
GV3 Developing vocabulary
LC5 Speaking coherently and confidently
LC6 Reading comprehension

FCSE links
Unit 8 Celebrations – (Various festivals, Special celebrations)

PLTS
E Effective participators
R Reflective learners

Resources
Audio files:
45_Kapitel2_Projektzone2_Aufgabe2
46_Kapitel2_Projektzone2_Aufgabe4

ActiveTeach:
Plenary resource

Starter

Aim

To practise giving presentations.

Pupils have three minutes to reflect on what makes a good presentation, making a note of at least three ideas. They then share these with their partner before sharing their combined ideas with another pair (think-pair-share). Collate ideas on the board. Pupils add any new ideas to their notes and make a checklist to use for self-assessment of their own presentations.

1 Finde die Paare. (Reading L2)

Reading. Pupils read the labels on the photos and match them to the text. They check their answers by listening to the audio in exercise 2.

Answers
1 b 2 d 3 g 4 a 5 f 6 c 7 e

2 Hör zu und überprüfe. (Listening L2)

Listening. Pupils listen to the audio and check their answers from exercise 1.

Audioscript
1 – b – *Wir sagen „Prost Neujahr".*
2 – d – *Wir machen ein Feuerwerk.*
3 – g – *Wir essen Linsensuppe und Schweinefleisch.*
4 – a – *Wir machen eine Party.*
5 – f – *Wir machen eine Wanderung.*
6 – c – *Wir feiern um Mitternacht.*
7 – e – *Wir trinken Sekt oder Limo.*

3 Lies die Texte und beantworte die Fragen. (Reading L3)

Reading. Pupils read the texts that accompany the two photos and answer the questions.

Some vocabulary is glossed for support.

Answers
1 31 December
2 Sekt
3 *Prost Neujahr!* or *Guten Rutsch!*
4 at midnight
5 They go for a walk.
6 It brings good luck for the New Year.

4 Hör zu und finde die Paare. (1–6) (Listening L3)

Listening. Pupils listen to the audio and match the pairs.

Audioscript
1 – *Was machst du am 31. Dezember?*
  – *Am 31. Dezember machen wir eine Party.*
2 – *Was machst du zu Silvester?*
  – *Zu Silvester tanze ich auf einer Party.*
3 – *Wie ist das Feuerwerk zu Silvester?*
  – *Oh, das große Feuerwerk um Mitternacht ist cool.*
4 – *Was trinkst du zu Silvester?*
  – *Zu Silvester trinke ich Limonade.*
5 – *Was machst du am 1. Januar?*
  – *Am 1. Januar mache ich eine Wanderung.*
6 – *Und was machst du zu Neujahr?*
  – *Zu Neujahr essen wir am Abend zusammen.*

Answers
1 c 2 d 3 e 4 b 5 a 6 f

© Pearson Education Ltd 2013. Copying permitted for purchasing institution only. This material is not copyright free.

Prost Neujahr! | **Familie und Tiere –** KAPITEL

5 Lies den Text und beantworte die Fragen. (Reading L4)

Reading. Pupils read the text and answer the multiple-choice questions.

Some vocabulary is glossed for support.

Answers
1 b 2 a 3 c 4 b 5 a 6 a

6 Was machst du zu Weihnachten und Neujahr? Mach eine kurze Präsentation. (Speaking L3–4)

Speaking. Pupils prepare and give a short presentation about what they do at a festival of their choice, such as Christmas, New Year, Diwali, Eid, Hanukkah, etc.

Plenary
Aim
For pupils to give each other feedback on their presentations.
Pupils take it in turns to make their presentations to the class and the rest of the class fill in the grid (Plenary resource). One pupil then feeds back to the pupil about their presentation.

Familie und Tiere – **KAPITEL 2**

Extra (Pupil Book pp. 122–123)

Self-access reading and writing

A Reinforcement

1 Schreib die Namen der Tiere richtig auf und finde die Paare. (Writing L1)

Writing. Pupils solve the anagrams to find the 'hidden' animal and then match the vocabulary to the illustration.

> **Answers**
> 1 ein Hund – e
> 2 eine Katze – c
> 3 ein Pferd – f
> 4 ein Kaninchen – a
> 5 ein Hamster – d
> 6 ein Meerschweinchen – b

2 Schreib die Zahlen als Wörter auf. Dann sag die Zahlen. (Writing L2)

Writing. Pupils say the number as a word and then write the word down.

> **Answers**
> 1 achtunddreißig
> 2 fünfundsechzig
> 3 sechsundachtzig
> 4 vierundsiebzig

3 Schreib die Telefonnummern als Wörter auf. (Writing L2)

Writing. Pupils write out the telephone numbers as words.

The *Tip* box gives some information about the format for writing and saying telephone numbers in German.

> **Answers**
> 1 54 13 29 37 42 – vierundfünfzig dreizehn neunundzwanzig siebenunddreißig zweiundvierzig
> 2 76 94 68 81 53 – sechsundsiebzig vierundneunzig achtundsechzig einundachtzig dreiundfünfzig
> 3 20 75 10 04 11 – zwanzig fünfundsiebzig zehn null vier elf

> **Extension**
> The international code for the UK is +44. Some pupils might like to find out what it is for Germany, Austria, Switzerland and Namibia.

4 Welche Farbe? Vervollständige die Sätze. (Reading L2)

Reading. Pupils read the sentences and look at the illustration. They then complete the gap-fill sentences with the correct colour words.

Some vocabulary is glossed for support.

> **Answers**
> 1 Das Sofa ist sehr bunt. Es ist weiß, lila, **rot**, **grün**, **orange**, **gelb** und **rosa**.
> 2 Die Balkons sind **orange** (*or* **rot**), **grün** und **gelb**.
> 3 Die Maske ist sehr bunt. Sie ist hellblau, lila, grau, rosa, gelb, … [as many colours as pupils can name]

B Extension

1 Lies das Gedicht und full die Lücken aus. (Reading L3)

Reading. Pupils read the poem and then complete it using the words from the box.

To help, the *Tip* box points out that each pair of lines rhymes.

Some vocabulary is glossed for support.

> **Answers**
> Dreißig Tage hat September,
> **April**, Juni und **November**.
> **Februar** hat achtundzwanzig,
> nur im Schaltjahr **neunundzwanzig**.
> Alle anderen ohne Frage
> haben **einunddreißig Tage**.

2 Schreib vier Sätze mit Wörtern aus jedem Kasten. Dann schreib die Sätze auf Englisch. (Writing L3)

Writing. Using the table in the pupil book, pupils write out four sentences with one element from each column in the table. They then translate the sentences into English.

© Pearson Education Ltd 2013. Copying permitted for purchasing institution only. This material is not copyright free.

Extra | **Familie und Tiere –** KAPITEL

3 Lies die E-Mail und beantworte die Fragen auf Englisch. (Reading L4)

Reading. Pupils read the email and answer the questions in English.

> **Answers**
> **1** in Basel, Switzerland **2** Leo **3** Jessica **4** very lazy **5** 42 **6** Leo's grandparents

4 Schreib ein Blog über deine Familie. Benutze Leos E-Mail als Vorlage. (Writing L3-4)

Writing. Pupils write a blog all about their family, using Leo's email as a model.

Pupils can make things up if they want to!

© Pearson Education Ltd 2013. Copying permitted for purchasing institution only. This material is not copyright free.

KAPITEL 3

(Pupil Book pp. 52–73)

Freizeit – juhu!

Unit & Learning objectives	Programme of Study references	Key Language	Grammar and other language features
1 Bist du sportlich? (pp. 54–55) • Talking about which sports you play • Using *gern* with the verb *spielen*	**GV2** Grammatical structures (*gern + spielen*) **GV3** Opinions and discussions	Was spielst du? Ich spiele … Badminton Basketball Fußball Wasserball Eishockey Tennis Volleyball Tischtennis Handball Bist du sportlich? Ich bin sehr/ziemlich/nicht sehr sportlich.	• Full paradigm of *spielen* • Using *gern/nicht gern* • Pronunciation of cognates • Changing information from 1st person to 3rd person • Forming a question
2 Freizeit ist toll! (pp. 56–57) • Talking about leisure activities • Giving your opinion	**GV2** Grammatical structures (irregular verbs and sentence structure) **LC3** Conversation **LC4** Expressing ideas (writing)	Was machst du gern? Ich fahre Rad. Ich spiele Gitarre. Ich lese. Ich schwimme. Ich fahre Skateboard. Ich mache Judo. Ich sehe fern. Ich tanze. Ich reite. Wie findest du das? Ich finde es … Es ist … irre super toll cool gut nicht schlecht okay langweilig nervig stinklangweilig furchtbar	• More on using *gern* • Irregular verbs *fahren*, *lesen*, *sehen* • Extra 'e' in *finden*

© Pearson Education Ltd 2013. Copying permitted for purchasing institution only. This material is not copyright free.

Freizeit – juhu! – KAPITEL

Unit & Learning objectives	Programme of Study references	Key Language	Grammar and other language features
3 In meiner Freizeit (pp. 58–59) • Talking about how often you do activities • Using correct word order	**GV2** Grammatical structures (word order) **LC6** Translation into English **LC8** Translation into German	Was machst du in deiner Freizeit? Ich gehe ins Kino. Ich höre Musik. Ich gehe einkaufen. Ich spiele Xbox oder Wii. Ich gehe in den Park. Ich gehe in die Stadt. Ich esse Hamburger oder Pizza. Ich chille. Ich mache Sport. Wann machst du das? Wie oft machst du das? am Abend am Wochenende (sehr/ziemlich/nicht so) oft jeden Tag einmal pro Woche zweimal pro Woche dreimal pro Woche einmal pro Monat	• Word order after time expressions • Using sentence structure to make text more interesting

© Pearson Education Ltd 2013. Copying permitted for purchasing institution only. This material is not copyright free.

Freizeit – juhu! — **KAPITEL 3**

Unit & Learning objectives	Programme of Study references	Key Language	Grammar and other language features
4 Ich bin online (pp. 60–61) • Talking about mobiles and computers • Talking about the future using the present tense	**GV2** Grammatical structures (sentence structure) **LC5** Accurate pronunciation and intonation **LC8** Translation into German	Was machst du am Computer oder auf deinem Handy? Ich chatte mit Freunden auf Facebook. Ich mache Fotos oder Filme. Ich suche und lese Infos für die Hausaufgaben. Ich simse. Ich lade Musik herunter. Ich sehe Videos. Ich surfe im Internet. Ich spiele Computerspiele. Ich telefoniere mit Freunden. immer manchmal nie jeden Morgen heute morgen am Montag nächste Woche in zwei Wochen	• The *wir* and *Sie/sie* forms • Talking about the future using the present tense + future time phrase • Pronunciation tips • Conversation tip
5 Listening Skills: Wir sind Freunde (pp. 62–63) • Developing prediction strategies • Understanding longer listening texts	**GV3** Developing vocabulary **LC1** Listening and responding **LC4** Expressing ideas (speaking)		• Using textual and visual clues • Thinking about possible content • Thinking about what is being asked for • Combining pre-listening strategies • Concentrating on familiar language
6 Writing Skills: Brieffreunde (pp. 64–65) • Making your writing interesting and varied • Writing about your free time	**GV2** Grammatical structures (various) **LC2** Transcription **LC4** Expressing ideas (writing)		• Using different ways to express opinions • Vary writing by including what other people do/like • Using correct word order • Using a checklist
Lernzieltest und Wiederholung (pp. 66–67) Pupils' checklist and practice exercises			• Keeping a conversation going

© Pearson Education Ltd 2013. Copying permitted for purchasing institution only. This material is not copyright free.

Freizeit – juhu! – KAPITEL

Unit & Learning objectives	Programme of Study references	Key Language	Grammar and other language features
Grammatik (pp. 68–69) Detailed grammar summary and practice exercises			• Verbs – the present tense • Irregular verbs – the present tense • Word order • The *wir* and *Sie/sie* forms • Future plans with the present tense
Projektzone: Ich sammle! (pp. 72–73) • Learning about collections • Researching and describing an unusual collection	**GV3** Developing vocabulary **LC2** Transcription **LC4** Expressing ideas (speaking)		• Translating compound nouns • Vocabulary for *not* collecting • Reusing familiar vocabulary

© Pearson Education Ltd 2013. Copying permitted for purchasing institution only. This material is not copyright free.

Freizeit – juhu! – KAPITEL 3

1 Bist du sportlich? (Pupil Book pp. 52–55)

Learning objectives
- Talking about which sports you play
- Using *gern* with the verb *spielen*

Programme of Study
GV2 Grammatical structures (*gern + spielen*)
GV3 Opinions and discussions

FCSE links
Unit 1 – Relationships, Family and Friends (Hobbies/free-time activities)
Unit 4 – Leisure (Hobbies, Free time/hobbies, Hobbies/activities)
Unit 5 – Healthy lifestyle (Activities)

Grammar
Full paradigm of *spielen*
Using *gern/nicht gern*

PLTS
I Independent enquirers

Key Language
Was spielst du?
Ich spiele …
Badminton
Basketball
Fußball
Wasserball
Eishockey
Tennis
Volleyball
Tischtennis
Handball
Bist du sportlich?
Ich bin sehr/ziemlich/nicht sehr sportlich.

Cross-curricular
Physical Education: information about different sports that pupils take part in

Resources
Audio files:
47_Kapitel3_Einheit1_Aufgabe1
48_Kapitel3_Einheit1_Aufgabe4
Workbooks:
Übungsheft 1 A&B, page 26
ActiveTeach:
Starter 1 resource
Starter 2 resource
p.054 Grammar presentation
p.054 Flashcards
p.055 Exercise 5 grid
Plenary resource
ActiveLearn:
Listening A, Listening B
Reading A, Reading B
Grammar, Vocabulary

Kapitel 3 Quiz pp. 52–53

Answers

1 Finde einen Nationalsport für …
1 Deutschland – b (Fußball)
2 Österreich – g (alpiner Skilauf)
3 die Schweiz – f (Schwingen)
4 England – a (Cricket)
5 Irland – d (Hurling)
6 Schottland – c (Golf)
7 Wales – e (Rugby)

2 Was für ein Sport ist das? Schreib die richtigen Buchstaben auf.

Pupils should use a dictionary if necessary. Various answers are possible.

1 Handball a, b 2 Skifahren b, c, e 3 Cricket a, b, f 4 Rugby a, b, e 5 Badminton b, c 6 Kanufahren b, c, d 7 Leichtathletik b, c, f 8 Wasserball a, b, d 9 Segeln b, c, d 10 Boxen c 11 Tischtennis a, b, c 12 Curling b, e

3 Wie viele Spieler hat eine Mannschaft? Finde die Paare.
1 e (15) 2 c (11) 3 d (7) 4 f (18) 5 b (5) 6 a (4)

Extension

There are several follow-up questions you could try, for example:

Wie viele Wintersportarten machst du?

Wie viele Spieler sind in einem Team?

Wie groß ist das Spielfeld/das Tor?

Wie lang ist das Spiel (in Minuten)? (numbers to be written out in full)

As an extra resource, make panels or cards in the style of Top Trumps that include numbers and facts for pupils to guess what goes with what; for example, what the number of players is.

© Pearson Education Ltd 2013. Copying permitted for purchasing institution only. This material is not copyright free.

Bist du sportlich? | **Freizeit – juhu!** – KAPITEL

Starter 1

Aim

To introduce the new vocabulary from the unit and to encourage pupils to make logical guesses about the meaning of new vocabulary.

Pupils decide which word is the odd-one-out (Starter 1 resource) and explain why they have made this choice. The explanations can be given in English or German (depending on the class). Other examples could be used and pupils could also be asked to make up their own odd-one-out puzzles as an extension task.

Go back to the principles of pronunciation here as there are so many cognates. (There is more information on pronunciation of cognates on pupil book p. 38). For example, in an audio task:

1 predict pronunciation, then listen to check
2 listen and decide whether the word is in German or English.

Answers

1 = *Skifahren* because it's not a ball sport.
2 = *Cricket* because it's not a water sport.
3 = *Leichtathletik* because it's not a ball sport.
4 = *Boxen* because it's not a winter sport.

1 Hör zu. Was passt zusammen? Schreib die richtigen Buchstaben auf. (1–6) (Listening L2)

Listening. Pupils listen to the audio. They decide which of the sports illustrated the speakers play.

Refer pupils to the *Aussprache* box. It reminds pupils that many sports have the same name in English and German, but with a different pronunciation.

Audioscript

1 – *Was spielst du?*
 – *Ich spiele Fußball und Tennis. Fußball im Winter und Tennis im Sommer.*
2 – *Und du? Was spielst du?*
 – *Ich spiele Basketball.*
 – *Du spielst Basketball … super.*
3 – *Ich spiele Tischtennis.*
 – *Tischtennis ist gut. Ich spiele auch Tischtennis.*
4 – *Was spielst du?*
 – *Also, ich spiele Volleyball und auch Badminton.*
 – *Schön, Volleyball und Badminton. Du bist sportlich!*
5 – *Und du, was spielst du?*
 – *Ich spiele Wasserball.*
 – *Du spielst Wasserball! Das ist ja toll.*
 – *Und ich spiele auch Eishockey.*
 – *Eishockey? Cool!*
6 – *Spielst du Fußball?*
 – *Nein, Fußball spiele ich nicht, aber ich spiele Handball. Ich finde es super.*
 – *Ja, Handball ist gut.*

Answers

1 c, f 2 b 3 h 4 g, a 5 d, e 6 i

Grammatik

The *Grammatik* box introduces the full paradigm for the regular verb *spielen*. There is more information and practice on *spielen* in the grammar unit on pupil book p. 68

2 Umfrage. Stell in der Klasse Fragen und mach Notizen. (Speaking L3)

Speaking. Pupils carry out a survey on the kind of sports that their classmates are involved in (or not).

3 Schreib ein paar Sätze über vier Freunde. (Writing L2)

Writing. Pupils write a couple of sentences about four pupils/friends of their choice.

This activity can be omitted if you don't want to use the third person yet.

The *Tip* box reminds pupils how to change the first person into the third person.

Starter 2

Aim

To review the formation of verbs in the present tense.

Pupils play a game of noughts and crosses (Starter 2 resource) in pairs, conjugating the verbs to earn the nought or the cross. The game can be printed out and laminated to be played with whiteboard pens. To play as a whole-class game in teams, display the grid on the board.

© Pearson Education Ltd 2013. Copying permitted for purchasing institution only. This material is not copyright free.

Bist du sportlich? | Freizeit – juhu! – **KAPITEL 3**

4 Hör zu. Was spielen sie gern? Schreib den Sport auf und zeichne ein Gesicht. (1–6) (Listening L3)

Listening. Pupils listen to the audio. They then draw a picture of the sport that is mentioned and an emoticon to show whether the speaker likes the sport or not.

Audioscript

1 – *Spielst du gern Handball?*
   – *Hmm, ja, ich spiele ziemlich gern Handball, aber das ist nicht mein Lieblingssport.*
2 – *He, Fabian. Wir spielen Fußball. Kommst du mit?*
   – *Oh nein. Ich spiele nicht gern Fußball.*
   – *Okay, dann tschüs!*
3 – *Spielst du Wasserball?*
   – *Ja, ich spiele gern Wasserball.*
4 – *Ich spiele Tischtennis. Spielst du auch Tischtennis?*
   – *Ja, ich spiele sehr gern Tischtennis!*
   – *Super! Also los!*
5 – *Was spielst du gern?*
   – *Ich spiele gern Badminton.*
   – *Ja? Ich auch.*
6 – *Spielst du gern Volleyball?*
   – *Ja, also … ich spiele ziemlich gern Volleyball.*

Answers
1 Handball ☺ (ziemlich gern)
2 Fußball ☹ (nicht gern)
3 Wasserball ☺ (gern)
4 Tischtennis ☺ ☺ (sehr gern)
5 Badminton ☺ (gern)
6 Volleyball ☺ (ziemlich gern)

5 Lies das Blog. Schreib die Tabelle ab und füll sie auf Englisch aus. (Reading L3)

Reading. Pupils read a blog. They then copy out the table and complete it in English.

Answers
sehr gern: *football*
gern: *table tennis*
ziemlich gern: *volleyball, handball*
nicht gern: *basketball, tennis*

Grammatik

Use the *Grammatik* box to go over ways of saying that you like to play a sport using *gern + spielen*. There is more information and practice on pupil book p. 56.

6 Partnerarbeit. Was spielst du gern oder nicht gern? (Speaking L3)

Speaking. Working in pairs, pupils take it in turns to ask each other questions about the sports that they like and dislike doing following the example in the pupil book.

The *Tip* box reminds pupils to put the verb before the subject when forming a question.

Extension

For the more able, extend exercise 6 to include the third person and some plurals (*er/sie spielt …; wir spielen …*).

7 Schreib Sätze. Beantworte die Fragen. (Writing L3–4)

Writing. Pupils write down answers to general questions about sport.

Some questions could be omitted if you only want to use the first person.

Plenary

Aim

For pupils to establish whether they have met the lesson objective of talking about which sports they like to play.

Pupils play a battleships game in pairs. They draw four boats on their grid (Plenary resource). The only way to guess where the boats are is by asking a question in German using the clues. Pupils will also need to know key phrases such as *getroffen/nicht getroffen/gesunken*.

Example conversation:
A: *Spielst du sehr gern Badminton?*
B: *Nein. Nicht getroffen!*
A: *Spielst du gern Badminton?*
B: *Ja, ich spiele gern Badminton. Getroffen!*

Alternative plenary

Use ActiveTeach p.055 Grammar practice to review word order with *gern*.

Bist du sportlich? | Freizeit – juhu! – KAPITEL

Workbook A, page 26

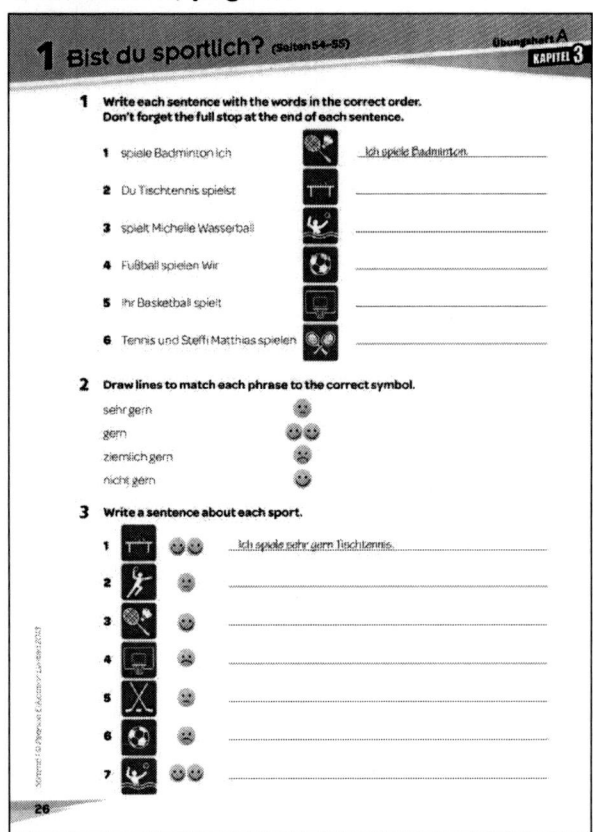

Answers

1.
   1. Ich spiele Badminton.
   2. Du spielst Tischtennis.
   3. Michelle spielt Wasserball.
   4. Wir spielen Fußball.
   5. Ihr spielt Basketball.
   6. Steffi und Matthias spielen Tennis.

2. sehr gern – ☺☺
   gern – ☺
   ziemlich gern – 😐
   nicht gern – ☹

3.
   1. Ich spiele sehr gern Tischtennis.
   2. Ich spiele ziemlich gern Handball.
   3. Ich spiele gern Federball.
   4. Ich spiele nicht gern Basketball.
   5. Ich spiele ziemlich gern (Eis)Hockey.
   6. Ich spiele nicht gern Fußball.
   7. Ich spiele sehr gern Wasserball.

Workbook B, page 26

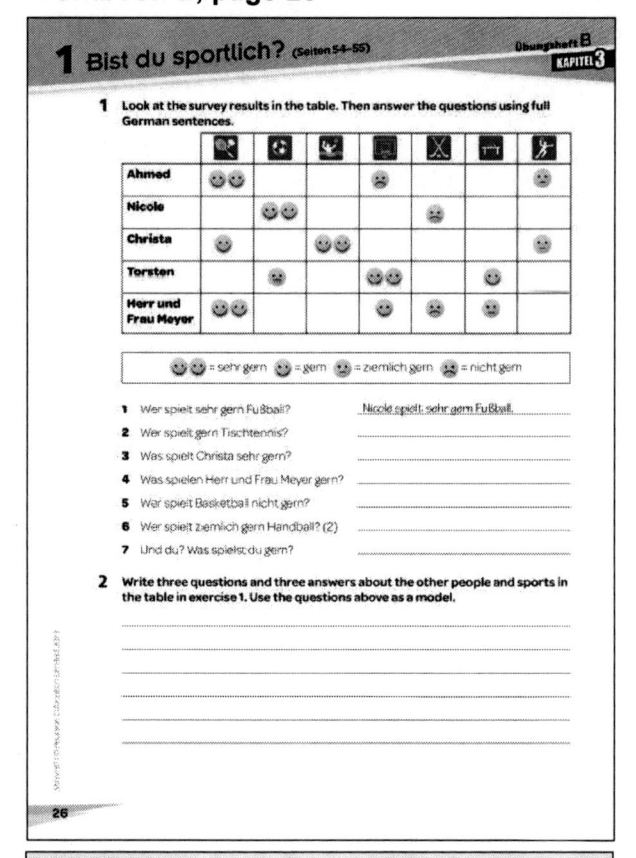

Answers

1.
   1. Nicole spielt sehr gern Fußball.
   2. Torsten spielt gern Tischtennis.
   3. Christa spielt sehr gern Wasserball.
   4. Herr und Frau Meyer spielen gern Basketball.
   5. Ahmed spielt nicht gern Basketball.
   6. Ahmed und Christa spielen ziemlich gern Handball.
   7. Pupils' own answers: Ich spiele gern …

2. Possible questions and answers:
   1. Wer spielt sehr gern Federball? Ahmed und Herr und Frau Meyer spielen sehr gern Federball.
   2. Spielt Torsten gern Fußball? Nein, er spiel nicht gern Fußball.
   3. Wer spielt nicht gern Eishockey? Nicole und Herr und Frau Meyer spielen nicht gern Eishockey.

© Pearson Education Ltd 2013. Copying permitted for purchasing institution only. This material is not copyright free.

Freizeit – juhu! – **KAPITEL 3**

2 Freizeit ist toll! (Pupil Book pp. 56–57)

Learning objectives	Key Language	Resources
• Talking about leisure activities • Giving your opinion **Programme of Study** **GV2** Grammatical structures (irregular verbs and sentence structure) **LC3** Conversation **LC4** Expressing ideas (writing) **FCSE links** Unit 4 – Leisure (Free time/hobbies, Hobbies/activities) **Grammar** More on using *gern* Irregular verbs *fahren, lesen, sehen* **PLTS** **T** Team workers	Was machst du gern? Ich fahre Rad. Ich spiele Gitarre. Ich lese. Ich schwimme. Ich fahre Skateboard. Ich mache Judo. Ich sehe fern. Ich tanze. Ich reite. Wie findest du das? Ich finde es … Es ist … irre super toll cool gut nicht schlecht okay langweilig nervig stinklangweilig furchtbar	**Audio files:** 49_Kapitel3_Einheit2_Aufgabe1 50_Kapitel3_Einheit2_Aufgabe3 51_Kapitel3_Einheit2_Aufgabe4 **Workbooks:** Übungsheft 1 A&B, page 27 **ActiveTeach:** Starter 2 resource p.056 Flashcards p.057 Grammar presentation p.057 Extension worksheet p.057 Video: Episode 5 Plenary resource **ActiveLearn:** Listening A, Listening B Reading A, Reading B Grammar, Vocabulary

Starter 1

Aim

To review vocabulary from the previous unit and to work on memorisation skills.

This game works a little like 'I went to the market and I bought …' Pupils work in two teams, one for each side of the class. The first pupil gives an opinion on a sport of their choice, for example:

A: *Ich heiße Jamie und ich spiele gern Wasserball.*

The second pupil then has to remember what the first pupil has said before adding their own sentence, for example:

B: *Ich heiße Tom und ich spiele gern Wasserball. Ich spiele nicht gern Fußball.*

For a greater challenge, pupils could be asked to change the verbs, for example:

B: *Er heißt Jamie und er spielt gern Wasserball. Ich heiße Tom und ich spiele nicht gern Fußball.*

The third pupil then has to remember what the first two players have said before adding their own sentence.

Teams score points depending on how far they get with the game, i.e. the number of people who correctly remember the sports and people.

1 Hör zu. Welches Bild ist das? (1–9) (Listening L2)

Listening. Pupils listen to the audio and match the speaker to the illustration.

Audioscript

1 – Was machst du gern?
  – Ich schwimme. Ich schwimme sehr gern.
2 – Und du, was machst du gern?
  – Was ich gern mache? Ich tanze, ja, ich tanze gern.
3 – Was machst du gern?
  – Ich reite. Das ist super! Ich reite sehr gern.
4 – Und du, was machst du gern?
  – Ich fahre Skateboard. Cool, nicht?
5 – Hallo! Was machst du gern?
  – Ich fahre Rad. Das ist toll. Ich fahre gern Rad.
6 – Und du, was machst du gern?

© Pearson Education Ltd 2013. Copying permitted for purchasing institution only. This material is not copyright free.

Freizeit ist toll! | Freizeit – juhu! – **KAPITEL**

– *Ich lese. Ich lese viele Comics und Magazine.*
7 – *Was machst du gern?*
– *Ich sehe fern. Das finde ich interessant. Ich sehe gern fern.*
8 – *Was machst du gern?*
– *Ich spiele Gitarre. Hör mal zu! Ich spiele gern Gitarre.*
9 – *Und du, was machst du gern?*
– *Ich mache Judo. Aua! Ich mache ziemlich gern Judo!*

Answers
1 d 2 h 3 i 4 e 5 a 6 c 7 g 8 b 9 f

Grammatik

Use the *Grammatik* box to remind pupils how to say you like or do not like playing a sport using *gern*, and to explain how to use *gern* with other verbs.

2 Partnerarbeit. Zeig auf die Bilder in Aufgabe 1. Stell Fragen. (Speaking L3)

Speaking. Working in pairs, pupils use the illustrations in exercise 1 and take it in turns to ask each other questions, concentrating on using *gern*.

3 Hör zu. Sieh dir die Bilder in Aufgabe 1 an. Finde die Aktivität und schreib die Meinung auf. (1–8) (Listening L3)

Listening. Pupils listen to the audio and, looking at the illustrations in exercise 1, decide which activity the speaker is talking about. They note down what the speakers think of the activity using the key language in the swingometer.

As a follow-up, make a large version of the swingometer as a wall display.

Audioscript

1 – *Ich schwimme sehr gern. Es ist toll.*
2 – *Ich spiele nicht gern Gitarre. Ich finde es langweilig.*
3 – *Wie findest du Judo?*
– *Es ist nicht schlecht. Ich mache ziemlich gern Judo.*
4 – *Was machst du nicht gern?*
– *Ich reite nicht gern. Ich finde es nervig.*
5 – *Was machst du gern?*
– *Ich lese sehr gern. Es ist irre!*
6 – *Ich fahre ziemlich gern Rad. Es ist okay.*
7 – *Ich tanze nicht gern. Ich finde es furchtbar.*
8 – *Was machst du gern?*
– *Ich fahre sehr gern Skateboard. Ich finde es super!*

Answers
1 d, toll 2 b, langweilig 3 f, nicht schlecht 4 i, nervig 5 c, irre 6 a, okay 7 h, furchtbar 8 e, super

4 Hör zu und lies den Text. Wie viele Adjektive findest du? (Listening L4)

Listening. Pupils listen to the audio and read the text. They then find as many adjectives as they can.

Some vocabulary is glossed for support.

Audioscript

– *Familie und Freizeit*
– *Ich heiße Susi. Ich schwimme gern und ich spiele Fußball – ich bin ziemlich sportlich und ich finde es super. Mein Bruder Ruben liest viele Comics und Magazine – er findet es irre, aber ich lese nicht gern, es ist stinklangweilig.*
– *Meine Schwester Lea spielt Handball und sie findet es fantastisch. Sie fährt auch sehr gern Rad. Ich finde es okay, aber es ist nicht mein Lieblingssport.*
– *Ich finde Fernsehen nervig, aber Lea sieht sehr gern fern. Ruben auch. Er findet es cool.*
– *Und was macht deine Familie? Wie findest du das?*

Answers

sportlich, super, irre, stinklangweilig, fantastisch, okay, nervig, cool

Grammatik

Use the *Grammatik* box to look at the irregular verbs *fahren*, *lesen* and *sehen*, pointing out the spelling changes in the *du* and *er/sie/es* forms.

There is more information and practice in the grammar unit on pupil book p. 68.

5 Lies den Text noch einmal. Finde die vier falschen Sätze. (Reading L4)

Reading. Pupils read the text again and decide which four statements are incorrect. You may choose to play the audio from exercise 4 again.

© Pearson Education Ltd 2013. Copying permitted for purchasing institution only. This material is not copyright free.

Freizeit ist toll! | Freizeit – juhu! – **KAPITEL 3**

Answers

3, 4, 5 and 7 are incorrect.

Extension

More able pupils could be encouraged to have a go at correcting the incorrect statements.

Starter 2

Aim

To review the vocabulary for free-time activities.

Pupils play a game of aural dominoes in groups of four. One team member times the game. The group that completes the game the fastest wins, then demonstrates to the rest of the class. This can also be played as a whole-class game.

Pupils are given a card or cards (more able pupils get more cards) (Starter 2 resource). Pupils don't look at each other's cards. One domino card is marked as *Anfang* and the pupil with this card starts by reading out their German sentence. Whichever pupil has the English translation then reads it out before reading out the second half of their domino (another German sentence). The aim is to keep reading aloud sentences until pupils reach the last domino, marked *Ende*.

Alternative starter 2

Use ActiveTeach p.056 Flashcards to review and practise language for leisure activities.

6 Gruppenarbeit. Wie findest du das? Mach einen Dialog über deine Meinung. Die dritte Person ist der Reporter.
(Speaking L4)

Speaking. In groups of three, pupils create a dialogue about their opinions following the example in the pupil book. The third member of the group reports back, i.e. using the third person.

The *Tip* box points out that the verb *finden* adds an extra 'e' in the *du* and the *er/sie/es* forms to make it easier to say.

Extension

More able pupils should be encouraged to ask questions using the *du* form of verbs, e.g. *Siehst du fern? Wie findest du das?* or the third person, e.g. *Fährt dein Bruder Rad? Wie findet er das?*

7 Schreib eine Antwort auf Susis E-Mail (Aufgabe 4). (Writing L3–4)

Writing. Pupils answer Susi's questions posed in the email in exercise 4. They write them down using full sentences.

Plenary

Aim

For pupils to establish whether they have met the lesson objectives of talking about leisure activities.

Pupils play a game of consequences. Each pupil is given a piece of paper containing a sentence to be completed in German (Plenary resource). Each pupil takes it in turn to complete the sentence in German before folding down the paper over their sentence and passing it to the next person. The original person then unfolds the paper, reads the paragraph and translates it into English. Pupils can be truthful or can make up silly sentences. Pupils should be encouraged to vary the opinion phrases used and to use connectives where appropriate.

Workbook A, page 27

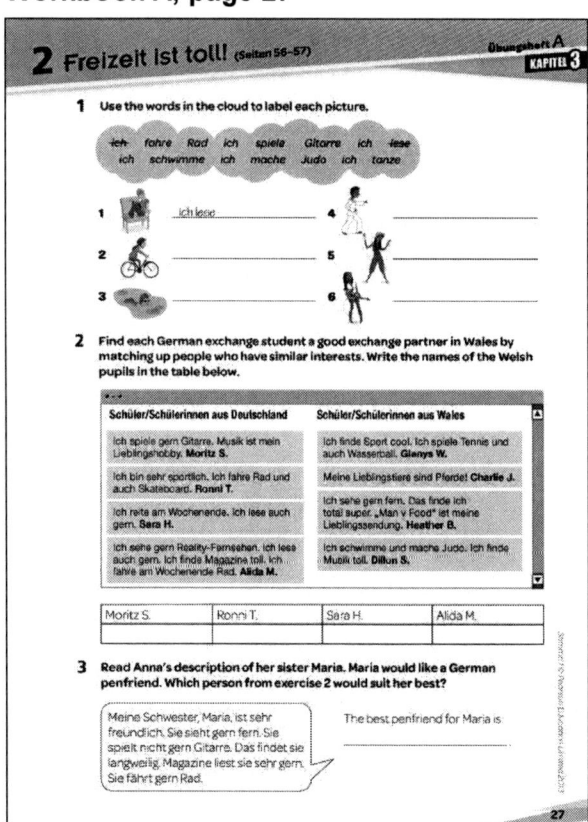

© Pearson Education Ltd 2013. Copying permitted for purchasing institution only. This material is not copyright free.

Freizeit ist toll! | Freizeit – juhu! – **KAPITEL**

Answers

1. 1 ich lese 2 ich fahre Rad 3 ich schwimme
   4 ich mache Judo 5 ich tanze
   6 ich spiele Gitarre
2. Moritz S. – Dillon S.
   Ronni T. – Glenys W.
   Sara H. – Charlie J.
   Alida M. – Heather B.
3. The best penfriend for Maria is: Alida M.

Workbook B, page 27

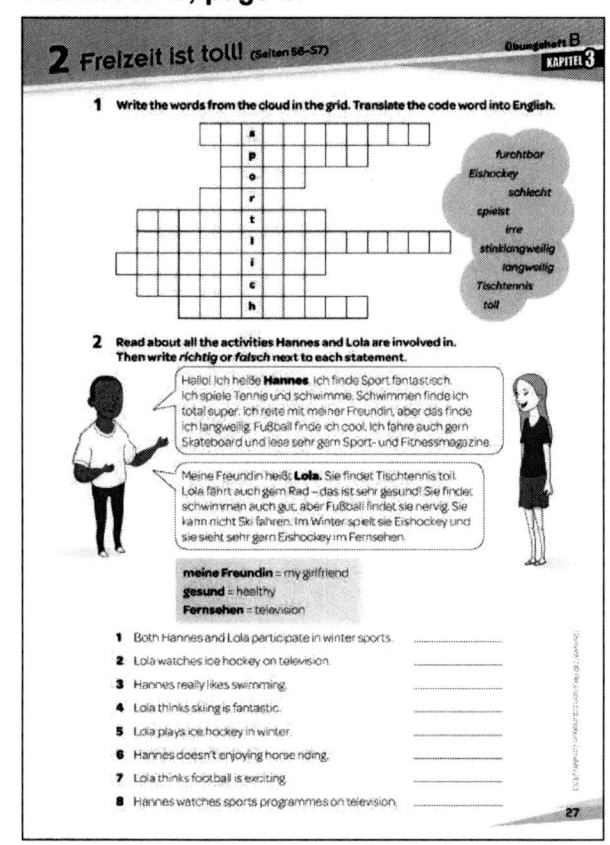

Answers

1. Tischtennis spielst toll ire furchtbar stinklangweilig langweilig schlecht Eishockey
   Code word: sportlich = sporty
2. 1 falsch 2 richtig 3 richtig 4 falsch
   5 richtig 6 richtig 7 falsch 8 falsch

Worksheet

Extension: Out of this world!

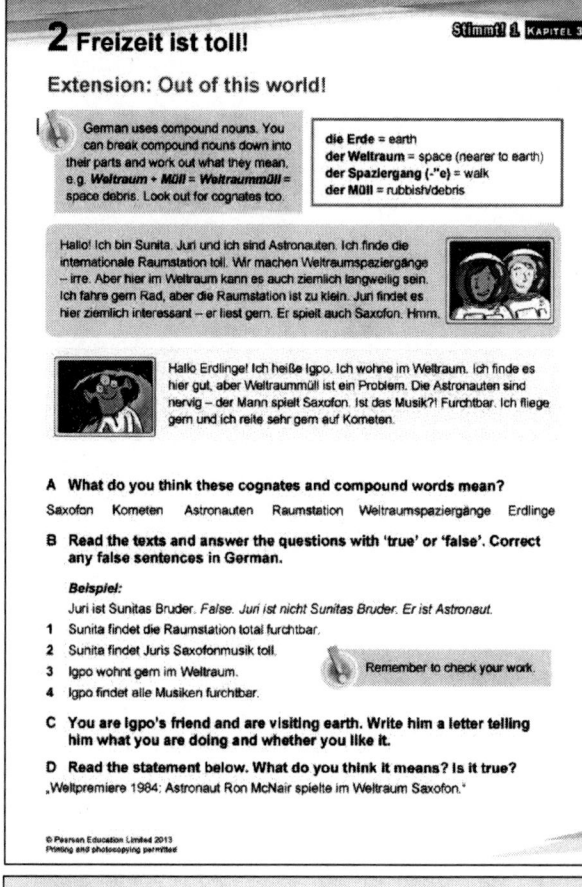

Answers

A Saxofon – saxophone
   Kometen – comets
   Astronauten – astronauts
   Raumstation – space station
   Weltraumspaziergänge – space walks

B Encourage pupils to really think about and discuss these. These are intended to extend the pupils' ability to make inferences as well as to understand the words.

1 Juri ist Sunitas Bruder.
The example indicates that this is false, and it probably is – it would be a strong coincidence for a brother and sister to become astronauts and serve on the ISS at the same time. But it's not logically impossible or implausible, just unlikely.

2 Sunita findet die Raumstation total furchtbar.
False. Sunita findet die Raumstation (meistens) toll, aber es kann langweilig sein.

© Pearson Education Ltd 2013. Copying permitted for purchasing institution only. This material is not copyright free.

Freizeit ist toll! | Freizeit – juhu! – **KAPITEL 3**

Also nicht total furchtbar.

3 Sunita findet Juris Saxofonmusik toll.
False. Her 'hmm' indicates that she does not find it wonderful (and in such a small space, who can blame her?).

4 Igpo wohnt gern im Weltraum.
Richtig (except for the irritant of the space Debris).

5 Igpo findet alle Musiken furchtbar.
False. Igbo findet Juris Saxofonmusik furchtbar. He says, 'Ist das Musik?!' This implies that there is other music he likes. (Some pupils may argue that music doesn't work in space without air.)

C Answers may vary.

D World premier 1984: Astronaut Ron McNair plays saxophone in space.
Astronaut Ron McNair was an accomplished saxophonist. It was intended that he would record a saxophone solo on board the Space Shuttle Challenger, but he died when the shuttle was destroyed shortly after lift-off.

1 No, they don't play. Audrey says 'Ich spiele nicht Eishockey' and Mesut says 'Ich spiele auch nicht Eishockey'.

2 Mesut thinks that judo is stupid and brutal. He says, 'Judo ist doof. Judo ist brutal.'

3 She says table tennis is for grannies. He doesn't like this because it's his favourite sport.

4 She is saying 'what a load of rubbish'.

5 Pupils' own opinion.

Video

Episode 5

Audrey and Mesut are watching a game of ice hockey and talking to some of the players about the sports they do.

Answers

A Before watching
Answers will vary.

B Watch
1 Audrey – judo Mesut – table tennis
Luca – ice hockey
2 Paula doesn't go riding.

C Watch again
1 Three times a week.
2 She thinks they're awful.
3 She swims every morning.
4 The best!
5 He plays guitar and in the evening he watches TV.

D Discuss with your partner

3 In meiner Freizeit (Pupil Book pp. 58–59)

Freizeit – juhu! – **KAPITEL**

Learning objectives
- Talking about how often you do activities
- Using correct word order

Programme of Study
GV2 Grammatical structures (word order)
LC6 Translation into English
LC8 Translation into German

FCSE links
Unit 4 – Leisure (Free time/hobbies)

Grammar
Word order after time expressions

PLTS
C Creative thinkers

Key Language
Was machst du in deiner Freizeit?
Ich gehe ins Kino.
Ich höre Musik.
Ich gehe einkaufen.
Ich spiele Xbox oder Wii.
Ich gehe in den Park.
Ich gehe in die Stadt.
Ich esse Hamburger oder Pizza.
Ich chille.
Ich mache Sport.
Wann machst du das?
Wie oft machst du das?
am Abend
am Wochenende
(sehr/ziemlich/nicht so) oft
jeden Tag
einmal pro Woche
zweimal pro Woche
dreimal pro Woche
einmal pro Monat

Resources
Audio files:
52_Kapitel3_Einheit3_Aufgabe1
53_Kapitel3_Einheit3_Aufgabe4
Workbooks:
Übungsheft 1 A&B, page 28
ActiveTeach:
p.058 Exercise 1 grid
p.058 Flashcards
p.059 Thinking skills worksheet
p.059 Grammar presentation
ActiveLearn:
Listening A, Listening B
Reading A, Reading B
Grammar, Vocabulary

Starter 1
Aim
To review vocabulary from the previous unit.
Pupils are given a set of words to put into order to make a sentence. For an extra challenge they add an opinion to each sentence.

Ich / Rad / gern / fahre
Musik / gern / Ich / höre
Ich / Gitarre / gern / spiele
fahre / Ich / gern / Skateboard
gern / reite / Ich
tanze / gern / Ich

1 Wie oft hörst du die Aktivitäten? Schreib die Tabelle ab und füll sie aus. Mach eine Strichliste. (1–5)
(Listening L2)

Listening. Pupils copy the tally chart and then listen to the audio. They record the number of times that they hear each activity mentioned in the tally chart.

Audioscript

1 – Was machst du in deiner Freizeit?
  – Ich spiele Xbox, ich gehe in die Stadt und … ja … ich chille.
2 – Und du, was machst du in deiner Freizeit?
  – Ich gehe in die Stadt … ähm … ich gehe einkaufen, ich esse Pizza oder Hamburger … und ich höre Musik.
3 – Und was machst du?
  – In meiner Freizeit?
  – Ja, in deiner Freizeit.
  – Also, ich chille … ich gehe in den Park und ich mache Sport – Fußball oder Tennis. Und ich höre Musik.
4 – Und du, was machst du in deiner Freizeit?
  – Ich … ich höre Musik … ich gehe in die Stadt … ich gehe ins Kino … und ich chille.
5 – Und du?
  – Was ich in meiner Freizeit mache? Ja, also, ich spiele Wii, ich höre Musik, ich gehe einkaufen … oh ja, und ich gehe in den Park.

Answers
a 1 b 4 c 2 d 2 e 2 f 3 g 1 h 3 i 1

© Pearson Education Ltd 2013. Copying permitted for purchasing institution only. This material is not copyright free.

In meiner Freizeit | Freizeit – juhu! – **KAPITEL 3**

2 Schreib die Tabelle noch einmal ab und mach eine Umfrage. Welche Aktivität ist am populärsten?
(Speaking L3)

Speaking. Pupils make a copy of the tally chart, and carry out their own survey to find out what their friends do. Which is the most popular activity?

> **Extension**
>
> As a class, discuss which activities the pupils do most and least using *sehr gern* and *ziemlich/nicht sehr gern*.

3 Sieh dir die Liste an. Wie heißt das auf Deutsch? (Reading L2)

Reading. Pupils translate the time expressions into German, using the key language box.

> **Answers**
>
> 1 am Wochenende 2 jeden Tag 3 am Abend 4 sehr oft 5 einmal pro Monat 6 einmal pro Woche 7 dreimal pro Woche 8 zweimal pro Woche

4 Lies die Sätze und hör zu. Wer sagt was? (1–4) (Listening L3)

Listening. Pupils listen to the audio, read the sentences and work out who says what.

> **Audioscript**

1 – Hallo Rakin! Was machst du in deiner Freizeit?
   – Ich spiele gern Xbox und ich chille auch sehr gern.
   – Wie oft machst du das?
   – Ich spiele sehr oft Xbox und ich chille am Wochenende.

2 – Und du, Hannah, was machst du in deiner Freizeit?
   – Ich habe ein Pony und ich reite gern.
   – Cool! Wie oft machst du das?
   – Ich reite zweimal pro Woche. Ich sehe auch gern fern.
   – Ja? Wann machst du das?
   – Ich sehe am Abend fern.

3 – Sebastian, was machst du in deiner Freizeit?
   – Ich bin sehr sportlich und ich gehe auch ziemlich gern ins Kino.
   – Okay, wie oft machst du das?

   – Ich mache jeden Tag Sport und ich gehe einmal pro Monat ins Kino.

4 – Hallo Mai! Was machst du in deiner Freizeit?
   – Ich schwimme sehr gern. Das ist mein Lieblingssport.
   – Super. Wie oft machst du das?
   – Ich schwimme dreimal pro Woche.
   – Das ist toll.
   – Ja, und Pizza finde ich auch toll! Ich esse einmal pro Woche Pizza. Mmm, lecker!

> **Answers**
>
> 1 Rakin, c, b 2 Hannah, f, a 3 Sebastian d, h 4 Mai g, e

> **Starter 2**
>
> **Aim**
>
> To review time phrases.
>
> Pupils play a game of bingo. They write down four time phrases from the previous lesson. Call out sentences in German using time phrases (pupil book p. 58), e.g *Ich chille am Abend*. The pupils cross off their time phrase if it is used. The first person to cross off all their time phrases is the winner. More able pupils could play this game in pairs.
>
> **Alternative starter 2**
>
> Use ActiveTeach p.058 Flashcards to review and practise language for talking about free time.

5 Partnerarbeit. Übersetze die Texte von Sophie und Dominik. Dein Partner/Deine Partnerin übersetzt die Texte von Linus und Alima. Vergleiche dann die Freizeitaktivitäten.
(Reading L4)

Reading. Pupils work in pairs, each translating two of the extracts from the message board. They then compare the leisure activities mentioned in their texts.

Some vocabulary is glossed for support.

As a pre-reading exercise pupils could make a list in English of all the leisure activities they can find.

> **Answers**
>
> **Sophie**: I swim three times a week and I think it's super. I also like going to the cinema at the weekend.

In meiner Freizeit | **Freizeit – juhu!** – KAPITEL

Dominik: In my free time I really like playing the clarinet. I play every day. Once a month I give a concert. I also play the guitar twice a week, but the clarinet is my favourite instrument.

Linus: I am not very sporty, but I like skiing and snowboarding. At the weekend I read a lot and I listen to music every day.

Alima: Once a week I do karate. It's OK, but it's also a bit boring. In the evening I often play Xbox.

Extension

A nice follow-up exercise would be for pupils to say in German the activities that they have found. Pupils will need help as they initially only know how to say, e.g. '*Ich schwimme*' and not '*schwimmen*'.

Grammatik

The *Grammatik* box looks at the way word order in German changes, for example when a time expression is positioned at the start of a sentence. There is more information and practice in the grammar unit on pupil book p. 69.

6 Wann machst du das? Beginn mit der Zeitangabe und liese die Sätze vor. (Speaking L2)

Speaking. Pupils make sentences about their activities, beginning with a time phrase.

Answers

1 Am Wochenende spiele ich Wii.

2 Jeden Tag höre ich Musik.

3 Einmal pro Monat gehe ich ins Kino.

4 Am Abend esse ich Pizza.

5 Zweimal pro Woche chille ich mit Freunden.

7 Schreib ein Paar Sätze über deine Freizeit. (Writing L3–4)

Writing. Pupils write a few sentences about what they do in their free time.

Refer pupils to the *Tip* box. It gives tips on making writing more interesting by varying sentence structure.

Plenary

Aim

For pupils to establish whether they have met the lesson objectives of talking about how often they do things and using correct word order.

A selection of A4 cards each with either a pronoun, a verb, an object or a time phrase are distributed around the class. Pupils are asked to stand up one at a time and to stand in order making a sentence with a pronoun, verb and object (where appropriate). One pupil with a time phrase card is then asked to stand at the start of the 'sentence'. Pupils are then asked to move if they think they need to in order to respect word order conventions. This is a good visual representation of the word order rules and what happens when you put a time phrase at the start of the sentence. Pupils are asked to reflect on what has moved (the pronoun) and what hasn't (the verb, because the verb is always second).

Workbook A, page 28

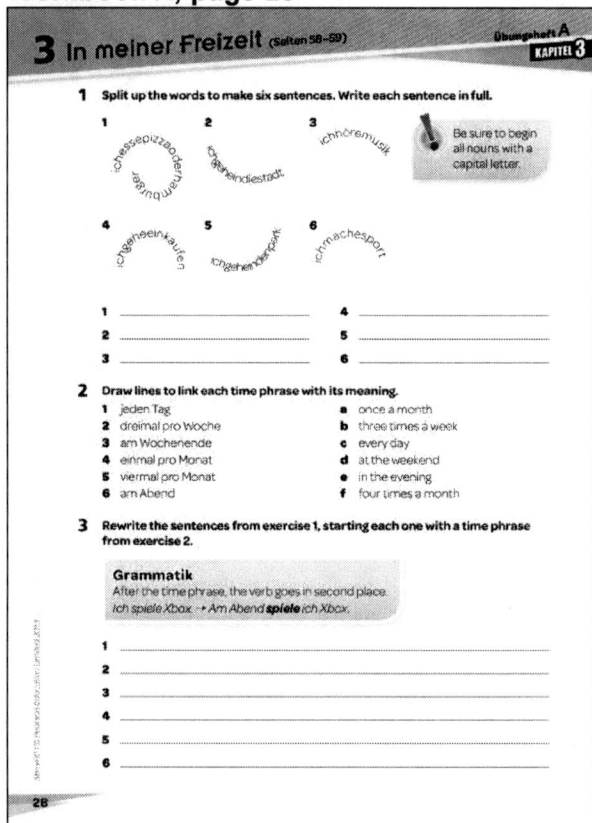

Answers

1 1 Ich esse Pizza oder Hamburger.

2 Ich gehe in die Stadt.

3 Ich höre Musik.

4 Ich gehe einkaufen.

5 Ich gehe in den Park.

6 Ich mache Sport.

2 1 c 2 b 3 d 4 a 5 e 6 f

3 Possible answers:

1 Einmal pro Monat esse ich Pizza oder Hamburger.

© Pearson Education Ltd 2013. Copying permitted for purchasing institution only. This material is not copyright free.

In meiner Freizeit | Freizeit – juhu! – **KAPITEL 3**

2 Viermal pro Monat gehe ich in die Stadt.
3 Jeden Tag höre ich Musik.
4 Dreimal pro Woche gehe ich einkaufen.
5 Am Wochenende gehe ich in den Park.
6 Am Abend mache ich Sport.

4 a – Jeden Tag mache ich Sport.
5 c – Einmal pro Woche esse ich Pizza.
6 d – Einmal pro Monat gehe ich ins Kino.

Worksheet

Thinking skills: It's only logical

Workbook B, page 28

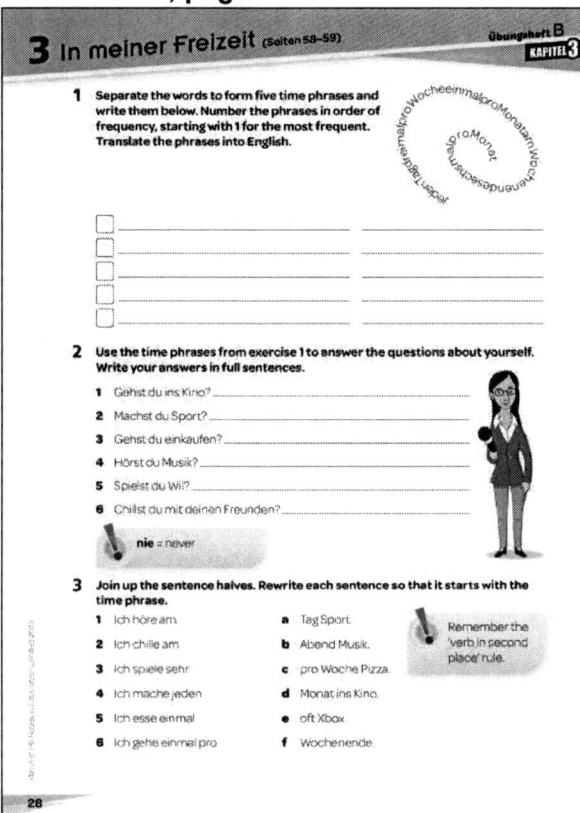

Answers

1 1 jeden Tag / every day
   2 dreimal pro Woche / three times a week
   5 einmal pro Monat / once a month
   3 am Wochenende / at the weekend
   4 sechsmal pro Monat / six times a month
2 Possible answers:
   1 Ich gehe einmal pro Monat ins Kino.
   2 Ich mache sechsmal pro Monat Sport. Ich spiele Tennis.
   3 Ich gehe dreimal pro Woche einkaufen.
   4 Ich höre jeden Tag Musik.
   5 Ich spiele dreimal pro Woche Wii.
   6 Ich chille am Wochenende mit meinen Freunden.
3 1 b – Am Abend höre ich Musik.
   2 f – Am Wochenende chille ich.
   3 e – Sehr oft spiele ich Xbox.

Answers

A Felix: Fußball, Karate
   Marie: Snowboard, Skateboard
   Selma: Handball, Snowboard
   Finn: Fußball, Karate
   Lukas: Fußball, Snowboard
B 1 Felix und Finn machen Karate.
   2 Marie, Selma und Lukas fahren Skateboard.
   3 Lukas spielt Fußball und fährt Snowboard.
C 1 and 5   2 and 4   3 and 6

© Pearson Education Ltd 2013. Copying permitted for purchasing institution only. This material is not copyright free.

4 Ich bin online (Pupil Book pp. 60–61)

Freizeit – juhu! – KAPITEL

Learning objectives
- Talking about mobiles and computers
- Talking about the future using the present tense

Programme of Study
GV2 Grammatical structures (sentence structure)
LC5 Accurate pronunciation and intonation
LC8 Translation into German

FCSE links
Unit 4 – Leisure (Free time/hobbies)

Grammar
The *wir* and *Sie/sie* forms
Talking about the future using the present tense + future time phrase

PLTS
C Creative thinkers

Key Language
Was machst du am Computer oder auf deinem Handy?
Ich chatte mit Freunden auf Facebook.
Ich mache Fotos oder Filme.
Ich suche und lese Infos für die Hausaufgaben.
Ich simse.
Ich lade Musik herunter.
Ich sehe Videos.
Ich surfe im Internet.
Ich spiele Computerspiele.
Ich telefoniere mit Freunden.
immer
manchmal
nie
jeden Morgen
heute
morgen
am Montag
nächste Woche
in zwei Wochen

Resources
Audio files:
54_Kapitel3_Einheit4_Aufgabe2
55_Kapitel3_Einheit4_Aufgabe4
Workbooks:
Übungsheft 1 A&B, page 29
ActiveTeach:
Starter 1 resource
Starter 2 resource
p.060 Flashcards
p.061 Extension reading activity
p.061 Grammar presentation
p.061 Video: Episode 6
p.061 Grammar worksheet
Plenary resource
ActiveLearn:
Listening A, Listening B
Reading A, Reading B
Grammar, Vocabulary

Starter 1

Aim

To classify new vocabulary from unit 4.

Pupils are given a set of phrases to put into a Venn diagram (Starter 1 resource). They will need to deduce what the new phrases mean. Ask the pupils why they have classified the words in the way they have. Once the new phrases have been presented to the class, pupils then go back to their Venn diagram and see if there are any phrases they would move, now they are sure of the meanings.

Conversion of the first person to the third person and singular verbs for free-time activities could also be revised.

1 Sieh dir die Aktivitäten an. Wie sagt man das? Versuch es mal. (Speaking L2)

Speaking. Pupils look at the illustrations showing different activities and decide how the German for each one is pronounced. Pupils check their ideas in exercise 2.

The *Tip* box points pupils to the key phonics words (see pupil book p. 8) to help them work out how to pronounce some of the new words presented in this unit.

2 Hör zu und überprüfe. (Listening L2)

Listening. Pupils listen to the audio and check their pronunciation of the activities from exercise 1.

Audioscript

- a – Ich chatte mit Freunden auf Facebook.
- b – Ich mache Fotos oder Filme.
- c – Ich suche und lese Infos für die Hausaufgaben.
- d – Ich simse.
- e – Ich lade Musik herunter.
- f – Ich sehe Videos.
- g – Ich surfe im Internet.
- h – Ich spiele Computerspiele.
- i – Ich telefoniere mit Freunden.

3 Partnerarbeit. Mach Dialoge. (Speaking L3)

Speaking. Pupils work in pairs to create dialogues based on the example in the pupil book.

The *Tip* box gives pupils the vocabulary for asking for more information.

© Pearson Education Ltd 2013. Copying permitted for purchasing institution only. This material is not copyright free.

Ich bin online | Freizeit – juhu! – **KAPITEL 3**

4 Hör dir die Interviews an und sieh dir die Aktivitäten in Aufgabe 1 an. Mach Notizen. Welche zwei Aktivitäten machen sie und wie oft? (1–4)
(Listening L3)

Listening. Pupils listen to the audio and, using the information about the activities presented in exercise 1, note down which two activities each speaker does and how often.

Audioscript

1 – Hallo! Ich heiße Timo. Ich bin ein großer Internet-Fan. Ich surfe jeden Tag im Internet. Ich finde Musik total cool und zweimal pro Woche lade ich meine Lieblingsmusik herunter.
2 – Hi! Ich bin Nina. Ich mache ziemlich viel auf meinem Handy ... ich simse jeden Tag und ich telefoniere oft mit Freunden.
3 – Guten Tag! Ich heiße Dominik. Ich spiele jeden Tag Computerspiele ... online, auf der Wii, auf meinem Handy ... Und einmal pro Woche suche und lese ich Infos für die Hausaufgaben.
4 – Hallo! Ich heiße Franziska. Ich chatte am Abend mit Freunden auf Facebook oder MSN. Ich mache am Wochenende viele Fotos oder Filme für Facebook.

Answers
1 g – every day, e – twice a week
2 d – every day, i – often
3 h – every day, c – once a week
4 a – in the evenings, b – at the weekend

5 Lies den Text und die Fragen. Wähl die richtigen Antworten aus. (Reading L4)

Reading. Pupils read the text and answer the questions, selecting the correct answer from a choice of two.

Some vocabulary is glossed for extra support.

Answers
1 Andrea 2 Andrea 3 Andrea und Emil
4 Andreas Vater 5 Andreas Vater
6 Andreas Mutter

Extension

An alternative version of this reading activity is provided on ActiveTeach (p.061 Extension reading activity, Reading L4).

Pupils read the text, which is slightly different, and answer the questions using German sentences

Some vocabulary is glossed for support.
Answers
1 Andrea telefoniert oft über Skype.
2 Andrea und Emil spielen gern Wii.
3 Andreas Vater schreibt ein Blog.
4 Emil/Andreas Bruder liest nicht gern.
5 Andrea sucht Infos online.
6 Emil/Andreas Bruder mag Sport.
7 Andreas Vater sieht gern Musikvideos.
8 Andreas Mutter liest gern E-Books.
9 Emil/Andreas Bruder fährt gern Skateboard.

Starter 2
Aim
To review word order with time phrases.

Pupils play the same word-order game as in unit 2, this time using key phrases from unit 4. The game is now more complex because pupils also have to match the pronoun to the conjugated verb.

A selection of A4 cards, each with either a pronoun, a verb, an object or a time phrase, are distributed around the class (Starter 2 resource). Pupils are asked to stand up one at a time and to stand in order making a sentence with a pronoun, verb and object (where appropriate). One pupil with a time phrase card is then asked to stand at the start of the 'sentence'. Pupils are then asked to move if they think they need to in order to respect word order conventions. This is a good visual representation of the word order rules and what happens when you put a time phrase at the start of the sentence. Pupils are asked to reflect on what has moved (the pronoun) and what hasn't (the verb, because the verb is always second).

Alternative starter 2

Use ActiveTeach p.060 Flashcards to review and practise language for talking about mobiles and computers.

Grammatik

The *Grammatik* box reminds pupils that the *wir* and *Sie/sie* forms of the verb are always the same as the infinitive – except for the irregular verb *sein*. There is more information and practice in the grammar unit on pupil book p. 69.

6 Lies den Text noch mal und füll die Lücken mit dem richtigen Zeitausdruck aus. (Reading L4)

Ich bin online | Freizeit – juhu! – **KAPITEL**

Reading. Pupils read the text from exercise 5 once again and complete the sentences with the correct time expression.

Answers
1 Andrea geht **jeden Tag** ins Internet.
2 Sie macht **immer** Hausaufgaben am Computer.
3 Emil liest **nie**.
4 **Jeden Morgen** schreibt Andreas Vater sein Blog.
5 Er sieht **am Wochenende** Musikvideos.
6 **Am Abend** liest Andreas Mutter E-Books.

Grammatik
The *Grammatik* box shows pupils how to talk about the future by using the present tense with a future time phrase. There is more information and practice in the grammar unit on pupil book p. 69.

7 Schreib diese Sätze auf Deutsch.
(Writing L3)

Writing. Pupils translate six sentences into German.

Answers
1 Wir telefonieren morgen über Skype.
2 Am Montag macht sie Hausaufgaben am Computer.
3 Nächste Woche fährt er Ski.
4 Andreas Vater schreibt in zwei Wochen ein Blog.
5 Er sieht am Abend Musikvideos.
6 Am Wochenende liest Andreas Mutter E-Books.

Plenary

Aim
For pupils to establish whether they have met the lesson objectives of talking about mobiles and computers and talking about the future using the present tense.

This can be played as a beat-the-teacher game or in pairs (if the grid is photocopied).

The grid is displayed on the board (Plenary resource). Choose one word from each box to make a sentence. Pupils take it in turns to guess a word or phrase. They have five guesses. If their guess is wrong, the phrase is crossed out; if it is right, then it is highlighted. The pupil who correctly guesses the final part of the sentence reads out the whole sentence and translates it into English.

Workbook A, page 29

Answers
1
  1 Ich lade Musik herunter.
  2 Ich suche Infos im Internet.
  3 Wir sehen Videos auf YouTube.
  4 Wir chatten auf Facebook.
  5 Ich mache mit meinem Handy Fotos. / Ich mache Fotos mit meinem Handy.
2 1 a 2 c 3 b
3
  1 Nächste Woche machen wir Filme.
  2 Am Montag suche ich Infos im Internet.
  3 Morgen chattest du auf Facebook.
  4 In zwei Wochen laden sie Musik herunter.
  5 Am Wochenende sieht Bronwyn Katzenvideos auf YouTube.

© Pearson Education Ltd 2013. Copying permitted for purchasing institution only. This material is not copyright free.

Ich bin online | Freizeit – juhu! – KAPITEL 3

Workbook B, page 29

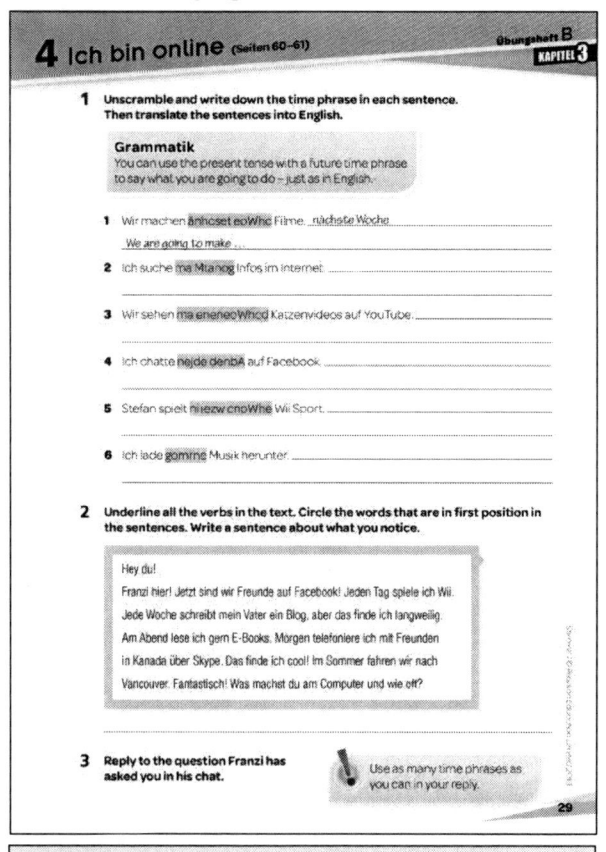

Answers

1
1 nächste Woche / We are going to make films next week.
2 am Montag / I am looking for information online on Monday.
3 am Wochenende / We are watching cat videos on YouTube at the weekend.
4 jeden Abend / I chat on Facebook every evening.
5 in zwei Wochen / Stefan is going to play Wii Sport in two weeks.
6 morgen / I am downloading music tomorrow.

2 Verbs: sind, spiele, schreibt, finde, lese, telefoniere, finde, fahren, machst

Key time phrases in first position: Jetzt, Jeden Tag, Jede Woche, Am Abend, Morgen, Im Sommer

Possible answers:
Most of the words in first position are time phrases. The verb and the subject are inverted after time phrases at the beginning of a sentence.

3 Possible answer:
Ich surfe oft im Internet. Ich sehe sehr gern Videos auf YouTube und ich chatte jeden Abend auf Facebook.

Worksheet

Grammar: Using the present tense to express future plans

© Pearson Education Ltd 2013. Copying permitted for purchasing institution only. This material is not copyright free.

Ich bin online | Freizeit – juhu! – KAPITEL

Answers

A Ich mache meine Hausaufgaben nächste Woche.
In zwei Wochen fahre ich Snowboard.

B Answers may vary.
1 Timo spielt morgen Computerspiele.
2 Nächste Woche telefonieren Mika und Marlis über Skype.
3 Er lädt morgen Musik herunter.
4 Amrei und Kuno chatten am Montag auf Facebook
5 Wir simsen nächste Woche.
6 In zwei Wochen macht sie Filme.

C Existing phrases translated. Pupils' future phrases may vary.
1 Timo spielt Computerspiele. / Timo is playing Computer games. /
2 Mika und Marlis telefonieren über Skype. / Mika and Marlis are skyping.
3 Er lädt Musik herunter. / He is downloading music
4 Amrei und Kuno chatten oft auf Facebook. / Amrei and Kuno often chat on Facebook
5 Wir simsen jeden Tag. / We text (each other) every day.
6 Zweimal pro Woche macht sie Filme. / She makes films twice a week.

Video

Episode 6

Ciara and Benno have come to a hip-hop dance school to talk to some German teenagers about their hobbies and have a go at dancing!

Answers

A Before watching
Answers will vary.

B Watch
1 horse riding, downloading music, playing guitar, reading, chatting on Facebook
2 horse riding: Dominik
going to the cinema: Sonja
dancing: both
playing Wii: Dominik
using Internet or Facebook: both

C Watch again
1 a) true; b) false; c) true; d) false; e) true
2 He invites them to join in and asks if they can dance.
3 Three times during the week and then in the disco at the weekend.
4 She is going to Dominik's concert.

D Discuss with your partner
1 They both like going to the cinema and reading.
2 You really can't dance.
3 It's fun.
4 Yes. Benno wants to go again next week as he found it fun, they both like dancing, and they both got dates for the weekend.

© Pearson Education Ltd 2013. Copying permitted for purchasing institution only. This material is not copyright free.

Freizeit – juhu! – **KAPITEL 3**

5 Listening Skills: Wir sind Freunde

(Pupil Book pp. 62–63)

Learning objectives	Key Language	Resources
• Developing prediction strategies • Understanding longer listening texts **Programme of Study** GV3 Developing vocabulary LC1 Listening and responding LC4 Expressing ideas (speaking) **FCSE links** Unit 1 – Relationships, Family and Friends (Family/friends)	No new key language. Pupils develop listening skills using key language from the chapter. **PLTS** C Creative thinkers	**Audio files:** 56_Kapitel3_Einheit5_Aufgabe2 57_Kapitel3_Einheit5_Aufgabe4 58_Kapitel3_Einheit5_Aufgabe5 59_Kapitel3_Einheit5_Aufgabe7 60_Kapitel3_Einheit5_Aufgabe8 **ActiveTeach:** Starter 2 resource

Starter 1

Aim

To work on prediction skills and review vocabulary from previous units.

Pupils are given five categories. In groups of four, they mind-map the different categories, trying to think of as many words as possible that they have either already seen in the pupil book or heard of elsewhere, for example German car manufacturers or football teams. They are given a countdown clock of ten minutes to do the activity before passing their mind-maps to another group to be marked. Suggestions are collated on the board. Pupils get one point for each word, two points if they are the only group to have thought of the word.

1 Lies die Titel. Welches Thema ist das? (Reading L3)

Reading. Pupils read the headlines and work out what the subject matter is.

Refer pupils to the skills feature on using any clues available to help with understanding, for example from pictures or titles.

The answers are given in exercise 2.

2 Hör zu. Überprüfe deine Antworten aus Aufgabe 1. (1–5) (Listening L3)

Listening. Pupils listen to the audio and check their answers from exercise 1.

Audioscript

1 – Meine Familie ist toll, aber mein Bruder nervt total.
2 – Tiere in Cafés? Ja, natürlich. Jetzt gibt es die neuen Katzen-Cafés in Tokio in Japan.
3 – Das neue Auto von Mercedes. Superschnell, super Technik, supertoll!
4 – Tennis? Volleyball? Handball? Egal. Sport macht fit und fit macht froh. Also, mach Sport!
5 – Fußball. Drei zu eins für Borussia Dortmund gegen Bayern München. Das ist also total schlecht für Bayern …

Answers

1 Familie 2 Tiere 3 Autos 4 Sport 5 Fußball

3 Partnerarbeit. Was sagen sie? Rate mal. (Speaking L3)

Speaking. In pairs, pupils look at the illustrations and emoticons and try to decide what the people are saying. They listen for the answers in exercise 4.

Refer pupils to the skills feature. The prediction activity primes pupils for what to listen out for, but their answers may not match the transcript exactly. It is useful to remind pupils of this before and after doing exercise 3. In feedback encourage pupils to share their different answers.

4 Hör zu und überprüfe. (1–5) (Listening L2)

Listening. Pupils listen to the audio and check their answers for exercise 3.

Audioscript

1 – Ich spiele gern Handball. Ich finde es gut.
2 – Ich spiele nicht gern Volleyball. Es ist stinklangweilig.
3 – Ich spiele sehr gern Fußball. Es ist toll.
4 – Ich spiele ziemlich gern Eishockey. Ich finde es nicht schlecht.
5 – Ich spiele sehr gern Wasserball. Es ist mein Lieblingssport.

© Pearson Education Ltd 2013. Copying permitted for purchasing institution only. This material is not copyright free.

Wir sind Freunde | **Freizeit – juhu!** – KAPITEL

> **Starter 2**
>
> **Aim**
>
> To review vocabulary from the unit and to focus on listening skills.
>
> Pupils have either a question or an answer card (Starter 2 resource). The cards are colour-coded, with one colour for question cards and one colour for answer cards. Pupils circulate around the classroom. If they have a question card, they must read their question to each person they meet. If they have an answer card, they read their answer once they've been asked the question. If the question and answer match, the pair then sit down together.
>
> This activity can be used to make pairs for further activities, encouraging pupils to work with different partners. It can also be used to make ability pairings.

5 Hör zu und füll die Lücken aus. Wähl aus dem Kasten. (Listening L4)

Listening. Pupils copy out the profiles. They then listen to the audio and fill in the gaps using words or phrases from the box provided.

Refer pupils to the skills feature. It suggests that pupils focus their listening by looking at the questions first to discover what type of information they need to look for.

Audioscript

- Herzlich willkommen. Heute hören wir ein Interview mit Martina und Christian, zwei Teenagern aus Stuttgart. Hallo, ihr beiden!
- Hallo!/Hi!
- Also wir machen ein Interview über Freizeit und Hobbys. Martina, wie bist du?
- Na ja, ich bin sehr laut und ziemlich sportlich.
- Laut und sportlich. Okay. Und welche Sportarten machst du gern?
- Eishockey ist mein Lieblingssport. Tennis spiele ich gern und ich finde Boxen super!
- Boxen! Tja, so was! Hast du noch andere Hobbys?
- Ja, ich habe viele Hobbys. Ich fahre Rad und ich tanze auch gern.
- Und was machst du am Computer?
- Auch ganz viel. Ich surfe oft im Internet und ich chatte mit Freunden.
- Danke Martina. Und Christian, wie bist du?
- Tja, also, ich bin ziemlich intelligent und auch kreativ.
- Intelligent und kreativ, okay, danke. Und bist du auch sportlich?
- Ich mache nicht so gern Sport, aber ich mache einmal pro Woche Judo. Badminton spiele ich auch manchmal.
- Und hast du noch andere Hobbys?
- Ja, Musik! Ich spiele zu Hause Keyboard und ich lese auch gern, vor allem Science-Fiction-Bücher.
- Und gehst du oft ins Internet?
- Ja, ich gehe jeden Tag ins Internet. Ich mache gern Fotos und Filme und ich lade am Wochenende immer meine Lieblingssongs herunter.
- Also Christian und Martina, vielen Dank für das Interview und auf Wiedersehen.
- Tschüs!

Answers

1 laut **2** Boxen **3** Rad fahren **4** mit Freunden chatten **5** kreativ **6** Badminton **7** lesen **8** Musik herunterladen

Extension

More able pupils could be directed to cover the word box and fill in the gaps by transcribing.

6 Tanja sucht einen Brieffreud oder eine Brieffreundin. Sieh dir das Bild an. Was sagt sie? Mach ein Brainstorming auf Deutsch. (Writing L2)

Writing. Pupils look at the picture and the information provided in the profile and brainstorm ideas on what the girl might be saying.

© Pearson Education Ltd 2013. Copying permitted for purchasing institution only. This material is not copyright free.

Wir sind Freunde | **Freizeit – juhu!** – KAPITEL 3

7 Partnerarbeit. Hör zu und mach Notizen auf Englisch. Dann vergleiche die Antworten mit einem Partner/einer Partnerin. Hör noch mal zu. Kannst du alle Details finden? (Listening L4)

Listening. Working in pairs, pupils listen to the audio and make notes on the contents in English. They then compare their answers with a partner and see if they can pick up on all the details.

Point out the skills feature, which advises pupils to combine all their pre-listening strategies – using visual and textual clues, predicting language and thinking about possible answers – to help with longer, open-ended tasks.

A second skills feature reminds pupils not to be put off by things they don't understand, rather to concentrate on what they *do* know!

Audioscript

– OK, wir suchen einen Brieffreund oder eine Brieffreundin für Tanja. Also, Tanja, beschreib dich ein bisschen.

– Na ja, also, ich heiße Tanja. Ich bin dreizehn Jahre alt und ich wohne zusammen mit meiner Familie in Bad Hersfeld in Deutschland. Es gibt fünf Personen in meiner Familie. Da sind meine Eltern, mein Bruder Finn, meine Schwester Selina und ich. Ich bin ziemlich lustig und laut. Ich bin auch kreativ und musikalisch. Ich finde Tiere toll und ich habe drei Katzen zu Hause. Ich bin nicht sehr sportlich, aber ich finde Badminton und Tischtennis okay. Musik hören ist mein Lieblingshobby. Ich sehe manchmal fern. Ich habe eine Digitalkamera und ich fotografiere gern.

Answers

Name: *Tanja*

Family (4): 5 people; parents; brother Finn; sister Selina

Personality (4): quite funny; loud; creative; musical

Pets (2): likes animals a lot; has 3 cats

Sport (3): not very sporty; thinks that badminton and table tennis are OK

Hobbies (3): favourite hobby is listening to music; sometimes watches TV; likes photography

8 Sieh dir die Profile in Aufgabe 5 an und hör Tanja noch mal zu. Wer ist der beste Brieffreund/die beste Brieffreundin für Tanja und warum? (Listening L4)

Listening. Pupils listen to the audio again. They then refer to the profiles in exercise 5 and decide who would make the best penfriend for Tanja.

Audioscript

For transcript see exercise 5.

Answers

The best penfriend match for Tanja is Christian. They have the following things in common:

kreativ

musikalisch

nicht sehr sportlich

Badminton

Fotografieren

The only attribute Tanja and Martina share is being *laut*.

Plenary

Aim

For pupils to establish whether they have met the lesson objectives of developing prediction strategies and understanding longer listening texts.

Pupils work individually and make a list of at least three tips for understanding longer listening texts. They then share their ideas with a partner and add to their lists. Finally, they share their ideas with their group of four to make a longer list. Each group then shares their best idea with the whole class (think-pair-share).

© Pearson Education Ltd 2013. Copying permitted for purchasing institution only. This material is not copyright free.

Freizeit – juhu! – KAPITEL

6 Writing Skills: Brieffreunde (Pupil Book pp. 64–65)

Learning objectives
- Making your writing interesting and varied
- Writing about your free time

Programme of Study
GV2 Grammatical structures (various)
LC2 Transcription
LC4 Expressing ideas (writing)

Key Language
No new key language. Pupils develop writing skills using key language from the chapter.

PLTS
S Self-managers

Resources
Audio files:
061_Kapitel3_Einheit6_Aufgabe1
Workbooks:
Übungsheft 1 A&B, page 30
ActiveTeach:
Starter 1 resource
Starter 2 resource
p.064 Exercise 4 grid

Starter 1

Aim

To work on making writing interesting and varied.

Pupils are given six categories of words in a grid (Starter 1 resource). In groups of four, they fill in the different categories, trying to think of as many words as possible that they have either already seen in the pupil book or that they have heard of which would add interest and variety to their written work.

They are given a countdown clock of ten minutes to do the activity, after which they pass their grids to another group to be marked.

Suggestions are collated on the board. Groups get one point for each word, two points if they are the only group to have thought of the word.

Further questioning can be done on the link between the different categories and NC levels (e.g. What would you need to include if you were trying to get a level 3?).

---

1 Hör zu und lies die E-Mail von Daniel. (Listening L4)

Listening. Pupils listen to the audio and read the email from Daniel.

Some vocabulary is glossed for support.

All the exercises in this unit use this text as source material.

Audioscript

Liebe Emily,

danke für deine E-Mail. Wie geht's?

Ich spiele sehr gern Eishockey. Das ist mein Lieblingssport und meine Lieblingsmannschaft ist EHC München. Sie spielen toll!

Meine Schwester spielt jeden Tag Volleyball, aber ich finde das total langweilig. Wir spielen am Wochenende zusammen Badminton. Ich spiele sehr gern Badminton. Und du? Machst du gern Sport?

Mein Vater fährt zweimal oder dreimal pro Woche Rad und ich fahre auch gern Rad. Wir fahren nächste Woche BMX-Rad in Dortmund – ich finde das cool! Ich sehe nicht so oft fern, aber ich sehe sehr gern Filme. Hast du einen Lieblingsfilm?

Ich gehe jeden Tag ins Internet. Ich spiele sehr gern Online-Spiele und ich suche oft Infos für die Hausaufgaben. Meine Mutter ist auch ein großer Internet-Fan. Sie schreibt ein Blog und liest gern E-Books.

Was machst du gern in deiner Freizeit?

Schreib bald!

Liebe Grüße

Daniel

2 Finde diese Wörter in Daniels E-Mail. (Reading L3)

Reading. Pupils re-read the email text from exercise 1 and look for the German of a selection of phrases.

With the help of the *Tip* box pupils should be made aware that they are dealing with informal ways of addressing people.

Answers
a Liebe **b** Danke für deine E-Mail **c** Wie geht's?
d Schreib bald! **e** Liebe Grüße

3 Lies die E-Mail noch mal. Welcher Absatz ist das? (Reading L4)

Reading. Pupils re-read the email from exercise 1 and work out in which paragraph Daniel covers the topics displayed.

Some vocabulary is glossed for support.

© Pearson Education Ltd 2013. Copying permitted for purchasing institution only. This material is not copyright free.

Brieffreunde | Freizeit – juhu! – **KAPITEL 3**

Answers

Beginn – Absatz 1

andere Sportarten – Absatz 3

Ende – Absatz 6

Lieblingssport – Absatz 2

Online-Interessen – Absatz 5

andere Hobbys – Absatz 4

4 Lies den Text noch mal. Schreib die Tabelle ab und vervollständige sie auf Deutsch. Schreib jedes Wort nur einmal auf. (Reading L4)

Reading. Pupils look at the email in exercise 1. They copy the table and complete it by selecting connectives, time expressions and questions that they find in the email. They may use each expression once only!

The skills feature points out that to make the *language* of their writing interesting and varied pupils should first recognise the features of a good piece of writing from a model and then adapt them. Exercises 4–7 help them to do this.

Answers

Connectives: *und*, aber, oder, auch

Time/frequency phrases: *jeden Tag*, am Wochenende, zweimal oder dreimal pro Woche, nicht so oft, oft

Questions: *Wie geht's?*, Und du?, Machst du gern Sport?, Hast du einen Lieblingsfilm?, Was machst du gern in deiner Freizeit?

Starter 2

Aim

To focus on writing about free time to a penfriend.

Pupils are given a model text in pairs (Starter 2 resource). This could be on paper or it could be laminated and used with whiteboard pens. They are asked to go through the model text and highlight examples of connectives, time phrases, frequency phrases, intensifiers, opinions and questions using different colours.

Each pair then works with another pair to share their answers and see if there is anything else which could be highlighted.

Finally, the group give the written work an NC level and write down what they think the writer has done well and suggestions for improvement targets.

5 Lies die E-mail. Schreib die Sätze ab und füll die Lücken aus. Dann schreib sie auf Englisch auf. (Reading L4)

Reading. Pupils read the email. They complete the sentences and then translate them into English.

The skills feature reminds pupils that there are lots of different ways to say you like – or dislike – something.

Answers

*1 Ich spiele **sehr gern** Eishockey. I really like playing ice hockey.*

*2 Das ist mein **Lieblingssport**. It is my favourite sport.*

*3 Ich **finde** das total **langweilig**. I find it totally boring.*

*4 Ich spiele **sehr gern** Badminton. I really like playing badminton.*

*5 Ich **finde** das cool! I think it's cool!*

*6 Meine Mutter ist auch ein großer Internet-**Fan**. My mother is also a big internet fan.*

6 Lies den Text. Finde die Sätze auf Deutsch und schreib sie auf. (Writing L2)

Writing. Pupils read the email and look for specific German sentences, which they write down.

The skills feature reminds pupils that they can vary their writing by including what people do and like.

Answers

1 Sie spielen toll!

2 Meine Schwester spielt jeden Tag Volleyball.

3 Wir spielen am Wochenende zusammen Badminton.

4 Mein Vater fährt zweimal oder dreimal pro Woche Rad.

5 Sie schreibt ein Blog.

6 Sie liest gern E-Books.

7 Sieh dir den Text noch mal an. Schreib Sätze. Beginn mit den unterstrichenen Wörtern. (Writing L3)

Writing. Using the email in exercise 1 as a source, pupils write out six sentences in German, rearranging the words to put the underlined phrase at the beginning of their sentence.

The skills feature reminds pupils that in German the verb always comes in second place, so they need to remember to put the words in the right order, for example after time expressions.

© Pearson Education Ltd 2013. Copying permitted for purchasing institution only. This material is not copyright free.

Brieffreunde | Freizeit – juhu! – **KAPITEL**

Answers

1 Jeden Tag spielt meine Schwester Volleyball.

2 Das finde ich total langweilig.

3 Am Wochenende spielen wir zusammen Badminton.

4 Nächste Woche fahren wir BMX-Rad in Dortmund.

5 Das finde ich cool!

6 Jeden Tag gehe ich ins Internet.

8 Schreib eine Antwort an Daniel über deine Freizeit. Benutze die Checkliste. (Writing L4)

Writing. Pupils write an answering email to Daniel, telling him about what they do in their own free time.

The skills feature points up a strategy for pupils to keep track of their answer, suggesting that they tick off items on the checklist as they include them in their work. This will help ensure that they cover everything.

9 Partnerarbeit. Überprüfe die E-Mail mit Hilfe der Checkliste. (Reading L4)

Reading. Working in pairs, pupils check their partner's work, using the checklist to guide them.

Plenary

Aim

For pupils to establish whether they have met the lesson objective of adding interest and variety to written work.

Pupils are given five sentences.

1 Ich spiele Tennis.
2 Meine Mutter geht schwimmen.
3 Mein Vater fährt Rad.
4 Wir fahren Skateboard.
5 Mein Bruder liest Comics.

The aim is to make the sentences as interesting as possible by using key words from the unit (connectives, time phrases, frequency phrases, intensifiers, opinions and questions).
Merits/prizes are awarded for the best sentences, which could be written up on A4 paper and displayed for the next lesson.

Alternative plenary

Use ActiveTeach p.065 Class Game to review word order.

Workbook A, page 30

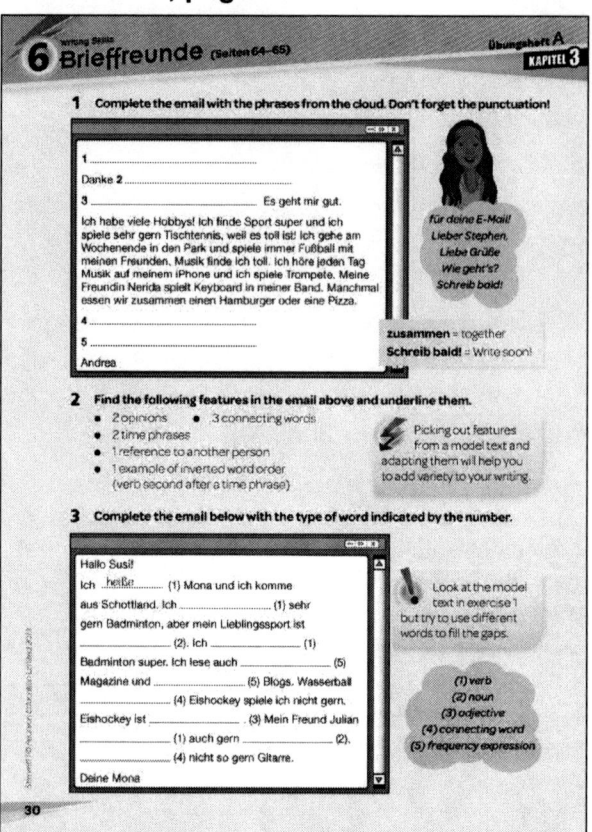

Answers

1 1 Lieber Stephen,
   2 für deine E-Mail!
   3 Wie geht's?
   4 Schreib bald!
   5 Liebe Grüße

2 2 opinions: Ich finde Sport super …; Musik finde ich toll.
   2 time phrases: am Wochenende; jeden Tag
   1 reference to another person: Meine Freundin Nerida …
   1 example of inverted word order: Manchmal essen wir …
   3 connecting words: und; weil; oder

3 Possible answers:
   heiße; spiele; Tennis; finde; oft; manchmal; und; langweilig; spielt; Flöte; aber

© Pearson Education Ltd 2013. Copying permitted for purchasing institution only. This material is not copyright free.

Workbook B, page 30

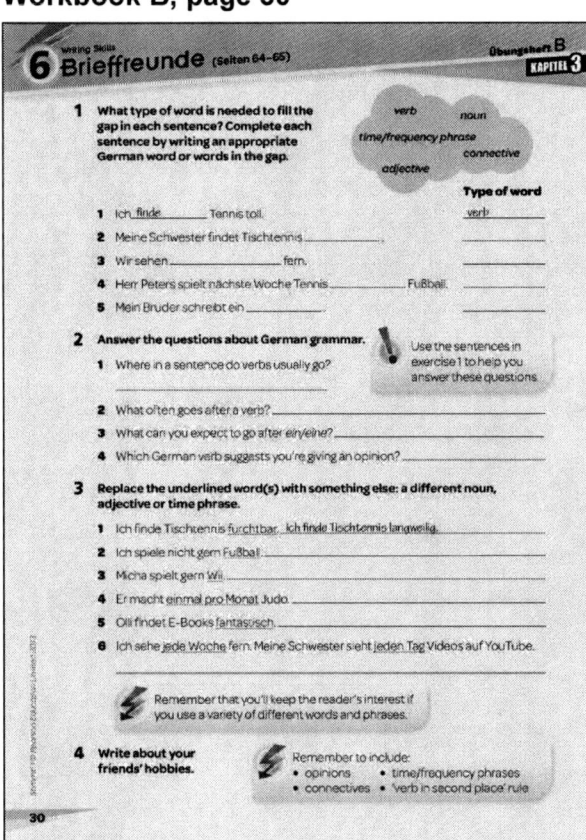

Answers

1 Possible answers:

  1 finde – verb

  2 doof – adjective

  3 oft – time/frequency phrase

  4 oder – connective

  5 Buch – noun

2 1 in second position

  2 a time/frequency phrase

  3 a noun

  4 finden

3 Possible answers:

  1 Ich finde Tischtennis **langweilig**.

  2 Ich spiele nicht gern **Badminton**.

  3 Micha spielt gern **Tischtennis**.

  4 Er macht **zweimal pro Woche** Judo.

  5 Olli findet E-Books **toll**.

  6 Ich sehe **manchmal** fern. Meine Schwester sieht **am Abend** Videos auf YouTube.

4 Pupils' own answers.

Freizeit – juhu! – KAPITEL

Lernzieltest und Wiederholung (Pupil Book pp. 66–67)

Lernzieltest
Pupils use this checklist to review language covered in the chapter, working on it in pairs in class or on their own at home. There is a Word version on ActiveTeach which can be printed out and given to students. Encourage them to follow up any weakness they identify. There are Target Setting Sheets included in the Assessment Pack, and an opportunity for pupils to record their own levels and targets on the *Mein Fortschritt* page in the Workbooks. You can also use the *Lernzieltest* checklist as an end-of-chapter plenary option.

Wiederholung
These revision exercises can be used for assessment purposes or for pupils to practise before tackling the assessment tasks in the Assessment Pack.

Resources
Audio files:
62_Kapitel3_Wiederholung_Aufgabe1
Workbooks:
Übungsheft 1 A&B, pages 31–32
ActiveTeach:
p.066 Lernzieltest checklist

1 Hör zu. Schreib den richtigen Buchstaben auf. (1–6) (Listening L2)

Listening. Pupils listen to the audio and match the illustrations to the speaker.

Audioscript

1 – Elena, was machst du gern in deiner Freizeit?
– Ich gehe gern einkaufen.
– Und was machst du gern am Computer?
– Ich spiele gern Computerspiele.
2 – Adrian, was machst du gern mit deinen Freunden?
– Wir chillen gern zusammen.
– Und was machst du gern auf deinem Handy?
– Ich mache Fotos.
3 – Was machst du gern in deiner Freizeit, Sara?
– Ich gehe gern ins Kino.
– Und was machst du gern am Computer?
– Ich sehe Videos.
4 – Was machst du gern mit deinen Freunden, Timo?
– Wir gehen schwimmen.
– Und was machst du gern am Computer?
– Ich surfe am Internet.
5 – Was machst du gern mit deinen Freunden, Nina?
– Wir spielen Tennis.
– Und was machst du gern auf deinem Handy?
– Ich lade Musik herunter.
6 – Dominik, was machst du gern in deiner Freizeit?
– Ich spiele Gitarre.
– Und was machst du gern am Computer?
– Ich suche Infos für die Hausaufgaben.

Answers
1 c 2 f 3 a 4 b 5 e 6 d

2 Gruppenarbeit. Mach Dialoge. (Speaking L3–4)

Speaking. Working in groups, pupils talk about what they do in their free time.

The *Tip* box gives the pupils some ideas on how to keep the conversation going.

3 Lies die E-Mail. Welche vier Sätze sind richtig? (Reading L3)

Reading. Pupils read the text and work out which of the four statements are correct.

Answers
1, 4, 6 and 7 are correct.

© Pearson Education Ltd 2013. Copying permitted for purchasing institution only. This material is not copyright free.

Lernzieltest und Wiederholung | Freizeit – juhu! – **KAPITEL 3**

4 Beantworte Pauls Fragen. Was willst du Paul noch fragen? Schreib eine E-Mail. Schreib 50–70 Wörter. (Writing L3–4)

Writing. Pupils write a return email, answering Paul's questions from the email in exercise 3 and including some questions of their own.

Pupils who need a framework to support their writing can first be given (or asked to come up with in groups) a content checklist of key words to cover, using the questions that Paul asks. They can be referred back to unit 6 too. Ask pupils to write 1–2 short sentences for each question, referring back to the relevant units in chapter 3. After that, they can be asked to check what they have written against the quality of language checklist (see below). They will probably not have included the references to other people or example of inverted word order, so they can then add to their work by doing this. Individual support can be offered at each stage, where appropriate.

Beginn ✓	4 opinions
Tennis	3 linking words
Lieblingssport	3 frequency expressions
Computer	2 questions
Wochenende	2 references to other people
mit Freunden	1 example of inverted word order
Ende	

Extension

Pupils who are more independent at this stage can be referred back to the checklist on p. 65. After writing, pupils can swap work for checking.

Workbook A, page 31

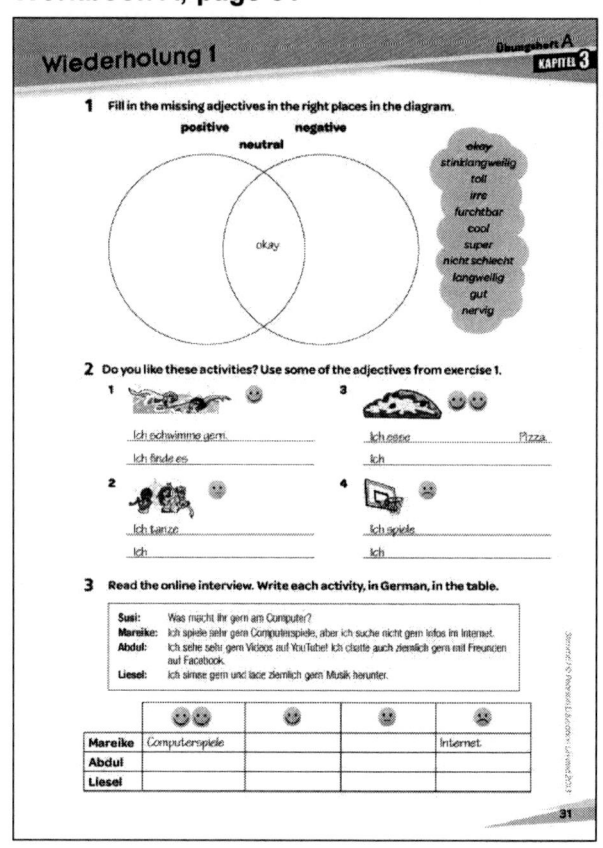

Answers

1 positive: toll; irre; cool; super; gut

   neutral: okay; nicht schlecht

   negative: stinklangweilig; furchtbar; langweilig; nervig

2 Possible answers:

   1 Ich schwimme gern. Ich finde es toll.

   2 Ich tanze ziemlich gern. Ich finde es okay.

   3 Ich esse sehr gern Pizza. Ich finde Pizza super.

   4 Ich spiele nicht gern Basketball. Ich finde es furchtbar.

3 Mareike: Computerspiele (sehr gern), Internet (nicht gern)

   Abdul: Videos auf YouTube (sehr gern), chatten (ziemlich gern)

   Liesel: simsen (gern), Musik herunterladen (ziemlich gern)

© Pearson Education Ltd 2013. Copying permitted for purchasing institution only. This material is not copyright free.

Lernzieltest und Wiederholung | Freizeit – juhu! – KAPITEL

Workbook B, page 31

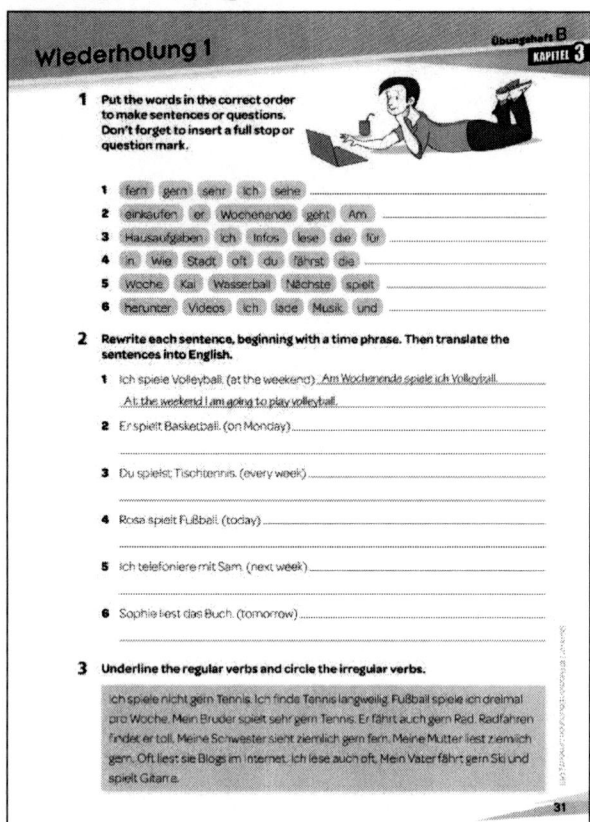

Wiederholung 1 — Übungsheft B, KAPITEL 3

1 Put the words in the correct order to make sentences or questions. Don't forget to insert a full stop or question mark.
  1 fern gern sehr Ich sehe
  2 einkaufen er Wochenende geht Am
  3 Hausaufgaben Ich Infos lese die für
  4 in Wie Stadt oft du fährst die
  5 Woche Kai Wasserball Nächste spielt
  6 herunter Videos Ich lade Musik und

2 Rewrite each sentence, beginning with a time phrase. Then translate the sentences into English.
  1 Ich spiele Volleyball. (at the weekend) Am Wochenende spiele ich Volleyball. At the weekend I am going to play volleyball.
  2 Er spielt Basketball. (on Monday)
  3 Du spielst Tischtennis. (every week)
  4 Rosa spielt Fußball. (today)
  5 Ich telefoniere mit Sam. (next week)
  6 Sophie liest das Buch. (tomorrow)

3 Underline the regular verbs and circle the irregular verbs.
  Ich spiele nicht gern Tennis. Ich finde Tennis langweilig. Fußball spiele ich dreimal pro Woche. Mein Bruder spielt sehr gern Tennis. Er fährt auch gern Rad. Radfahren findet er toll. Meine Schwester sieht ziemlich gern fern. Meine Mutter liest ziemlich gern. Oft liest sie Blogs im Internet. Ich lese auch oft. Mein Vater fährt gern Ski und spielt Gitarre.

Workbook A, page 32

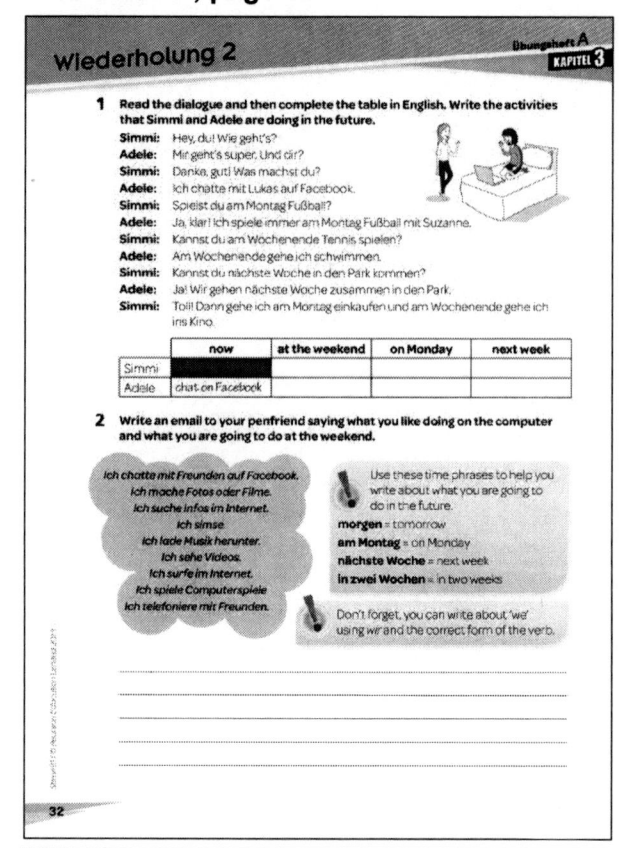

Wiederholung 2 — Übungsheft A, KAPITEL 3

1 Read the dialogue and then complete the table in English. Write the activities that Simmi and Adele are doing in the future.
  Simmi: Hey, du! Wie geht's?
  Adele: Mir geht's super. Und dir?
  Simmi: Danke, gut! Was machst du?
  Adele: Ich chatte mit Lukas auf Facebook.
  Simmi: Spielst du am Montag Fußball?
  Adele: Ja, klar! Ich spiele immer am Montag Fußball mit Suzanne.
  Simmi: Kannst du am Wochenende Tennis spielen?
  Adele: Am Wochenende gehe ich schwimmen.
  Simmi: Kannst du nächste Woche in den Park kommen?
  Adele: Ja! Wir gehen nächste Woche zusammen in den Park.
  Simmi: Toll! Dann gehe ich am Montag einkaufen und am Wochenende gehe ich ins Kino.

	now	at the weekend	on Monday	next week
Simmi				
Adele	chat on Facebook			

2 Write an email to your penfriend saying what you like doing on the computer and what you are going to do at the weekend.

  Ich chatte mit Freunden auf Facebook.
  Ich mache Fotos oder Filme.
  Ich suche Infos im Internet.
  Ich simse.
  Ich lade Musik herunter.
  Ich sehe Videos.
  Ich surfe im Internet.
  Ich spiele Computerspiele.
  Ich telefoniere mit Freunden.

  Use these time phrases to help you write about what you are going to do in the future.
  morgen = tomorrow
  am Montag = on Monday
  nächste Woche = next week
  in zwei Wochen = in two weeks

  Don't forget, you can write about 'we' using *wir* and the correct form of the verb.

Answers

1 1 Ich sehe sehr gern fern.
   2 Am Wochenende geht er einkaufen.
   3 Ich lese Infos für die Hausaufgaben.
   4 Wie oft fährst du in die Stadt?
   5 Nächste Woche spielt Kai Wasserball.
   6 Ich lade Musik und Videos herunter.

2 1 Am Wochenende spiele ich Volleyball. / At the weekend I play volleyball.
   2 Am Montag spielt er Basketball. / On Monday he plays basketball.
   3 Jede Woche spielst du Tischtennis. / Every week you play table tennis.
   4 Heute spielt Rosa Fußball. / Today Rosa plays football.
   5 Nächste Woche telefoniere ich mit Sam. / I'll call Sam next week.
   6 Morgen liest Sophie das Buch. / Tomorrow Sophie will read the book.

3 Regular verbs: spiele, finde, spiele, spielt, findet, spielt
   Irregular verbs: fährt, sieht, liest, liest, lese, fährt

Answers

1 **Simmi:** cinema (at the weekend), shopping (on Monday), park with Adele (next week)
  Adele: chat on Facebook (now), swimming (at the weekend), football with Suzanne (on Monday), park with Simmi (next week)

2 Pupils' own answers.

© Pearson Education Ltd 2013. Copying permitted for purchasing institution only. This material is not copyright free.

Lernzieltest und Wiederholung | Freizeit – juhu! – KAPITEL 3

Workbook B, page 32

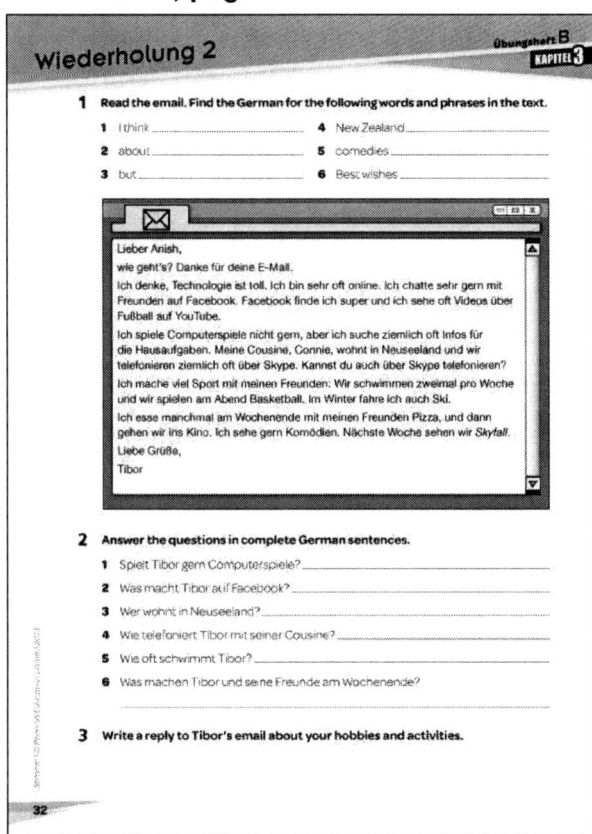

Wiederholung 2 — Übungsheft B, KAPITEL 3

1 Read the email. Find the German for the following words and phrases in the text.

1 I think _____ 4 New Zealand _____
2 about _____ 5 comedies _____
3 but _____ 6 Best wishes _____

> Lieber Anish,
> wie geht's? Danke für deine E-Mail.
> Ich denke, Technologie ist toll. Ich bin sehr oft online. Ich chatte sehr gern mit Freunden auf Facebook. Facebook finde ich super und ich sehe oft Videos über Fußball auf YouTube.
> Ich spiele Computerspiele nicht gern, aber ich suche ziemlich oft Infos für die Hausaufgaben. Meine Cousine, Connie, wohnt in Neuseeland und wir telefonieren ziemlich oft über Skype. Kannst du auch über Skype telefonieren?
> Ich mache viel Sport mit meinen Freunden: Wir schwimmen zweimal pro Woche und wir spielen am Abend Basketball. Im Winter fahre ich auch Ski.
> Ich esse manchmal am Wochenende mit meinen Freunden Pizza, und dann gehen wir ins Kino. Ich sehe gern Komödien. Nächste Woche sehen wir *Skyfall*.
> Liebe Grüße,
> Tibor

2 Answer the questions in complete German sentences.

1 Spielt Tibor gern Computerspiele? _____
2 Was macht Tibor auf Facebook? _____
3 Wer wohnt in Neuseeland? _____
4 Wie telefoniert Tibor mit seiner Cousine? _____
5 Wie oft schwimmt Tibor? _____
6 Was machen Tibor und seine Freunde am Wochenende? _____

3 Write a reply to Tibor's email about your hobbies and activities.

Answers

1 1 Ich denke 2 über 3 aber
4 Neuseeland 5 Komödien
6 Liebe Grüße

2 1 Nein. Tibor spielt nicht gern Computerspiele.
2 Er chattet mit (seinen) Freunden auf Facebook.
3 Seine Cousine, Connie, wohnt in Neuseeland.
4 Tibor telefoniert mit seiner Cousine über Skype.
5 Er schwimmt zweimal pro Woche.
6 Er isst mit (seinen) Freunden Pizza und geht dann ins Kino.

3 Pupils' own answers.

© Pearson Education Ltd 2013. Copying permitted for purchasing institution only. This material is not copyright free.

Freizeit – juhu! – KAPITEL

Grammatik (Pupil Book pp. 68–69)

The *Stimmt!* Grammatik section provides a more detailed summary of key grammar covered in the chapter, along with further exercises to practise these points.

Grammar topics
Verbs – the present tense
Irregular verbs – the present tense
Word order
The *wir* and *Sie/sie* forms
Future plans with the present tense

Resources
Workbooks:
Übungsheft 1 A&B, page 33

Verbs – the present tense

1 Write out *spielen* with the correct verb endings. Check the endings for *wohnen* on page 35 if you need to. (Writing L2)

Answers
ich spiel**e**
du spiel**st**
er/sie/es spiel**t**
wir spiel**en**
ihr spiel**t**
Sie spiel**en**
sie spiel**en**

2 Translate each sentence into German, using the correct form of *spielen*. Think carefully about the subject. (Writing L3)

The *Tip* box reminds pupils to think carefully about who is doing the action (i.e. I, we, they, etc.).

Answers
1 Ich **spiele** Fußball.
2 Meine Schwester **spielt** Hockey.
3 Mein Bruder und ich **spielen** Wii.
4 Meine zwei Katzen spielen jeden Tag.
5 **Spielst** du Computerspiele?
6 Mario **spielt** gern Tennis.
7 Frau Pfannkuch, **spielen** Sie Keyboard?
8 Lisa und Max, ihr **spielt** Keyboard!

Irregular verbs – the present tense

3 Write out these sentences, changing the subject to that shown in brackets. Then translate the sentences. (Writing L4)

Answers
1 *Er fährt gern Rad.* He likes to cycle.
2 *Meine Schwester sieht jeden Abend fern.* My sister watches TV every evening.
3 *Angelika, liest du gern?* Angelika, do you like reading?
4 *Dan, fährst du gern Rad?* Dan, do you like riding a bike?

Word order

4 Write out these sentences, starting with the time phrase. (Writing L4)

Answers
1 Einmal pro Woche lese ich.
2 Am Wochenende fahren wir Rad.
3 Dreimal pro Woche schwimmt er.
4 Einmal pro Monat machen sie Judo.
5 Am Abend spiele ich oft Xbox.
6 Jeden Tag tanzen wir in der Schule.

The wir and Sie/sie forms

5 Fill in the gaps with the correct form of the verb given in brackets. (Writing L3)

Answers
1 Wir **telefonieren** über Skype.
2 Wir **sind** gute Freunde.
3 Sie **spielen** oft zusammen Tennis.
4 Meine Eltern **sind** cool.

© Pearson Education Ltd 2013. Copying permitted for purchasing institution only. This material is not copyright free.

Future plans with the present tense

6 Substitute the present tense time phrase for the future one in brackets to change the meaning from present to future. Write out the English meaning of the new sentences. (Writing L4)

> **Answers**
>
> *1 Ich schwimme morgen.* I'm going swimming tomorrow.
>
> *2 Wir sehen am Wochenende fern.* We're going to watch TV at the weekend.
>
> *3 Er fährt in zwei Wochen Skateboard.* He's going skateboarding in two weeks.
>
> *4 Sie spielen am Montag Tischtennis.* They're going to play table tennis on Monday.
>
> *5 Sie spielt nächste Woche Volleyball.* She's going to play volleyball next week.
>
> *6 Wir gehen in drei Wochen ins Kino.* We're going to the cinema in three weeks.

7 Choose four of your sentences from exercise 6 and rewrite them, beginning with the time phrase. Think carefully about word order! (Writing L4)

> **Possible answers**
>
> 1 Morgen schwimme ich.
>
> 2 Am Wochenende sehen wir fern.
>
> 3 In zwei Wochen fährt er Skateboard.
>
> 4 Am Montag spielen sie Tischtennis.
>
> 5 Nächste Woche spielt sie Volleyball.
>
> 6 In drei Wochen gehen wir ins Kino.

Workbook A, page 33 to follow

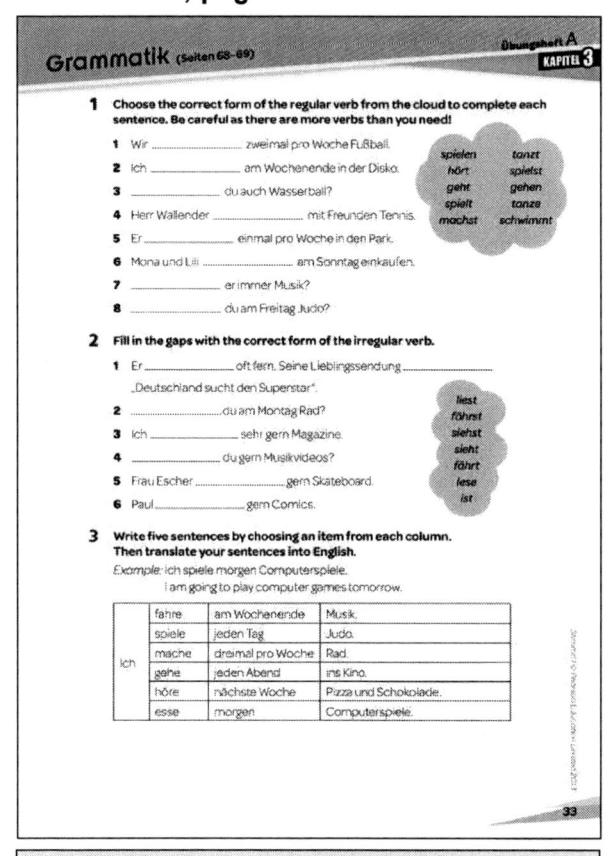

> **Answers**
>
> 1 1 spielen 2 tanze 3 Spielst 4 spielt
>   5 geht 6 gehen 7 Hört 8 Machst
>
> 2 1 sieht; ist 2 Fährst 3 lese 4 Siehst
>   5 fährt 6 liest
>
> 3 Possible answers:
>
>   Ich fahre ... Rad.
>
>   Ich spiele ... Computerspiele.
>
>   Ich mache ... Judo.
>
>   Ich gehe ... ins Kino.
>
>   Ich höre ... Musik.
>
>   Ich esse ... Pizza und Schokolade.

Workbook B, page 33

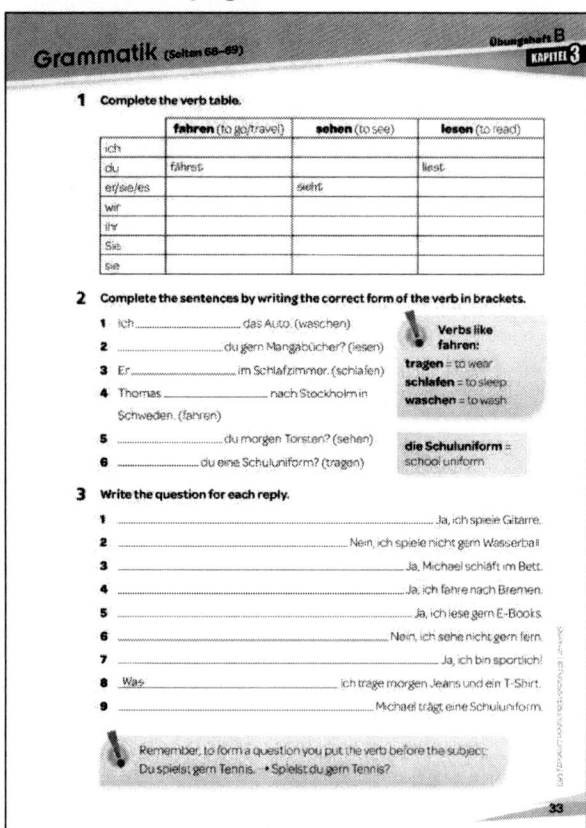

Grammatik (Seiten 68–69)

1 Complete the verb table.

	fahren (to go/travel)	**sehen** (to see)	**lesen** (to read)
ich			
du	fährst		liest
er/sie/es		sieht	
wir			
ihr			
Sie			
sie			

2 Complete the sentences by writing the correct form of the verb in brackets.

1 Ich .... das Auto. (waschen)
2 .... du gern Mangabücher? (lesen)
3 Er .... im Schlafzimmer. (schlafen)
4 Thomas .... nach Stockholm in Schweden. (fahren)
5 .... du morgen Torsten? (sehen)
6 .... du eine Schuluniform? (tragen)

Verbs like **fahren**:
tragen = to wear
schlafen = to sleep
waschen = to wash

die Schuluniform = school uniform

3 Write the question for each reply.

1 .... Ja, ich spiele Gitarre.
2 .... Nein, ich spiele nicht gern Wasserball.
3 .... Ja, Michael schläft im Bett.
4 .... Ja, ich fahre nach Bremen.
5 .... Ja, ich lese gern E-Books.
6 .... Nein, ich sehe nicht gern fern.
7 .... Ja, ich bin sportlich!
8 Was .... ich trage morgen Jeans und ein T-Shirt.
9 .... Michael trägt eine Schuluniform.

Remember, to form a question you put the verb before the subject:
Du spielst gern Tennis. → Spielst du gern Tennis?

Answers

1 fahre / fährst / fährt / fahren / fahrt / fahren / fahren

sehe / siehst / sieht / sehen / seht / sehen / sehen

lese / liest / liest / lesen / lest / lesen / lesen

2 1 wasche 2 Liest 3 schläft 4 fährt
5 Siehst 6 Trägst

3 1 Spielst du Musik?
2 Spielst du gern Wasserball?
3 Schläft Michael im Bett?
4 Fährst du nach Bremen?
5 Liest du gern E-Books?
6 Siehst du gern fern?
7 Bist du sportlich?
8 Was trägst du morgen?
9 Was trägt Michael?

Freizeit – juhu! – KAPITEL 3

Projektzone: Ich sammle! (Pupil Book pp. 72–73)

The *Projektzone* is one or two optional units in which no new grammar is introduced, but in which the chapter topic is extended into an exciting cultural and practical context which allows for cross-curricular and project work. **Learning objectives** • Learning about collections • Researching and describing an unusual collection	**Programme of Study** **GV3** Developing vocabulary **LC2** Transcription **LC4** Expressing ideas (speaking) **FCSE links** Unit 4 – Leisure (Free time/hobbies) **PLTS** **I** Independent enquirers	**Resources** **Audio files:** 63_Kapitel3_Projektzone_Aufgabe2 64_Kapitel3_Projektzone_Aufgabe3 **ActiveTeach:** p.072 Exercise 3 grid Starter 2 resource Plenary resource

Starter 1

Aim

To reflect on what people collect.

Pupils mind-map individually for three minutes, reflecting on the different types of things people collect. They use a dictionary to find out how to say these things in German. After three minutes they share ideas with a partner, adding to their mind-map. They then share their joint ideas with another pair (think-pair-share). All ideas are collated on the board.

1 Man kann alles sammeln! Was passt zusammen? (1–9) (Reading L2)

Reading. Pupils match the photos to the vocabulary. They listen to the audio in exercise 2 to check their answers.

The *Tip* box highlights a feature of German in which several nouns can be joined together to make one word (compound nouns). Pupils can help solve the problem of translation by splitting the words up into perhaps more familiar individual words.

Answers
1 f 2 g 3 a 4 e 5 i 6 h 7 b 8 d 9 c

2 Hör zu und überprüfe. (1–9) (Listening L2)

Listening. Pupils listen to the audio and check their answers from exercise 1.

Audioscript

1 – Ich sammle Postkarten.
2 – Ich sammle Freundschaftsbänder.
3 – Ich habe eine Modellautosammlung.
4 – Ich sammle Fossilien.
5 – Ich sammle Tassen.
6 – Ich sammle Modellelefanten.
7 – Ich habe eine Mangasammlung.
8 – Ich habe eine Fußballkartensammlung.
9 – Ich sammle Computerspiele.

Starter 2

Aim

To build compound nouns and to think about meanings and gender with compound nouns.

A set of cards is distributed around the class (Starter 2 resource). Pupils put the nouns together as a jigsaw puzzle. The cards could be enlarged so that the activity could be done as a whole class activity. Pupils work out the meanings of the words they have built without referring to a dictionary and make a list in their books in German and English. They highlight the article. Ask pupils how they decided what the words meant and why they think the particular articles have been used.

3 Hör zu. Was sammeln sie? Wie viele Dinge haben sie in ihrer Sammlung? Schreib die Tabelle ab und füll sie aus. (1–4) (Listening L3)

Listening. Pupils listen to the audio and identify what the speakers collect and how many they have in their collection. They complete a table with this information.

Audioscript

1 – Tina, sammelst du etwas?
  – Ja, ich habe eine tolle Mangasammlung. Manga ist das japanische Wort für Comics. Ich habe siebenundneunzig Mangabücher.
  – Siebenundneunzig! Wow!
2 – Elias, hast du eine Sammlung?
  – Ja. Ich sammle Fußballkarten. Ich habe vierundfünfzig Karten in meiner Sammlung.

© Pearson Education Ltd 2013. Copying permitted for purchasing institution only. This material is not copyright free.

Ich sammle! | Freizeit – juhu! – KAPITEL

3 – *Brigitte, sammelst du etwas?*
– *Nein, aber mein Vater sammelt Tassen. Er hat fünfundachtzig.*
– *Fünfundachtzig Tassen. Das ist aber interessant!*

4 – *Anton, hast du eine Sammlung?*
– *Ja. Ich sammle Computerspiele für meine Xbox. Ich habe achtzehn Xboxspiele.*
– *Wie viele? Achtzehn!?! Super!*

Answers
1 Mangabücher, 97
2 Fußballkarten, 54
3 Tassen, 85
4 Xboxspiele/Computerspiele, 18

4 Gruppenarbeit. Diskutiere deine Meinung mit deiner Gruppe. (Speaking L3–4)

Speaking. Working in groups, pupils talk about what they collect and what they think about their collections.

Some vocabulary is glossed for support.

The *Tip* box gives pupils the vocabulary for saying that they *don't* collect anything.

5 Lies die Texte. Korrigiere die Sätze. (Reading L3)

Reading. Pupils read the four texts and correct the sentences at the side.

Some vocabulary is glossed for support.

Answers
1 Johanna wohnt **(in Graz)** in Österreich.
2 Johanna sammelt **Bananenaufkleber**.
3 Markus sammelt **Elefanten**.
4 Gregor hat **87** Fußballkarten.
5 Melanie sammelt seit **2007** Schokoladenpapiere.
6 Melanies Sammlung ist **groß**.

6 Sieh dir die Infos an. Schreib Sätze. (Writing L4)

Writing. Pupils look at the information provided in the three profiles and write a few sentences about each person.

7 Suche Infos online. Finde (oder erfinde) eine interessante Sammlung. Mach ein Poster mit Texten und Bildern. (Writing L4)

Writing. Pupils explore online to gather information about a collection that interests them. They then use this information to put together a poster with text and images.

The *Tip* box reminds pupils to look back through their textbook and reuse some familiar language.

Plenary

Aim

For pupils to establish whether they have met the lesson objective of describing an unusual collection.

Pupils have the gap-fill text on paper (Plenary resource). They fill in the missing words and then compare with a partner. For less able pupils the necessary verbs could also be given. Different gap-fill texts could be given, depending on whether the focus should be on verb formation, nouns or adjectives. Pupils could then be asked to reflect on how the texts might further be improved (e.g. by adding connectives, time phrases, opinions).

© Pearson Education Ltd 2013. Copying permitted for purchasing institution only. This material is not copyright free.

Freizeit – juhu! – **KAPITEL 3**

Extra (Pupil Book pp. 124–125)

Self-access reading and writing

A Reinforcement

1 Finde die Paare. (Reading L2)

Reading. Pupils match the sentence halves.

Answers
1 d   2 c   3 f   4 e   5 a   6 b

2 Ist das positiv ☺, negativ ☹ oder dazwischen ☻? (Reading L3)

Reading. Pupils read the sentences and decide if they are positive, negative or neutral in mood.

Answers
1 negative   2 positive   3 negative   4 in between
5 negative   6 positive

3 Sieh dir Halims Zimmer an. Stell dir vor, du bist Halim. Schreib sechs Sätze über dich. (Writing L4)

Writing. Pupils look at the illustration of Halim's room. Imagining that they are Halim, they write six sentences about themselves.

Answers
Ich spiele gern Wii.
Ich bin sehr sportlich.
Ich spiele gern Fußball und Basketball.
Mein Lieblingssport ist Basketball.
Ich lese gern.
Ich spiele Gitarre.
Ich fahre Skateboard.
Ich mache Judo.
Ich höre gern Musik.
Ich fahre gern Rad.
Ich spiele Computerspiele.
(Pupils' answers may vary.)

B Extension

1 Finde einen englischen Freund/eine englische Freundin für die deutschen Jungen und Mädchen. (Reading L3)

Reading. Pupils look at the texts and illustrations and find a suitable English penfriend for the German people.

Answers
Lilian + Georgia
Dominik + Deepesh
Alina + Hannah
Serkan + Nathalie
Mia + Luke

2 Sieh dir die fünf deutschen Texte an. Wer ist das? (Reading L4)

Reading. Pupils look at the German sentences and decide which of the young people from exercise 1 the sentence refers to.

The *Tip* box reminds pupils to look carefully at the pronoun and verb in questions 2 and 6 to work out how many people *sie machen* and *sie hören* refer to.

Answers
1 Mia   2 Dominik und Alina   3 Serkan   4 Dominik
5 Lilian   6 Lilian und Alina

3 Schreib ein Interview über deine Freizeit. (Writing L4)

Writing. Pupils write an interview about how they spend their free time.

The pupil book provides some stimulus ideas and words to help.

© Pearson Education Ltd 2013. Copying permitted for purchasing institution only. This material is not copyright free.

KAPITEL 4

(Pupil Book pp. 74–95)

Schule ist klasse!

Unit & Learning objectives	Programme of Study references	Key Language	Grammar and other language features
1 Ich mag Deutsch! (pp. 76–77) • Talking about school subjects • Using *weil* to give reasons and opinions	**GV2** Grammatical structures (word order with *weil*) **LC5** Accurate pronunciation and intonation **LC6** Reading comprehension	Ich mag … Ich mag … nicht. Deutsch Englisch Mathe Naturwissenschaften Informatik Erdkunde Geschichte Sport Kunst Musik Theater Technik Mein Lieblingsfach ist … Ich mag auch … und … Ich mag … sehr. Ich liebe …, aber ich hasse … Warum magst du das (nicht)? Ich liebe/mag (Mathe), weil es … ist. Ich hasse (Mathe)/mag (Mathe) nicht, weil es … ist. einfach faszinierend gut interessant nützlich supercool toll furchtbar langweilig nervig nutzlos schwierig stinklangweilig	• Word order with *weil* • Using familiar words to help pronounce unfamiliar words • Putting a comma before *weil*

Schule ist klasse! – KAPITEL 4

Unit & Learning objectives	Programme of Study references	Key Language	Grammar and other language features
2 Was und wann? (pp. 78–79) • Talking about days and times • More about word order	**GV2** Grammatical structures (word order) **LC4** Expressing ideas (writing) **LC6** Translation into English	Sieben Tage in der Woche: Montag Dienstag Mittwoch Donnerstag Freitag Samstag Sonntag Was hast du am Montag? Am Montag/Heute/Morgen … … habe ich/haben wir … … Deutsch/Sport/keine Schule. Wie viel Uhr ist es? Es ist acht Uhr. Es ist zehn Uhr zwanzig. Wann hast du/haben wir (Englisch)? Um wie viel Uhr hast du/haben wir (Englisch)? Um (8) Uhr (15). in der ersten/zweiten/dritten Stunde vor der Pause nach der Mittagspause	• Word order with time expressions • Ways of remembering the days of the week • Ordinal numbers

© Pearson Education Ltd 2013. Copying permitted for purchasing institution only. This material is not copyright free.

Schule ist klasse! – KAPITEL

Unit & Learning objectives	Programme of Study references	Key Language	Grammar and other language features
3 Lehrer und Lehrerinnen (pp. 80–81) • Describing your teachers • Using *sein* (his) and *ihr* (her)	**GV2** Grammatical structures (possessive pronouns *sein/ihr*) **LC3** Conversation **LC4** Expressing ideas (writing)	freundlich streng jung alt launisch fair unpünktlich arrogant nervig lustig cool streng Mein Lehrer/Englischlehrer heißt … Meine Lehrerin/Deutschlehrerin heißt … Er/Sie ist … (zu/sehr/ziemlich/ein bisschen/nicht) …	• How to say 'his' and 'her' • Connectives and qualifiers
4 Im Klassenzimmer (pp. 82–83) • Talking about school facilities and rules • Using the prepositions *in*, *an*, *auf*, *neben*	**GV2** Grammatical structures (prepositions) **LC4** Expressing ideas (writing) **LC6** Reading comprehension	das Klassenzimmer der Tisch der Stuhl der Computer das Whiteboard das Poster das Fenster die Wand die Tür der Korridor in der Schule im Klassenzimmer im Korridor auf dem Tisch an der Wand am Fenster neben der Tür neben dem Computer	• Prepositions of position *in*, *an*, *auf*, *neben* • The irregular verb *dürfen* • Learning the plurals of nouns • How to say where something is 'not' • *Es gibt* + accusative
5 Reading Skills: Mein Lieblingstag (pp. 84–85) • Understanding longer reading texts • Looking up words you don't know	**GV3** Developing vocabulary **LC6** Reading comprehension		• Prediction techniques • Focus reading and skimming skills • Help with translating unfamiliar words • Use a dictionary

© Pearson Education Ltd 2013. Copying permitted for purchasing institution only. This material is not copyright free.

Schule ist klasse! – KAPITEL 4

Unit & Learning objectives	Programme of Study references	Key Language	Grammar and other language features
6 Speaking Skills: Meine Traumschule (pp. 86–87) • Talking at length about a topic • Improving your pronunciation	**LC4** Expressing ideas (speaking) **LC5** Speaking coherently and confidently		• Strategies for successful pronunciation • Putting together a presentation and making it interesting • The significance of *ie* and *ei* for pronunciation • Tackling tongue-twisters • Key points for asking questions
Lernzieltest und Wiederholung (pp. 88–89) Pupils' checklist and practice exercises			• Tips for making speech fluent and interesting
Grammatik (pp. 90–91) Detailed grammar summary and practice exercises			• Word order with *weil* • Word order with expressions of time • *sein/ihr* • Prepositions • *es gibt* • *dürfen* • Identifying the main verb • Check gender and plurals in unit 4
Projektzone: Sonne, Mond und Erde (pp. 94–95) • Finding out about the solar system • Making a display about the solar system	**GV3** Developing vocabulary **LC4** Expressing ideas (writing) **LC6** reading comprehension		• Pronunciation of new words • Practising dictionary skills • Using a comma and a space instead of a decimal point and comma in large numbers • Using what pupils know

© Pearson Education Ltd 2013. Copying permitted for purchasing institution only. This material is not copyright free.

Schule ist klasse! – **KAPITEL**

1 Ich mag Deutsch! (Pupil Book pp. 74–77)

Learning objectives
- Talking about school subjects
- Using *weil* to give reasons and opinions

Programme of Study
GV2 Grammatical structures (word order with *weil*)
LC5 Accurate pronunciation and intonation
LC6 Reading comprehension

FCSE links
Unit 2 – Education and Future Plans (School subjects, Opinions)

Grammar
Word order with *weil*

PLTS
C Creative thinkers

Key Language
Ich mag … (nicht).
Deutsch
Englisch
Mathe
Naturwissenschaften
Informatik
Erdkunde Geschichte
Sport
Kunst
Musik
Theater
Technik
Mein Lieblingsfach ist …
Ich mag auch … und …
Ich mag … sehr.
Ich liebe …, aber ich hasse …
Warum magst du das (nicht)?
Ich liebe/mag (Mathe), weil es … ist.
Ich hasse (Mathe)/mag (Mathe) nicht, weil es … ist.
gut
einfach / schwierig
faszinierend / stinklangweilig
interessant / langweilig
nützlich / nutzlos
supercool / furchtbar
toll / nervig

Resources
Audio files:
65_Kapitel4_Einheit1_Aufgabe2
66_Kapitel4_Einheit1_Aufgabe3
67_Kapitel4_Einheit1_Aufgabe5
Workbooks:
Übungsheft 1 A&B, page 37
ActiveTeach:
Starter 1 resource
p.076 Flashcards (1)
p.076 Flashcards (2)
p.077 Grammar presentation
Plenary resource
ActiveLearn:
Listening A, Listening B
Reading A, Reading B
Grammar, Vocabulary

Kapitel 4 Quiz pp. 74–75

Answers

1 Die Schule ist in:
b Deutschland

2 Welcher Satz past?
b Es gibt eine Uniform.

3 Ich gehe in Deutschland in die Schule:
c Ich bin sechs Jahre alt.

4 Ich spiele Tischtennis …
a in der Pause.

5 In deutschen Schulen spielt man oft …
a Handball.

6 „Sitzen bleiben" in Deutschland heißt:
c Ich komme nicht in die nächste Klasse.

Starter 1

Aim

To introduce the new vocabulary from the unit and to encourage pupils to make logical guesses about the meaning of new vocabulary.

Pupils match the German and English words (Starter 1 resource). They then compare with a partner and discuss why they have made the guesses they have. They then share their ideas in groups of four (think-pair-share).

1 Lies die Namen der Schulfächer. Wie sagt man das? Versuch es mal.
(Reading L1, Speaking L1)

Reading/Speaking. Pupils read the German words for the school subjects and try to pronounce them.

They check their ideas in exercise 2.

The *Tip* box reminds pupils to think about words that they know already. You can also refer them to their key phonics in chapter 1, pupil book p. 8.

© Pearson Education Ltd 2013. Copying permitted for purchasing institution only. This material is not copyright free.

Ich mag Deutsch! | **Schule ist klasse!** – KAPITEL 4

2 Hör zu und überprüfe. (a–l) (Listening L2)

Listening. Pupils listen to the audio and check their ideas on the pronunciation of the German words presented in exercise 1.

Audioscript

- a – Deutsch. Ich mag Deutsch.
- b – Englisch. Ich mag Englisch.
- c – Mathe. Ich mag Mathe nicht.
- d – Naturwissenschaften. Ich mag Naturwissenschaften.
- e – Informatik. Ich mag Informatik.
- f – Erdkunde. Ich mag Erdkunde nicht.
- g – Geschichte. Ich mag Geschichte.
- h – Sport. Ich mag Sport.
- i – Kunst. Ich mag Kunst nicht.
- j – Musik. Ich mag Musik.
- k – Theater. Ich mag Theater.
- l – Technik. Ich mag Technik nicht.

3 Hör zu. Sieh dir die Bilder in Aufgabe 1 an. Welche Fächer hörst du? Schreib auch „mag" oder „mag nicht". (1–8) (Listening L2)

Listening. Pupils listen to the audio and note which subject(s) (referring to the illustrations in exercise 1) the speakers mention.

Audioscript

1 – Was ist dein Lieblingsfach?
 – Mein Lieblingsfach ist Englisch. Ja, ich mag Englisch. Es ist super.
2 – Was magst du in der Schule?
 – Ich mag Technik. Das ist toll. Technik ist mein Lieblingsfach.
3 – Wie findest du Naturwissenschaften?
 – Also … Naturwissenschaften. Ich mag Naturwissenschaften sehr.
4 – Magst du Deutsch?
 – Oh ja, das ist ganz einfach! Mein Lieblingsfach ist Deutsch.
 – Super, Deutsch ist cool!
5 – Wie findest du Sport?
 – Ich mag Sport nicht. Mein Lieblingsfach ist Informatik. Ich liebe Informatik.
 – Also, du magst Sport nicht, aber du magst Informatik sehr.

6 – Ich mag Mathe und Musik.
 – Ist Mathe dein Lieblingsfach?
 – Ja, aber ich liebe auch Musik.
7 – Wie findest du Kunst?
 – Ich bin sehr kreativ – mein Lieblingsfach ist Kunst.
 – Du magst Kunst. Gut.
 – Ja, und ich mag auch Theater.
 – Also, du magst Kunst und Theater.
8 – Magst du Geschichte?
 – Geschichte? Oh nein, ich hasse Geschichte! Geschichte ist furchtbar!
 – Was magst du denn?
 – Mein Lieblingsfach ist Erdkunde.
 – Du magst Erdkunde, aber du magst Geschichte nicht.
 – Richtig!

Answers

1 b – mag **2** l – mag **3** d – mag **4** a – mag **5** h – mag nicht, e – mag **6** c – mag, j – mag **7** i – mag, k – mag **8** g – mag nicht, f – mag

4 Umfrage. Stell Fragen und mach Notizen. (Speaking L3)

Speaking. Pupils ask questions and make notes on the answers they receive.

5 Hör zu. Finde die Paare. (1–8) (Listening L2)

Listening. Pupils listen to the audio and match the speakers to the illustrations.

Some pupils could also be asked to listen out for the subject.

Audioscript

1 – Ich finde Mathe einfach.
2 – Ich finde Musik langweilig.
3 – Ich finde Deutsch toll.
4 – Ich finde Technik nützlich.
5 – Ich finde Informatik interessant.
6 – Ich finde Naturwissenschaften schwierig.
7 – Ich finde Sport furchtbar.
8 – Ich finde Geschichte nutzlos.

Answers

1 e **2** d **3** a **4** g **5** c **6** f **7** b **8** h

© Pearson Education Ltd 2013. Copying permitted for purchasing institution only. This material is not copyright free.

Ich mag Deutsch! | **Schule ist klasse!** – KAPITEL

Starter 2

Aim

To introduce the new vocabulary from the unit and to encourage pupils to make logical guesses about the meaning of new vocabulary.

Pupils write the adjectives below one of two headings – *positiv/negativ*. They then discuss with a partner why they have made these choices and what they think the adjectives might mean. For extension they can add in any other opinion words they know:

toll

furchtbar

interessant

langweilig

einfach

schwierig

nützlich

nutzlos

faszinierend

nervig

Alternative starter 2

Use ActiveTeach p.076 Flashcards to review and practise language for giving opinions about school subjects.

6 Lies die Texte und beantworte die Fragen auf Englisch. (Reading L3)

Reading. Pupils read the texts and answer the questions.

Answers

1 Anton 2 It's useful, interesting and easy. 3 technology 4 Zoe and Anton 5 Because it's not difficult. 6 (open ended)

Grammatik

The *Grammatik* box draws pupils' attention to the effect on the word order when sentences are joined using *weil*. It is probably a good idea to teach *weil* more inductively, for example by showing pupils sentences and asking them what the pattern is. Pupils could be encouraged to come up with their own way of remembering the rule.

There is more information and practice in the grammar unit on pupil book p. 90.

7 Was magst du und was magst du nicht? Warum? Schreib Sätze mit „weil". (Writing L3)

Writing. Following the icons in the pupil book, pupils write out the six pairs of sentences, joining each one using *weil*.

The *Tip* box reminds pupils to include a comma before *weil*.

Answers

1 Ich mag Deutsch sehr, weil es interessant ist.

2 Ich mag Musik, weil es einfach ist.

3 Ich mag Theater nicht, weil es furchtbar ist.

4 Ich mag Kunst nicht, weil es nutzlos und langweilig ist.

8 Mach Dialoge. (Speaking L3)

Speaking. Pupils make dialogues following the example in the pupil book.

9 Was magst du und was magst du nicht? Warum? Schreib Sätze. (Writing L4)

Writing. Pupils write about the things that they do and do not like. They should include reasons.

Some pupils could be encouraged to use more complicated expressions and different word order, e.g. *Ich finde Mathe toll, weil es einfach ist. Sport hasse ich, weil …*

Plenary

Aim

For pupils to establish whether they have met the lesson objective of using *weil* to give reasons for likes and dislikes.

Pupils play a racing game in two teams. Each person has an A4 word or punctuation card (Plenary resource). Pupils stand on either side of the classroom in their teams, initially making two sentences separated by a full stop. Pupils read out their word and the full-stop pupil says *Punkt*. By saying *weil*, prompt the pupil holding the *weil* card to go to the middle of the sentence and to (gently) push out the full stop. The full-stop pupil and the pupil holding the second verb card move to the end of the sentence. When they arrive at the end, the pupils again read out their words or punctuation. The first team to correctly make and read out their sentence gets the point. This can be repeated several times with different words.

© Pearson Education Ltd 2013. Copying permitted for purchasing institution only. This material is not copyright free.

Ich mag Deutsch! | **Schule ist klasse!** – KAPITEL 4

For a bit of fun, pupils could walk through the game first and every time the *weil* pupil appears he or she could be booed, as if they were a pantomime villain, thus underlining the idea that '*weil* is vile'.

Workbook A, page 37

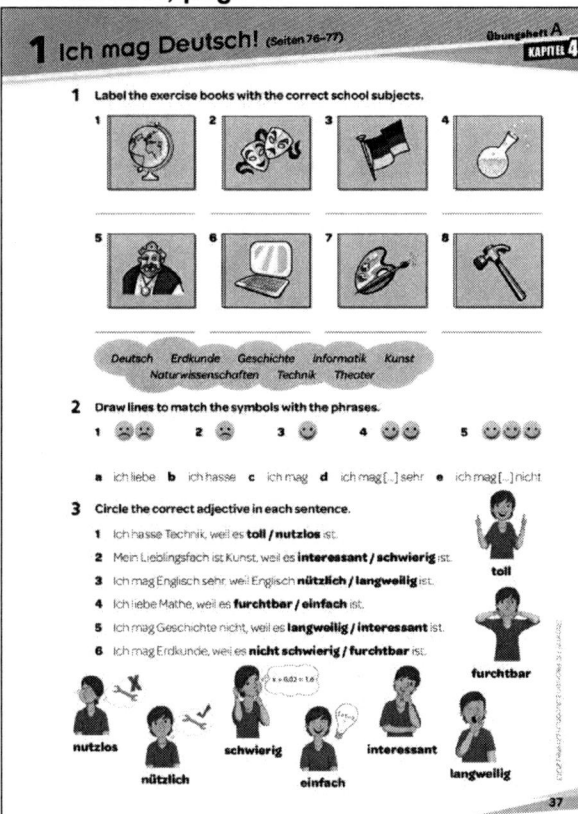

Answers

1 **1** Erdkunde **2** Theater **3** Deutsch
 4 Naturwissenschaften **5** Geschichte
 6 Informatik **7** Kunst **8** Technik

2 **1** b **2** e **3** c **4** d **5** a

3 **1** nutzlos **2** interessant **3** nützlich
 4 einfach **5** langweilig **6** nicht schwierig

Workbook B, page 37

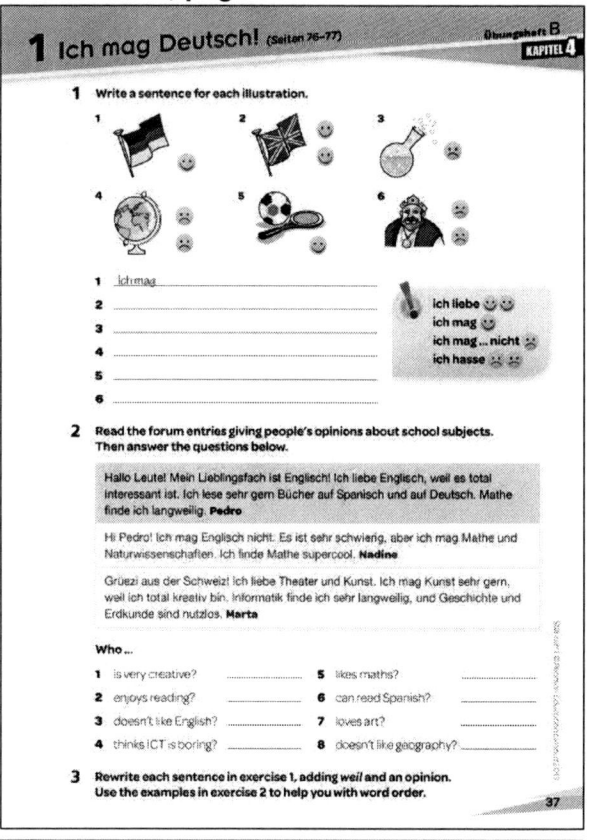

Answers

1 **1** Ich mag Deutsch.
 2 Ich liebe Englisch.
 3 Ich mag Naturwissenschaften nicht.
 4 Ich hasse Erdkunde.
 5 Ich mag Sport.
 6 Ich hasse Geschichte.

2 **1** Marta **2** Pedro **3** Nadine **4** Marta
 5 Nadine **6** Pedro **7** Marta **8** Marta

3 Pupils' own answers.

© Pearson Education Ltd 2013. Copying permitted for purchasing institution only. This material is not copyright free.

2 Was und wann? (Pupil Book pp. 78–79)

Schule ist klasse! – KAPITEL

Learning objectives
- Talking about days and times
- More about word order

Programme of Study
GV2 Grammatical structures (word order)
LC4 Expressing ideas (writing)
LC6 Translation into English

FCSE links
Unit 2 – Education and Future Plans (School timetable)

Grammar
Word order with time expressions

PLTS
C Creative thinkers

Cross-curricular
Mathematics: telling the (digital) time

Key Language
Sieben Tage in der Woche:
Montag
Dienstag
Mittwoch
Donnerstag
Freitag
Samstag
Sonntag
Was hast du am Montag?
Am Montag/Heute/Morgen …
… habe ich/haben wir …
… Deutsch/Sport/keine Schule.
Wie viel Uhr ist es?
Es ist acht Uhr.
Es ist zehn Uhr zwanzig.
Wann hast du/haben wir (Englisch)?
Um wie viel Uhr hast du/haben wir (Englisch)?
Um (8) Uhr (15).
in der ersten/zweiten/dritten Stunde
vor der Pause
nach der Mittagspause

Resources
Audio files:
68_Kapitel4_Einheit2_Aufgabe1
69_Kapitel4_Einheit2_Aufgabe5
70_Kapitel4_Einheit2_Aufgabe6
71_Kapitel4_Einheit2_Aufgabe9

Workbooks:
Übungsheft 1 A&B, page 38

ActiveTeach:
Starter 1 resource
p.078 Grammar worksheet
p.079 Exercise 6 grid
p.079 Exercise 8 grid
p.079 Flashcards
Plenary resource

ActiveLearn:
Listening A, Listening B
Reading A, Reading B
Grammar, Vocabulary

Starter 1

Aim

To review giving and justifying your opinion with *weil*.

Pupils make the longest sentence they can using the words from the board (Starter 1 resource). They can change the subject, opinion, reason or connective. If they wish, as an extension activity they can add in extra details, opinions, intensifiers or connectives.

Audioscript
- *Montag, Dienstag,*
- *Montag, Dienstag,*
- *Mittwoch, Donnerstag,*
- *Mittwoch, Donnerstag,*
- *Freitag, Samstag, Sonntag,*
- *Freitag, Samstag, Sonntag,*
- *Sieben Tage … in der Woche.*

1 Hör zu und sing mit!
(Listening/Speaking L1)

Listening/Speaking. Pupils listen to the audio and sing along.

This can be sung as a team game with the verses getting faster and seeing who can keep up best. It can also be sung as a round.

The *Tip* box looks in more detail at the component parts of *Mittwoch*, and encourages pupils to think about the ways the words are formed in order to help them devise ways of remembering them.

2 Welcher Tag ist das? Verbinde die Bilder (1–6) mit dem genannten Tag (a–f). Wähle dann zwei Texte und übersetze sie ins Englische.
(Reading L3)

Reading. Pupils match the subject illustrations (1–6) to the speech bubbles with sentences which each contain a day of the week (a–f). They then choose two of the sentences and translate them into English.

Explain the word order; the verb comes second, and therefore after time expressions.

Was und wann? | Schule ist klasse! – **KAPITEL 4**

Answers

1 e Donnerstag
Today is Thursday, my favourite day. On Thursday we have English and history. Super!

2 f Dienstag
On Tuesday we have ICT and sport. That's cool! Tuesday is my favourite day.

3 a Montag
On Monday we have maths. I think it's great. We also have sport.

4 c Sonntag
Tomorrow we don't have school. Sunday is my favourite day.

5 d Freitag
On Friday we have German and music. It's not bad.

6 b Mittwoch
My favourite day is Wednesday, because we have music and art. On Wednesday I like going to school.

Extension

Ask pupils to highlight the verb in the more complicated sentences and give them more practice joining sentences together, etc.

Grammatik

The *Grammatik* box points out that the time expression 'on Monday' often comes at the start of a sentence. Remind pupils that if the time expression comes first, then the verb must come next.

There is more information and practice in the grammar unit on pupil book pp. 90.

3 Partnerarbeit. Stell und beantworte Fragen. (Speaking L3)

Speaking. Working in pairs, pupils take it in turns to ask and answer questions about when they have certain subjects and what they think of them.

Starter 2

Aim

To review telling the time.

Revise numbers up to 60 and present digital times.

A series of sentences giving the time are displayed on the board. Pupils play a game of pass-the-parcel, passing along a parcel (this could be empty or perhaps full of small prizes) with music being played (ideally German music, of course!). When the music stops the pupil holding the parcel translates the first sentence into English. If they get it right, they win a prize/merit. If they get it wrong, the pupil to their left translates it for them. The game then continues. This game is good for differentiation, as the music can be stopped at certain times to enable different pupils to translate slightly easier or more complex times.

Example sentences:

Es ist fünf Uhr.

Es ist einundzwanzig Uhr.

Es ist zehn Uhr fünfzehn.

Es ist drei Uhr zwanzig.

Es ist neun Uhr vierzig.

Es ist sechs Uhr fünfundvierzig.

Es ist neunzehn Uhr zehn.

4 Wie viel Uhr ist es? (Reading L2)

Reading. Pupils match the times to the illustrations of digital clocks. Pupils check their answers by listening to the audio in exercise 5.

Answers

1 c **2** a **3** e **4** b **5** f **6** d

5 Hör zu und überprüfe. (1–6) (Listening L2)

Listening. Pupils listen to the audio and check their answers to exercise 4.

Audioscript

1 – c – *Es ist sieben Uhr.*
2 – a – *Es ist zehn Uhr.*
3 – e – *Es ist zwanzig Uhr.*
4 – b – *Es ist fünfzehn Uhr dreißig.*
5 – f – *Es ist neun Uhr fünfzehn.*
6 – d – *Es ist achtzehn Uhr zwanzig.*

6 Hör zu. Was passt zusammen? Schreib die Tabelle ab und füll sie aus. Benutze die Bilder. (1–6) (Listening L3)

Listening. Pupils listen to the audio. They match the subject to the time and complete the table.

Was und wann? | Schule ist klasse! – KAPITEL

Audioscript

1 – Wann hast du Geschichte?
– Um acht Uhr. Ich habe Geschichte um acht Uhr.
2 – Um wie viel Uhr haben wir Sport?
– Sport haben wir um zwölf Uhr zehn.
– Um zwölf Uhr zehn. Danke.
3 – Was haben wir um zehn Uhr fünfzehn?
– Ähm … um zehn Uhr fünfzehn haben wir Informatik.
4 – Um wie viel Uhr haben wir Mathe?
– Um neun Uhr fünfundvierzig.
– Okay, Mathe um neun Uhr fünfundvierzig. Danke.
5 – Haben wir heute Musik?
– Ja, um dreizehn Uhr fünfzig.
– Um dreizehn Uhr fünfzig. Okay, bis dann.
6 – Was hast du heute um vierzehn Uhr fünfundzwanzig?
– Um vierzehn Uhr fünfundzwanzig? Wir haben Englisch.

Answers
1 c 2 d 3 a 4 f 5 b 6 e

7 Sieh dir Aufgabe 6 an. Sag, wann du die Fächer hast. (Speaking L2)

Speaking. Pupils look at the subjects in exercise 6 and say what time they have these subjects.

8 Lies die Texte. Schreib den Stundenplan ab und füll ihn aus. (Reading/Listening L3)

Reading/Listening. Pupils read the text. Then they copy out and complete the timetable.

Pupils check their answers by listening to the audio in exercise 9.

The *Tip* box refers pupils to pupil book p. 39 to remind them how to say first, second, third, etc.

Answers
a Deutsch b Erdkunde c Informatik d Sport

9 Hör zu und überprüfe. (Listening L3)

Listening. Pupils listen to the audio and check their answers to exercise 8.

Audioscript

– Hier ist mein Stundenplan für Montag:
– In der ersten Stunde habe ich Deutsch.
– Vor der Pause, in der zweiten Stunde, habe ich Mathe.
– Ich habe Erdkunde nach der Pause, in der dritten Stunde.
– Vor der Mittagspause, in der vierten Stunde, haben wir Informatik.
– Nach der Mittagspause, in der fünften Stunde, haben wir Englisch.
– Und in der sechsten Stunde haben wir Sport.

10 Was ist dein Lieblingstag? Warum? Was hast du wann? Schreib Sätze. (Writing L4)

Writing. Pupils write a few sentences about their favourite day at school, giving the day and the times when they have subjects. They should also include some reasons for liking that day.

Plenary

Aim

For pupils to establish whether they have met the lesson objectives of talking about days and times.

Pupils complete a gap-fill speaking activity, where they have two halves of a school timetable and have to fill in the gaps by asking a partner questions (Plenary resource).

For example:

A: *Was hast du um acht Uhr fünfzig?*
B: *Ich habe Religion. Was hast du um acht Uhr?*
A: *Ich habe Deutsch.*

Alternative plenary

Use ActiveTeach p.079 Class Game to review language for talking about time.

© Pearson Education Ltd 2013. Copying permitted for purchasing institution only. This material is not copyright free.

Was und wann? | **Schule ist klasse!** – KAPITEL 4

Workbook A, page 38

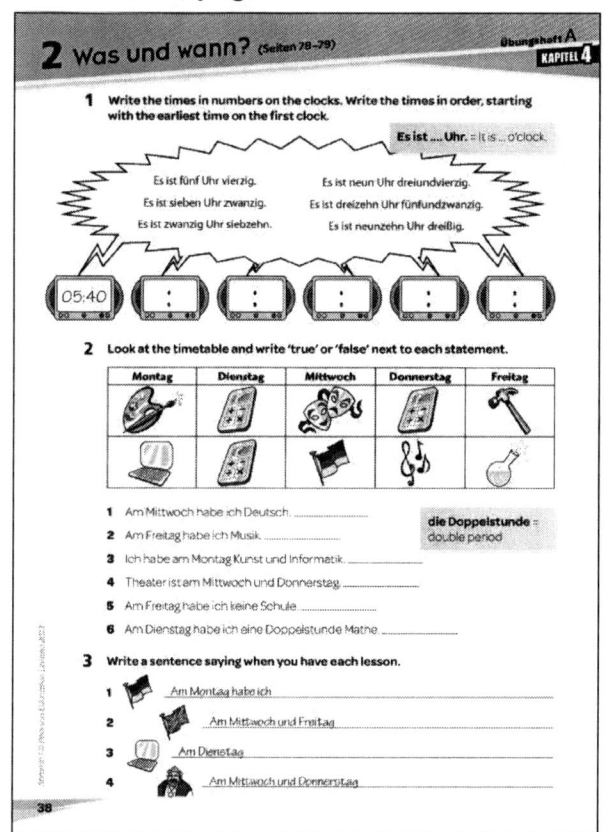

Answers

1 05:40 Uhr / 07:20 Uhr / 09:43 Uhr / 13:25 Uhr / 19:30 Uhr / 20:17 Uhr

2 **1** true **2** false **3** true **4** false **5** false **6** true

3 **1** Am Montag habe ich Deutsch.
   2 Am Mittwoch und Freitag habe ich Englisch.
   3 Am Dienstag habe ich Informatik.
   4 Am Mittwoch und Donnerstag habe ich Geschichte.

Workbook B, page 38

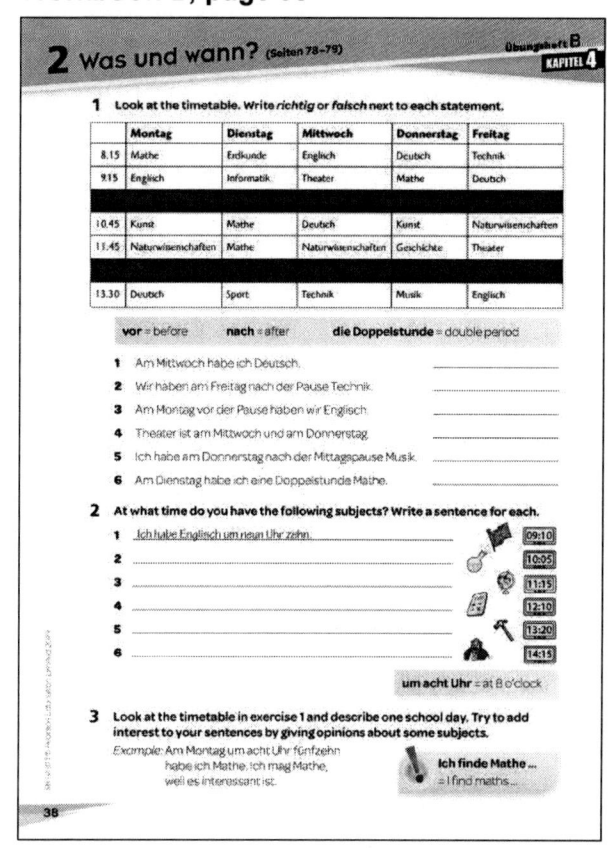

Answers

1 **1** richtig **2** falsch **3** richtig **4** falsch **5** richtig **6** richtig

2 **1** Ich habe Englisch um neun Uhr zehn.
   2 Ich habe Naturwissenschaften um zehn Uhr fünf.
   3 Ich habe Erdkunde um elf Uhr fünfzehn.
   4 Ich habe Mathe um zwölf Uhr zehn.
   5 Ich habe Technik um dreizehn Uhr zwanzig.
   6 Ich habe Geschichte um vierzehn Uhr fünfzehn.

3 Pupils' own answers.

© Pearson Education Ltd 2013. Copying permitted for purchasing institution only. This material is not copyright free.

Was und wann? | **Schule ist klasse!** – KAPITEL

Worksheet

Grammar: Word order

2 Was und wann?
Stimmt! 1 KAPITEL 4

Grammar: Word order

A Tick the correct sentence from each pair.
Beispiel:
Am Mittwoch wir haben Deutsch. ☐
Am Mittwoch haben wir Deutsch. ☑

Grammatik
Remember the verb second rule: if the time expression comes first, the verb comes afterwards.

1 Am Freitag habe ich Kunst. ☐
Am Freitag ich habe Kunst. ☐

2 Habe ich am Dienstag Mathe. ☐
Ich habe am Dienstag Mathe. ☐

3 Mein Lieblingstag Donnerstag ist. ☐
Mein Lieblingstag ist Donnerstag. ☐

4 Um 10 Uhr haben wir Geschichte. ☐
Um 10 Uhr wir haben Geschichte. ☐

B Add the time phrases to the beginning of these sentences. Make sure you change the word order so that the verb comes second.

1 Wir haben Kunst und Mathe. (Am Donnerstag)
2 Ich habe Geschichte. (Vor der Pause)
3 Wir haben Informatik. (In der zweiten Stunde)
4 Du hast Sport. (Um 12 Uhr)
5 Wir haben Musik. (Um 8 Uhr 35)

C Join these pairs of sentences with *weil*.

Grammatik
Remember that after *weil* the verb goes to the end of the sentence.

1 Mittwoch ist mein Lieblingstag. Ich habe Mathe.
2 Musik ist mein Lieblingsfach. Es ist interessant.
3 Mein Lieblingstag ist Sonntag. Wir haben keine Schule.
4 Am Freitag hasse ich die Schule. Ich habe Kunst.
5 Am Montag gehe ich gern in die Schule. Ich habe Informatik.

D Translate your answers from activity C into English.

© Pearson Education Limited 2013
Printing and photocopying permitted

Answers

A 1 Am Freitag habe ich Kunst.
2 Ich habe am Dienstag Mathe.
3 Mein Lieblingstag ist Donnerstag.
4 Um 10 Uhr haben wir Geschichte.

B 1 Am Donnerstag haben wir Kunst und Mathe.
2 Vor der Pause habe ich Geschichte.
3 In der zweiten Stunde haben wir Informatik.
4 Um 12 Uhr hast du Sport.
5 Um 8 Uhr 35 haben wir Musik.

C 1 Mittwoch ist mein Lieblingstag, weil ich Mathe habe
2 Musik ist mein Lieblingsfach, weil es interessant ist.
3 Mein Lieblingstag ist Sonntag, weil wir keine Schule haben.
4 Am Freitag hasse ich die Schule, weil ich Kunst habe.
5 Am Montag gehe ich gern in die Schule, weil ich Informatik habe.

D 1 Wednesday is my favourite day because I have maths.
2 Music is my favourite subject because it is interesting.
3 My favourite day is Sunday because we don't have school.
4 On Friday I hate school because I have art.
5 On Monday I like going to school because we have ICT.

© Pearson Education Ltd 2013. Copying permitted for purchasing institution only. This material is not copyright free.

Schule ist klasse! – KAPITEL 4

3 Lehrer und Lehrerinnen (Pupil Book pp. 80–81)

Learning objectives	Key language	Resources
• Describing your teachers • Using *sein* (his) and *ihr* (her) **Programme of Study** **GV2** Grammatical structures (possessive pronouns *sein/ihr*) **LC3** Conversation **LC4** Expressing ideas (writing) **FCSE links** Unit 2 – Education and Future Plans (School – teachers) **Grammar** How to say 'his' and 'her' **PLTS** **R** Reflective learners	freundlich streng jung alt launisch fair unpünktlich arrogant nervig lustig cool Mein Lehrer/Englischlehrer heißt … Meine Lehrerin/Deutschlehrerin heißt … Er/Sie ist … (zu/sehr/ziemlich/ein bisschen/nicht) …	**Audio files:** 72_Kapitel4_Einheit3_Aufgabe1 73_Kapitel4_Einheit3_Aufgabe4 **Workbooks:** Übungsheft 1 A&B, page 39 **ActiveTeach:** Starter 2 resource p.080 Flashcards p.081 Grammar presentation p.081 Video: Episode 7 Plenary resource **ActiveLearn:** Listening A, Listening B Reading A, Reading B Grammar, Vocabulary

Starter 1

Aim

To reflect on the language needed to describe teachers and consider the language they already know which can be recycled.

Pupils mind-map describing teachers, making notes in English of the sorts of things they might want to say. They then expand their mind-maps in a different colour in German, adding in words and phrases seen in previous units (descriptions of hair and eyes are an example of this). They then compare their mind-map with a partner's before comparing with another pair (think-pair-share). Ideas are collated on the board or on a large piece of sugar paper. This could be added to during the lesson. Pupils are encouraged to add the German to their mind-maps during the course of the lesson. Suggested starting points are: descriptions, hair and eyes, opinions and basic personal info (name, age, where they live).

1 Hör zu. Was ist die richtige Reihenfolge? (1–4) (Listening L3)

Listening. Pupils listen to the audio and sort out the adjectives according to the order they hear them.

Read through the adjectives first with the pupils and get them to try out the pronunciation.

The key language feature reminds pupils of the way in which qualifiers such as *zu* alter the meaning of a sentence slightly. It points out that pupils can expand their vocabulary quickly by using a prefix such as *un-* with an adjective.

Audioscript

1 – *Mein Lieblingslehrer heißt Herr Brünger. Er ist freundlich und fair.*
2 – *Meine Sportlehrerin heißt Frau Strick. Sie ist sehr streng und manchmal unpünktlich.*
3 – *Meine Deutschlehrerin heißt Frau Grünwald. Sie ist ein bisschen alt, aber sie ist meine Lieblingslehrerin, weil sie sehr lustig ist.*
4 – *Ich mag meinen Mathelehrer nicht. Herr Zinke ist ziemlich jung, aber er ist nervig, weil er zu launisch ist.*

Answers

1 a, f **2** b, g **3** d, i **4** c, h, e

2 Wie sind deine Lehrer und Lehrerinnen? Mach Dialoge. (Speaking L4)

Speaking. Pupils create dialogues about their teachers following the example in the pupil book.

Starter 2

Aim

To review masculine and feminine in the context of possessive pronouns.

Pupils have illustrations of two hot-air balloons, one with the masculine/neuter possessive pronouns on the basket and one with the feminine/plural possessive pronouns on the basket (Starter 2 resource). They also have a set of words (which can be cut up as cards if required). They write or stick the words onto the correct balloon. Pupils can also look back at the

Lehrer und Lehrerinnen | **Schule ist klasse!** – KAPITEL

previous balloons for other examples or add some words of their own.

Alternative starter 2

Use ActiveTeach p.080 Flashcards to review and practise language for talking about teachers.

3 Diese Lehrer und Lehrerinnen haben ein Geheimnis. Was ist es? Rate mal! (Reading L3)

Reading. Pupils look at the texts and the pictures and try to guess what secret it is that each teacher has.

Some vocabulary is glossed for support.

Pupils discover the answers in exercise 4.

4 Hör zu und überprüfe. (1–6) (Listening L4)

Listening. Pupils listen to the audio and find out the secrets from exercise 3.

Audioscript

1 – e – Mein Lieblingslehrer ist Herr Arnold, mein Musiklehrer. Er ist ziemlich jung und freundlich. Seine Schwester ist ein berühmtes Model.
2 – a – Frau Wörth ist meine Mathelehrerin. Sie kann sehr gut Gitarre spielen und sie spielt in einer Band. Ihre Band heißt „Verrückt".
3 – b – Mein Englischlehrer heißt Herr Daler und er ist lustig. Seine Lieblingstiere sind Katzen – er hat dreiundzwanzig Katzen im Haus.
4 – f – Frau Friedrichs ist meine Deutschlehrerin, aber sie ist auch sehr sportlich. Ihr Lieblingssport ist Handball. Sie spielt in der Nationalmannschaft.
5 – c – Mein Kunstlehrer, Herr Grüner, ist ziemlich alt, aber er ist supercool. Er hat nur ein Haustier, aber sein Haustier ist ein Schwein!
6 – d – Frau Hellmann ist meine Lieblingslehrerin, weil sie fair und nicht launisch ist. Sie mag BMWs und ihr Auto ist siebzig Jahre alt!

Answers

1 e 2 a 3 b 4 f 5 c 6 d

Grammatik

The *Grammatik* box looks at the way to say 'his' and 'her' in German.

There is more information and practice in the grammar unit on pupil book p. 90.

5 Füll die Lücken aus und finde den Avatar. (Reading L3)

Reading. Pupils fill in the gaps in the texts with the correct pronoun and then match the text to the illustration.

Some vocabulary is glossed for support.

Answers

1 *Sein*, d 2 Ihre, a 3 Sein, f 4 Ihr, b 5 Seine, e 6 Ihre, c

6 Beschreib einen Lehrer und eine Lehrerin. Zeichne seinen/ihren Avatar. (Writing L4)

Writing. Pupils write out a description of a male teacher and a female teacher. They then draw the avatars. Exercises 3 and 5 provide models for pupils to base their answers upon if they wish.

Plenary

Aim

For pupils to establish whether they have met the lesson objective of describing teachers.

Pupils write a description of a teacher but leave out the name. They have five minutes in which to do this and must write in silence without telling anyone who they have chosen. Collect the descriptions and redistribute them, so each pupil has someone else's written work. The pupils then read the descriptions they've been given and in a different colour write the name of the teacher they think it is. They also peer assess the written work, giving ticks and a target for the quality of the writing. The grid (Plenary resource) could be used to give more guidance.

Alternative plenary

Use ActiveTeach p.081 Grammar practice to review *sein* and *ihr*.

© Pearson Education Ltd 2013. Copying permitted for purchasing institution only. This material is not copyright free.

Lehrer und Lehrerinnen | Schule ist klasse! – **KAPITEL 4**

Workbook A, page 39

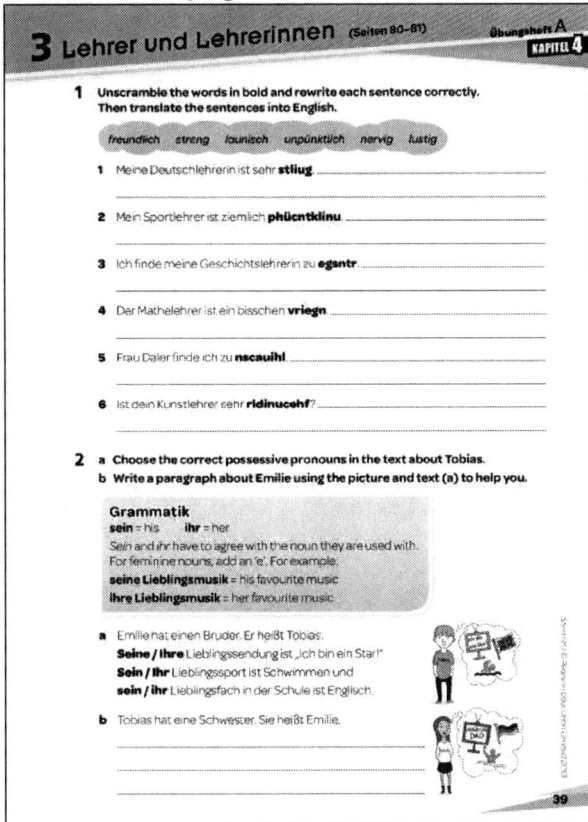

3 Lehrer und Lehrerinnen (Seiten 80–81) — Übungsheft A, KAPITEL 4

1 Unscramble the words in bold and rewrite each sentence correctly. Then translate the sentences into English.

freundlich streng launisch unpünktlich nervig lustig

1 Meine Deutschlehrerin ist sehr **stliug**.
2 Mein Sportlehrer ist ziemlich **phücntklinu**.
3 Ich finde meine Geschichtslehrerin zu **egsntr**.
4 Der Mathelehrer ist ein bisschen **vriegn**.
5 Frau Daler finde ich zu **nscauihl**.
6 Ist dein Kunstlehrer sehr **ridinuceohf**?

2 a Choose the correct possessive pronouns in the text about Tobias.
b Write a paragraph about Emilie using the picture and text (a) to help you.

Grammatik
sein = his **ihr** = her
Sein and ihr have to agree with the noun they are used with. For feminine nouns, add an 'e'. For example:
seine Lieblingsmusik = his favourite music
ihre Lieblingsmusik = her favourite music

a Emilie hat einen Bruder. Er heißt Tobias.
 Seine / Ihre Lieblingssendung ist „Ich bin ein Star!"
 Sein / Ihr Lieblingssport ist Schwimmen und
 sein / ihr Lieblingsfach in der Schule ist Englisch.

b Tobias hat eine Schwester. Sie heißt Emilie.

Answers

1 1 Meine Deutschlehrerin ist sehr lustig. / My (female) German teacher is very funny.
2 Mein Sportlehrer ist ziemlich unpünktlich. / My (male) PE teacher is quite unpunctual.
3 Ich finde meine Geschichtslehrerin zu streng. / I find my (female) history teacher too strict.
4 Der Mathelehrer ist ein bisschen nervig. / The (male) maths teacher is a little bit annoying.
5 Frau Daler finde ich zu launisch. / I find Frau Daler too moody.
6 Ist dein Kustlehrer sehr freundlich? / Is your (male) art teacher very friendly?

2 a Seine; Sein; sein
b Ihre Lieblingssendung ist „American Dad". Ihr Lieblingssport ist Wasserpolo und Ihr Lieblingsfach in der Schule ist Deutsch.

Workbook B, page 39

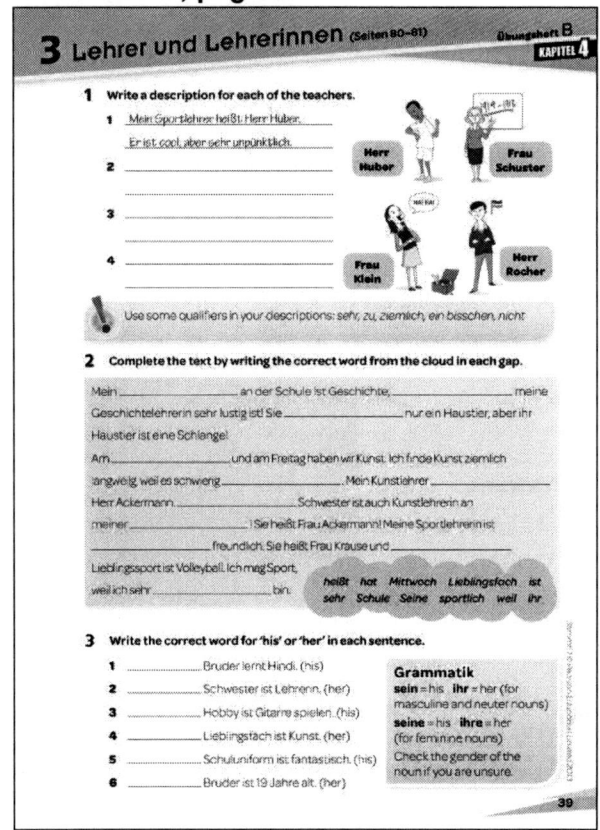

3 Lehrer und Lehrerinnen (Seiten 80–81) — Übungsheft B, KAPITEL 4

1 Write a description for each of the teachers.
1 Mein Sportlehrer heißt Herr Huber. Er ist cool, aber sehr unpünktlich.
2
3
4

Herr Huber, Frau Schuster, Frau Klein, Herr Rocher

Use some qualifiers in your descriptions: sehr, zu, ziemlich, ein bisschen, nicht

2 Complete the text by writing the correct word from the cloud in each gap.

Mein _____ an der Schule ist Geschichte, _____ meine Geschichtelehrerin sehr lustig ist! Sie _____ nur ein Haustier, aber ihr Haustier ist eine Schlange! Am _____ und am Freitag haben wir Kunst. Ich finde Kunst ziemlich langweilig, weil es schwierig _____. Mein Kunstlehrer Herr Ackermann _____ Schwester ist auch Kunstlehrerin an meiner _____! Sie heißt Frau Ackermann! Meine Sportlehrerin ist _____ freundlich. Sie heißt Frau Krause und _____ Lieblingssport ist Volleyball. Ich mag Sport, weil ich sehr _____ bin.

heißt hat Mittwoch Lieblingsfach ist sehr Schule Seine sportlich weil ihr

3 Write the correct word for 'his' or 'her' in each sentence.
1 _____ Bruder lernt Hindi. (his)
2 _____ Schwester ist Lehrerin. (her)
3 _____ Hobby ist Gitarre spielen. (his)
4 _____ Lieblingsfach ist Kunst. (her)
5 _____ Schuluniform ist fantastisch. (his)
6 _____ Bruder ist 19 Jahre alt. (her)

Grammatik
sein = his **ihr** = her (for masculine and neuter nouns)
seine = his **ihre** = her (for feminine nouns)
Check the gender of the noun if you are unsure.

Answers

1 Possible answers:
1 Mein Sportlehrer heißt Herr Huber. Er ist cool, aber sehr unpünktlich.
2 Meine Geschichtslehrerin heißt Frau Schuster. Sie ist ziemlich streng, aber intelligent.
3 Meine Techniklehrerin heißt Frau Klein. Sie ist sehr lustig.
4 Mein Französischlehrer heißt Herr Rocher. Er ist ein bisschen launisch.

2 Mein **Lieblingsfach** an der Schule ist Geschichte, **weil** meine Geschichtslehrerin sehr lustig ist! Sie **hat** nur ein Haustier, aber ihr Haustier ist eine Schlange! Am **Mittwoch** und am Freitag haben wir Kunst. Ich finde Kunst ziemlich langweilig, weil es schwierig **ist**. Mein Kunstlehrer **heißt** Herr Ackermann. **Seine** Schwester ist auch Kunstlehrerin an meiner **Schule**! Sie heißt Frau Ackermann!

> Meine Sportlehrerin ist **sehr** freundlich. Sie heißt Frau Krause und **ihr** Lieblingssport ist Volleyball. Ich mag Sport, weil ich sehr **sportlich** bin.
>
> 3 1 Sein 2 Ihre 3 Sein 4 Ihr 5 Seine
>   6 Ihr

Video

Episode 7

Felix and Katharina are trying to organise an interview with their favourite teachers, but it does not go according to plan ...

> **Answers**
>
> **A** Before watching
>   Answers will vary.
>
> **B** Watch
>   **1** his German teacher
>   **2** her English teacher
>   **3** the audio recorder/dictaphone
>   **4** her English teacher isn't in today.
>   **6** No, they don't have an interview recorded.
>
> **C** Watch again
>   **1 a)** Felix has German on Tuesday at 8.15 a.m.
>   **b)** Katharina has English on Monday at 13.15 p.m.
>   **c)** Katharina has maths last lesson today.
>   **d)** Felix has art fifth lesson today.
>   **2** c – auf dem Stuhl
>   **3 a)** false **b)** true **c)** false **d)** true
>
> **D** Discuss with your partner
>   **1** "That's tomorrow. That's a bit too late."
>   **2** The microphone is missing. Katarina decides to use her mobile phone to record the interview instead.
>   **3** His mobile phone is broken.
>   **4** They haven't recorded an interview and Audrey is expecting one.
>   **5** Audrey has the microphone under the table in her classroom and so they are going to record the interview tomorrow.

Schule ist klasse! – KAPITEL 4

4 Im Klassenzimmer (Pupil Book pp. 82–83)

Learning objectives	Key Language	Resources
• Talking about school facilities and rules • Using the prepositions *in*, *an*, *auf*, *neben* **Programme of Study** GV2 Grammatical structures (prepositions) LC4 Expressing ideas (writing) LC6 Reading comprehension **FCSE links** Unit 2 – Education and Future Plans (School facilities) **Grammar** Prepositions of position *in*, *an*, *auf*, *neben* The irregular verb *dürfen* **PLTS** C Creative thinkers	das Klassenzimmer der Tisch der Stuhl der Computer das Whiteboard das Poster das Fenster die Wand die Tür der Korridor in der Schule im Klassenzimmer im Korridor auf dem Tisch an der Wand am Fenster neben der Tür neben dem Computer	**Audio files:** 74_Kapitel4_Einheit4_Aufgabe2 75_Kapitel4_Einheit4_Aufgabe3 **Workbooks:** Übungsheft 1 A&B, page 40 **ActiveTeach:** Starter 2 resource p.082 Grammar presentation p.082 Flashcards p.083 Grammar presentation (1) p.083 Grammar presentation (2) p.083 Video: Episode 8 p.083 Extension worksheet Plenary resource **ActiveLearn:** Listening A, Listening B Reading A, Reading B Grammar, Vocabulary

Starter 1

Aim

To use new language from the unit and work out the meanings of new vocabulary.

Find a picture of a classroom and give a copy to each pair of pupils. Pupils have a set of cards with which to label the different items of furniture. They are given a countdown clock (five minutes or less depending on the class) in which to complete the activity and it is a race, with the first pair to correctly label all the items being declared the winners.

Extension

Pupils could find out the German words for other items they see in the classroom, such as the map.

1 Sieh dir das Klassenzimmer an. Wie sagt man das? Versuch es mal.
(Speaking/Reading L1)

Speaking/Reading. Pupils look at the illustration of a classroom and try to pronounce the items that it shows. Pupils check their pronunciation by listening to the audio in exercise 2.

The *Tip* box reminds pupils to learn the plurals when they learn their vocabulary.

2 Hör zu und überprüfe. (1–10)
(Listening L2)

Listening. Pupils listen to the audio to check their pronunciation of the vocabulary presented in exercise 1.

Audioscript

1 – das Klassenzimmer
2 – der Tisch
3 – der Stuhl
4 – der Computer
5 – das Whiteboard
6 – das Poster
7 – das Fenster
8 – die Wand
9 – die Tür
10 – der Korridor

3 Hör zu. Welches Bild ist das? (1–8)
(Listening L2)

Listening. Pupils listen to the audio and match the sentences to the illustrations.

Audioscript

1 – *Der Computer ist auf dem Tisch.*
2 – *Der Lehrer ist neben der Tür.*
3 – *Es gibt ein Whiteboard im Klassenzimmer.*
4 – *Ein Buch ist neben dem Computer.*
5 – *Es gibt hundert Klassenzimmer in der Schule.*
6 – *Es gibt zwei Stühle im Korridor.*

© Pearson Education Ltd 2013. Copying permitted for purchasing institution only. This material is not copyright free.

Im Klassenzimmer | **Schule ist klasse!** — KAPITEL

7 – *Mein Tisch ist am Fenster.*
8 – *Viele Poster sind an der Wand.*

Answers
1 d 2 g 3 b 4 h 5 a 6 c 7 f 8 e

Grammatik

To help with describing the position of something, the *Grammatik* box introduces the prepositions *in*, *an*, *auf* and *neben*. It explains that the word for 'the' changes when it follows these.

There is more information and practice in the grammar unit on pupil book p. 91.

Starter 2

Aim

To review the use of the accusative after *es gibt*.

Pupils are given a short text where a German pupil describes her classroom (Starter 2 resource). Put a giant *EN* on the board and ask pupils to complete a think-pair-share activity where they have to write a reason why the letters are on the board.

- Think = the pupils have three minutes to individually think in silence about the letters.
- Pair = the pupils compare their ideas in pairs to decide on a reason.
- Share = the pupils work in groups of four to write out a reason which is then shared with the class.

This relates back to the first time pupils met the accusative in chapter 1. Pupils are asked to highlight any examples in the text they have where they think the *en* is relevant. Lead a class discussion about what pupils have noticed, what the significance of the *en* is and what examples they have found in the text.

Alternative starter 2

Use ActiveTeach p.082 Flashcards to review and practise language for classroom objects.

Extension

Pupils could be asked to translate the text into English or could be asked questions about the classroom.

4 Wo ist Sophie Spinne? Schreib es heimlich auf. Dein Partner/Deine Partnerin muss raten. (Speaking L3)

Speaking. Pupils decide for themselves where Sophie Spider is hiding, and a partner has to guess.

This gives lots of practice of using the expressions introduced in the unit in a fun way. It can be done as group or pair work, possibly using a big cut-out spider to stick in various places. Points could also be awarded for how quickly they guess.

The *Tip* box points out that you just need to put *nicht* before a phrase to say where something is 'not'.

5 Lies die Tweets über Schulregeln und beantworte die Fragen. (Reading L4)

Reading. Pupils read the tweets about school rules and answer questions.

The *Tip* box introduces the expression *es gibt* and explains that masculine words that follow this expression change the indefinite article *ein* to *einen*. There is more information and practice in the grammar unit on pupil book p. 91.

Some vocabulary is glossed for support.

Answers
1 @katrina_seiler
2 in the German lesson
3 in the school yard/playground
4 He thinks it's unfair that you can't use phones in school.

Grammatik

The *Grammatik* box introduces the singular paradigm of the irregular verb *dürfen*.

It includes tips on how to use it, for example that it is used with an infinitive at the end of the sentence.

It is also used with *man* to describe what people generally do.

There is more information and practice in the grammar unit on pupil book p. 91.

6 Was darf man in deiner Schule machen oder nicht machen? Wie findest du das? Schreib Tweets (maximal 140 Zeichen!). (Writing L4)

Writing. Pupils write tweets about what they are allowed to do in the classroom – or not!

© Pearson Education Ltd 2013. Copying permitted for purchasing institution only. This material is not copyright free.

Im Klassenzimmer | **Schule ist klasse!** – KAPITEL 4

Plenary

Aim

For pupils to establish whether they have met the lesson objective of using the prepositions *in*, *an*, *auf*, *neben*.

Pupils play a game with mini whiteboards and whiteboard pens. Each pupil (ideally) has their own mini whiteboard. Display a series of gapped sentences, one at a time (Plenary resource). Pupils have to write the missing article on their mini whiteboards and the first pupil to show the correct article gets a point. At the end of the game the pupil with the most points is the winner.

Workbook A, page 40

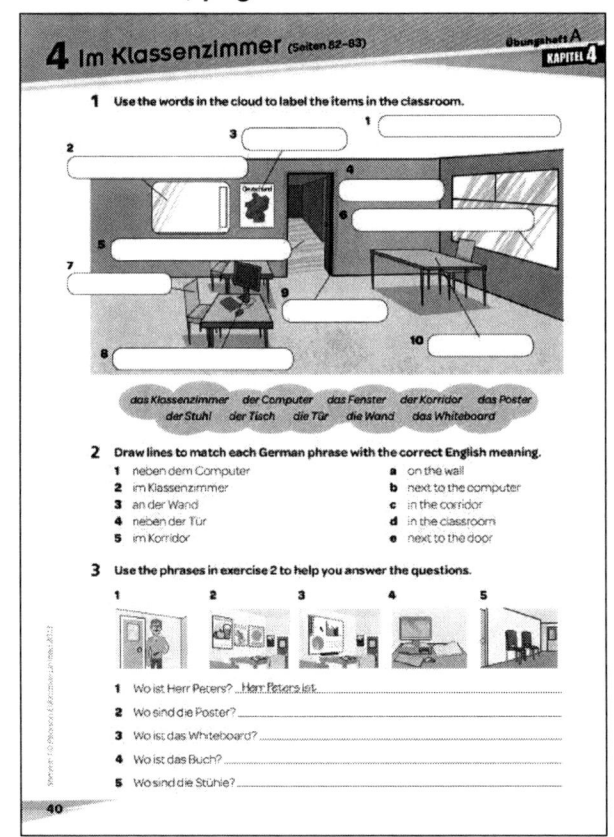

Answers

1. 1 das Klassenzimmer 2 das Whiteboard
   3 das Poster 4 die Wand 5 der Korridor
   6 das Fenster 7 der Stuhl 8 der Computer
   9 die Tür 10 der Tisch
2. 1 b 2 d 3 a 4 e 5 c
3. 1 Herr Peters ist neben der Tür.
   2 Die Poster sind an der Wand.
   3 Das Whiteboard ist im Klassenzimmer.
   4 Das Buch ist auf dem Tisch, neben dem Computer.
   5 Die Stühle sind im Korridor.

Workbook B, page 40

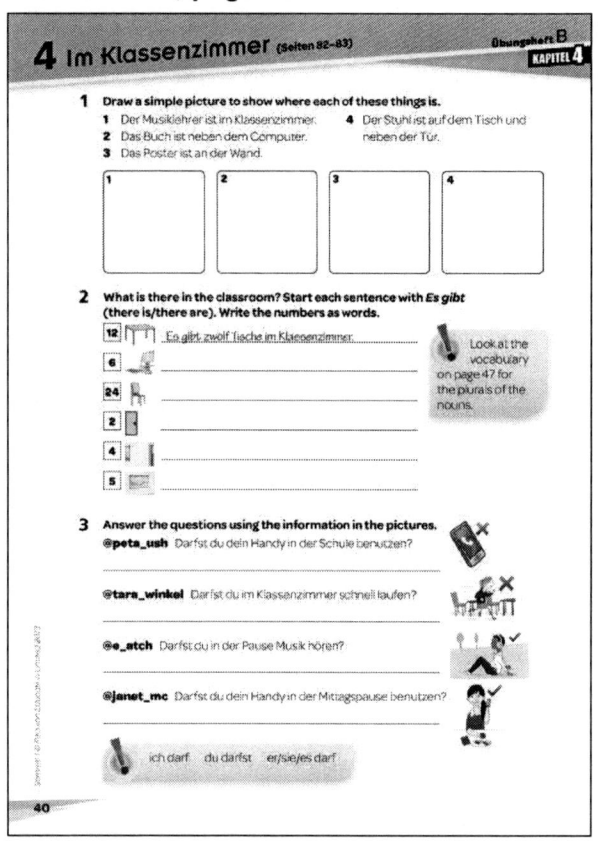

Answers

1. Illustrations:
   1 Music teacher inside the classroom.
   2 Book next to computer.
   3 Poster on the wall.
   4 Chair on table, next to the door.
2. Es gibt zwölf Tische im Klassenzimmer.
   Es gibt sechs Computer im Klassenzimmer.
   Es gibt vierundzwanzig Stühle im Klassenzimmer.
   Es gibt zwei Türen im Klassenzimmer.
   Es gibt vier Wände im Klassenzimmer.
   Es gibt fünf Fenster im Klassenzimmer.
3. 1 Nein. Ich darf nicht mein Handy benutzen.
   2 Nein. Ich darf nicht im Klassenzimmer schnell laufen.
   3 Ja! Ich darf in der Pause Musik hören.
   4 Ja! Ich darf mein Handy in der Mittagspause benutzen.

© Pearson Education Ltd 2013. Copying permitted for purchasing institution only. This material is not copyright free.

Im Klassenzimmer | **Schule ist klasse!** – KAPITEL

Worksheet

Extension: In Lisa's room

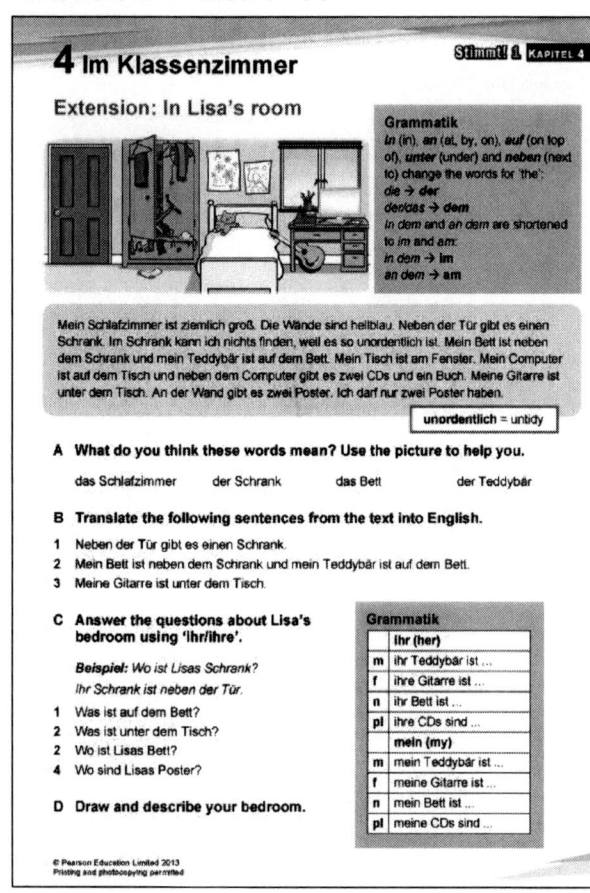

Answers

A Das Schlafzimmer – bedroom
der Schrank – wardrobe / cupboard
das Bett – bed
der Teddybär – teddy (bear)

B 1 Next to (by) the door there is a wardrobe.
2 My bed is next to (by) the wardrobe and my teddy is on the bed.
3 My guitar is under the table.

C 1 Ihr Teddy ist auf dem Bett.
2 Ihre Gitarre ist unter dem Tisch.
3 Ihr Bett ist neben dem Schrank.
4 Ihre Poster sind an der Wand.

Video

Episode 8

The German pupils are discussing school rules and their opinions about these rules.

Answers

A Before watching
Answers will vary.

B Watch
1 playing computer games at break ✓
playing football in the playground ✓
using mobile phones at break ✗
2 playing computer games: Leoni
playing football with friends: Benno
gets hungry in lessons: Ciara

C Watch again
1 It's dangerous to run in corridors.
2 Benno complains that Leoni is always on the computers during break and so he and the others can never go on them.
3 He uses the adjective *gemein* which means 'mean'.
4 Ciara finds mobile phones irritating.
5 Audrey says you're not allowed to wear stupid hats. Mesut replies that you're not allowed to be so cheeky, to which Audrey replies that you're not allowed to be so boring. However, Mesut disagrees and says that he is intellectual.

D Discuss with your partner
1 "Can you hear us?"
2 "I'll start."
3 Benno likes sitting on tables, but he also likes standing on the tables so that everyone can see and hear him.
4 "Das finde ich …"
5 Yes, you can learn more about their likes and dislikes, what they do in their spare time and what annoys them.

© Pearson Education Ltd 2013. Copying permitted for purchasing institution only. This material is not copyright free.

5 Reading Skills: Mein Lieblingstag

(Pupil Book pp. 84–85)

Schule ist klasse! – **KAPITEL 4**

Learning objectives	Key Language	Resources
• Understanding longer reading texts • Looking up words you don't know **Programme of Study** GV3 Developing vocabulary LC6 Reading comprehension	No new key language. Pupils develop reading skills using key language from the chapter. **PLTS** S Self-managers	**Workbooks:** Übungsheft 1 A&B, page 41 **ActiveTeach:** Starter 1 resource p.084 Extension reading activity p.085 Learning skills worksheet Plenary resource

Starter 1

Aim

To review vocabulary for school rules from unit 4.

Pupils are given a list of infinitives and a blank table with the headings *darf man* and *darf man nicht* (Starter 1 resource). They write the infinitives under the correct heading, depending on whether they are allowed or not allowed to do them in their school. Some vocabulary has been recycled from previous units of the book.

1 Lies den Text und beantworte die Fragen auf Englisch. (Reading L4)

Reading. Pupils read the main text and answer the questions.

The skills feature introduces prediction skills, reminding pupils to use any clues on the page to get an idea about the topic before even starting to read, for example the title, paragraph headings and pictures.

Answers
1 b 2 a 3 yes 4 b

2 Sieh dir die Texte an. (Reading L4)

Reading. Pupils look at the main text.

a Schreib drei Informationen über jede Person auf Deutsch auf.

Pupils write three key facts in German about each of the characters.

b Vergleiche die Informationen mit einem Partner/einer Partnerin.

Pupils compare their key facts with a partner.

The skills feature reminds pupils to check the nature of the task so that they can focus their understanding and reading. It introduces the idea of skimming.

Extension

More able pupils could do further work on dealing with extended sentences:

- Break sentences down into smaller sentences/clauses.
- Work on word order: look for the verb, subject, connective, etc.

They could be challenged to find five facts about each of the characters.

Starter 2

Aim

To work on building up vocabulary by looking at word-families.

Pupils are given the root-word *Schul-*. They then look through unit 5 to find examples of words belonging to this word-family. They can also look back through the chapter and see if they can find any other words belonging to the word-family. They then use a dictionary and look in the German–English section to find additional words to add to the word-family. Explain that word-families can help identify the meaning of new words and reminds pupils about compound nouns in German and how useful it is to identify the component nouns.

3a Schreib die Wörter in alphabetischer Reihenfolge auf. (Reading L2)

Reading. Pupils write out a list of words in alphabetical order.

b Sind sie Verben, Substantive oder Adjektive? (Reading L2)

Pupils say whether the words are verbs, nouns or adjectives and look up the English meaning in a dictionary.

The skills feature helps pupils with dictionary skills and gives tips on how to work out what an unknown word might mean.

© Pearson Education Ltd 2013. Copying permitted for purchasing institution only. This material is not copyright free.

Mein Lieblingstag | **Schule ist klasse!** – KAPITEL

Answers
anfangen – verb – to begin
Arbeit – noun – work
Beruf – noun – job
Hausmeister – noun – caretaker
sauber – adjective/adverb – clean
tun – verb – to do
Turnen – noun – gymnastics

Extension
More work can be done on dictionary skills:
- Put words in alphabetical order.
- Find the right meaning where a word has several different meanings. This is a particularly valuable skill.
- More on the actual dictionary entries and the abbreviations used.

4 Beantworte die Fragen auf Englisch. (Reading L4)

Reading. Pupils answer the questions about the text in English.

The *Tip* box suggests pupils look up any words they need to know to answer the questions and have another go, if necessary.

Answers
1 Tuesday, Wednesday and Thursday
2 any three of: plays golf, listens to music, goes to cinema, watches TV
3 organise them
4 because the next day is Saturday
5 because he lives in a house next to/near the school
6 12 hours
7 *either* makes sure everything is clean and safe *or* repairs anything broken
8 Sunday

Extension
An alternative version of this reading activity is provided on ActiveTeach (p.084 Extension reading activity, Reading L5).

Pupils read a different version of the texts and answer the question, deciding for each sentence which of the characters is talking.

Answers
1 Frau Stiegler
2 Herr Dahlke
3 Niklas Grüber
4 Herr Dahlkes Katze
5 Niklas Grüber
6 Frau Stiegler und Herr Dahlke
7 Niklas Grüber
8 Frau Stiegler
9 Herr Dahlkes Katze
10 Herr Dahlke

This could also lead nicely into some writing about their own favourite days or that of an imaginary character.

Plenary
Aim

To use reading skills to understand longer reading texts.

Pupils are given the text (Plenary resource). They highlight the items in the checklist and go on to discuss the text in pairs, taking it in turns to translate a sentence.

Display the text on the board and ask pupils to take it in turns to come and highlight the items. Ask pupils which sentences were difficult to understand and why this might have been.

Pupils then help to draw up a list of top ten tips for understanding longer reading texts.

© Pearson Education Ltd 2013. Copying permitted for purchasing institution only. This material is not copyright free.

Mein Lieblingstag | **Schule ist klasse!** – KAPITEL 4

Workbook A, page 41

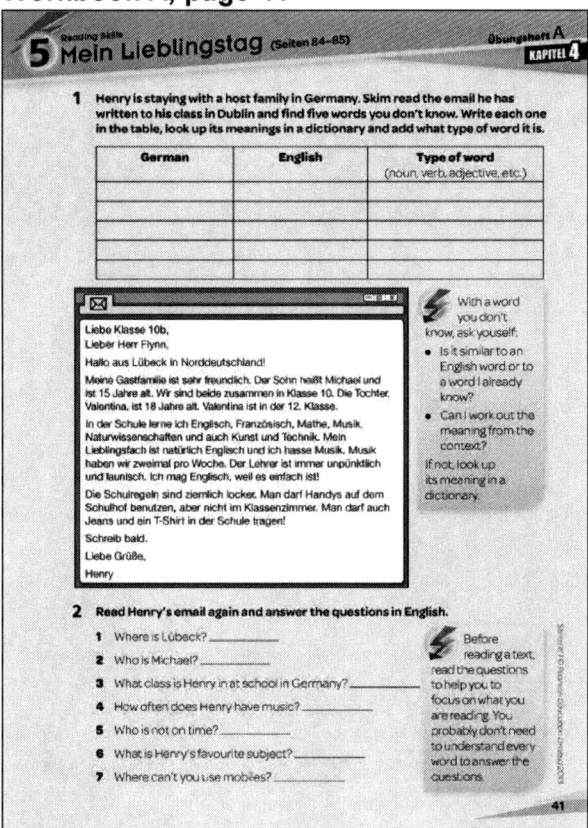

Answers

1 Pupils' own answers.

2 1 In northern Germany.

2 The son in his host family. / His exchange partner.

3 Year 10.

4 Twice a week.

5 The music teacher.

6 English, because it's easy.

7 In the classroom.

Workbook B, page 41

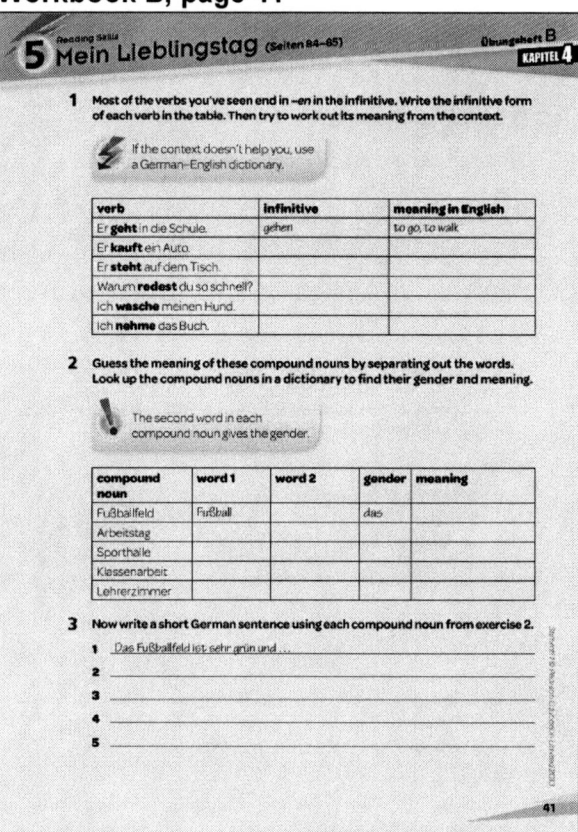

Answers

1 kaufen / to buy

stehen / to stand

reden / to speak, talk

waschen / to wash

nehmen / to take

2 Fußball / Feld / das / football pitch

Arbeit(s) / Tag / der / work day

Sport / Halle / die / sports hall

Klassen / Arbeit / die / class test

Lehrer / Zimmer / das / staff room

3 Possible answers:

1 Das Fußballfeld ist sehr grün und nicht sehr alt.

2 Mein Arbeitstag ist ziemlich lang.

3 Die Sporthalle in der Schule ist ganz modern.

4 Am Montag gibt es eine Klassenarbeit in der Schule.

5 Das Lehrerzimmer ist nicht sehr groß.

© Pearson Education Ltd 2013. Copying permitted for purchasing institution only. This material is not copyright free.

Mein Lieblingstag | **Schule ist klasse!** – KAPITEL

Worksheet

Learning skills: Dealing with new words

5 Mein Lieblingstag — Stimmt! 1 KAPITEL 4

Learning skills: Dealing with new words

You can work out some new words without a dictionary by thinking about:
- **cognates** – words that sound and look the same in German and English
- **near cognates** – words that sound and look so similar to the English words that you can make a good guess about their meaning. But beware of false friends!

A Draw a line to match the German words to their English translations. Think about cognates and near cognates.

Feld   reparieren   Affe   Adresse   Piep   danken   Diamant   Erde

Field   earth   address   beep   diamond   repair   thank   ape

B Read the information about dictionary entries, then look up the words below in a dictionary and complete the table.

Schaf [ʃaːf] *nt* –(e)s, –e sheep; twit (Brit coll.)

[ʃaːf] – pronunciation   *nt* – neuter (*das Schaf*)
–(e)s – ignore this bit for now   –e – plural (*ein Schaf, zwei Schafe*)

sheep; twit – the English meanings of *Schaf*. It is important to use the context to pick the right meaning. For instance, you are unlikely to find a field full of twits, or a school full of sheep!

	Gender	Plural	Meaning(s)
Affe	m (der)	-n (Affen)	ape
Karte			card/ticket/map/menu
Raum			
Stunde			

Remember: words in a dictionary are arranged in alphabetical order!

C Translate these sentences into English. Use the context to work out what *Karte* means in each case. Don't forget to look out for cognates and near cognates to help you!

1 Im Restaurant: „Herr Kellner, die Karte bitte!"   **Kellner = waiter**
2 Meine SIM-Karte funktioniert nicht.
3 Eine Karte von Berlin nach Leipzig, bitte.
4 Haben Sie eine Deutschlandkarte?
5 Der Kartentrick ist einfach.

© Pearson Education Limited 2013
Printing and photocopying permitted

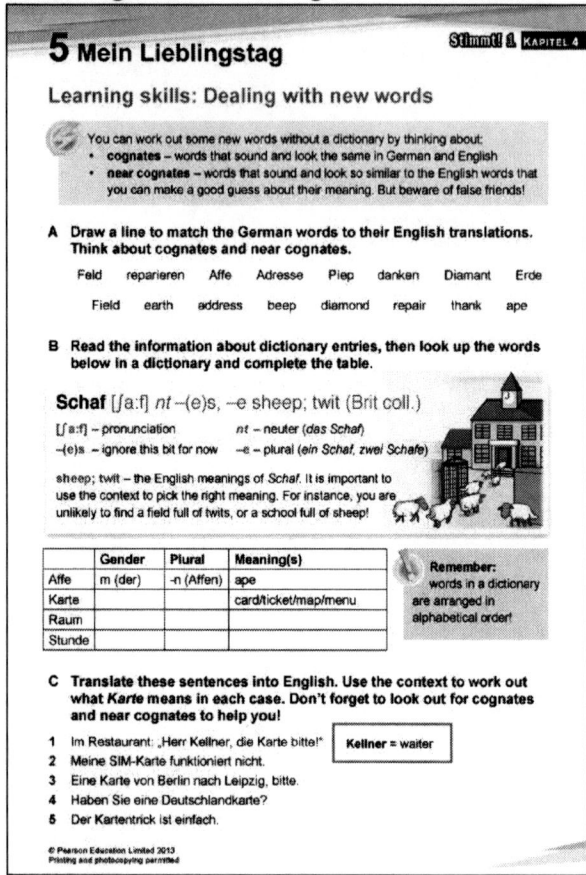

Answers

A Feld – field   reparieren – repair
Affe – ape   Adresse – address
Piep – beep   danken – thank
Diamant – diamond   Erde – earth

B Affe: m (der), -n (Affen), ape
Karte: f (die), -n (Karten), card / ticket / map / menu
Raum: m (der), "-e (Räume), room / space / area / expanse / scope
Stunde: f (die), -n (Stunden), hour / lesson / time

C 1 In the restaurant: Waiter, the menu please!
2 My SIM card isn't working.
3 A ticket from Berlin to Leipzig, please.
4 Do you have a map of Germany?
5 The card trick is easy.

Schule ist klasse! – **KAPITEL 4**

6 Speaking Skills: Meine Traumschule

(Pupil Book pp. 86–87)

Learning objectives	Key Language	Resources
• Talking at length about a topic • Improving your pronunciation **Programme of Study** **LC4** Expressing ideas (speaking) **LC5** Speaking coherently and confidently **FCSE links** Unit 2 – Education and Future Plans (School facilities)	No new key language. Pupils develop speaking skills using key language from the chapter. **PLTS** **E** Effective participators	**Audio files:** 76_Kapitel4_Einheit6_Aufgabe2 **ActiveTeach:** Starter 1 resource Starter 2 resource Plenary resource

Starter 1

Aim

To review question words.

Pupils match the questions to the answers (Starter 1 resource).

Extension

Pupils make up their own answers to the questions.

1 Partnerarbeit. Wie sagt man die Zungenbrecher? Versuch es mal!
(Speaking L2)

Speaking. Working in pairs, pupils try out the tongue-twisters presented in the pupil book.

Use the tongue-twisters to warm up and get pupils thinking about the sounds they know.

If preferred, pupils could be given the unfamiliar vocabulary (below) or follow up the dictionary skills from unit 5 by asking pupils to look up the words.

mehrere – several

riesen- – huge

der Reisebus(-se) – coach

fleißig – hard-working

die Fließband – conveyor belt

der Arbeiter(–) – worker

ziehen – to pull

zahm – tame

die Ziege(-n) – goat

der Zentner(–) – hundredweight (50 kg)

der Zucker(–) – sugar

der Zug(-¨e) – train

weinen – to cry

der Spruch(-¨e) – saying

The *Tip* box notes the important difference in pronunciation between *ei* and *ie*.

The skills feature helps pupils with some strategies for successful pronunciation and speaking.
(source:
Text 2: www.uebersetzung.at/twister/de.htm
Text 4: adapted from www.
www.uebersetzung.at/twister/de.htm)

2 Hör zu und wiederhole. (1–5)
(Listening/Speaking L2)

Listening/Speaking. Pupils listen to the audio and repeat the tongue-twisters. They could peer assess one another in pairs, groups or as a class awarding stars for:

• pronunciation of *ei*, *ie*, *z*, *w*, *ch*, *sch*, *ü*, *ä*
• trying to sound German
• speaking clearly
• getting all the words in without stumbling.

Ask pupils to make constructive suggestions for improvement.

The *Tip* box provides assistance on tackling tongue-twisters and pronunciation.

Audioscript

1 – *In einem Riesenreisebus sitzen vierundfünfzig fleißige Fließbandarbeiter.*
2 – *Am zehnten zehnten um zehn Uhr zehn ziehen zehn zahme Ziegen zehn Zentner Zucker zum Züricher Zoo-Zug.*
3 – *Wiebke weint, weil Wiebkes Wände schwarz-weiß sind.*
4 – *Schnellsprechsprüche spreche ich schnell.*

© Pearson Education Ltd 2013. Copying permitted for purchasing institution only. This material is not copyright free.

Meine Traumschule | **Schule ist klasse!** – KAPITEL

3 Partner- oder Gruppenarbeit. Stell dir deine Traumschule vor. Mach eine Liste von Fragen für deinen Partner/deine Partnerin oder Gruppe über ihre Traumschule. (Speaking/Writing L4)

Speaking/Writing. Working in pairs or small groups, pupils imagine what their own dream school would be like. They then make a list of questions to ask about their partner's or group's dream school. Collate the questions before moving on to exercise 4. This might be too difficult for some, in which case go straight to exercise 4.

The *Tip* box notes the key points to remember when forming questions.

4 Partnerarbeit. Stelle deinen Partner/deine Partnerin deine Fragen (Aufgabe 3) und beantworte ihre Fragen. Benutze die Beispiele. (Speaking L4)

Speaking. Working in pairs or small groups, pupils take it in turns to ask each other some of their questions from exercise 3, and to answer them.

Some vocabulary is glossed for support and suggestions are provided in tabular form.

> **Starter 2**
>
> **Aim**
>
> To assess a written text and make suggestions for improvement.
>
> Pupils read the text (Starter 2 resource) and use the checklist to assess it. They then add in extra detail in a different colour to improve the text.

5 Mach eine kurze Präsentation über deine Traumschule. (Speaking L4)

Speaking. Pupils give a short presentation about their dream school.

Pupils could record themselves speaking on their phones, either in the classroom or for homework.

A video blog could work well for describing school/dream schools.

Refer pupils to the skills feature. It not only helps with tactics for making the presentation sound fluent and interesting, but also helps to cope with unfamiliar language and unexpected responses during questions from the class.

> **Plenary**
>
> **Aim**
>
> To focus on pronunciation.
>
> Pupils work in groups of four. One pupil is nominated reader and the other three pupils divide up the sound cards between them (Plenary resource). The reader reads aloud the text below (adapted from the starter activity). If the reader makes a mistake with the pronunciation, the pupil with that particular sound card holds it up and the reader must go back to the start of their sentence and read the sentence again, correcting the mistake. All four pupils take it in turns to be the reader.

© Pearson Education Ltd 2013. Copying permitted for purchasing institution only. This material is not copyright free.

Schule ist klasse! – KAPITEL 4

Lernzieltest und Wiederholung (Pupil Book pp. 88–89)

Lernzieltest
Pupils use this checklist to review language covered in the chapter, working on it in pairs in class or on their own at home. There is a Word version on ActiveTeach which can be printed out and given to pupils. Encourage them to follow up any weakness they identify. There are Target Setting Sheets included in the Assessment Pack, and an opportunity for pupils to record their own levels and targets on the *Mein Fortschritt* page in the Workbooks. You can also use the *Lernzieltest* checklist as an end-of-chapter plenary option.

Wiederholung
These revision exercises can be used for assessment purposes or for pupils to practise before tackling the assessment tasks in the Assessment Pack.

Resources
Audio files:
77_Kapitel4_Wiederholung_Aufgabe1
Workbooks:
Übungsheft 1 A&B, pages 42–43
ActiveTeach:
p.088 Lernzieltest checklist
p.089 Exercise 1 grid

---

1 Hör zu. Schreib den Stundenplan ab und füll ihn aus. Wähl aus dem Kasten. (Listening L3)

Listening. Pupils listen to the audio and complete a copy of the table from the pupil book, choosing subjects from the box provided.

Audioscript
- Am Montag habe ich Deutsch in der ersten Stunde.
- Am Dienstag haben wir Mathe in der ersten Stunde und in der zweiten Stunde. Das ist furchtbar!
- Am Montag haben wir Technik in der fünften Stunde. Technik ist mein Lieblingsfach. Und dann haben wir Sport! Toll!
- Am Dienstag haben wir Englisch und Geschichte nach der Pause: Englisch in der dritten Stunde und Geschichte in der vierten Stunde.
- Am Montag haben wir Informatik in der dritten Stunde.
- Am Montag habe ich Musik vor der Mittagspause.
- Ich habe Naturwissenschaften am Dienstag in der sechsten Stunde.
- Theater ist mein Lieblingsfach. Wir haben Theater am Dienstag nach der Mittagspause.

Answers
	Mo.	Di.
1. Stunde:	**Deutsch**	*Mathe*
2. Stunde:	*Erdkunde*	**Mathe**
Pause		
3. Stunde:	**Informatik**	*Englisch*
4. Stunde:	**Musik**	*Geschichte*
Mittagspause		
5. Stunde:	**Technik**	**Theater**
6. Stunde:	*Sport*	**Naturwiss.**

2 Partnerarbeit. Beschreib einen Lehrer/eine Lehrerin. Dein Partner/Deine Partnerin schreibt alles auf. (Listening L2)

Speaking. Working in pairs, pupils take it in turns to describe one of the teachers in the illustrations. The partner transcribes the descriptions.

Write adjectives up on the board for pupils who might struggle; the more able can attempt the task independently.

The *Tip* box reminds pupils to say as much as possible and to use connectives.

Possible answers
1 Herr Grün ist mein Mathelehrer. Er ist klein und hat braune Haare. Er ist ziemlich streng, aber er ist auch freundlich. Sein Bruder spielt Fußball in der deutschen Nationalmannschaft.

2 Frau Braun ist meine Sportlehrerin. Sie ist ziemlich jung, groß und sie hat lange blonde Haare. Sie ist sehr sportlich, aber sie ist zu launisch und arrogant. Ihr Lieblingsauto ist ein VW.

3 Herr Schwarz ist mein Deutschlehrer. Er ist ziemlich alt, mittelgroß und hat graue Haare. Er ist sehr fair und lustig und er mag Katzen.

© Pearson Education Ltd 2013. Copying permitted for purchasing institution only. This material is not copyright free.

Lernzieltest und Wiederholung | **Schule ist klasse!** – KAPITEL

3 Lies das Blog und beantworte die Fragen. (Listening L3)

Reading. Pupils read the blog and answer the questions in English.

Answers
1 in the classroom
2 listen to music
3 maths, German, English, science
4 their favourite subjects
5 no homework
6 at 2 p.m.

4 Schreib einige Sätze über deine Schule. (Listening L4)

Writing. Pupils write a few sentences describing their school. Some starter ideas are supplied.

Workbook A, page 42

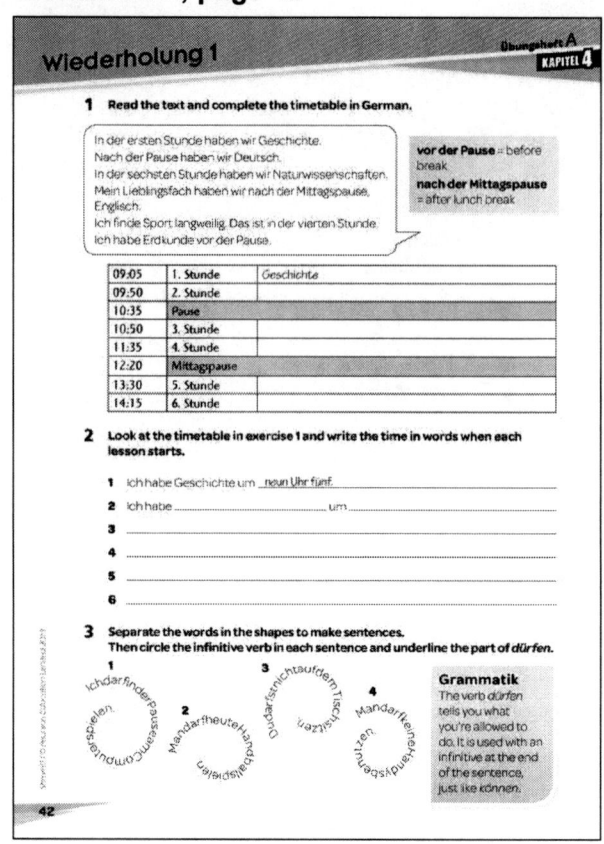

Answers

1 1. Stunde: Geschichte
   2. Stunde: Erdkunde
   3. Stunde: Deutsch
   4. Stunde: Sport
   5. Stunde: Englisch
   6. Stunde: Naturwissenschaften

2 1 Ich habe Geschichte um neun Uhr fünf.
   2 Ich habe Erdkunde um neun Uhr fünfzig.
   3 Ich habe Deutsch um zehn Uhr fünfzig.
   4 Ich habe Sport um elf Uhr fünfunddreißig.
   5 Ich habe Englisch um dreizehn Uhr dreißig.
   6 Ich habe Naturwissenschaften um vierzehn Uhr fünfzehn.

3 1 Ich <u>darf</u> in der Pause am Computer **spielen**.
   2 Man <u>darf</u> heute Handball **spielen**.
   3 Du <u>darfst</u> nicht auf dem Tisch **sitzen**.
   4 Man <u>darf</u> keine Handys **benutzen**.
   (Infinitives presented here in bold rather than circled.)

© Pearson Education Ltd 2013. Copying permitted for purchasing institution only. This material is not copyright free.

Lernzieltest und Wiederholung | **Schule ist klasse!** – KAPITEL 4

Workbook B, page 42

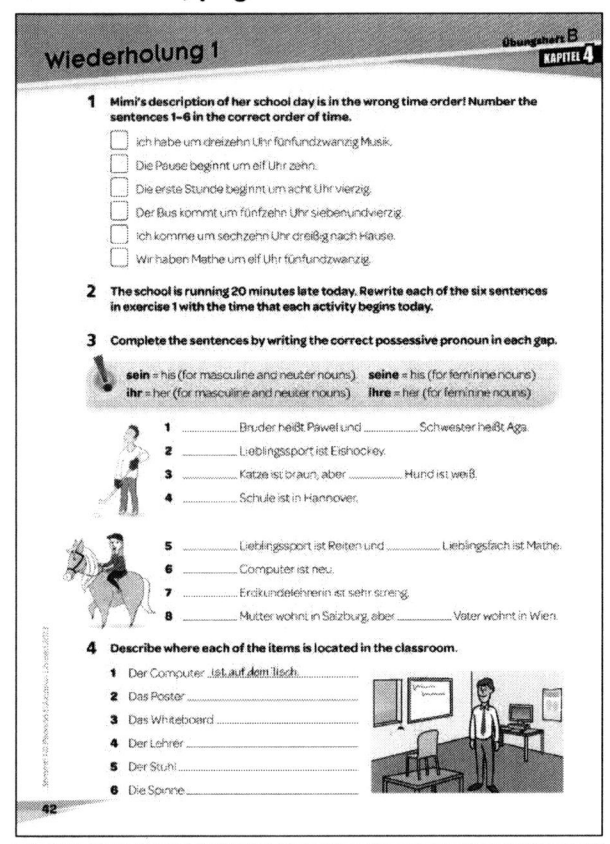

Workbook A, page 43

Answers

1 4; 2; 1; 5; 6; 3

2 Ich habe um 13:45 Uhr Musik.
Die kleine Pause beginnt um 11:30 Uhr.
Die erste Stunde beginnt um 9:00 Uhr.
Der Bus kommt um 16:07 Uhr.
Ich komme um 16:50 Uhr nach Hause.
Wir haben Mathe um 11:45 Uhr.

3 1 Seine, seine
2 Sein
3 Seine, sein
4 Seine
5 Ihr, ihr
6 Ihr
7 Ihre
8 Ihre, ihr

4 1 Der Computer ist auf dem Tisch.
2 Das Poster ist an der Wand/neben dem Computer.
3 Das Whiteboard ist neben dem Fenster.
4 Der Lehrer ist im Klassenzimmer/neben dem Tisch.
5 Der Stuhl ist auf dem Tisch.
6 Die Spinne ist neben dem Fenster.

Answers

1 Pupils' own answers.

2 1 Ich lerne gern Mathe, weil es sehr nützlich ist.
2 Wir machen Sport, weil es super ist.
3 Ich liebe Englisch, weil der Lehrer lustig ist.
4 Frau Wörth spielt Volleyball, weil sie sportlich ist.

3 Pupils' own answers.

© Pearson Education Ltd 2013. Copying permitted for purchasing institution only. This material is not copyright free.

Workbook B, page 43

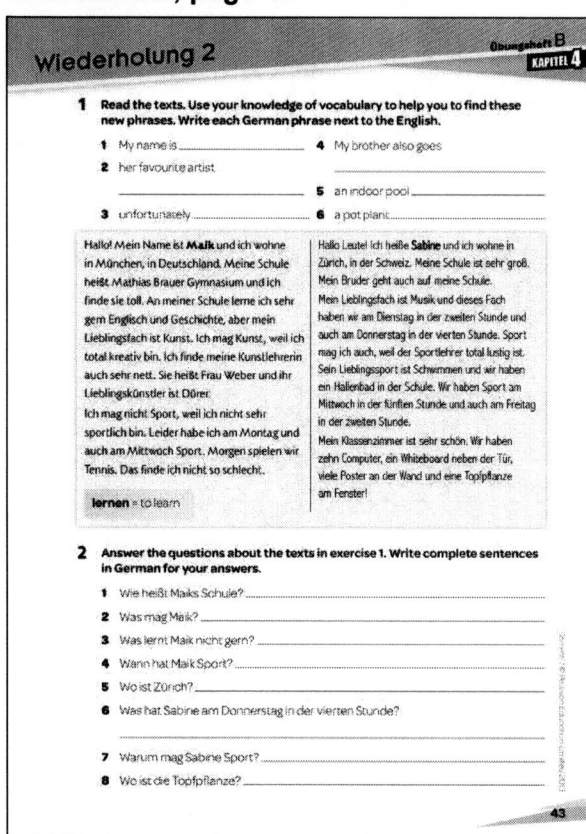

Wiederholung 2 — Übungsheft B, KAPITEL 4

1 Read the texts. Use your knowledge of vocabulary to help you to find these new phrases. Write each German phrase next to the English.

1 My name is _____
2 her favourite artist _____
3 unfortunately _____
4 My brother also goes _____
5 an indoor pool _____
6 a pot plant _____

> Hallo! Mein Name ist **Maik** und ich wohne in München, in Deutschland. Meine Schule heißt Mathias Brauer Gymnasium und ich finde sie toll. An meiner Schule lerne ich sehr gern Englisch und Geschichte, aber mein Lieblingsfach ist Kunst. Ich mag Kunst, weil ich total kreativ bin. Ich finde meine Kunstlehrerin auch sehr nett. Sie heißt Frau Weber und ihr Lieblingskünstler ist Dürer.
> Ich mag nicht Sport, weil ich nicht sehr sportlich bin. Leider habe ich am Montag und auch am Mittwoch Sport. Morgen spielen wir Tennis. Das finde ich nicht so schlecht.
>
> **lernen** = to learn

> Hallo Leute! Ich heiße **Sabine** und ich wohne in Zürich, in der Schweiz. Meine Schule ist sehr groß. Mein Bruder geht auch auf meine Schule.
> Mein Lieblingsfach ist Musik und dieses Fach haben wir am Dienstag in der zweiten Stunde und auch am Donnerstag in der vierten Stunde. Sport mag ich auch, weil der Sportlehrer total lustig ist. Sein Lieblingssport ist Schwimmen und wir haben ein Hallenbad in der Schule. Wir haben Sport am Mittwoch in der fünften Stunde und auch am Freitag in der zweiten Stunde.
> Mein Klassenzimmer ist sehr schön. Wir haben zehn Computer, ein Whiteboard neben der Tür, viele Poster an der Wand und eine Topfpflanze am Fenster!

2 Answer the questions about the texts in exercise 1. Write complete sentences in German for your answers.

1 Wie heißt Maiks Schule? _____
2 Was mag Maik? _____
3 Was lernt Maik nicht gern? _____
4 Wann hat Maik Sport? _____
5 Wo ist Zürich? _____
6 Was hat Sabine am Donnerstag in der vierten Stunde? _____
7 Warum mag Sabine Sport? _____
8 Wo ist die Topfpflanze? _____

Answers

1
1 Mein Name ist …
2 ihr Lieblingskünstler
3 leider
4 Mein Bruder geht auch
5 ein Hallenbad
6 eine Topfpflanze

2
1 Maiks Schule heißt Mathias Brauer Gymnasium.
2 Maik mag Kunst, weil er kreativ ist/weil die Lehrerin sehr nett ist.
3 Maik lernt nicht gern Sport.
4 Maik hat am Montag und am Mittwoch Sport.
5 Zürich ist in der Schweiz.
6 Sabine hat Musik am Donnerstag in der vierten Stunde.
7 Sabine mag Sport, weil der Lehrer sehr lustig ist.
8 Die Topfpflanze ist am Fenster im Klassenzimmer.

Schule ist klasse! – KAPITEL 4

Grammatik (Pupil Book pp. 90–91)

The *Stimmt!* Grammatik section provides a more detailed summary of key grammar covered in the chapter, along with further exercises to practise these points.

Grammar topics
Word order with *weil*
Word order with expressions of time
sein/ihr
Prepositions
es gibt
dürfen

Resources
Workbooks:
Übungsheft 1 A&B, page 44

Word order with weil

1 Join the sentences using *weil*, then translate the full sentences into English. (Writing L4)

Some pupils could omit question 5.

The *Tip* box reminds pupils to identify the main verb that needs to go to the end of the sentence in the more complicated question 5.

> **Answers**
> 1 Ich mag Mittwoch, weil wir Englisch und Sport haben. *I like Wednesday, because we have English and sport.*
> 2 Herr König ist cool, weil er nicht sehr streng ist. *Mr King is cool, because he is not very strict.*
> 3 Mein Lieblingstag ist Samstag, weil ich Tennis im Park spiele. *My favourite day is Saturday, because I play tennis in the park.*
> 4 Frau Haller hat viele Freunde, weil sie sehr lustig ist. *Mrs Heller has many friends, because she is very funny.*
> 5 Informatik ist mein Lieblingsfach, weil man am Computer spielen darf. *ICT is my favourite subject, because you are allowed / one is allowed to play on the computer.*

Word order with expressions of time

2 Rewrite the sentences. Begin with the underlined words. (Writing L4)

The nouns are colour coded to help with gender.

> **Answers**
> 1 <u>Am Montag</u> haben wir Mathe.
> 2 <u>Heute</u> haben wir keine Schule.
> 3 <u>In der dritten Stunde</u> hast du Erdkunde.
> 4 <u>Um 10 Uhr</u> spielen Lukas und seine Freunde Fußball.
> 5 <u>Jeden Tag</u> haben wir Englisch, aber <u>nur am Montag</u> haben wir Technik.

sein/ihr

3 Copy the sentences and fill in the gaps with *sein(e)* or *ihr(e)*. (Writing L3)

> **Answers**
> 1 Jonas mag Karate, aber **sein** Lieblingssport ist Judo.
> 2 Sara und **ihre** Mutter singen zusammen.
> 3 Das ist Lukas. **Seine** Großeltern wohnen in Österreich.
> 4 Mina hat viele Tiere. Ich finde **ihr** Pferd freundlich und **ihre** Mäuse so niedlich.

Prepositions

4 Look at the pictures. Where are they? Write sentences. (Writing L3)

> **Answers**
> 1 Der Lehrer ist neben der Tür.
> 2 Der Tisch ist am (neben dem) Fenster.
> 3 Der Computer ist auf dem Tisch.
> 4 Das Poster ist an der Wand.
> 5 Der Stuhl ist im Korridor.
> 6 Die Katze ist auf dem Stuhl.

es gibt

5 Translate these sentences into German. (Writing L3)

The *Tip* box reminds pupils to check the gender and plural of nouns on p. 82 if they need to.

> **Answers**
> 1 Es gibt ein Poster an der Wand.
> 2 Es gibt einen Computer auf dem Tisch.
> 3 Es gibt einen Tisch neben der Tür.
> 4 Es gibt 50 (fünfzig) Klassenzimmer in der Schule.

© Pearson Education Ltd 2013. Copying permitted for purchasing institution only. This material is not copyright free.

Grammatik | Schule ist klasse! – KAPITEL

dürfen

6 Write the English. Underline your translation of *dürfen*. (Writing L2)

Answers
1 <u>I'm allowed</u> to play tennis today.
2 The teacher <u>is allowed</u> to sit on the table.
3 <u>Are you allowed</u> to go to the cinema today?
4 At school <u>you/we/people are not allowed</u> to bully.

Workbook A, page 44

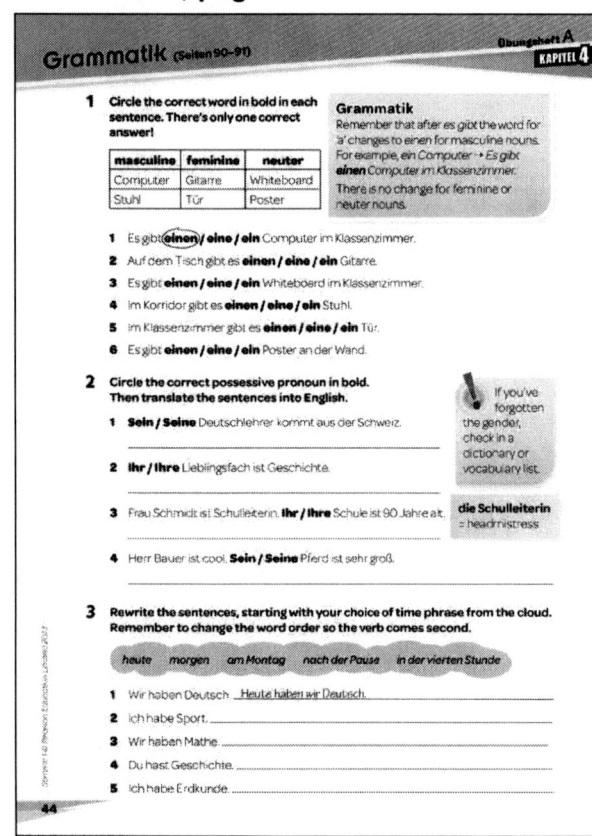

2 Morgen habe ich Sport.
3 In der vierten Stunde haben wir Mathe.
4 Am Montag hast du Geschichte.
5 Nach der Pause habe ich Erdkunde.

Workbook B, page 44

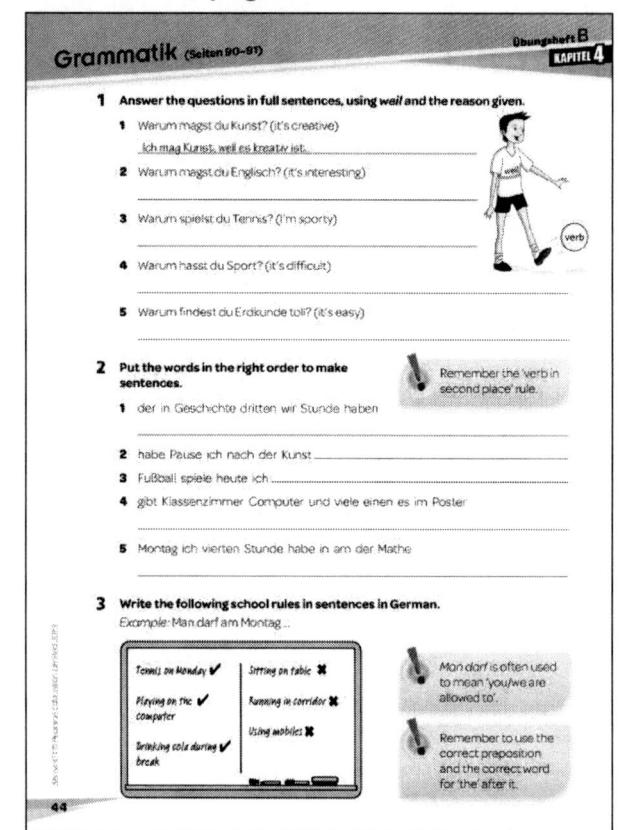

Answers
1 1 Ich mag Kunst, weil es kreativ ist.
   2 Ich mag Englisch, weil es interessant ist.
   3 Ich spiele Tennis, weil ich sportlich bin.
   4 Ich hasse Sport, weil es schwierig ist.
   5 Ich finde Erdkunde toll, weil es einfach ist.
2 1 Wir haben in der dritten Stunde Geschichte. / In der dritten Stunde haben wir Geschichte.
   2 Ich habe nach der Pause Kunst. / Nach der Pause habe ich Kunst.
   3 Ich spiele heute Fußball. / Heute spiele ich Fußball.
   4 Es gibt einen Computer und viele Poster im Klassenzimmer. / Im Klassenzimmer gibt es einen Computer und viele Poster.
   5 Ich habe am Montag in der vierten Stunde Mathe. / Am Montag in der vierten Stunde habe ich Mathe.

Answers
1 1 einen 2 eine 3 ein 4 einen 5 eine 6 ein
2 1 Sein – His German teacher comes from Switzerland.
   2 Ihr – Her favourite subject is History.
   3 Ihre – Frau Schmidt is a head teacher. Her school is 90 years old.
   4 Sein – Herr Bauer is cool. His horse is very big.
3 Possible answers:
   1 Heute haben wir Deutsch.

© Pearson Education Ltd 2013. Copying permitted for purchasing institution only. This material is not copyright free.

Grammatik | **Schule ist klasse!** – KAPITEL 4

3 Man darf am Montag Tennis spielen.
Man darf am Computer spielen.
Man darf Cola in der Pause trinken.
Man darf nicht auf dem Tisch sitzen.
Man darf nicht im Korridor laufen.
Man darf keine Handys benutzen.

Schule ist klasse! – **KAPITEL**

Projektzone: Sonne, Mond und Erde

(Pupil Book pp. 94–95)

The *Projektzone* is one or two optional units in which no new grammar is introduced, but in which the chapter topic is extended into an exciting cultural and practical context which allows for cross-curricular and project work.

Learning objectives

- Finding out about the solar system
- Making a display about the solar system

Programme of Study

GV3 Developing vocabulary
LC4 Expressing ideas (writing)
LC6 Reading comprehension

PLTS
E Effective participators

Cross-curricular
Science: **astronomy**

Resources

Audio files:
78_Kapitel4_Projektzone_Aufgabe5

ActiveTeach:
Starter 2 resource
Plenary resource

Starter 1

Aim

To find out what pupils already know about the solar system.

Pupils work individually and have three minutes to write down as many facts as they can about the solar system. They then have three minutes to share their ideas with their partners before having a further three minutes to discuss and share their ideas with another group. This will be useful in establishing what pupils know and preparing them for the texts on the solar system in German.

1 Man findet die Sonne und den Mond in vielen Wörtern. Was passt zusammen? (Reading L2)

Reading. Pupils match the German to the English translation.

The *Tip* box reminds pupils to use their dictionary skills to help.

Answers
1 b   2 d   3 e   4 g   5 a   6 h   7 f   8 c

Extension

Look up other words with *Sonne*, *Mond* and perhaps also *Erde* (Erdbeere, Erdbeben, Erdgeschoss …).

2 Sieh dir die Daten und Bilder an. Finde die Paare und füll die Lücken mit den Zahlen aus. (Reading L2)

Reading. Pupils match up the text and the pictures, and then fill in the gaps in the sentences with the correct numbers.

The *Tip* box points out that in German you use a comma rather than a decimal point – and therefore a space (not a comma) to separate thousands and millions.

Some vocabulary is glossed for support.

Answers
1 d (150)   2 f (384,000)   3 b (24)   4 c (29,53)   5 e (365,24)   6 a (4,54)

3 Lies den Text und schreib die Planeten in der richtigen Reihenfolge auf. (Reading L3)

Reading. Pupils read the text and write out the planets in their order of distance from the sun (nearest first). The planet names are included in a box.

Some vocabulary is glossed for support.

The mnemonic sentence is used in German schools to aid pupils in memorising the planets.

Answers
Merkur, Venus, Erde, Mars, Jupiter, Saturn, Uranus, Neptun

Starter 2

Aim

To understand a text containing unfamiliar vocabulary.

Pupils read the text in German first (Starter 2 resource) and highlight any new vocabulary. They then complete the gap-fill translation in English, working out the meaning of the new words. Once they have completed the translation, they compare with a partner and fill in any remaining gaps together.

© Pearson Education Ltd 2013. Copying permitted for purchasing institution only. This material is not copyright free.

Projektzone: Sonne, Mond und Erde | **Schule ist klasse!** – **KAPITEL 4**

> **Answers**
>
> Mars is the fourth **planet** in our **solar system**.
>
> Its diameter is 6,800 km. Mars is the second smallest planet in the **solar system**. It is 228 km **from** the sun.
>
> Mars is **orange** and is often called the **red** planet. The planet is **orange** because it has iron oxide on the surface and in the **atmosphere**.
>
> Mars has two small **moons**: Phobos and Deimos.

4 Wie sagt man die deutschen Namen der Planeten? Versuch es mal. (Speaking L2)

Speaking. Pupils are encouraged to try and say the names of the planets using the correct German pronunciation. Pupils check their pronunciation in exercise 5.

The *Aussprache* box gives some tips on how to work out the correct pronunciation if pupils don't already know.

5 Hör zu und überprüfe. (Listening L1)

Listening. Pupils listen to the audio to check the pronunciation of the names of the planets.

> **Audioscript**
>
> – Merkur
> – Venus
> – Erde, Mars
> – Jupiter
> – Saturn
> – Uranus
> – Neptun

6 Partnerarbeit. Sag drei Planeten. Dein Partner/Deine Partnerin schreibt die Namen auf. (Speaking L1)

Speaking. Pupils work in pairs. One selects three planets from exercise 3 and says them out loud. The other one transcribes the names of the planets. They then evaluate each other's speaking and writing respectively:

- pronunciation of *e, j, r, s, u* sounds
- sounding German
- spelling correctly.

If possible, video a group of nine people doing the sentence. The 'sun' says the whole sentence and the eight 'planets' call out their names and move into the correct position from the sun.

> **Extension**
>
> Some pupils could be encouraged to close their books and say the rhyme (exercise 3) from memory. Their partner writes down what they say.

> **Extension**
>
> Instead of (or as well as) this exercise, some pupils might be able to make up their own German rhyme or sentence for remembering the names and order of the planets.

7 Mach ein Poster über das Sonnensystem (auf Deutsch natürlich!). (Writing L1–4)

Writing. Pupils design and produce a poster about the solar system. They can use their own information, and perhaps some from the *Weißt du das?* feature.

Include some examples of writing about the solar system to support the poster activity, for example a simple poem:

Die Erde – grün und blau,

Der Mond ist weiß und grau,

Die Sonne liebe ich,

Sie ist ziemlich freundlich.

The *Tip* box reminds pupils to try and use words and phrases that they already know rather than look up new material.

> **Plenary**
>
> **Aim**
>
> To peer assess a written text about the solar system.
>
> Pupils peer assess their written work on the solar system before it is handed in to the teacher.
>
> Whilst reading their partner's work on the solar system, pupils should give as much feedback as possible using the grid supplied (Plenary resource). They should give a mark out of 10 for each category and suggest how their partner could improve.

Schule ist klasse! – KAPITEL

Extra (Pupil Book pp. 126–127)

Self-access reading and writing

A Reinforcement

1 Entschlüssle die Schulfächer und schreib die Namen richtig auf, dann finde die Paare. (Reading L1)

Reading. Pupils decipher the school subject words using the code provided. They then match the pairs.

The *Tip* box provides the key to the code.

> **Answers**
> 1 Deutsch – c
> 2 Mathe – e
> 3 Erdkunde – a
> 4 Informatik – f
> 5 Kunst – b
> 6 Naturwissenschaften – d

2 Schreib die Sätze ab und vervollständige sie. (Reading L3)

Writing. Pupils copy and complete the sentences.

> **Answers**
> 1 Ich habe **Englisch** am **Montag** um **zehn Uhr fünfzehn**.
> 2 Ich habe **Geschichte** am **Mittwoch** um **dreizehn Uhr dreißig**.
> 3 Wir haben **Sport** am **Freitag** um **elf Uhr zwanzig**.
> 4 Um **acht Uhr fünfundvierzig** habe ich **Musik**.
> 5 Ich habe **Theater** am **Dienstag** in der **fünften** Stunde.
> 6 Am **Donnerstag** in der **dritten** Stunde habe ich **Technik**.

3 Lies die Meinung. Ist sie positiv ☺ oder negativ ☹? (Reading L2)

Reading. Pupils read the opinions and decide whether they are positive or negative.

> **Answers**
> 1 positive 2 negative 3 negative 4 positive
> 5 negative 6 positive

4 Schreib deine Meinung über drei Lehrer auf. (Writing L3)

Writing. Pupils write their opinion of three teachers.

B Extension

1 Was ist das? Schreib die fett gedruckten Wörter richtig auf. (Reading L1)

Reading. Pupils read the sentences and solve the anagrams (in bold).

> **Answers**
> 1 Der Computer 2 Der Stuhl 3 Der Tisch
> 4 Das Poster 5 Die Lehrerin

2 Lies das Blog, dann finde die drei falschen Sätze. (Reading L4)

Reading. Pupils read the text and find the three incorrect statements.

Some vocabulary is glossed for support.

> **Answers**
> 1, 4 and 6 are incorrect

3 Korrigiere die drei falschen Sätze. (Writing L4)

Writing. Pupils write out correctly the three incorrect statements from exercise 2.

> **Possible answers**
> 1 Finn ist in der **8. (achten)** Klasse.
> 4 Mittwoch ist Finns Lieblingstag, weil er **eine Doppelstunde Mathe** hat.
> 6 In der Mittagspause **darf man** im Klassenzimmer bleiben.

4 Schreib ein Blog über deine Schule. (Writing L4)

Writing. Pupils write a blog about their school. They should include:

- their name and age
- the school name
- their favourite school day (including some of the lessons they have and when)
- their opinion of two of their subjects (give reasons)
- what there is in their German classroom.

KAPITEL 5

(Pupil Book pp. 96–119)

Gute Reise!

Unit & Learning objectives	Programme of Study references	Key Language	Grammar and other language features
1 In der Stadt (pp. 98–99) • Saying what there is/isn't in a town • Using *es gibt* + *ein/kein*	**GV2** Grammatical structures (*es gibt* + *ein/kein*) **LC1** Listening and responding **LC6** Reading comprehension	der Bahnhof der Park der Marktplatz die Kirche die Imbissstube die Kegelbahn das Kino das Schwimmbad das Schloss Es gibt einen/keinen … Es gibt eine/keine … Es gibt ein/kein …	• Sentences with *es gibt* … • Negative sentences with *kein* • Using key phonics to help with pronunciation • Compound words • Using the *Wörter* section to check plurals
2 Wir gehen einkaufen! (pp. 100–101) • Saying what souvenirs you want to buy • Using *ich möchte* to say what you would like	**GV2** Grammatical structures (*möchten* with the infinitive) **LC2** Transcription **LC3** Conversation (using modes of address)	der Kuli der Schlüsselanhänger der Aufkleber die Tasse die Postkarte die Kappe das Freundschaftsband das Trikot das Kuscheltier Ich möchte … (kaufen). Du möchtest … (kaufen). Er/Sie möchte … (kaufen).	• *möchten* with the infinitive • Making numbers into prices • Pronouncing cognates • When to use *du* and when to use *Sie* • Extending your answer
3 Mmm, lecker! (pp. 102–103) • Buying snacks and drinks • More practice with euros and cents	**GV3** Developing vocabulary **GV3** Opinions and discussions **LC6** Reading comprehension	Was möchtest du? Was möchten Sie? Etwas zu essen? Etwas zu trinken? Ich möchte … Ich hätte gern … einmal Bratwurst (mit …), bitte zweimal … dreimal … der Hamburger der Tee die Bratwurst die Cola die Pizza die Pommes das Eis das Mineralwasser	• *man kann* + infinitive • *ich hätte gern* … and *ich möchte* … • Working out the meaning of compound words

© Pearson Education Ltd 2013. Copying permitted for purchasing institution only. This material is not copyright free.

Gute Reise! – KAPITEL

Unit & Learning objectives	Programme of Study references	Key Language	Grammar and other language features
4 In den Sommerferien (pp. 104–105) • Talking about holiday plans • Using *werden* to form the future tense	**GV1** Tenses (forming the future using *werden*) **LC5** Speaking coherently and confidently **LC8** Writing creatively	Was wirst du in den Sommerferien machen? Ich werde … Wir werden … segeln klettern an den Strand gehen wandern im See baden tauchen windsurfen rodeln im Meer schwimmen In den Sommerferien werde ich mit … Wir werden … nach … fahren Wir werden … Wochen bleiben Wir werden … und auch … Dort gibt es … und …, aber kein … Man kann dort … und … Am Montag/Freitag … Ich möchte auch …	• Using *werden* + infinitive • Beware of words that look similar to the English but have different meanings • *wohin*
5 Listening Skills: Auf geht's! (pp. 106–107) • Understanding longer, more varied spoken texts • Focusing on high-frequency words	**GV3** Developing vocabulary **LC1** Listening and responding		• High-frequency words • Pre-listening strategies • Listening strategies • Key words *ein*, *kein* and *nicht* and their effect on meaning • Word order
6 Writing Skills: Willkommen! (pp. 108–109) • Writing at length about a topic • Adapting a model	**GV3** Developing vocabulary **LC2** Transcription **LC8** Writing creatively		• Add variety by using adjectives • Adding variety by varying sentence structure • Adapting a model to help structure writing • Using a checklist
Lernzieltest und Wiederholung (pp. 110–111) Pupils' checklist and practice exercises			• Listening and responding to each other • Adapting a model to structure work

© Pearson Education Ltd 2013. Copying permitted for purchasing institution only. This material is not copyright free.

Gute Reise! – KAPITEL 5

Unit & Learning objectives	Programme of Study references	Key Language	Grammar and other language features
Grammatik (pp. 112–113) Detailed grammar summary and practice exercises			• Negative sentences with *kein* • *möchten* with the infinitive • Using *gern* with a variety of verbs • Using *werden* to form the future tense • Checking the gender of nouns in the pupil book • The *wir* form of the present tense is the same as the infinitive • Sentence structure following a time expression
Projektzone 1: Infos für Touristen (pp. 116–117) • Researching German-speaking places • Creating a tourist brochure	**LC3** Conversation (dealing with the unexpected) **LC5** Speaking coherently and confidently **LC8** Writing creatively		• Speaking spontaneously • Extra words that make speech sound spontaneous • Thinking before speaking
Projektzone 2: Lass uns spielen! (pp. 118–119) • Using familiar language in a new context • Creating your own board game	**LC1** Listening and responding **LC3** Conversation		• Use the *Wörter* pages or a dictionary to check words

© Pearson Education Ltd 2013. Copying permitted for purchasing institution only. This material is not copyright free.

Gute Reise! – KAPITEL

1 In der Stadt (Pupil Book pp. 98–99)

Learning objectives
- Saying what there is/isn't in a town
- Using *es gibt + ein/kein*

Programme of Study
GV2 Grammatical structures (*es gibt + ein/kein*)
LC1 Listening and responding
LC6 Reading comprehension

FCSE links
Unit 7 – Local Area and Environment (Facilities)

Grammar
Sentences with *es gibt …*
Negative sentences with *kein*

PLTS
C Creative thinkers

Cross-curricular
Geography: town planning

Key Language
der Bahnhof
der Park
der Marktplatz
die Kirche
die Imbissstube
die Kegelbahn
das Kino
das Schwimmbad
das Schloss
Es gibt einen/keinen …
Es gibt eine/keine …
Es gibt ein/kein …

Resources
Audio files:
79_Kapitel5_Einheit1_Aufgabe3
80_Kapitel5_Einheit1_Aufgabe4
81_Kapitel5_Einheit1_Aufgabe7
82_Kapitel5_Einheit1_Aufgabe8
Workbooks:
Übungsheft 1 A&B, page 48
ActiveTeach:
Starter 1 resource
Starter 2 resource
p.098 Grammar presentation
p.098 Flashcards
p.099 Video: Episode 9
Plenary resource
ActiveLearn:
Listening A, Listening B
Reading A, Reading B
Grammar, Vocabulary

Kapitel 5 Quiz pp. 96–97

Answers

1 Neuschwanstein ist ein …
c Schloss

2 Neuschwanstein ist in …
a Deutschland

3 Neuschwanstein ist über … Jahre alt.
a 100

4 Neuschwanstein ist die Inspiration für …
c Cinderella Schloss

5 Was für eine Stadt ist das? Verbinde die Stadt mit der richtigen Kategorie.
1 Baden-Baden – eine Mittelstadt
2 Binningen – eine Kleinstadt
3 Hamburg – eine Millionenstadt
4 Ulm – eine Großstadt
5 Mariental – eine Kleinstadt
6 Wien – eine Hauptstadt

6 Ist das eine Megastadt oder nicht? Schreib die Namen der vier Megastädte auf.
Tokio, Mexiko-Stadt, New York City, Rio de Janeiro

Starter 1

Aim

To introduce new vocabulary from the unit and to encourage pupils to make logical guesses about the meaning of new vocabulary.

Pupils are given cards with the new vocabulary from the unit (Starter 1 resource). Working in small groups, pupils put the words into one of three categories. They can decide which category to put them in, but must be able to justify their reasons. Ask each group why they have placed the words in their chosen categories.

1 Wie heißt das auf Deutsch? Schreib die Wörter auf. (Writing L1)

Writing. Pupils write out the German word for the buildings in the photos. The vocabulary is provided to choose from.

Pupils check their answers in exercise 3.

Answers
a das Schwimmbad b das Schloss c die Imbissstube d der Bahnhof e die Kegelbahn f der Park g die Kirche h der Marktplatz i das Kino

© Pearson Education Ltd 2013. Copying permitted for purchasing institution only. This material is not copyright free.

In der Stadt | **Gute Reise!** – KAPITEL 5

2 Wie spricht man das aus? Sag die Wörter aus Aufgabe 1. (Speaking L1)

Speaking. Pupils work out how to pronounce the vocabulary presented in exercise 1.

The *Tip* box reminds pupils to use their key phonics from p. 8 of the pupil book to help them with their pronunciation.

3 Hör zu und überprüfe. (1–9) (Listening L2)

Listening. Pupils listen to the audio and check the pronunciation of the vocabulary presented in exercise 1.

Audioscript

1 – der Bahnhof
2 – der Marktplatz
3 – der Park
4 – die Kirche
5 – die Imbissstube
6 – die Kegelbahn
7 – das Kino
8 – das Schwimmbad
9 – das Schloss

Starter 2

Aim

To review the use of *es gibt + ein/kein*.

Pupils read the short text (see worksheet on ActiveTeach) and highlight in one colour all the things that the town has and in another colour all the things that the town does not have. They compare their lists with a partner before sharing with another pair (think-pair-share).

Alternative starter 2

Use ActiveTeach p.098 Flashcards to review and practise language for places in town.

Extension

Pupils could highlight all the adjectives and connectives in the text and give suggestions on how it might be improved.

Grammatik

The *Grammatik* box explains the use of *es gibt einen/eine/ein* to say 'there is …' (pupils have already met this in a classroom context in chapter 4) and introduces the word *kein* to mean 'not a' or 'no', giving the pupils the vocabulary for building sentences that talk about what there is and isn't.

There is more information and practice in the grammar unit on pupil book p. 112.

4 Sieh dir die Fotos in Aufgabe 1 an. Hör zu. Was gibt es in der Stadt und was gibt es nicht? (1–3) (Listening L3)

Listening. Pupils listen to the audio. Using the photos in exercise 1, they note what there is and is not in each town.

Pupils could be paired to do this listening activity, so that one pupil listens out for what there is and the other for what there is not. Pupils can then share answers, and perhaps also swap roles when they listen again to check each other's answers, before feeding back. This strategy often changes the perception of the activity from 'individual test' to 'pair task'.

Audioscript

1 – Ich wohne in Battenberg, in Hessen in Deutschland. In meiner Stadt gibt es einen Marktplatz und ein Schloss. Es gibt aber kein Kino und kein Schwimmbad.
2 – Meine Stadt heißt Mistelbach. Sie liegt in Österreich. Hier gibt es eine schöne Kirche, einen großen Park und eine tolle Imbissstube. In meiner Stadt haben wir leider kein Kino – das finde ich sehr schlecht!
3 – Ich wohne in Glückstadt in Norddeutschland. Hier gibt es ein Schwimmbad, einen Bahnhof und ein Kino. Das ist toll! Leider gibt es aber keine Kegelbahn.

Answers

1 h ✓ b ✗ i ✗ a ✗
2 g ✓ f ✓ c ✓ i ✗
3 a ✓ d ✓ i ✓ e ✗

5 Partnerarbeit. Sieh dir deine Antworten in Aufgabe 4 an und mach Dialoge. (Speaking L3)

Speaking. Working in pairs, pupils look at their answers to exercise 4 and create mini dialogues following the example in the pupil book.

6 Verbinde die Wörter in den Kästen und schreib die acht englischen Wörter auf Deutsch auf. (Writing L1, Reading L2)

Writing/Reading. Pupils combine the words in the boxes and write down the eight English words in German. Pupils check their combinations by listening to the audio in exercise 7.

The *Tip* box defines a compound word and reminds pupils how to decide which gender the resulting word should take.

In der Stadt | Gute Reise! – KAPITEL

> **Answers**
> 1 der Wasserpark 2 die Kunstgalerie 3 die Eisbahn 4 der Stadtpark 5 das Sportzentrum 6 der Radweg 7 das Kindertheater 8 der Fischmarkt

7 Hör zu und überprüfe. (1–8)
(Listening L1)

Listening. Pupils listen to the audio to see if their combinations are correct.

> **Audioscript**
>
> 1 – der Wasserpark
> 2 – die Kunstgalerie
> 3 – die Eisbahn
> 4 – der Stadtpark
> 5 – das Sportzentrum
> 6 – der Radweg
> 7 – das Kindertheater
> 8 – der Fischmarkt

8 Junge Reporter beschreiben eine Touristenstadt. Hör zu und lies.
(Listening L4, Reading L4)

Listening/Reading. Pupils listen to the audio and read the text.

Some vocabulary is glossed for support.

> **Audioscript**
>
> 1 – Hallo! Ich heiße Erika und ich bin heute in Binningen, einer kleinen Stadt in der Schweiz, in der Nähe von Basel. Binningen ist ziemlich klein, aber toll. Hier in der Stadtmitte gibt es ein Schloss, eine schöne Kirche und ein Automuseum. Man kann dort viele tolle Autos sehen. Es gibt aber kein Kino – das ist nicht gut! Jedes Jahr kommen viele Touristen nach Binningen. Die Gegend ist bekannt für den Zoo Basel. Sie ist auch die Heimatstadt von Roger Federer. Er ist natürlich der weltbekannte Tennisspieler. Ich bin Erika Meyer, für Junge Reporter Unterwegs, in Binningen.
>
> 2 – Guten Tag! Ich bin Heinrich und ich bin in Swakopmund im Westen von Namibia. Hier gibt es viele Restaurants und Cafés, drei Museen, eine Kunstgalerie, ein Aquarium und einen Schlangenpark! Es gibt kein Schwimmbad, aber man kann viele interessante Sportarten machen, zum Beispiel Sandboarden und Quad-Bike fahren! Ich bin Heinrich Keller, für Junge Reporter Unterwegs, in Swakopmund, Namibia.

9 Lies die Texte noch mal. Wo ist das? Binningen oder Swakopmund?
(Reading L4)

Reading. Pupils read the texts again and decide which town the sentences refer to.

Question 5 tests *kein* explicitly. Pupils who skim the key words will only notice *Aquarium* and may choose Swakopmund as the answer. This will provide a key learning opportunity to draw attention to the similarity between *kein* and *ein* and emphasise the need to look/listen carefully, as the difference in meaning is crucial.

> **Answers**
> 1 Binningen 2 Swakopmund 3 Swakopmund 4 Binningen 5 Binningen 6 Binningen

10 Wähl eine Stadt aus. Schreib einen Text als Reporter und mach eine Präsentation. (Speaking L4)

Speaking. Pupils write a talk about a town of their own choice and give a presentation.

The *Tip* box directs pupils to the *Wörter* section on pp. 114–115 of the pupil book for help with plurals.

Before attempting exercise 10 plurals should be revised.

> **Plenary**
>
> **Aim**
>
> For pupils to establish whether they have met the lesson objective of saying what there is and is not in a town.
>
> Pupils work with mini whiteboards. Read out (or show on the board) the sentences with missing words (Plenary resource). The first pupil to show the teacher the correct missing word wins the point. The ✓ and ✗ indicate whether there is or isn't this place in the town. This could be played as a team game.

© Pearson Education Ltd 2013. Copying permitted for purchasing institution only. This material is not copyright free.

Workbook A, page 48

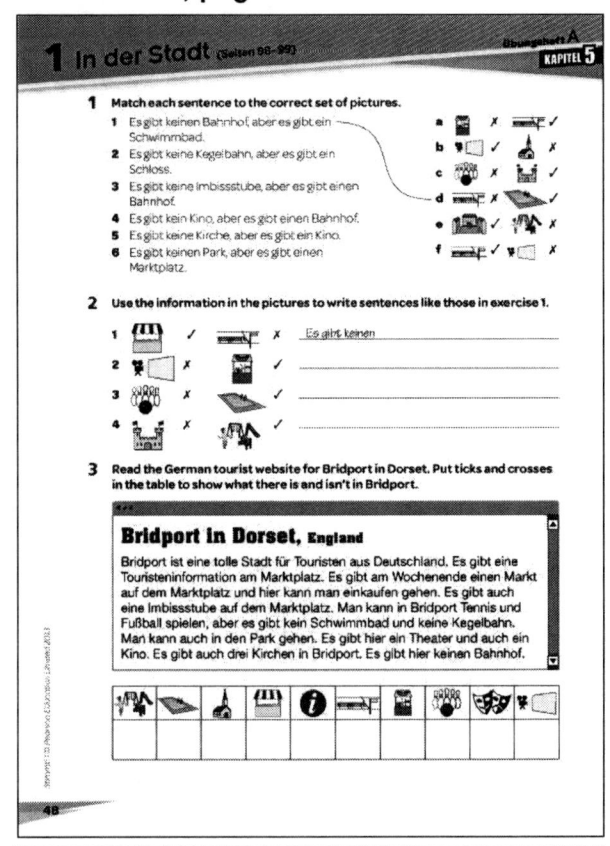

Answers

1 1 d 2 c 3 a 4 f 5 b 6 e

2 1 Es gibt keinen Bahnhof, aber es gibt einen Marktplatz.

2 Es gibt kein Kino, aber es gibt eine Imbissstube.

3 Es gibt keine Kegelbahn, aber es gibt ein Schwimmbad.

4 Es gibt kein Schloss, aber es gibt einen Park.

3 Ticks: tourist info; market square; snack stand; park; theatre; cinema; church

Crosses: swimming pool; bowling alley; railway station

Workbook B, page 48

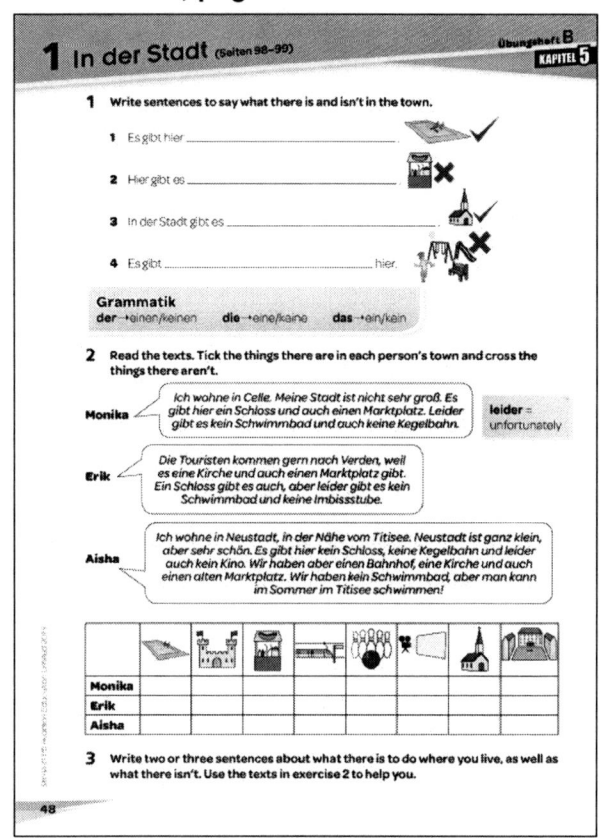

Answers ✓

1 1 Es gibt hier ein Schwimmbad.

2 Hier gibt es keine Imbissstube.

3 In der Stadt gibt es eine Kirche.

4 Es gibt einen Park hier.

2 Monika/Celle: castle ✓, marketplace ✓ swimming pool ×, bowling alley ×.

Erik: church ✓, marketplace ✓, castle ✓; swimming pool ×, snack stall ×.

Aisha: railway station ✓, church ✓, marketplace ✓; castle ×, bowling alley ×, cinema ×, swimming pool ×.

3 Pupils' own answers.

Ich wohne in Harrow, in der Nähe von London. Harrow ist ziemlich groß. Wir haben einen Bahnhof, aber kein … etc.

© Pearson Education Ltd 2013. Copying permitted for purchasing institution only. This material is not copyright free.

In der Stadt | Gute Reise! – KAPITEL

Video

Episode 9

Benno and Leoni are discussing countries where German is spoken, and talking about what you can do in these countries.

Answers

A Before watching
Answers will vary.

B Watch
1 She mentions, Hamburg, Austria, Switzerland, America and Scandinavia.
2 Hamburg: go to the zoo
Austria: visit the Mozart museum
Switzerland: snowboard
3 Pupils' own answers.

C Watch again
1 Hamburg is in the North of Germany.
2 You can't go sledding in Hamburg.
3 Ski and walk in the mountains.
4 In Austria you can do winter sports all year round. In Austria there are many high mountains. Here you can hike, climb and in the winter you can go skiing and sledding. In the summer you can go summer sledding on the summer sledge course and swim in the lake. There are many lovely towns in Austria, for example, the capital Vienna and Salzburg. Salzburg is the home town of Mozart. Austria is well known for good food, for example, Wiener schnitzel with potato salad and apple strudel.
5 Answer the questions about Switzerland:
a) Chocolate. There is a chocolate factory and a chocolate museum.
b) The Matterhorn is a mountain. In the summer you can ride bikes, climb or bathe in a lake, and in the winter you can go snowboarding.
c) Yes, you can.
d) Zermatt doesn't have a big airport.

D Discuss with your partner
1 At *Miniatur Wunderland*. All the places are there in miniature.
2 Pupils' own answers.
3 Leoni asks Emma where she wants to go, Hamburg, Austria or Switzerland? Benno says he will visit all of them in *Miniatur Wunderland*.
4 She means that there is something for everyone in Hamburg.
5 It means "it's known for".

© Pearson Education Ltd 2013. Copying permitted for purchasing institution only. This material is not copyright free.

Gute Reise! – **KAPITEL 5**

2 Wir gehen einkaufen! (Pupil Book pp. 100–101)

Learning opportunities
- Saying what souvenirs you want to buy
- Using *ich möchte* to say what you would like

Programme of Study
GV2 Grammatical structures (*möchten* with the infinitive)
LC2 Transcription
LC3 Conversation (using modes of address)

FCSE links
Unit 4 – Leisure (Around town)

Grammar
möchten with the infinitive

PLTS
T Team workers

Key Language
der Kuli
der Schlüsselanhänger
der Aufkleber
die Tasse
die Postkarte
die Kappe
das Freundschaftsband
das Trikot
das Kuscheltier
Ich möchte … (kaufen).
Du möchtest … (kaufen).
Er/Sie möchte … (kaufen).

Resources
Audio files:
83_Kapitel5_Einheit2_Aufgabe2
84_Kapitel5_Einheit2_Aufgabe4
Workbooks:
Übungsheft 1 A&B, page 49
ActiveTeach:
Starter 1 resource
Starter 2 resource
p.100 Flashcards
p.101 Extension writing activity
p.101 Extension worksheet
Plenary resource
ActiveLearn:
Listening A, Listening B
Reading A, Reading B
Grammar, Vocabulary

Starter 1

Aim

To review large numbers in anticipation of working on prices.

Pupils play a bingo game with the larger numbers in groups of four, with one pupil as the caller and the other three pupils as the players. This could be played a number of times to give each pupil an opportunity to be the caller; or the caller could be given the role as an extension task.

Caller cards and player cards (Starter 1 resource) can be laminated for future use. Pupils can cross off numbers with a whiteboard pen.

1 Partnerarbeit. Wie viel kostet das? Mach Dialoge. (Speaking L3)

Speaking. Pupils work in pairs to create dialogues following the example in the pupil book. Pupils check their answers by listening to the audio in exercise 2.

The *Tip* box shows pupils how to make numbers into prices.

The *Aussprache* box reminds pupils to say words using the German pronunciation, even for cognates.

2 Hör zu und überprüfe. Schreib den Namen des Souvenirs und den Preis auf. (1–9) (Listening L2)

Listening. Pupils listen to the audio and check their answers to exercise 1.

Audioscript

1 – *Wie viel kostet der Kuli?*
  – *Er kostet zwei Euro fünfzig.*
2 – *Wie viel kostet der Schlüsselanhänger?*
  – *Er kostet drei Euro fünfundneunzig. Ja, drei Euro fünfundneunzig.*
3 – *Und der Aufkleber? Wie viel kostet er?*
  – *Fünfundzwanzig Cent.*
4 – *Wie viel kostet die Tasse, bitte?*
  – *Sie kostet acht Euro fünfzig.*
5 – *Und die Postkarte?*
  – *Sie kostet sechzig Cent.*
6 – *Wie viel kostet die Kappe?*
  – *Zehn Euro.*
7 – *Und das Freundschaftsband? Wie viel kostet das?*
  – *Das Freundschaftsband? Drei Euro.*
8 – *Ich möchte das Trikot. Wie viel kostet es?*
  – *Es kostet fünfundfünfzig Euro.*
  – *Fünfundfünfzig Euro?! Oh je!*
9 – *Wie viel kostet das Kuscheltier?*
  – *Es kostet sechzehn Euro.*

Answers
1 der Kuli – €2,50
2 der Schlüsselanhänger – €3,95
3 der Aufkleber – €0,25
4 die Tasse – €8,50
5 die Postkarte – €0,60

© Pearson Education Ltd 2013. Copying permitted for purchasing institution only. This material is not copyright free.

Wir gehen einkaufen! | **Gute Reise!** – KAPITEL

> 6 die Kappe – €10,00
> 7 das Freundschaftsband – €3,00
> 8 das Trikot – €55,00
> 9 das Kuscheltier – €16,00

3 Wie viel kostet das? Wähl fünf Souvenirs aus und schreib Sätze. (Writing L3)

Writing. Pupils choose five of the souvenirs from exercise 1 and write sentences about how much they cost.

4 Hör zu und lies. Was kauft David? (Listening L4)

Listening. Pupils listen to the audio and follow the text in the pupil book to find out what David buys.

The *Tip* box reminds pupils that in German you use *du* when talking to one person you know well, and *Sie* when talking to people older than you or whom you do not know well.

Some words are glossed for support.

Audioscript

– *Guten Tag. Kann ich dir helfen?*
– *Guten Tag. Ich möchte ein Souvenir kaufen, vielleicht eine Kappe. Haben Sie Kappen?*
– *Ja, natürlich. Diese Kappe, zum Beispiel, kostet €9,90.*
– *Toll!*
– *Sonst noch etwas?*
– *Ja. Ich möchte noch einen Kuli für meine Schwester.*
– *Welche Farbe? Wir haben blau, grün, rot, schwarz und lila.*
– *Lila, bitte. Wie viel kostet das?*
– *Alles zusammen kostet das €11,95.*
– *Bitte sehr.*
– *Danke schön. Auf Wiedersehen.*

Answers
David buys a baseball cap and a (purple) pen.

Starter 2

Aim

To review the vocabulary for the souvenir items.

Pupils play a game of noughts and crosses with the vocabulary using the grid. This can be played in pairs or in two teams as a whole class. Pupils have to say in German which box they have selected and then give the name of the item in German. If they get it right, they draw their nought or cross. Once pupils have finished they could make their own grids using the vocabulary from the unit or from previous units. For an extra challenge prices could be added to the squares and pupils could also give the prices of the items in German.

Alternative starter 2

Use ActiveTeach p.100 Flashcards to review and practise language for souvenirs.

5 Lies den Dialog noch einmal. Beantworte die Fragen auf Deutsch. Schreib Sätze. (1–5) (Reading L4)

Reading. Pupils read the dialogue in exercise 4 and answer the questions in German in full sentences.

The *Tip* box reminds pupils to think carefully about which verb to use for the answer to question 4.

Answers
1 David (Er) möchte eine Kappe kaufen.
2 Die Kappe (Sie) kostet €9,90.
3 David (Er) möchte einen Kuli kaufen.
4 Der Kuli (für Davids Schwester) ist lila.
5 Alles zusammen kostet das €11,95.

Grammatik

The *Grammatik* box looks at the modal verb *möchten* and using it with the infinitive.

There is more information and practice on modal verbs in the grammar units on pupil book p. 45 and p. 112.

6 Partnerarbeit. Ein Gedächtnisspiel. Ich gehe einkaufen! (Speaking L3)

Speaking. Pupils work in pairs and play a memory game following the example in the pupil book. The first pupil begins by saying that they are going shopping and what they would like to buy. Their partner then repeats what has been said and adds whatever they would like to buy. They continue like this, adding an item on each time.

© Pearson Education Ltd 2013. Copying permitted for purchasing institution only. This material is not copyright free.

Wir gehen einkaufen! | Gute Reise! – **KAPITEL 5**

7 Lies den Dialog (Aufgabe 4) noch mal. Finde fünf Substantive, fünf Verben und fünf Adjektive. (Reading L4)

Reading. Pupils re-read the dialogue from exercise 4 and hunt out five nouns, five verbs and five adjectives.

> **Answers**
>
> Substantive – Souvenir, Kappe, Kuli, Schwester, Farbe, (Tag), (Euro), (Beispiel)
>
> Verben – (5 of) kann, helfen, möchte, kaufen, haben, kostet
>
> Adjektive – (5 of) toll, blau, grün, rot, schwarz, lila

8 Partnerarbeit. Schreib einen Dialog. Lern den Dialog auswendig und sag ihn auf. (Writing L4,)

Writing. Working in pairs, pupils write a dialogue based on the example given. They learn their dialogue by heart and then perform it.

For ideas on extending their dialogue, the *Tip* box suggests that pupils refer to exercise 4.

> **Extension**
>
> For a greater challenge to exercise 8, a more extensive dialogue is provided on ActiveTeach (p.101 Extension writing activity).

> **Plenary**
>
> **Aim**
>
> For pupils to establish whether they have met the lesson objectives of saying what souvenirs they want to buy and using *ich möchte* to say what they would like.
>
> Pupils play a snakes and ladders board game in groups of four (Plenary resource). If they land on a picture, they imagine they are the tourist asking for that item and have to make the sentence using *ich möchte* … If they land on *kaufen*, they have to make a sentence saying what the previous speaker is buying using *er kauft* … or *sie kauft* … If they land on a price, they have to say what the previous item costs: *es kostet* … If they land on a smiley face they go up one row and if they land on a sad face they go down one row.

Workbook A, page 49

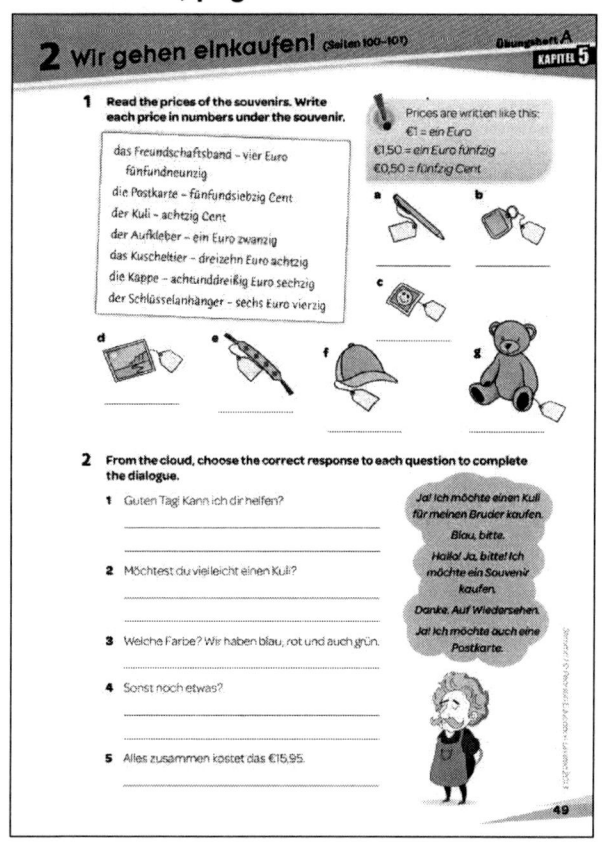

Answers

1 a €0,80 b €6,40 c €1,20 d €0,75
  e €4,95 f €38,60 g €13,80

2 1 Hallo! Ja, bitte! Ich möchte ein Souvenir kaufen.

  2 Ja! Ich möchte einen Kuli für meinen Bruder kaufen.

  3 Blau, bitte.

  4 Ja! Ich möchte auch eine Postkarte.

  5 Danke. Auf Wiedersehen.

© Pearson Education Ltd 2013. Copying permitted for purchasing institution only. This material is not copyright free.

Wir gehen einkaufen! | **Gute Reise!** – KAPITEL

Workbook B, page 49

> 10 Bitte sehr.
>
> 6 Ja. Ich möchte ein Fußballtrikot für meine Schwester.
>
> 8 Schwarz, bitte. Wie viel kostet das?

Worksheet

Extension: Modal verbs

Answers

1
1 Ich möchte einen Kuli.
2 Ich möchte einen Schlüsselanhänger.
3 Ich möchte einen Aufkleber.
4 Ich möchte eine Postkarte.
5 Ich möchte eine Kappe.
6 Ich möchte ein Freundschaftsband.
7 Ich möchte ein Kuscheltier.
8 Ich möchte eine Tasse.

2
1 Guten Tag! **Kann** ich dir helfen?
7 Welche **Farbe**? Wir haben blau, rot oder schwarz.
3 Ja, klar! Dieser **Elefant**, zum Beispiel, kostet nur €18,95.
4 Super!
11 Danke. Auf **Wiedersehen**.
5 Sonst noch etwas?
9 Alles **zusammen** kostet das €38,95.
2 Guten Tag! Ich möchte ein Souvenir **kaufen**, vielleicht ein Kuscheltier. Haben Sie **Kuscheltiere**?

Answers

A a) Ich möchte in die Stadt gehen, aber ich darf nicht.
b) Ella möchte in den Park gehen.
c) Mein Bruder kann gut Gitarre spielen.
d) Meine Schwester und ich dürfen in die Stadt gehen.
e) Was möchtet ihr machen?

B 1 Thomas is not allowed to play Xbox.
2 I can't do my homework.
3 I would like to go into town, but I'm not allowed.

C 1 Ich kann das Kuscheltier kaufen.
2 Wir möchten zehn Postkarten kaufen.
3 Erik und Hanna dürfen das Trikot nicht kaufen.

© Pearson Education Ltd 2013. Copying permitted for purchasing institution only. This material is not copyright free.

Gute Reise! – KAPITEL 5

3 Mmm, lecker! (Pupil Book pp. 102–103)

Learning objectives	Key Language	Resources
• Buying snacks and drinks • More practice with euros and cents **Programme of Study** GV3 Developing vocabulary GV3 Opinions and discussions LC6 Reading comprehension **FCSE links** Unit 6 – Food and Drink (Food/drink vocabulary items, Eating out) **Grammar** *Man kann* with the infinitive **PLTS** C Creative thinkers **Cross-curricular** **Mathematics:** numbers, prices and addition	Was möchtest du? Was möchten Sie? Etwas zu essen? Etwas zu trinken? Ich möchte … Ich hätte gern … einmal Bratwurst (mit …), bitte zweimal … dreimal … der Hamburger der Tee die Bratwurst die Cola die Pizza die Pommes das Eis das Mineralwasser	**Audio files:** 85_Kapitel5_Einheit3_Aufgabe2 86_Kapitel5_Einheit3_Aufgabe3 87_Kapitel5_Einheit3_Aufgabe4 **Workbooks:** Übungsheft 1 A&B, page 50 **ActiveTeach:** Starter 1 resource Starter 2 resource p.102 Flashcards **ActiveLearn:** Listening A, Listening B Reading A, Reading B Grammar, Vocabulary

Starter 1

Aim

To review numbers for prices.

Pupils read the prices, which are written as numbers (Starter 1 resource) and order the prices from cheapest to most expensive. The prices could be printed onto card and cut up for pupils to move into position.

1 Sieh dir die Speisekarte und die Fotos an. Schreib die Liste mit den Namen der Snacks ab und ordne die Preise zu. (Reading/Writing L1)

Reading/Writing. Pupils look at the menu and the photos and add the correct prices to the list of snacks that they copy out. They check their answers by listening to the audio in exercise 2.

Answers
1 Hamburger – €2,90
2 Bratwurst – €2,60
3 Pizza – €3,50
4 Pommes – €2,50
5 Salat – €2,00
6 Eis – €3,20
7 Cola – €2,20
8 Mineralwasser – €2,20
9 Tee – €2,10

2 Hör zu und überprüfe. (1–9) (Listening L2)

Listening. Pupils listen to the audio and check their answers to exercise 1.

Audioscript

1 – Hamburger – zwei Euro neunzig
2 – Bratwurst – zwei Euro sechzig
3 – Pizza – drei Euro fünfzig
4 – Pommes – zwei Euro fünfzig
5 – Salat – zwei Euro
6 – Eis – drei Euro zwanzig
7 – Cola – zwei Euro zwanzig
8 – Mineralwasser – zwei Euro zwanzig
9 – Tee – zwei Euro zehn

3 Hör zu. Was und wie viel(e) möchten sie? (1–5) (Listening L4)

Listening. Pupils listen to the audio and make notes on what the people want, and how much.

The *Tip* box points out that *ich hätte gern* is just another way of saying *ich möchte*.

Some vocabulary is glossed for support.

© Pearson Education Ltd 2013. Copying permitted for purchasing institution only. This material is not copyright free.

Mmm, lecker! | **Gute Reise!** – KAPITEL

Audioscript

1.
   - Guten Tag. Ich möchte zweimal Pizza und einmal Salat, bitte.
   - Möchtest du etwas zu trinken?
   - Ja, ich hätte gern eine Cola und ein Mineralwasser, bitte.
   - Das macht dreizehn Euro vierzig.
   - Bitte schön.
   - Danke schön. Tschüs.
   - Auf Wiedersehen.

2.
   - Guten Tag. Was darf es sein?
   - Hallo. Einmal Bratwurst mit Pommes, bitte.
   - Sonst noch etwas?
   - Ja, eine Tasse Tee. Was macht das?
   - Sieben Euro zwanzig.
   - Bitte schön.
   - Danke. Auf Wiedersehen.
   - Tschüs.

3.
   - Guten Tag. Ich möchte einmal Bratwurst mit Salat und ein Wasser, bitte.
   - Sonst noch etwas?
   - Nein, danke.
   - Also … sechs Euro achtzig, bitte.
   - Danke schön. Auf Wiedersehen.

4.
   - Hallo. Kann ich Ihnen helfen?
   - Guten Tag. Ich hätte gern einmal Hamburger mit Pommes und einmal Pizza mit Salat.
   - Möchten Sie etwas zu trinken?
   - Ja, zwei Cola, bitte.
   - Fünfzehn Euro dreißig, bitte.

5.
   - Hallo. Ein Schokoladeneis, bitte.
   - Und möchten Sie etwas zu trinken?
   - Nein, danke.
   - Drei Euro zwanzig.
   - Bitte schön.
   - Danke schön. Tschüs.

Answers
1 2 x Pizza, 1 x Salat, 1 x Cola, 1 x Mineralwasser
2 1 x Bratwurst, 1 x Pommes, 1 x Tee
3 1 x Bratwurst, 1 x Salat, 1 x Wasser
4 1 x Hamburger, 1 x Pommes, 1 x Pizza, 1 x Salat, 2 x Cola
5 1 x Eis

Starter 2
Aim

To review the concept of compound nouns and to introduce some words for snacks and drinks.

Pupils are given a list of words in jigsaw pieces (Starter 2 resource). They are then asked how many different compound nouns they can build with the jigsaw pieces in ten minutes. They try out different combinations and make a list in their books of all the different words they have found with the English translation. This can be done in pairs, groups or individually. Prizes or merits could be awarded to the pupil who has made the most words.

Alternative starter 2

Use ActiveTeach p.102 Flashcards to review and practise language for drinks and snacks.

4 Hör noch mal zu. Was kostet das? (1–5) (Listening L4)

Listening. Pupils listen to the audio from exercise 3 again and work out how much each person's snack cost.

Audioscript
For transcript see exercise 3.

Answers
1 €13,40 **2** €7,20 **3** €6,80 **4** €15,30 **5** €3,20

5 Partnerarbeit. Mach Dialoge im Schnellimbiss. (Speaking L4)

Speaking. Working in pairs, pupils create dialogues following the example in the pupil book.

Grammatik
The *Grammatik* box looks at the formula *man kann* + infinitive which is used to talk about what people in general do.

6 Lies die Texte und die Aussagen. Ist das Marcel, Lina oder sind das beide? (Reading L4)

Reading. Pupils read the texts and the statements and decide whether each statement is by Marcel, Lina or the two together.

Some vocabulary is glossed for support.

Mmm, lecker! | **Gute Reise!** – **KAPITEL 5**

Answers

1 Lina
2 Lina und Marcel (beide)
3 Lina
4 Marcel
5 Lina
6 Lina
7 Marcel
8 Lina

7 Sieh dir die Speisekarte an. Wie heißt das auf Englisch? (Reading L4)

Reading. Pupils read the menu and work out what the English translations are.

The *Tip* box reminds pupils to use a dictionary and that some German words are compound words. If they try to divide up the long words into their component parts they might have a better chance of understanding them.

Answers

1 crab claws in tomato sauce
2 avocado on toast
3 snails in butter
4 Mopane worms in chilli sauce
5 ostrich fillet with chips
6 shark steak with fried potatoes
7 oysters in white wine sauce

Plenary

Aim

For pupils to establish whether they have met the lesson objective of buying snacks and drinks.

Pupils work in pairs to see which pair can make the longest conversation in five minutes. The conversation is played as a game of verbal tennis, where each partner has to take it in turn to speak, so making a verbal rally of phrases. One person plays the waiter or waitress and the other plays the customer. The conversation should start with the phrase: *Guten Tag. Ich möchte …* and can include any phrases learnt in the unit plus any other phrases the pupils want to include. An example conversation might go:

A: *Guten Tag. Ich möchte einmal Pommes, bitte.*

B: *Sonst noch etwas?*

A: *Ja, ich hätte gern eine Cola.*

B: *Was möchten Sie noch essen?*

A: *Zweimal Schokoladeneis.*

B: *Möchten Sie noch etwas trinken?*

A: *Ja, wir möchten Kaffee.*

B: *Was ist dein Lieblingsessen?*

A: *Mein Lieblingsessen ist Bratwurst.*

And so on until the time limit (about five minutes) is up.

Extension

For an extra challenge pupils could be banned from using the same phrase twice.

Mmm, lecker! | **Gute Reise!** – KAPITEL

Workbook A, page 50

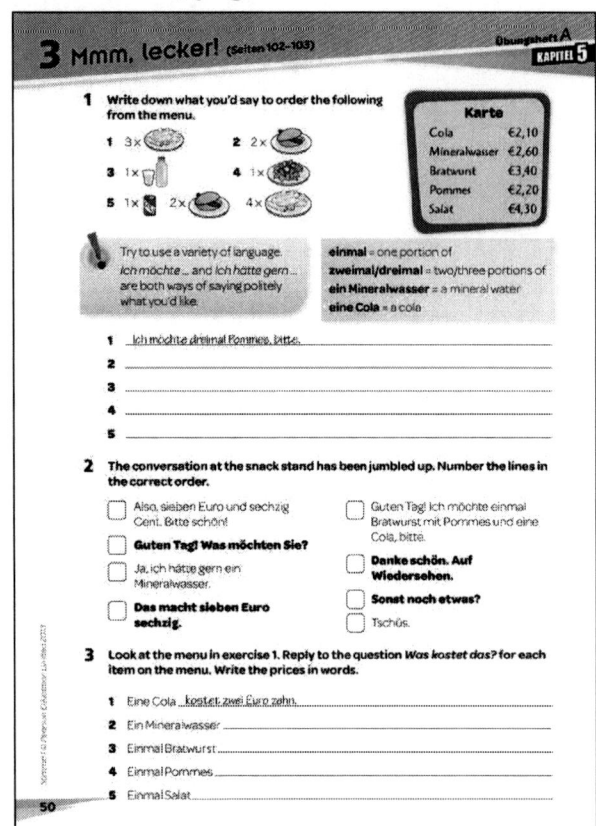

3 Mmm, lecker! (Seiten 102–103) — Übungsheft A — KAPITEL 5

1 Write down what you'd say to order the following from the menu.

1 3× 🥤   2 2× 🥐
3 1× 🍶   4 1× 🥗
5 1× 🥤 2× 🌭 4× 🍟

Karte
Cola   €2,10
Mineralwasser €2,60
Bratwurst   €3,40
Pommes   €2,20
Salat   €4,30

Try to use a variety of language. *Ich möchte …* and *Ich hätte gern …* are both ways of saying politely what you'd like.

einmal = one portion of
zweimal/dreimal = two/three portions of
ein Mineralwasser = a mineral water
eine Cola = a cola

1 Ich möchte dreimal Pommes, bitte.
2 _____
3 _____
4 _____
5 _____

2 The conversation at the snack stand has been jumbled up. Number the lines in the correct order.

☐ Also, sieben Euro und sechzig Cent. Bitte schön!
☐ Guten Tag! Was möchten Sie?
☐ Ja, ich hätte gern ein Mineralwasser.
☐ Das macht sieben Euro sechzig.
☐ Guten Tag! Ich möchte einmal Bratwurst mit Pommes und eine Cola, bitte.
☐ Danke schön. Auf Wiedersehen.
☐ Sonst noch etwas?
☐ Tschüs.

3 Look at the menu in exercise 1. Reply to the question *Was kostet das?* for each item on the menu. Write the prices in words.

1 Eine Cola kostet zwei Euro zehn.
2 Ein Mineralwasser _____
3 Einmal Bratwurst _____
4 Einmal Pommes _____
5 Einmal Salat _____

Answers

1
1 Ich möchte dreimal Pommes, bitte.
2 Ich möchte zweimal Bratwurst, bitte.
3 Ich möchte einmal Mineralwasser, bitte.
4 Ich möchte einmal Salat, bitte.
5 Ich möchte eine Cola, zweimal Bratwurst und viermal Pommes, bitte.

2
6 Also, sieben Euro und sechzig Cent. Bitte schön!
1 Guten Tag! Was möchten Sie?
4 Ja, ich hätte gern ein Mineralwasser.
5 Das macht sieben Euro sechzig.
2 Guten Tag! Ich möchte einmal Bratwurst mit Pommes und eine Cola, bitte.
7 Danke schön. Auf Wiedersehen.
3 Sonst noch etwas?
8 Tschüs.

3
1 Eine Cola kostet zwei Euro zehn.
2 Ein Mineralwasser kostet zwei Euro sechzig.
3 Einmal Bratwurst kostet drei Euro vierzig.
4 Einmal Pommes kostet zwei Euro zwanzig.
5 Einmal Salat kostet vier Euro dreißig.

Workbook B, page 50

3 Mmm, lecker! (Seiten 102–103) — Übungsheft B — KAPITEL 5

1 Write four short conversations between hungry customers and the owner of the snack stand. The price of each individual item is shown; don't forget to add up the total price.

1 🍔 ×1 drei Euro zehn   🥐 ×1 zwei Euro fünfunddreißig
2 🍟 ×2 zwei Euro sechzig   🌭 ×2 zwei Euro fünfundzwanzig
3 🥣 ×3 drei Euro zwanzig   🥤 ×1 ein Euro neunzig
4 🍕 ×4 drei Euro fünfundreißig   🥫 ×1 zwei Euro zehn

Ich möchte …/Ich hätte gern … I'd like …
Das kostet alles zusammen … All together that costs …

1 Guten Tag! Ich möchte einmal Hamburger und einmal Bratwurst, bitte.
   Das kostet alles zusammen € _____
2 _____
3 _____
4 _____

2 Write a short review of the menu, saying what there is to eat and drink and what you do and don't like.

Hamburger
Bratwurst
Pommes
Salat
Eis
Tee
Cola
Mineralwasser

Man kann … trinken/essen. You can eat/drink …
Ich esse/trinke gern … I like eating/drinking …
Ich esse/trinke nicht gern … I don't like eating/drinking …
Ich mag … I like …
Ich mag nicht … I don't like …

Answers

1
1 Guten Tag! Ich möchte einmal Hamburger und einmal Bratwurst, bitte.
Das kostet alles zusammen fünf Euro fünfundvierzig.
2 Guten Tag! Ich möchte zweimal Pommes und zweimal Salat, bitte.
Das kostet alles zusammen neun Euro siebzig.
3 Guten Tag! Ich möchte dreimal Eis und einmal Wasser, bitte.
Das kostet alles zusammen elf Euro fünfzig.
4 Guten Tag! Ich möchte viermal Pizza und einmal Cola, bitte.
Das kostet alles zusammen siebzehn Euro neunzig.

2 Pupils' own answers:
Es gibt hier Hamburger und Bratwurst zu essen, aber mein Lieblingsessen ist der Salat. Ich trinke auch sehr gern Cola, aber ich mag nicht Tee hier trinken. Man kann hier auch Eis kaufen, etc.

Gute Reise! – **KAPITEL 5**

4 In den Sommerferien (Pupil Book pp. 104–105)

Learning objectives
- Talking about holiday plans
- Using *werden* to form the future tense

Programme of Study
GV1 Tenses (forming the future using *werden*)
LC5 Speaking coherently and confidently
LC8 Writing creatively

FCSE links
Unit 3 – Holidays and Travel (Holidays, activities)

Grammar
Using *werden* + infinitive

PLTS
E Effective participators

Cross-curricular
Geography: countries around the world

Key Language
Was wirst du in den Sommerferien machen?
Ich werde …
Wir werden …
segeln
klettern
an den Strand gehen
wandern
im See baden
tauchen
windsurfen
rodeln
im Meer schwimmen
In den Sommerferien werde ich mit …
Wir werden … nach … fahren
Wir werden … Wochen bleiben
Wir werden … und auch …
Dort gibt es … und …, aber kein..
Man kann dort … und …
Am Montag/Freitag …
Ich möchte auch …

Resources
Audio files:
88_Kapitel5_Einheit4_Aufgabe1
89_Kapitel5_Einheit4_Aufgabe6
Workbooks:
Übungsheft 1 A&B, page 51
ActiveTeach:
Starter 1 resource
Starter 2 resource
p.104 Grammar worksheet
p.104 Exercise 1 grid
p.104 Grammar presentation
p.104 Flashcards
p.105 Learning skills worksheet
p.105 Video: Episode 10
p.105 Exercise 6 grid
p.105 Extension reading activity
Plenary resource
ActiveLearn:
Listening A, Listening B
Reading A, Reading B
Grammar, Vocabulary

Starter 1
Aim
To introduce the new vocabulary and for pupils to classify the new words
Pupils classify the sports (Starter 1 resource) according to what type of sport they are, deducing the meanings of the new vocabulary. Other sports could be added in.
Extension
Some rogue sports could be included which don't fit into any category, so pupils could be encouraged to make up their own categories.

1 Hör zu und sieh dir die Bilder an. Was werden Elias und Melina im Sommer machen? (Listening L4)
Listening. Pupils listen to the audio and, looking at the pictures, work out what Elias and Martina are going to be doing in the summer.
The *Tip* box warns pupils to beware of German words that look like English ones but which have a different meaning.

Audioscript
– Hallo! Ich heiße Elias. Ich werde in den Sommerferien mit meiner Familie nach St Wolfgang fahren. Das ist in Österreich. Ich werde im See baden, segeln und tauchen. Ich liebe Wassersport. Wir werden wandern gehen und wir werden auch zusammen auf der Sommerrodelbahn rodeln.

– Guten Tag! Ich heiße Melina. Ich wohne an der Nordseeküste in der Nähe von Bremen. Im Sommer werde ich jeden Tag an den Strand gehen und im Meer schwimmen. Hier kann man auch Wassersport machen. Wir werden windsurfen. Und im Sportzentrum kann man klettern. Ich werde klettern, weil es toll ist!

Answers
Elias – e, a, f, d, h
Melina – c, i, g, b

Grammatik
The *Grammatik* box introduces pupils to another way of talking about the future, using *werden* + infinitive.
There is more information and practice in the grammar unit on pupil book p. 113.

© Pearson Education Ltd 2013. Copying permitted for purchasing institution only. This material is not copyright free.

In den Sommerferien | Gute Reise! – KAPITEL

2 Sieh dir die Bilder an. Was werden wir machen? Schreib Sätze. (Writing L3)

Writing. Pupils look at the pictures and write sentences describing what the people are going to do (using *werden* + infinitive).

Answers

1 *Wir werden an den Strand gehen, Tennis spielen,* tauchen und im Meer schwimmen.

2 Wir werden windsurfen, im See baden, wandern und reiten.

3 Wir werden klettern, Rad fahren, segeln und rodeln.

3 Gruppenarbeit. Mach einen Dialog über deine Sommerpläne. Die dritte Person ist der Reporter. (Speaking L4)

Speaking. Working in groups of three, pupils create dialogues about their summer plans following the example in the pupil book. The third pupil summarises the dialogue.

Starter 2

Aim

To review word order in the future tense, with *möchten* and after time phrases.

Pupils unscramble the sentences (Starter 2 resource), putting the words into the correct order. The sentences form a paragraph which pupils could then use as a model for their own writing.

Alternative starter 2

Use ActiveTeach p.104 Flashcards to review and practise language for holiday activities.

Extension

Pupils make up sentences of their own to test their partner.

4 Lies den Text und füll die Lücken aus. Wähl aus dem Kasten. (Reading L5)

Reading. Pupils read the text and fill in the gaps, choosing words from the box.

Some vocabulary is glossed for support.

Answers

1 werde 2 fahren 3 gibt 4 werden 5 schwimmen 6 wandern 7 möchte 8 kann

Extension

An alternative version of this exercise is provided on ActiveTeach (p.105 Extension reading activity, Reading L5). Pupils read a longer text and fill the gaps, choosing the words from a box.

Answers

1 werde 2 fahren 3 wird 4 ist 5 gibt 6 machen 7 werden 8 schwimmen/baden 9 wandern 10 baden/schwimmen 11 wird 12 gehen 13 möchte 14 isst 15 kann

5 Lies den Text noch mal und beantworte mit ganzen Sätzen die Fragen auf Deutsch. (Writing L4)

Writing. Pupils re-read the text in exercise 4 and answer the questions in German, using full sentences.

The *Tip* box gives pupils the vocabulary for saying 'where … to' (*wohin*).

Answers

1 Sie werden nach Interlaken fahren.

2 Theresa und Sophie (Sie) werden Rad fahren und ein Picknick machen.

3 Man kann das Schloss besuchen.

4 Sie werden am letzten Tag (Freitag) Souvenirs kaufen.

5 Theresas Vater kann nicht nach Interlaken fahren.

6 Ferienpläne! Hör zu. Schreib die Tabelle ab und füll sie aus. (1–3) (Listening L5)

Listening. Pupils listen to the audio and complete a copy of the table.

Audioscript

1 – *Ich werde mit meinen Eltern und meinem Bruder nach Spanien fahren. Wir werden zwei Wochen dort bleiben. In der ersten Woche werden wir sehr aktiv sein. Wir werden jeden Tag dreißig Kilometer Rad fahren. Meine Familie und ich fahren sehr gern Rad. In der zweiten Woche werden wir an den Strand gehen und im Meer schwimmen. Es wird ganz toll sein!*

2 – *Ich werde mit meinen Großeltern nach Amerika fahren. Sie haben ein Haus in Florida. Ich werde dort sechs Wochen bleiben. Wir werden das Kennedy Space Center besuchen. Ich liebe Wassersport und*

© Pearson Education Ltd 2013. Copying permitted for purchasing institution only. This material is not copyright free.

In den Sommerferien | Gute Reise! – **KAPITEL 5**

ich werde tauchen und windsurfen. Das wird super sein!

3 – *In den Sommerferien werde ich nach Afrika fahren. Mein Onkel und meine Tante wohnen in Namibia. Ich werde drei Wochen bei ihnen wohnen. Ich werde viele neue Sportarten machen, zum Beispiel sandboarden und Quad-Bike fahren. Ich werde auch in den Schlangenpark gehen. Es wird fantastisch sein!*

Answers

1 Spain, parents + brother, 2 weeks, cycling; go to beach; swim in sea, great

2 America, grand-parents, 6 weeks, visit Kennedy Space Centre; diving; wind-surfing, super

3 Africa, (to stay with) aunt and uncle, 3 weeks, sand-boarding; quad-biking; visit snake park, fantastic

7 Sieh dir Aufgabe 4 an. Schreib über deine Ferienpläne. (Writing L4–5)

Writing. Using exercise 4 for guidance, pupils write about their own holiday plans.

8 Sieh dir Aufgabe 7 an. Schreib zehn Schlüsselwörter auf und zeichne fünf Bilder und mach eine Präsentation. (Speaking L4–5)

Speaking. Pupils prepare for a presentation by writing down ten key words and drawing five pictures. They then give their presentation.

Plenary

Aim

For pupils to establish whether they have met the lesson objective of talking about holiday plans.

Pupils are given a card with the picture of a celebrity. They have to imagine they are this person and that they have planned a holiday. Where would this person go and what would they do there? They have to explain to their partner in German what their plans are for their holiday in such a way that their partner can guess which celebrity card they have (the names of the celebrities could be listed on the board so that pupils can guess from a limited range of names).

Feedback is given on the quality of the presentation using a grid (Plenary resource).

An example presentation might be:
(Kylie Minogue)

In den Sommerferien werde ich nach Australien fahren.

Ich werde vier Wochen bleiben.

Wir werden singen und auch tanzen.

Dort gibt es das Opernhaus.

Man kann dort schwimmen und zum Strand gehen.

Ich möchte auch einkaufen gehen.

Workbook A, page 51

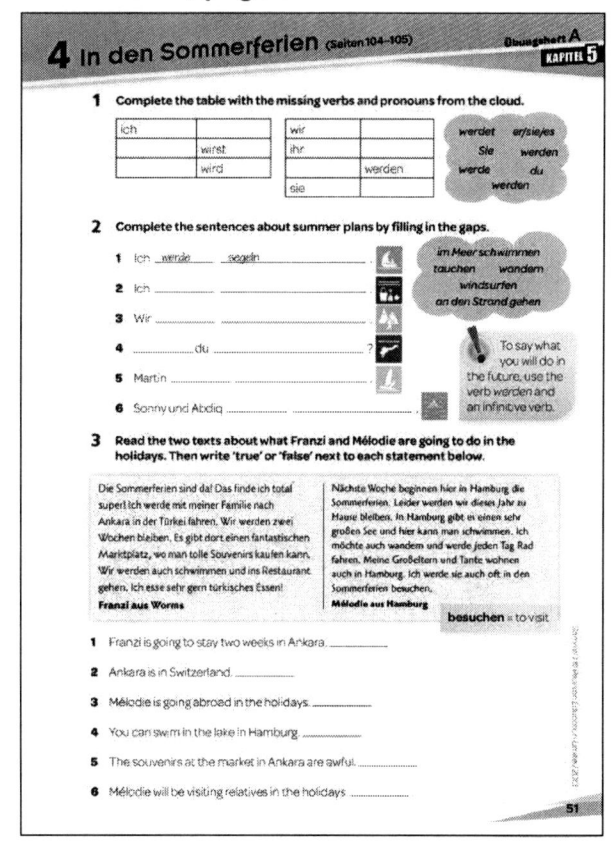

Answers

1 ich werde

du wirst

er/sie/es wird

wir werden

ihr werdet

Sie werden

sie werden

2 1 Ich werde segeln.

2 Ich werde an den Strand gehen.

3 Wir werden wandern.

4 Wirst du tauchen gehen?

5 Martin wird windsurfen.
6 Sonny und Abdiq werden im Meer schwimmen.
3 **1** true **2** false **3** false **4** true **5** false **6** true

Workbook B, page 51

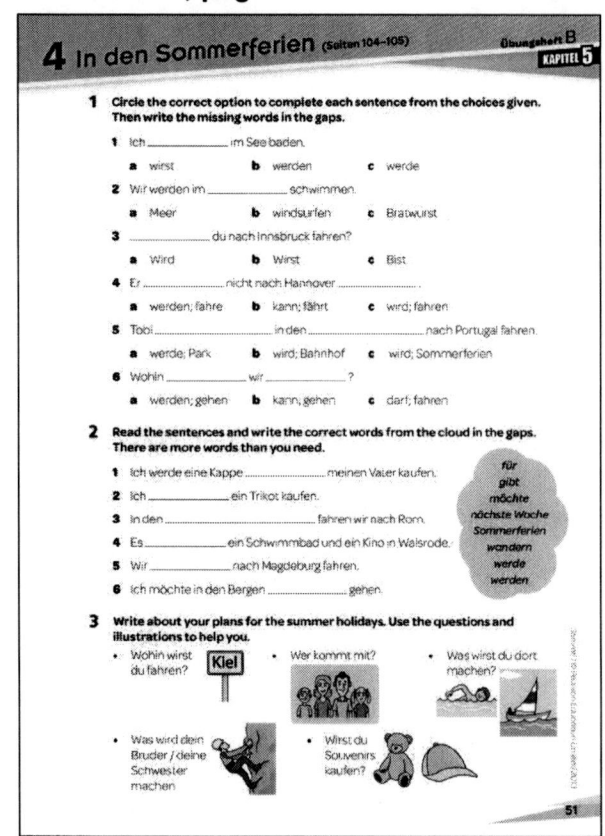

Answers
1 **1** c werde **2** a Meer **3** b Wirst
4 c wird; fahren **5** c wird; Sommerferien
6 a werden; gehen
2 **1** für **2** möchte **3** Sommerferien
4 gibt **5** werden **6** wandern
3 Possible answer:
In den Sommerferien werde ich nach Kiel fahren. Meine Familie kommt mit. Ich werde dort schwimmen und segeln. Mein Bruder wird klettern gehen. Ich werde ein Kuscheltier und eine Kappe als Souvenirs kaufen.

Worksheet 1

Grammar: The future tense

Answers
A 1, 2, 4, 6
B **1** Ich werde reiten.
2 Ich werde im See baden.
3 Timo wird in der Schweiz wandern.
4 Ella wird in Bayern klettern.
5 Luis und Razia werden einen Kletterwald besuchen.
6 Was wirst du machen?
C Answers will vary.

In den Sommerferien | Gute Reise! – **KAPITEL 5**

Worksheet 2

Learning skills: How do I remember everything?

Answers

1 Places to live: das Haus, das Schloss, die Wohnung, die Burg

Outside places: der Wald, der Park, der Berg,

Classroom items: der Gummi, das Buch, der Stift

2 masculine (blue): der Wald, der Park, der Berg, der Gummi, der Stift

feminine (red): die Wohnung, die Burg

neuter (green): das Haus, das Schloss, das Buch

3 column 1: die Häuser, die Schlösser, die Bücher, die Wälder

column 2: die Wohnungen, die Burgen

column 3: die Gummis, die Parks

column 4: die Stifte, die Berge

Video

Episode 10

The reporters are deciding what to order in a café, and are discussing their holiday plans.

Answers

A Before watching

Answers will vary.

B Watch

1 Hamburger with salad

2 Ciara: Holiday house in Italy (*Italien*)

Mesut: Camping in the Black Forest (*Schwarzwald*)

Alwin: Visiting a castle in Bavaria (*Bayern*)

Audrey: Going to America (*Amerika*)

C Watch again

1 Felix finally orders a pizza with salad and a coke.

2 Leoni and Benno are still filming.

3 €35,20

4 €4,80

5 An expedition in the Sahara, wild-water rafting on the Amazon, or climbing in the Alps.

6 Leoni asks where their food is.

D Discuss with your partner

1 He is saying "Oh, you're so healthy!" as Katharina only orders salad and mineral water. He is saying it to tease her.

2 "Would you like anything else?"

3 Pupils' own answers.

4 She has lots of friends in Italy.

5 Pupils' own answers.

6 Audrey suggests that they each do a report on their holiday with photos and video clips for Joe and their friends in Britain.

© Pearson Education Ltd 2013. Copying permitted for purchasing institution only. This material is not copyright free.

Gute Reise! – KAPITEL

5 Listening Skills: Auf geht's! (Pupil Book pp. 106–107)

Learning objectives
- Understanding longer, more varied spoken texts
- Focusing on high-frequency words

Programme of Study
GV3 Developing vocabulary
LC1 Listening and responding

FCSE links
Unit 7 – Local Area and Environment (Facilities)

Key Language
No new key language. Pupils develop listening skills using key language from the chapter.

PLTS
S Self-managers

Cross-curricular
Geography: towns and tourism

Resources
Audio files:
90_Kapitel5_Einheit5_Aufgabe2
91_Kapitel5_Einheit5_Aufgabe3
92_Kapitel5_Einheit5_Aufgabe4
93_Kapitel5_Einheit5_Aufgabe6
94_Kapitel5_Einheit5_Aufgabe7

Active Teach:
Plenary resource

Starter 1

Aim

To focus on high-frequency words.

Ask pupils what they think a high-frequency word is. A list of criteria is drawn up by the class as a checklist. Pupils work together in groups of four. They have a piece of paper, at least A3 size, on which they write as many high-frequency words as possible in English. They then move around the room anti-clockwise, looking at the sheets of other groups and adding any words they think the groups have missed before returning to their own places. Collate the words, with a discussion as to whether each meets the criteria set by the class at the end of the lesson. Pupils should then use the pupil book pages to find the German equivalents for their words (or a dictionary if time permits and deemed appropriate).

1 Lies den Satz. Benutze die Wörter, um so viele kurze Sätze wie möglich zu schreiben. (Writing L3)

Writing. Pupils read the sentence in the pupil book and use the words in it to make as many short sentences as possible.

The skills feature gives information on the type of high-frequency words that are most common in German (adverbs and pronouns or prepositions).

Possible answers

Ich schwimme nicht gern.
Ich gehe ins Schwimmbad.
Ich schwimme oft.
Es ist teuer.
Es ist zu teuer.
Ich gehe nicht oft.
Ich gehe nicht ins Schwimmbad.
Ich gehe sehr oft.
Ich schwimme gern.

2 Hör zu und wähl die richtige Antwort aus. (1–7) (Listening L4)

Listening. Pupils listen to the audio and for each English sentence select which of three words is used. This is to encourage careful listening.

Audioscript

1 – Ulm ist sehr bekannt für die Universität.
2 – Die Stadt ist ziemlich voll von Touristen.
3 – Am Donnerstag gibt es auf dem Marktplatz einen Markt.
4 – In meiner Stadt kann man nie Sport treiben.
5 – In Stuttgart ist alles sehr teuer.
6 – Köln ist nicht immer zu laut.
7 – Die Touristen können sonntags nicht die Kathedrale besuchen.

Answers

1 very **2** quite **3** Thursdays **4** never **5** everything **6** not always **7** cannot

3 Hör Tobi zu und wähl die richtige Antwort aus. (Listening L5)

Listening. Pupils listen to the boy speaking on the audio and choose the correct answer for the multiple-choice questions.

The skills feature gives some useful pre-listening strategies.

Audioscript

– Ich wohne in Fuschl am See, einem Dorf im Westen von Österreich, nicht weit von Salzburg. Hier kann man snowboarden und

© Pearson Education Ltd 2013. Copying permitted for purchasing institution only. This material is not copyright free.

Auf geht's! | **Gute Reise!** – KAPITEL 5

Ski fahren. Im Dorf gibt es nur einen kleinen Supermarkt – das findet meine Mutter nicht so gut. Wir können aber mit dem Auto nach Salzburg fahren, um in den Supermarkt zu gehen. Im Sommer kann man nicht so viel machen, aber man kann im See baden und Wassersport machen. Das ist toll! Ich wohne gern hier, aber meine Schwester findet es im Sommer langweilig. Diesen Sommer werden wir nach Sylt in Norddeutschland fahren. Meine Schwester und meine Mutter möchten jeden Tag an den Strand gehen und in der Sonne liegen.

Answers
1 b 2 a 3 a 4 c 5 b 6 b

Starter 2

Aim

To work on listening skills when listening to longer, more varied spoken texts.

Read out a short text in German. Any of the longer reading or listening texts from chapter 5 would be appropriate here, so this can be chosen to suit the ability level of each class. Each time pupils hear one of the high-frequency words, they stand up. Then ask one pupil which word they've heard and what it means in English.

4 Hör zu. Timo beschreibt seine Stadt. Was gibt es dort und was kann man machen? (5 Informationen auf Englisch). Was gibt es nicht und was kann man nicht machen? (3 Informationen). (Listening L4)

Listening. Pupils listen to the audio and pick out five details of what the town has and what you can do there and three details of what the town does not have and what you cannot do there.

The *Tip* box points out that it is important to differentiate between *ein* and *kein*, and that the word *nicht* changes the meaning from positive to negative. It is therefore important to watch out for these words.

Audioscript

– *Ich mag meine Stadt, weil sie historisch und schön ist. Hier gibt es zwei Museen und eine große Kirche. Es gibt kein Schloss, aber das finde ich in Ordnung. In der Stadtmitte kann man auch tolle Souvenirs kaufen. Leider gibt es keine Kegelbahn, aber es gibt ein sehr modernes Kino. Ich liebe Filme! Es gibt hier ein tolles Schwimmbad und man kann schwimmen gehen, aber Wintersport kann man nicht machen, weil es keinen Schnee gibt.*

Answers

Timo's town has two museums, a church, a cinema and a swimming pool.

You can buy great souvenirs there.

Timo's town does not have a castle or a bowling alley.

You can't do winter sports.

5 Partnerarbeit. Sieh dir die Vokabeln an und schreib fünf kurze Sätze auf Deutsch. Lies deine Sätze vor. Dein Partner/Deine Partnerin schreibt sie auf. (Writing L4)

Writing. Working in pairs, pupils use the vocabulary presented in the pupil book to write out five short sentences in German. They then read their sentences out loud and their partner writes down the German transcription.

The words are familiar and pupils can repeat their sentences several times if necessary. This can be differentiated downwards by suggesting that pupils read what their partner has written.

The *Tip* box reminds pupils to respect the word order when starting a sentence with a time expression.

Possible answers

Wir machen am Abend Hausaufgaben.

Mein Freund möchte Fußball spielen.

Ich kann nicht oft Fußball spielen.

Ich werde am Montag Hausaufgaben machen, aber ich möchte Fußball spielen.

Ich spiele gern Fußball.

6 Hör zu. Was kann man auf Sylt machen? Finde die zehn Unterschiede zwischen dem Text unten und dem Hörtext. (Listening L5)

Listening. Pupils listen to the audio and look at the text. They pick out ten differences between the audio and the written text. There is one error per paragraph.

The skills feature reminds pupils of some useful listening strategies.

Some vocabulary is glossed for support.

© Pearson Education Ltd 2013. Copying permitted for purchasing institution only. This material is not copyright free.

Auf geht's! | Gute Reise! – KAPITEL

Audioscript

1 – Ich werde im Sommer mit meiner Familie und drei Freunden nach Sylt fahren. Was kann man auf Sylt machen? Ich bin für jeden Tipp dankbar!
2 – Westerland hat ein großes Aquarium und man kann in Tinnum die Schokoladenfabrik besuchen.
3 – Man kann auch in die Stadt gehen, ins Schwimmbad und in die Sauna gehen und dann in einem schönen Restaurant essen – das sind doch tolle Ferien, oder?
4 – Essen gehen – es gibt in Hörnum einen tollen Fischimbiss. Er ist der Beste auf Sylt!
5 – Ins Wellenbad gehen – die Sylter Welle ist ein tolles Schwimmbad mit Sauna!
6 – In Tinnum gibt es einen Zoo mit über 400 Tieren und in Braderup gibt es einen Ponyhof.
7 – Man kann mit dem Schiff fahren und die Seehunde sehen.
8 – Man kann mit dem Bus fahren und das Rote Kliff besuchen.
9 – In Keitum gibt es ein Kunstmuseum und eine sehr schöne Kirche.
10 – In Westerland ins Restaurant gehen und Muscheln in Weißwein essen!

Answers

1 Ich werde im Sommer mit meiner Familie und **zwei** Freunden nach Sylt fahren. Was kann man auf Sylt machen? Ich bin für jeden Tipp dankbar!

2 Westerland hat ein **neues** Aquarium und man kann in Tinnum die Schokoladenfabrik besuchen.

3 Man kann auch **ins Kino** gehen, ins Schwimmbad und in die Sauna gehen und dann in einem schönen Restaurant essen – das sind doch tolle Ferien, oder?

4 Essen gehen – es gibt in Hörnum einen tollen **Imbiss**. Er ist der Beste auf Sylt!

5 Ins Wellenbad gehen – die Sylter Welle ist ein tolles **Sportzentrum** mit Sauna!

6 In Tinnum gibt es einen Zoo mit über **300** Tieren und in Braderup gibt es einen Ponyhof.

7 Man kann mit dem Schiff fahren und die **Seelöwen** sehen.

8 Man kann mit dem **Rad** fahren und das Rote Kliff besuchen.

9 In Keitum gibt es ein **Heimatmuseum** und eine sehr schöne Kirche.

10 In Westerland ins Restaurant gehen und Muscheln in **Rotwein** essen!

7 Hör noch mal zu. Schreib die zehn richtigen Wörter auf. (Listening L5)

Listening. Pupils listen to the audio again and write down the ten correct words.

Audioscript

For transcript see exercise 6.

Answers

1 drei 2 großes 3 in die Stadt 4 Fischimbiss 5 Schwimmbad 6 400 7 Seehunde 8 Bus 9 Kunstmuseum 10 Weißwein

Plenary

Aim

For pupils to establish whether they have met the lesson objective of understanding longer, more varied spoken texts.

Pupils play a game of aural dominoes (Plenary resource). Each pupil has the start and the end of a sentence (with the exception of the first and the last pupil). They read out their sentences, and the pupil who has the other half of their sentence then reads it out. This game can be played more than once and timed for an extra element of competition.

6 Writing Skills: Willkommen!

Gute Reise! – **KAPITEL 5**

(Pupil Book pp. 108–109)

Learning objectives
- Writing at length about a topic
- Adapting a model

Programme of Study
GV3 Developing vocabulary
LC2 Transcription
LC8 Writing creatively

FCSE links
Unit 7 – Local Area and Environment (Facilities)

Key Language
No new key language. Pupils develop writing skills using key language from the chapter.

PLTS
T Team workers

Cross-curricular
Geography: tourism

Resources
Audio files:
95_Kapitel5_Einheit6_Aufgabe2
96_Kapitel5_Einheit6_Aufgabe3
Workbooks:
Übungsheft 1 A&B, page 52
ActiveTeach:
Starter 1 resource
Starter 2 resource

Starter 1

Aim

To review adjectives and how they are used in sentences.

Pupils are given a set of sentences (Starter 1 resource). They are asked to add interest to the sentences by adding at least one adjective to each sentence. Collate suggestions and award points for the most inventive and interesting sentences.

1 Schreib zehn Adjektive auf, die eine Stadt beschreiben können. Vergleiche deine Adjektive mit einem Partner/einer Partnerin. (Writing L2)

Writing. Pupils write down ten adjectives that could be used to describe a town. They compare their list with that of their partner. Pupils listen to the audio in exercise 2 to check some of their ideas.

The skills feature reminds pupils to add variety and interest to their writing by using adjectives.

2 Hör zu und vergleiche. Hast du die gleichen Adjektive? Schreib die fehlenden Adjektive auf? (Listening L1)

Listening. Pupils listen to the audio and compare the adjectives they hear with their own list from exercise 1. They should add any to their list they hear that they may not have thought of.

Audioscript

- *interessant*
- *faszinierend*
- *toll*
- *supercool*
- *groß*
- *klein*
- *berühmt*
- *bekannt*
- *historisch*
- *touristisch*
- *modern*
- *alt*
- *schön*
- *familienfreundlich*

3 Hör zu und verbinde die Satzhälften. Schreib ganze Sätze. (Listening L5, Writing L3)

Listening/Writing. Pupils listen to the audio and match the sentence halves to make full sentences. They write the sentences out in full.

The skills feature reminds pupils of ways to add variety to their writing, in this case by varying sentence structure.

Audioscript

- *Willkommen in Cambridge, meiner Heimatstadt. Cambridge ist eine mittelgroße, touristische Stadt in Ostengland. Die Stadt ist bekannt für die Universität. Für Familien gibt es ein Schwimmbad, eine Kegelbahn und viele Parks. Für Touristen haben wir ein Museum, ein Theater und eine Kunstgalerie. Man kann hier gut einkaufen und Rad fahren. Cambridge ist nicht groß, aber hier ist immer viel los!*

- *Besuchen Sie Salisbury, meine Lieblingsstadt in Südengland. Salisbury hat für alle etwas – Kultur und Sport. In der Stadt gibt es einen schönen Marktplatz und viele Museen. Man kann in einem der vielen Parks ein Picknick machen. In der Nähe kann man auch die alten Ruinen von Stonehenge besuchen. Sie sind faszinierend! Kommen Sie nach Salisbury – meine Stadt ist eine Reise wert!*

© Pearson Education Ltd 2013. Copying permitted for purchasing institution only. This material is not copyright free.

Willkommen! | **Gute Reise!** – KAPITEL

> **Answers**
>
> **1** d Cambridge ist eine mittelgroße, touristische Stadt in Ostengland. **2** e Die Stadt ist bekannt für die Universität. **3** h Für Familien gibt es ein Schwimmbad, eine Kegelbahn und viele Parks. **4** a Man kann dort gut einkaufen und Rad fahren. **5** g Salisbury ist in Südengland. **6** c Salisbury hat für alle etwas – Kultur und Sport. **7** f In der Stadt gibt es einen schönen Marktplatz und viele Museen. **8** b In der Nähe kann man die alten Ruinen von Stonehenge besuchen.

4 Schreib so viele Satzanfänge wie möglich. (Writing L3)

Writing. Pupils write as many sentence starters as they can, using the vocabulary presented in the pupil book if they wish.

5 Lies den Text und beantworte die Fragen auf Deutsch. Schreib ganze Sätze. (Reading L5)

Reading. Pupils read the text and answer the questions in German, using full sentences.

Some vocabulary is glossed for support.

> **Answers**
>
> **1** Die Stadt heißt Wismar.
>
> **2** Wismar (Die Stadt) ist in Norddeutschland (an der Ostseeküste).
>
> **3** Für Familien gibt es einen tollen Zoo mit Wasserspielplatz und das „Wonnemar" Schwimmbad (mit Sauna, Fitnessraum und Turborutschen).
>
> **4** In der Innenstadt gibt es einen Marktplatz und eine alte Kirche.
>
> **5** In Wismar kann man einkaufen, Tennis spielen, schwimmen, angeln, eine Radtour machen und Wassersport machen (Wasserski, Windsurfen).

> **Starter 2**
>
> **Aim**
>
> To draw up a checklist for written work.
>
> Working in groups of four, pupils write a 'recipe' for a good piece of extended writing. Prompts can be given (Starter 2 resource). These recipes are then shared with the whole class and the class votes on their favourite recipe. This recipe could then be used for the peer assessment in the plenary as an alternative to the peer-assessment grid provided.

6 Du hast Glück. Du darfst allein die Sommerferien für deine Familie planen. Schreib deinen Plan auf. (Writing L4–5)

Writing. Pupils write about where they and their family are going to go for their summer holiday.

The pupil book includes a table in the final skills feature which pupils can fill in to help them with their planning. Extra support in the form of prompts could be provided by completing the second column of the table for the pupils. These can be displayed for pupils who require a more structured approach to the task.

The skills feature on adapting a model points out ways in which pupils can use sentences, vocabulary and structures from other texts to model their writing.

7 Partnerarbeit. Überprüfe den Text mit Hilfe der Checkliste. (Reading L4–5)

Reading. Working with a partner, pupils check each other's writing using the checklist.

A skills feature also notes that a checklist can help with planning.

> **Plenary**
>
> **Aim**
>
> For pupils to establish whether they have met the lesson objectives of writing at length about a topic and adapting a model.
>
> Pupils work in pairs. Each pair is given a text. This text could be a photocopied piece of homework written by a member of this class, a previous class or a parallel class. All names should be removed from the texts. Each pair of pupils could be given a different text depending on their level of ability. Pupils peer assess the text against the recipe from Starter 2 or the peer-assessment grid from the pupil book. Using different colours, pupils highlight the different items from the checklist and decide what level they would give the written work if it had been done as an assessed piece of writing, justifying why they would give it this level.
>
> Ideally, two pairs in the class would be given the same text to peer assess. This would enable pupils to then work in groups of four to compare their peer assessment and discuss the similarities or differences in their findings.

© Pearson Education Ltd 2013. Copying permitted for purchasing institution only. This material is not copyright free.

Workbook A, page 52

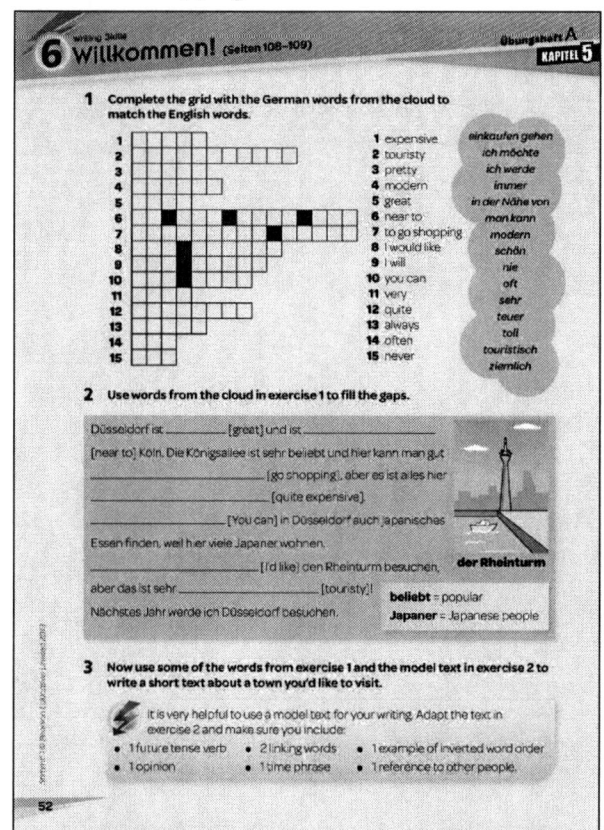

Answers

1 1 teuer 2 touristisch 3 schön 4 modern 5 toll 6 in der Nähe von 7 einkaufen gehen 8 ich möchte 9 ich werde 10 man kann 11 sehr 12 ziemlich 13 immer 14 oft 15 nie

2 Düsseldorf ist **toll** und ist **in der Nähe von** Köln. Die Königsallee ist sehr beliebt und hier kann man gut **einkaufen gehen**, aber es ist alles hier **ziemlich teuer**. **Man kann** in Düsseldorf auch japanisches Essen finden, weil hier viele Japaner wohnen. **Ich möchte** den Rheinturm besuchen, aber das ist sehr **touristisch**! Nächstes Jahr werde ich Düsseldorf besuchen.

3 Pupils' own answers.

Workbook B, page 52

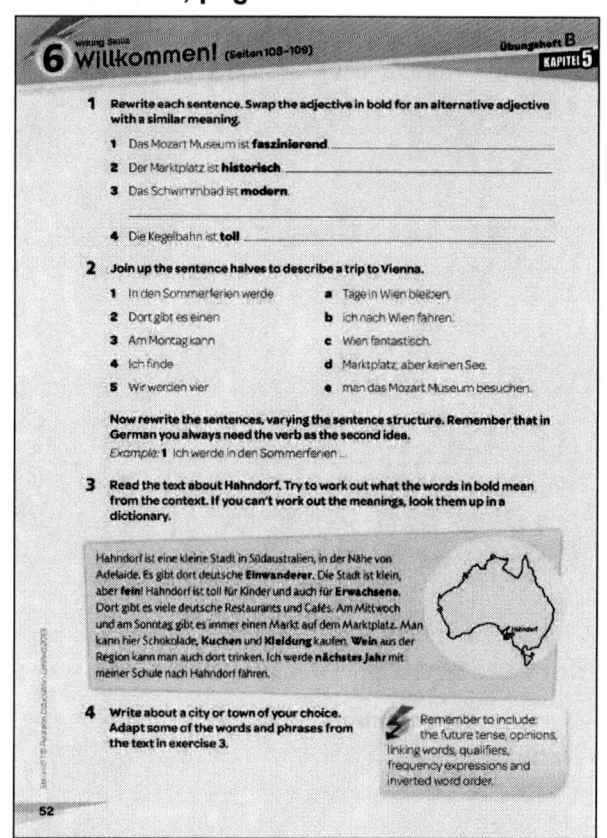

Answers

1 Possible answers:
  1 Das Mozart Museum ist fantastisch.
  2 Der Marktplatz ist alt.
  3 Das Schwimmbad ist neu.
  4 Die Kegelbahn ist super.

2 1 b 2 d 3 e 4 c 5 a
  1 Ich werde in den Sommerferien nach Wien fahren.
  2 Es gibt dort einen Marktplatz, aber keinen See.
  3 Man kann am Montag das Mozart Museum besuchen.
  4 Wien finde ich fantastisch.
  5 In Wien werden wir vier Tage bleiben.

3 der Einwanderer – immigrant
  fein – fine   der Erwachsene – adult
  der Kuchen – cake   die Kleidung – clothing
  der Wein – wine   nächstes Jahr – next year

4 Pupils' own answers.

Gute Reise! – KAPITEL

Lernzieltest und Wiederholung (Pupil Book pp. 110–111)

Lernzieltest
Pupils use this checklist to review language covered in the chapter, working on it in pairs in class or on their own at home. There is a Word version on ActiveTeach which can be printed out and given to pupils. Encourage them to follow up any weakness they identify. There are Target Setting Sheets included in the Assessment Pack, and an opportunity for pupils to record their own levels and targets on the *Mein Fortschritt* page in the Workbooks. You can also use the *Lernzieltest* checklist as an end-of-chapter plenary option.

Wiederholung
These revision exercises can be used for assessment purposes or for pupils to practise before tackling the assessment tasks in the Assessment Pack.

Resources
Audio files:
Kapitel5_Wiederholung_Aufgabe1.mp3
Kapitel5_Wiederholung_Aufgabe2.mp3
Workbooks:
Übungsheft 1 A&B, pages 53–54
ActiveTeach:
p.110 Lernzieltest checklist

---

1 Hör zu. Schreib den richtigen Buchstaben auf. (1–5) (Listening L2)

Listening. Pupils listen to the audio and match the illustrations to the speakers.

Audioscript

1 – Guten Tag. Ich möchte einmal Bratwurst mit Pommes und eine Cola, bitte.
  – Einmal Bratwurst mit Pommes … eine Cola … Das macht sieben Euro dreißig.
2 – Guten Tag. Ich möchte ein Eis und ein Mineralwasser.
  – Ein Vanilleeis oder Schokoladeneis?
  – Ein Schokoladeneis, bitte.
  – Fünf Euro vierzig.
  – Bitte schön.
  – Danke. Auf Wiedersehen.
  – Tschüs.
3 – Hallo. Ich hätte gern einmal Hamburger mit Salat, bitte.
  – Etwas zu trinken?
  – Ja, eine Cola.
  – Sieben Euro zehn, bitte.
4 – Hallo. Ich möchte einmal Pizza mit Pommes und einen Tee, bitte.
  – Einmal Pizza mit Pommes … Tee … Acht Euro zehn, bitte.

5 – Guten Tag. Was möchten Sie?
  – Einmal Pommes mit Salat, bitte.
  – Etwas zu trinken?
  – Ja, ein Mineralwasser.
  – Das macht sechs Euro siebzig.

Answers

1 b **2** d **3** a **4** e **5** c

2 Hör noch mal zu. Schreib den richtigen Preis auf. (1–5) (Listening L2)

Listening. Pupils listen to the audio again and write down the correct price for each snack.

Audioscript

For transcript see exercise 1.

Answers

1 €7,30 **2** €5,40 **3** €7,10 **4** €8,10 **5** €6,70

3 Partnerarbeit. Du bist im Urlaub! Mach ein Interview über Souvenirs. (Speaking L3–4)

Speaking. Working in pairs, pupils interview each other about souvenirs, using the illustrations and texts in the pupil book as stimuli.

The *Tip* box reminds pupils to listen to one another and reply in order to keep the conversation going.

© Pearson Education Ltd 2013. Copying permitted for purchasing institution only. This material is not copyright free.

Lernzieltest und Wiederholung | Gute Reise! – **KAPITEL 5**

4 Lies die E-Mail. Welche vier Sätze sind richtig? Korrigiere die anderen Sätze. (Reading L5)

Reading. Pupils read the text and work out which four sentences below it are the correct ones. They then correct the remaining sentences.

It would be useful to elicit good features of this text from pupils as preparation for the writing activity in exercise 5. Features include:

1 Appropriate start/finish
2 Opinions
3 A variety of sentence structures, including starting with a phrase and swapping the verb
4 A variety of different verbs, e.g. *man kann …*
5 Future tense
6 Referring to persons other than yourself, e.g. *meine Schwester möchte …*, *wir werden …*
7 Inclusion of questions.

Pupils could be asked to suggest any improvements to the text. One suggestion might be to include a reason/justification using *weil*.

Exploiting the reading text in this way as preparation for writing will give pupils the structured guidance they need to produce a quality checklist that they can use as they plan and write their postcard in exercise 5.

> **Answers**
> Sentences 1, 4, 6 and 7 are correct.
> Corrected sentences:
> **2 In der Nähe** gibt es einen großen Wasserpark.
> **3** In München kann man **sehr** viel sehen.
> **5 Monikas Schwester** möchte eine Tasse oder ein Freundschaftsband kaufen.

5 Es ist Sommer und du hast Ferien. Schreib eine Postkarte. (Writing L5)

Writing. Pupils write a postcard from their summer holiday. A framework is presented in the pupil book.

The *Tip* box reminds pupils to refer back to their own previous work and to exercise 4 for a model to help them with their writing.

Workbook A, page 53

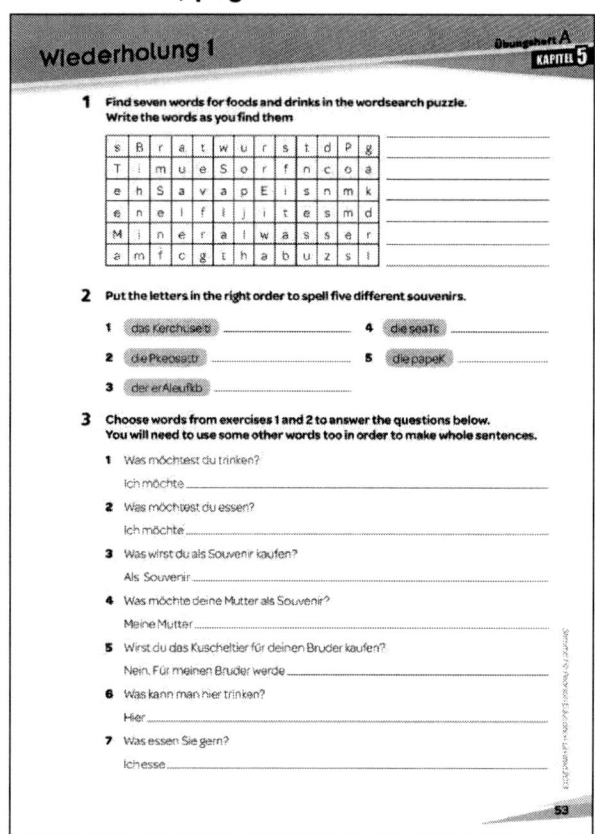

Wiederholung 1

1 Find seven words for foods and drinks in the wordsearch puzzle. Write the words as you find them

s	B	r	a	t	w	u	r	s	t	d	P	g
T	i	m	u	e	S	o	r	f	n	c	o	a
e	h	S	a	v	a	p	E	i	s	n	m	k
e	n	e	l	f	i	j	i	t	e	s	m	d
M	i	n	e	r	a	l	w	a	s	s	e	r
a	m	f	c	g	t	h	a	b	u	z	s	l

2 Put the letters in the right order to spell five different souvenirs.

1 das Kerchusetr .... 4 die seaTs ....
2 die Pkeosstr .... 5 die papeK ....
3 der erAleufkb ....

3 Choose words from exercises 1 and 2 to answer the questions below. You will need to use some other words too in order to make whole sentences.

1 Was möchtest du trinken?
Ich möchte ....
2 Was möchtest du essen?
Ich möchte ....
3 Was wirst du als Souvenir kaufen?
Als Souvenir ....
4 Was möchte deine Mutter als Souvenir?
Meine Mutter ....
5 Wirst du das Kuscheltier für deinen Bruder kaufen?
Nein. Für meinen Bruder werde ....
6 Was kann man hier trinken?
Hier ....
7 Was essen Sie gern?
Ich esse ....

Answers

1 Bratwurst; Mineralwasser; Tee; Eis; Pommes; Salat; Senf

2 1 das Kuscheltier
   2 die Postkarte
   3 der Aufkleber
   4 die Tasse
   5 die Kappe

3 Possible answers:
   1 Ich möchte eine Cola trinken.
   2 Ich möchte Pommes essen.
   3 Als Souvenir werde ich ein Kuscheltier kaufen.
   4 Meine Mutter möchte eine Tasse als Souvenir.
   5 Nein. Für meinen Bruder werde ich einen Aufkleber kaufen.
   6 Hier kann man Mineralwasser trinken.
   7 Ich esse gern Salat.

Lernzieltest und Wiederholung | **Gute Reise!** – KAPITEL

Workbook B, page 53

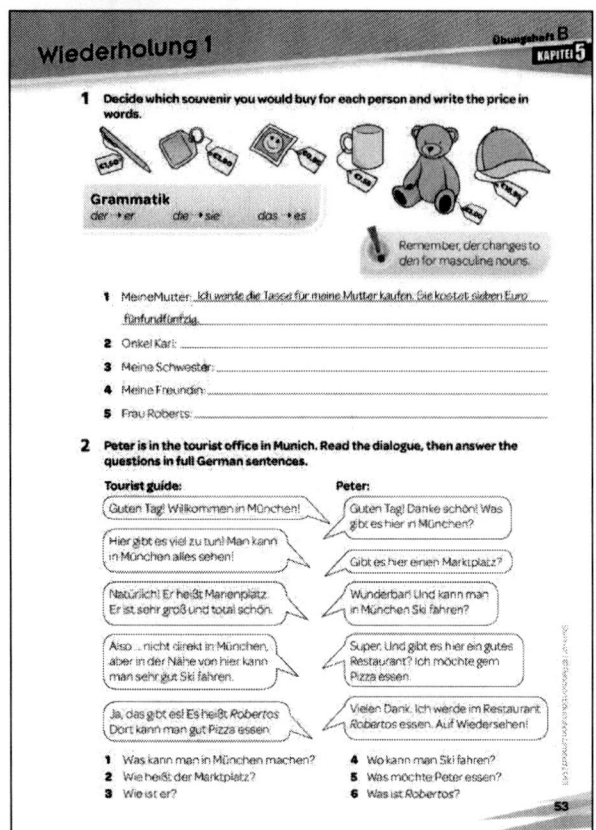

Answers

1 Possible answers:
   1 Ich werde die Tasse für meine Mutter kaufen. Sie kostet sieben Euro fünfundfünfzig.
   2 Ich werde den Schlüsselanhänger für Onkel Karl kaufen. Er kostet drei Euro neunzig.
   3 Ich werde das Kuscheltier für meine Schwester kaufen. Es kostet drei Euro.
   4 Ich werde den Kuli für meine Freundin kaufen. Er kostet einen Euro fünfzig.
   5 Ich werde den Aufkleber für Frau Roberts kaufen. Er kostet fünfundneunzig Cent.

2 1 In München kann man den Marienplatz sehen/alles sehen/in der Nähe Ski fahren/gut essen.
   2 Der Marktplatz heißt Marienplatz.
   3 Der Marktplatz ist sehr groß und total schön.
   4 Man kann in der Nähe von München Ski fahren.
   5 Peter möchte eine Pizza essen.
   6 *Robertos* ist ein gutes Restaurant in München.

Workbook A, page 54

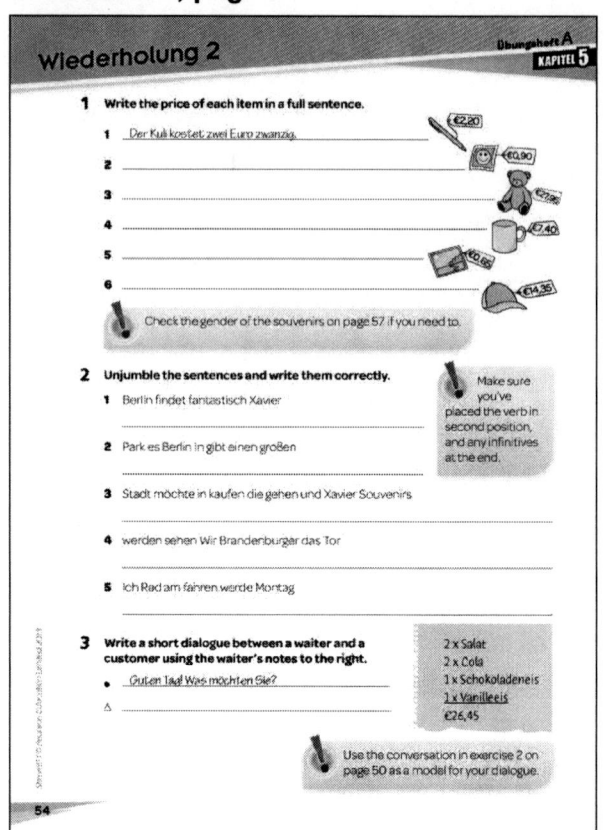

Answers

1 1 Der Kuli kostet zwei Euro zwanzig.
   2 Der Aufkleber kostet neunzig Cent.
   3 Das Kuscheltier kostet siebenundzwanzig Euro fünfundneunzig.
   4 Die Tasse kostet sieben Euro vierzig.
   5 Die Postkarte kostet fünfundsechzig Cent.
   6 Die Kappe kostet vierzehn Euro fünfunddreißig.

2 1 Xavier findet Berlin fantastisch.
   2 In Berlin gibt es einen großen Park.
   3 Xavier möchte in die Stadt gehen und Souvenirs kaufen.
   4 Wir werden das Brandenburger Tor sehen.
   5 Ich werde am Montag Rad fahren.

3 Pupils' own answers.

© Pearson Education Ltd 2013. Copying permitted for purchasing institution only. This material is not copyright free.

Workbook B, page 54

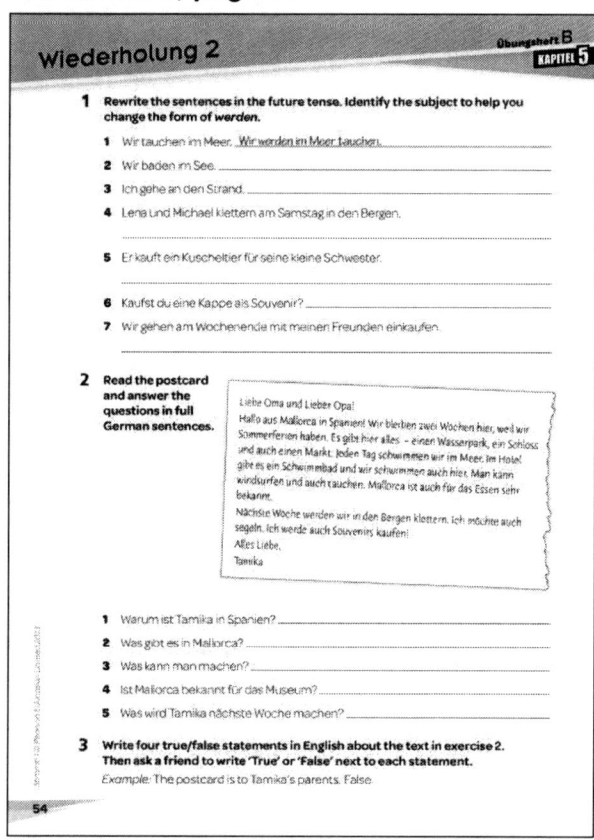

Wiederholung 2 — Übungsheft B — KAPITEL 5

1 Rewrite the sentences in the future tense. Identify the subject to help you change the form of **werden**.

1 Wir tauchen im Meer. _Wir werden im Meer tauchen._
2 Wir baden im See. _____
3 Ich gehe an den Strand. _____
4 Lena und Michael klettern am Samstag in den Bergen. _____
5 Er kauft ein Kuscheltier für seine kleine Schwester. _____
6 Kaufst du eine Kappe als Souvenir? _____
7 Wir gehen am Wochenende mit meinen Freunden einkaufen. _____

2 Read the postcard and answer the questions in full German sentences.

> Liebe Oma und Lieber Opa!
> Hallo aus Mallorca in Spanien! Wir bleiben zwei Wochen hier, weil wir Sommerferien haben. Es gibt hier alles – einen Wasserpark, ein Schloss und auch einen Markt. Jeden Tag schwimmen wir im Meer. Im Hotel gibt es ein Schwimmbad und wir schwimmen auch hier. Man kann windsurfen und auch tauchen. Mallorca ist auch für das Essen sehr bekannt.
> Nächste Woche werden wir in den Bergen klettern. Ich möchte auch segeln. Ich werde auch Souvenirs kaufen!
> Alles Liebe,
> Tamika

1 Warum ist Tamika in Spanien? _____
2 Was gibt es in Mallorca? _____
3 Was kann man machen? _____
4 Ist Mallorca bekannt für das Museum? _____
5 Was wird Tamika nächste Woche machen? _____

3 Write four true/false statements in English about the text in exercise 2. Then ask a friend to write 'True' or 'False' next to each statement.
Example: The postcard is to Tamika's parents. False.

Answers

1
1 Wir werden im Meer tauchen.
2 Wir werden im See baden.
3 Ich werde an den Strand gehen.
4 Lena und Michael werden am Samstag in den Bergen klettern.
5 Er wird ein Kuscheltier für seine kleine Schwester kaufen.
6 Wirst du eine Kappe als Souvenir kaufen?
7 Wir werden am Wochenende mit meinen Freunden einkaufen gehen.

2
1 Sie hat Sommerferien.
2 Es gibt einen Wasserpark, ein Schloss und auch einen Markt.
3 Man kann schwimmen, windsurfen und tauchen.
4 Nein. Mallorca ist für das Essen bekannt.
5 Tamika wird in den Bergen klettern, segeln und Souvenirs kaufen.

3 Pupils' own answers.

Grammatik (Pupil Book pp. 112–113)

Gute Reise! – **KAPITEL**

The *Stimmt!* Grammatik section provides a more detailed summary of key grammar covered in the chapter, along with further exercises to practise these points.

Grammar topics
Negative sentences with *kein*
möchten with the infinitive
Using *gern* with a variety of verbs
Using *werden* to form the future tense

Resources
Workbooks:
Übungsheft 1 A&B, page 55

Negative sentences with kein

1 Complete the sentences with the correct form of *kein*. (Writing L2)

Answers
1 Ich habe **keinen** Hamburger.
2 Mein Freund Timo hat **keine** Geschwister.
3 Ich möchte **keinen** Schlüsselanhänger kaufen.
4 Wir essen **kein** Eis.
5 Meine Freundin Jessica trinkt **keine** Cola.
6 Wir möchten **keinen** Hund.
7 In der Stadt gibt es **kein** Schwimmbad.
8 Sie hat **keine** Gitarre.

2 What is/isn't there in Ulm? Write sentences. (Writing L3)

The *Tip* box reminds pupils they can check the gender of these nouns on pupil book p. 98.

Answers
1 Es gibt kein Schloss in Ulm.
2 Es gibt kein Schwimmbad in Ulm.
3 Es gibt kein Kino in Ulm.
4 Es gibt keinen Wasserpark in Ulm.
5 Es gibt keine Kegelbahn in Ulm.

möchten with the infinitive

3 Put these words in the correct order. Write out the sentences and translate them into English. (Writing L2–3)

Answers
1 *Wir möchten Eis essen.* – We would like to eat some ice cream.
2 *Möchtest du Cola trinken?* – Would you like to drink Cola?
3 *Ich möchte ins Kino gehen.* – I would like to go to the cinema.
4 *Ich möchte ein Freundschaftsband kaufen.* – I would like to buy a friendship bracelet.
5 *Wir möchten schwimmen und Rad fahren* (or *… Rad fahren und schwimmen*). – We would like to go swimming and cycling.
6 *Sie möchte in Berlin wohnen.* – She would like to live in Berlin.

4 Translate these sentences into German. (Writing L3)

Answers
1 Ich möchte eine Kappe kaufen.
2 Wir möchten schwimmen.
3 Sie möchte eine Cola trinken.
4 Möchtest du Rad fahren?

Using gern with a variety of verbs

5 Look at the pictures and write sentences. (Writing L3)

The *Tip* box reminds pupils that the *wir* form of the present tense is the same as the infinitive for that verb.

Answers
1 *Wir gehen gern an den Strand.*
2 Ich windsurfe nicht gern.
3 Er taucht gern.
4 Wir schwimmen gern im Meer.
5 Wir segeln nicht gern.
6 Ich fahre gern Rad.

© Pearson Education Ltd 2013. Copying permitted for purchasing institution only. This material is not copyright free.

Grammatik | Gute Reise! – KAPITEL 5

Using werden *to form the future tense*

6 Write the English. Underline your translation of *werden*. (Writing L2)

Some vocabulary is glossed for support.

> **Answers**
>
> *1* <u>I am going to</u> (or <u>I will</u>) play tennis today.
>
> *2* <u>He is going to</u> (or <u>He will</u>) go to Italy in the summer holidays.
>
> *3* Mrs Grünemeier, <u>are you going to</u> (or <u>will you</u>) go walking in the summer?
>
> *4* Next year <u>we are going to</u> (or <u>will</u>) go to the beach every day.
>
> *5* Max, what <u>are you going to</u> (or <u>will you</u>) do in July?
>
> *6* <u>My family and I are going to</u> (or <u>will</u>) bathe in the lake.

7 Look at the pictures and write sentences. (Writing L4–5)

The *Tip* box revises sentence structure and verb position, reminding pupils that when a sentence starts with a time expression, the verb and subject swap position.

> **Answers**
>
> *1 Normalerweise fahren wir nach Spanien, aber nächstes Jahr werden wir nach Österreich fahren.*
>
> *2 Normalerweise tauchen wir, aber nächstes Jahr werden wir segeln.*
>
> *3 Normalerweise gehen wir an den Strand, aber nächstes Jahr werden wir wandern.*
>
> *4 Normalerweise spielen wir Tennis, aber nächstes Jahr werden wir rodeln.*
>
> *5 Normalerweise schwimmen wir im Meer, aber nächstes Jahr werden wir im See baden.*
>
> *6* (pupil's own answer)

Workbook A, page 55

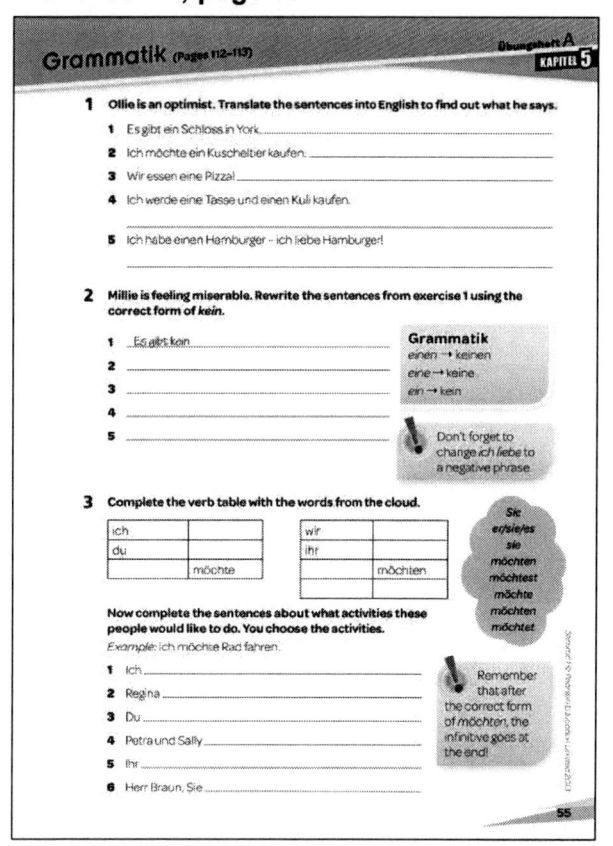

> **Answers**
>
> **1** 1 There's a castle in York.
>
> 2 I'd like to buy a stuffed toy.
>
> 3 We're eating a pizza!
>
> 4 I will buy a mug and a pen.
>
> 5 I've got a hamburger – I love hamburgers!
>
> **2** 1 Es gibt kein Schloss in York.
>
> 2 Ich möchte kein Kuscheltier kaufen.
>
> 3 Wir essen keine Pizza!
>
> 4 Ich werde keine Tasse und keinen Kuli kaufen.
>
> 5 Ich habe keinen Hamburger – Ich hasse Hamburger!
>
> **3** ich möchte   du möchtest   er/sie/es möchte
>
> wir möchten   ihr möchtet   Sie möchten
>
> sie möchten
>
> Possible answers:
>
> 1 Ich möchte Rad fahren.
>
> 2 Regina möchte einkaufen gehen.
>
> 3 Du möchtest angeln gehen.
>
> 4 Petra und Sally möchten Eis essen.
>
> 5 Ihr möchtet ins Kino gehen.
>
> 6 Herr Braun, Sie möchten etwas zu trinken?

Grammatik | Gute Reise! – KAPITEL

Workbook B, page 55

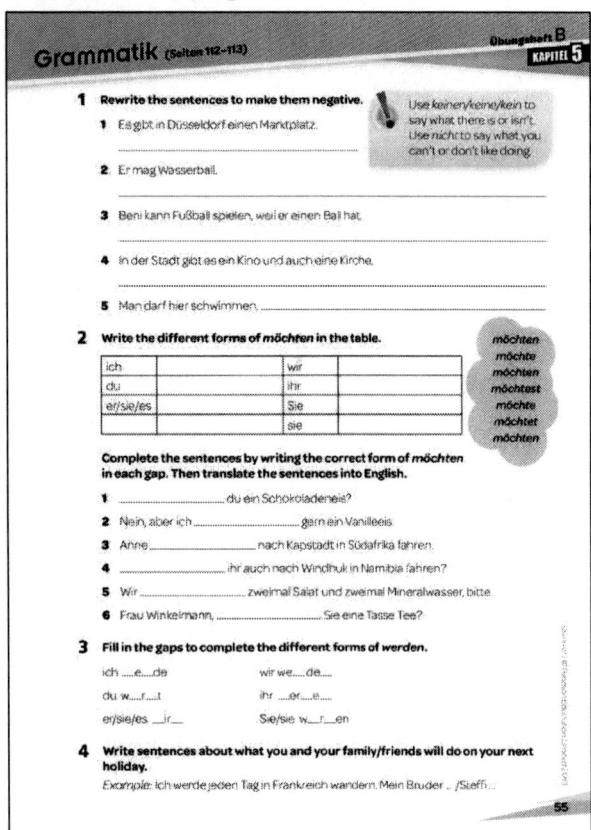

Answers

1 1 Es gibt in Düsseldorf keinen Marktplatz.
2 Er mag nicht Wasserball.
3 Beni kann nicht Fußball spielen, weil er keinen Ball hat.
4 In der Stadt gibt es kein Kino und auch keine Kirche.
5 Man darf nicht hier schwimmen.

2 ich möchte   du möchtest   er/sie/es möchte
wir möchten   ihr möchtet   Sie möchten
sie möchten

1 Möchtest 2 möchte 3 möchte
4 Möchtet 5 möchten 6 möchten

3 ich werde   du wirst   er/sie/es wird
wir werden   ihr werdet   Sie/sie werden

4 Pupils' own answers.

© Pearson Education Ltd 2013. Copying permitted for purchasing institution only. This material is not copyright free.

Gute Reise! – **KAPITEL 5**

Projektzone 1: Infos für Touristen

(Pupil Book pp. 116–117)

The Projektzone is one or two optional units in which no new grammar is introduced, but in which the chapter topic is extended into an exciting cultural and practical context which allows for cross-curricular and project work.

Learning objectives
- Researching German-speaking places
- Creating a tourist brochure

Programme of Study
LC3 Conversation (dealing with the unexpected)
LC5 Speaking coherently and confidently
LC8 Writing creatively

FCSE links
Unit 3 – Holidays and Travel (Destination, Activities)

PLTS
I Independent enquirers

Cross-curricular
Geography: tourism in German-speaking places

Resources
Audio files:
99_Kapitel5_Projektzone1_Aufgabe1
100_Kapitel5_Projektzone1_Aufgabe3
101_Kapitel5_Projektzone1_Aufgabe4

ActiveTeach:
p.116 Exercise 1 grid

Starter 1

Aim

To look at what makes a good brochure.

Pupils brainstorm what they think is important in a tourist brochure (think-pair-share). They draw up a list of essential qualities for a brochure.

The teacher shows pupils some brochures from a variety of German (or German-speaking) tourist resorts. Alternatively, tourist office websites could be used if pupils have access to an ICT suite.

Pupils then rate the brochures they have seen on a scale of 1–10 for the essential qualities they have listed.

Example qualities might be:
- Front cover (eye-catching?)
- Layout
- Pictures
- Text (clear and easy to read)
- Maps
- Contents
- Interesting and or unusual
- Genuinely informs the reader about the tourist resort
- Information on where to stay
- Information on events
- Information on transport

1 Hör zu. Was sagt Markus? Verbinde die Bilder mit den richtigen Satzanfängen. (1–5) (Listening L2)

Listening. Pupils listen to the audio and match the pictures to the sentence starters.

Audioscript

1 – *Fünf, vier, drei, zwei, eins, stop! OK, Markus, was kannst du über Ulm sagen?*
  – *OK … Ulm ist in Süddeutschland.*
2 – *Es gibt dort eine große Kirche – das Ulmer Münster.*
3 – *Man kann dort das Brotmuseum besuchen.*
4 – *Ich möchte eine Einstein-Tasse kaufen.*
5 – *Im September werde ich den Einstein-Marathon machen.*

Answers
1 d 2 a 3 c 4 b 5 e

2 Partnerarbeit. Wähl ein Bild aus. Mach das Buch nach zehn Sekunden zu. Was kannst du über Wien oder Baden-Baden sagen? Dein Partner/Deine Partnerin überprüft deine Antwort. Dann tauscht die Rollen. (Speaking L4–5)

Speaking. Working with a partner, pupils take it in turns to choose a picture and to talk about either Vienna or Baden-Baden. Their partner checks their work.

Exercise 3 provides a model 'talk' for pupils to listen to.

The skills feature gives the pupils some guidance on speaking spontaneously.

© Pearson Education Ltd 2013. Copying permitted for purchasing institution only. This material is not copyright free.

Infos für Touristen | **Gute Reise!** – KAPITEL

3 Hör zu und vergleiche. (Listening L3)

Listening. Pupils listen to a model talk about Vienna and Baden-Baden.

The *Tip* box suggests that pupils try to listen specifically for a selection of extra words that make the text sound more spontaneous.

dort – 2

er heißt – 1

auch – 2

im Sommer – 2

und – 2

als Souvenir – 2

Audioscript

- Wien ist in Österreich. Es gibt dort einen Park – er heißt Wiener Prater. Man kann auch das Schokomuseum besuchen – mmm, lecker! Ich werde im Sommer rodeln und ich möchte als Souvenir einen Wiener Schlüsselanhänger kaufen.
- Baden-Baden ist in Südwestdeutschland. Es gibt dort einen Marktplatz. Man kann auch das Schloss besuchen. Ich werde im Sommer im See baden und ich möchte als Souvenir eine Baden-Baden-Kappe kaufen.

Starter 2

Aim

To look for key words using authentic texts, which can then be adapted in their own writing.

Pupils use the brochures they have been given (or the websites) to find some key words they may need when drawing up their own brochures.

Suggested words for pupils to look for might be:

- Town
- Region/local area
- Activities
- Accommodation
- Practical information
- Worth seeing
- Top excursions

Alternatively, pupils could suggest their own list of useful vocabulary to look for.

Extension

Pupils look through the brochures and find any other vocabulary they think they might want to include.

4 Hör zu und lies. (Listening L4)

Listening. Pupils listen to an advertising text about Lungern and follow the text in the pupil book.

Some vocabulary is glossed for support.

Audioscript

- Lungern – Sommerparadies in der Schweiz!
- Das Ferienhaus
- Komfortables Ferienhaus direkt am Lungernsee in der Nähe von Interlaken in der Mitte der Schweiz. Das Haus ist ideal für große Familien mit Kindern.
- Das Dorf
- In Lungern gibt es einen kleinen Marktplatz, ein Souvenirgeschäft, Restaurants und eine schöne Kirche. Im Souvenirgeschäft kann man T-Shirts, Kulis, Tassen und Kappen kaufen.
- Das Seebad Lungern
- Das kleine Seebad ist ideal für Kinder. Hier gibt es einen Strand, eine Wasserrutschbahn, Tischfußball, Tischtennis und ein Restaurant.
- Am See
- Man kann im See baden, windsurfen, segeln und Pedalos mieten.
- In der Gegend
- Man kann Rad fahren und wandern. Einen Minigolfplatz gibt es auch.

5 Partnerarbeit. Mach ein Interview über Lungern. Benutze den Text aus Aufgabe 4 und die Fragen aus Aufgabe 6 als Hilfe. (Speaking L3–5)

Speaking. Working in pairs, pupils carry out an interview about Lungern. They use the material from exercise 4 and the questions presented in exercise 6 for support.

The *Tip* box reminds pupils that it is OK to think before they speak/answer, using fillers such as *und* or *äh* and *ähm!*

Infos für Touristen | **Gute Reise!** – KAPITEL 5

6 Wähl eine Stadt/eine Gegend aus der Liste aus. Suche Infos und mach eine Broschüre. (Writing L4–5)

Writing. Pupils create a tourist brochure about one of the towns or areas listed.

Prompt questions are provided for support.

Encourage pupils to produce accurate and creative brochures by researching facts and including visuals.

Plenary

Aim

For pupils to establish whether they have met the unit objective of creating a tourist brochure.

Pupils put their completed brochures at the back of the classroom, laid out as if they were in the tourist office. Each pupil has a set of Post-it notes, one for each brochure. They write on their Post-it notes **! (two stars and a target) for each brochure, assessing them against the criteria drawn up at the start of the lesson (see below for an example). Each pupil sticks their Post-it on the brochure they've been looking at. The teacher rings a bell (as in speed-dating) to let pupils know they need to move on to the next brochure. At the end of the designated time period (ten minutes or more at the teacher's discretion), pupils collect their own brochures and read the feedback given.

Suggested criteria:

- Front cover (eye-catching?)
- Layout
- Pictures
- Text (clear and easy to read)
- Maps
- Contents
- Interesting and or unusual
- Genuinely informs the reader about the tourist resort
- Information on where to stay
- Information on events
- Information on transport

Projektzone 2: Lass uns spielen!

(Pupil Book pp. 118–119)

Gute Reise! – **KAPITEL**

The Projektzone is one or two optional units in which no new grammar is introduced, but in which the chapter topic is extended into an exciting cultural and practical context which allows for cross-curricular and project work.

Learning objectives
- Using familiar language in a new context
- Creating your own board game

Programme of Study
LC1 Listening and responding
LC3 Conversation
PLTS
E Effective participators

Resources
Audio files:
102_Kapitel5_Projektzone2_Aufgabe2
103_Kapitel5_Projektzone2_Aufgabe4

Starter 1

Aim

To revise key vocabulary used in the board game.

Pupils use mini whiteboards. The teacher calls out one of the phrases below in English and the pupils have to write the number of the German phrase on their mini whiteboard. It can be done competitively with house-points or merits for the first to show the correct number.

Display these numbered German phrases in the classroom:

1. Es gibt
2. Man kann
3. Ich möchte
4. Ich werde
5. Wir werden
6. Zungenbrecher

1 Welches Feld ist das? Sieh dir das Brettspiel an und schreib die richtigen Zahlen auf. (Reading L2–3)

Reading. Pupils look at the board game illustrated and find the number that corresponds to the instruction.

(tongue twisters, source:
Text 2: www.uebersetzung.at/twister/de.htm
Text 4: adapted from www.
www.uebersetzung.at/twister/de.htm)

Answers

a Go forwards 3 spaces = 9
b Say a tongue-twister about the capital of Austria = 12
c Go to jail and miss a go = 8 & 14
d Say three activities that you will do in August = 18
e Say what there is in the city of Bonn = 13
f Go back three spaces = 16

2 Hör zu, sieh dir das Brettspiel an. Welches Feld ist das? (1–8) (Listening L3)

Listening. Pupils listen to the audio, look at the board game, and decide which space it is.

Audioscript

1 – *In den Sommerferien werde ich windsurfen und im See baden.*
2 – *Ich möchte einmal Bratwurst mit Pommes und eine Cola, bitte.*
3 – *Im Sommer werden wir nach Österreich fahren.*
4 – *In Heidelberg gibt es ein Schloss und einen Park.*
5 – *In Ulm, um Ulm und um Ulm herum!*
6 – *Ich möchte ein Kuscheltier und eine Kappe.*
7 – *In Interlaken gibt es einen Marktplatz und eine Imbissstube.*
8 – *Ich möchte einen Schlüsselanhänger und ein Freundschaftsband.*

Answers

1 15 *2* 11 *3* 2 *4* 19 *5* 7 *6* 4 *7* 6 *8* 10

3 Partnerarbeit. Du spielst und landest auf den folgenden Feldern. Was sagst du? Wechsel dich mit deinem Partner/deiner Partnerin ab. (Speaking L3–4)

Speaking. Working in pairs, pupils take it in turns to land on the spaces instructed and say out loud the sentence that the space gives them clues for.

They check their answers by listening to the audio in exercise 4.

Answers

a 2 – Im Sommer werden wir nach Österreich fahren.
b 10 – Ich möchte einen Schlüsselanhänger und ein Freundschaftsband.

© Pearson Education Ltd 2013. Copying permitted for purchasing institution only. This material is not copyright free.

Lass uns spielen! | Gute Reise! – **KAPITEL 5**

c 17 – Die Damen in Baden-Baden baden oft; baden Baden-Baden Herren mit?

d 3 – In Zell am See kann man im See baden und wandern.

e 5 – Ich möchte ein Eis und ein Mineralwasser.

f 12 – Man trinkt Wein in Wien.

4 Hör zu und überprüfe. (Listening L2)

Listening. Pupils listen to the audio and check their answers for exercise 3.

Audioscript

- a
- 2 – Im Sommer werden wir nach Österreich fahren.
- b
- 10 – Ich möchte einen Schlüsselanhänger und ein Freundschaftsband.
- c
- 17 – Die Damen in Baden-Baden baden oft; baden Baden-Baden Herren mit?
- d
- 3 – In Zell am See kann man im See baden und wandern.
- e
- 5 – Ich möchte ein Eis und ein Mineralwasser.
- f
- 12 – Man trinkt Wein in Wien.

Starter 2

Aim

To introduce phrases needed when playing a board game.

Display the German board game phrases from exercise 7 of this unit at the front of the class. Pupils work either individually or in pairs to work out what they mean. Encourage pupils to think about the context, and the sorts of phrases they use when playing board games. Pupils should be asked to reflect why they have translated the phrases in the way they have (cognates, familiar vocabulary they have learnt in other contexts, etc.). To make it more competitive the starter could be timed or treated as a quiz.

5 Du spielst und landest auf den folgenden Feldern. Schreib auf, was du sagen wirst. (Writing L3–4)

Writing. Pupils write down what they will say when they land on the spaces given.

Answers

a *In Bonn gibt es einen Bahnhof und eine Kirche.*

b *Ich möchte ein Kuscheltier und eine Kappe.*

c *In Heidelberg gibt es ein Schloss und einen Park.*

d *In Interlaken gibt es einen Marktplatz und eine Imbissstube.*

e *In den Sommerferien werde ich windsurfen und im See baden.*

6 Mach dein eigenes Brettspiel. Mach es authentisch und benutze deine Infos über deutschsprachige Länder und Städte. (Writing L4–5)

Writing. Pupils make their own board game based on the example given and using their own research on German-speaking countries and towns.

The teacher informs pupils that they can choose their own design.

The *Tip* box reminds pupils to use language that they already know by checking back through the *Wörter* pages, or to use a dictionary for any words that they don't know – making sure that they use the correct gender and article for nouns.

7 Gruppenarbeit. Spiel das Spiel. Du kannst folgende Phrasen benutzen. (Speaking L3–5)

Speaking. In small groups, pupils play the game (their own or the one in the pupil book).

The pupil book gives some phrases that will be useful when playing.

Plenary

Aim

To give feedback on a board game.

Pupils play the game created by another pupil, pair or group. Using the sentence starters below, they give oral feedback to the pupil, pair or group.

Ich spiele (gern/nicht gern) dein Brettspiel.

Ich finde dein Brettspiel (+ opinion/intensifier).

Die Bilder sind (+ opinion/intensifier).

Der Text ist (+ opinion/intensifier).

Es gibt (+ kein/keine/keinen) …(e.g gute Bilder/Zungenbrecher)

Gute Reise! – **KAPITEL**

Extra (Pupil Book pp. 128–129)

Self-access reading and writing

A Reinforcement

1 Schreib die Namen der Souvenirs richtig auf und finde die Paare. (Reading L1)

Reading. Pupils solve the anagrams and write out the words for the souvenirs correctly. They then find the pairs.

Answers
1 d – *die Tasse*
2 c – *das Trikot*
3 f – *der Aufkleber*
4 b – *die Kappe*
5 a – *das Kuscheltier*
6 e – *der Schlüsselanhänger*

2 Lies den Dialog. Schreib den Text ab und vervollständige die Sätze. (Reading L2)

Reading. Pupils read the dialogue. They copy it out and complete the gap-fill sentences.

The *Tip* box reminds pupils to look at the menu to help work out the prices.

Answers
Guten Tag. Ich möchte einmal **Pizza** und **zweimal** Salat, bitte.
Möchtest du etwas zu trinken?
Ja, ich hätte gern eine **Cola** und ein **Mineralwasser**, bitte.
Das macht **dreizehn** Euro **achtzig**.

3 Was gibt es dort? Sieh dir die Bilder an und schreib Sätze. (Writing L3)

Writing. Pupils look at the illustrations and write a sentence about each of three towns, describing what can be found there.

The four nouns in each answer may be listed in any order.

The *Tip* box reminds pupils to check the genders of the nouns they are using so that they use the correct form *einen*, *eine* or *ein* (or indeed *keinen*, *keine* or *kein*).

Answers
1 *In Bremen gibt es eine Imbissstube, ein Sportzentrum, eine Kirche und eine Kunstgalerie.*
2 *In Krefeld gibt es einen Park, eine Kegelbahn, einen Bahnhof und ein Schwimmbad.*
3 *In Augsburg gibt es ein Schloss, einen Marktplatz, einen Park und ein Kino.*

B Extension

1 Schreib sechs Sätze mit Wörtern aus jedem Kasten. Dann schreib die Sätze auf Englisch. (Writing L3)

Writing. Pupils write six sentences, using an element from each of the boxes in the table. They then translate their sentences into English.

The *Tip* box reminds pupils that *fahren* means 'to go' in the sense of 'to travel', otherwise you use *gehen*.

2 Lies den Text. Finde im Text: eine positive Meinung, zwei Adjektive, drei Gebäude, vier Aktivitäten. (Reading L4)

Reading. Pupils read the text and find:

- a positive opinion
- two adjectives
- three buildings
- four activities.

Some vocabulary is glossed for support.

Possible answers
eine positive Meinung: Die Stadt ist einfach toll.
zwei Adjektive: (any 2) alt, historisch, toll, schön, groß, modern
drei Gebäude: (any 3) Amphitheater, Theater, Kunstgalerie, Museum (Museen), Kino, Schwimmbad, Kegelbahn, Schloss
vier Aktivitäten: (any 4) das Schloss (or any of the other buildings) besuchen, Wassersport machen, segeln, Kanu fahren, tauchen, wandern, Rad fahren, reiten, (rodeln)

© Pearson Education Ltd 2013. Copying permitted for purchasing institution only. This material is not copyright free.

Extra | Gute Reise! – **KAPITEL 5**

3 Beantworte diese Fragen zum Text aus Aufgabe 2. (Reading L4)

Reading. Pupils re-read the text in exercise 2 and answer the questions.

> **Possible answers**
>
> **1** Die Stadt/Sie heißt Trier.
>
> **2** Die Stadt/Sie/Trier ist im Westen von Deutschland.
>
> **3** Für Touristen gibt es das Amphitheater und eine Kunstgalerie (any two suitable details accepted).
>
> **4** Für junge Leute gibt es eine Kegelbahn und eine Sommerrodelbahn (any two suitable details accepted).
>
> **5** Man kann dort Wassersport machen, tauchen und Rad fahren. (any three suitable details accepted).

4 Mach ein Interview über eine Stadt. Benutze die Fragen aus Aufgabe 3. Unten sind auch ein paar Wörter zur Hilfe. (Writing L4)

Writing. Pupils write an interview about a town of their choice. The questions in exercise 3 and the words displayed in the pupil book provide support.

The *Tip* box reminds pupils that they can choose any town – real or imaginary.